Special Relations

SPECIAL RELATIONS

The Americanization of Britain?

H. L. Malchow

Stanford University Press
Stanford, California

This book has been published with the assistance of Tufts University.

Stanford University Press
Stanford, California

Library of Congress Cataloging-in-Publication Data

Malchow, Howard L.
    Special relations: the Americanization of Britain? / H. L. Malchow
        pages   cm.
    Includes bibliographical references and index.
    ISBN 978-0-8047-7399-7 (cloth : alk. paper)
    1. Great Britain—Civilization—American influences.   2. Great Britain—Civilization—1945– .   3. Popular culture—History—20th century.   4. Social movements—History—20th century.   5. Great Britain—Relations—United States.   6. United States—Relations—Great Britain.   I. Title.

DA566.4.M34   2011
303.48'241073—dc22   2010043066

Typeset at Stanford University Press in 10/12.5 Minion

For my Mother,

who admires British gardens

but prefers the wildflowers of the Texas hill country in springtime

Acknowledgments

In the decade and more it has taken this work to evolve I have incurred a debt to many—to my colleagues and especially to my students at Tufts University, to those patient librarians who have assisted me in Britain and the United States, and to many friends who have talked of their experiences and listened to mine. I am particularly obliged to friends no longer living—Gerald R. Gill, Ann Lafferty, and Jaki Leverson—and to Benjamin Botnick, Virginia Drachman, Melanie Hall, Andrew Laing, Chad Andrew Martin, David Newell, Stan Rogerson, Michael Saler, Ann Imlah Schneider, Anna Thew and Martin Lugg, and John Thomas. Stephen Brooke and an anonymous reviewer solicited by Stanford University Press gave me valuable advice about improving the manuscript. I have long owed a debt of gratitude to Norris Pope at Stanford Press, and, as ever, to Peter Stansky for his patient encouragement and sage advice. Whatever flaws and weaknesses there may be here are mine and not theirs.

Contents

Illustrations

Preface: Trafalgar Square, 19/20 July 1969

Toward evening on Saturday, the 19th of July 1969, Trafalgar Square filled with a mostly youthful crowd. Only nine months earlier the square, historic site of both protest and celebration, had been packed with an agitated throng opposed to the Vietnam War and its technology of death, many of whom marched off to what proved to be the last of the great demonstrations at the American embassy in Grosvenor Square. This expectant, if anxious, crowd, however, had assembled to cheer the success of American technology, and to celebrate, as it were, the humanism of its modernity. A giant television screen had been erected before the National Gallery on the square's north side where, a little past 9:00 p.m. London time, live satellite images from NASA's space center in Houston would play out the drama of *Apollo XI*'s Moon landing. For the millions of others who would watch crowded around the family telly—a larger audience than that for the Queen's coronation in 1953 and probably rivaling the 25 million or so who watched Churchill's funeral in 1965—the event was, as for hundreds of millions around the world, high drama unfolding in their sitting rooms, and when it was over the national grid reported a critical surge of demand as, it was said, millions of electric tea kettles were simultaneously set to boil. Each of the three television channels in Britain scheduled intensive coverage for Saturday night and Sunday morning, and substantial coverage during the following three days before the *Apollo* crew returned to Earth.

By most accounts,[1] it was the commercial channel ITV, led by six hours of London Weekend Television's David Frost all Saturday night, that scored the best, at least most entertaining, reportage. As Michael Palin, who had watched the *Apollo* blastoff on the 16th and then all night on the 19th/20th, recalled, "The extraordinary thing about the evening" was that ITV somehow contrived to fill all those hours before Armstrong stepped out onto the Moon's surface.[2] BBC1 disappointingly chose to continue its regular programming up to the critical descent, shifting from *The Black and White Minstrel Show* just as the landing module separated from its mother ship. Instead of a night of expert talking heads interspersed with live feed from NASA, Frost chose a variety show format of "chat and audience participation" with performing celebrities like Cilla Black, Engelbert Humperdink, and Cliff Richards, while ITV cameras went to Trafalgar Square to interview among the crowd there. Amid commercials for dog food, soft drinks, toilet soap, corn flakes, and detergents, there was Prime Minister Harold Wilson, who chose ITV to address the nation, an enthusiastic eighty-six-year-old Dame Sybil Thorndike, telephone conversations with viewers, and an interview with a man who had in 1964 placed a £10 bet that Americans would land on the Moon by 1970 and now stood ready to win £10,000. Some thought all this trivializing, and the American science fiction writer Ray Bradbury walked out of the London Weekend Studios rather than participate in what he regarded as a vulgar irrelevance. But many apparently found Frost's show to be innovative and successful in breaking "the long presentation of facts." It was also the only program to raise in a sustained way the core issue of whether manned spaceflight was actually worth the expense. Around midnight a panel debated this, with the historian A. J. P. Taylor and the American black entertainer Sammy Davis, Junior, together ("a somewhat bizarre alliance" Michael Billington reasonably thought) attacking the value of lunar exploration. In the end, of course, it was what Peter Black, television reviewer for the *Daily Mail* called "those incredible flat American voices" from NASA and the Apollo mission itself, that provided the real drama, "terrific waves of anxiety and relief," "when one lost all awareness of anything not coming out of the TV screen."[3]

As it happened, those who watched amid the crowd in Trafalgar Square or from their sitting rooms had a better view than the party of American residents and tourists who were to assemble in the embassy's theater to watch live coverage there in Grosvenor Square. As the critical time approached the embassy's own internal power failed. Elsewhere there were myriad television parties public and private. The *Evening Standard* arranged a "Moon breakfast" at the Savoy where the expatriate painter David Hockney declared himself to be unimpressed with it all ("I fell asleep"), while its own advertisements, like ITV's commercials, eagerly exploited the media event of the century. A full-page ad of the Moon wreathed in cigarette smoke: "Congratulations from W. D. & H. D. Wills, pacemakers in tobacco on the historic achievement of Apollo XI."[4]

The era of satellite-relayed telecommunications that made the Moon landing an event of worldwide simultaneity had begun seven years earlier, on 11 July 1962, when the American AT&T *Telstar* satellite beamed its first live pictures to the British receiving station at Goonhilly in Cornwall. As one observer there at the receiving dish later recalled, "You felt as if you were really at the centre of something." Among some others, however, the historic moment evoked reflections of a rather different kind. The Conservative MP for Morecambe and Lonsdale, Basil de Ferranti, was simply annoyed that "the Americans had done it all. What a pity that we could not have been the pioneers as we always used to be."[5]

In Britain, satellite transmission itself did not mean a sudden access to American television; canned U.S. programs were already commonplace on both BBC and ITV. But it did presage less expensive and easier telephone traffic, the immediacy of live transmission, and generally a greater density of exposure to American popular culture. If the satellite revolution meant, potentially at any rate, wider and more immediate communication into as well as from the United States, the issue of how American life might be impacted by greater access to international news and sport was much less compelling than what easier access to America might mean for others. Two days after *Telstar* began its limited service (it was not in geosynchronous orbit and could relay only while in "sight"), the *Daily Telegraph* repeated concerns they claimed had been voiced in the States: "What impression of American life will be given when [both good and bad American programming] is a daily reality?"[6]

The Hughes Aircraft Company's *Syncom 2*, the first communications satellite in geosynchronous orbit (allowing round-the-clock contact), followed in July the next year. In 1965 Hughes's *Early Bird* satellite offered free television exchange for a few months, but then the international consortium imposed high charges that deterred commercial use until Atlantic-stationary *Intelsat III*s greatly increased capacity and lowered cost in the years after 1968. In Britain, where the G.P.O. had signed on as an original member of the Telstar group, receptor dishes proliferated in Cornwall (near Poldhu, where Marconi's radio mast had sent the first trans-atlantic message in 1901). They were given whimsical Camelot names—Arthur, Guinevere, and Merlin—and quickly became popular tourist sites.

In January 1965, all the U.S. networks were able to offer Americans intermittent, fifteen-minute live broadcasts of the Churchill funeral as *Telstar* swung into range. By 1968, when reception from the Intel system was continuous, the British could see live broadcasts of the presidential election of that year, and in the summer of 1969 early-rising American tennis fans could watch Rod Laver defeat John Newcomb live at Wimbledon. As Laver would later boast to Bud Collins, "Maybe more people watched me on this day in 1969 than ever watched all the tennis matches ever played before because Tel-Star [*sic*] was carrying it around the world."[7] By that time the system had doubled its capacity; there were further improvements the following year, and in the seventies live broadcasting became relatively cheap and commonplace. There were also significant reductions in the cost of telephone communication, and international direct dialing between Britain and North America was introduced in 1970.[8]

The Moon landing, nearly everyone agreed, was somehow an era-defining event, but what, exactly, did it mean? On an emotional level it was simply science fiction and boys' adventure fantasy made real, as Michael Palin put down in his diary: "To bed at 5.00 with the image in my mind of men in spacesuits . . . just like the images in my mind after reading Dan Dare in the old *Eagle* comics—only this time it's true."[9] British dreams and American fact? Indeed, the ability to view the landing, live, in Britain, owed something perhaps to the British science fiction writer and futurologist Arthur Clarke, who had anticipated the synchronous orbit communications satellite as early as 1945.[10] But Britain's own drive to modernization, most graphically represented perhaps in London by the thrusting G.P.O. tower with its microwave transmitters, had seemed to falter by the late sixties, and it was little consolation to observe, as Reginald Turnill, the BBC's man in Houston during the _Apollo XI_ drama, improbably did to a Radio 4 audience in December, that the "astonishing thing about America's post-Apollo space plans is that they are being drawn up largely by Englishmen."[11]

There was some irony, perhaps, in the fact that the same satellite technology that brought the Moon landing from Houston to London, had four years earlier sent to an expectant American audience live images of the funeral of "the greatest Englishman"—the End of Empire versus the Dawn of the Space Age. For Americans, this was a Britain of the past, heritage Britain, an anticipation perhaps, amid the media hype of "swinging London," of the coming decade's fascination not with British Pop but with transatlantic nostalgia. For the British viewing the Apollo mission, satellites brought an America of thundering Saturn rockets, of power and modernity, and if Britain could reciprocate by at least receiving those signals, as a plugged-in partner, the closest it itself could actually get to space travel was the London studio where the American director Stanley Kubrick had turned Arthur Clarke's fiction, _2001, A Space Odyssey_, into at least celluloid reality.

As image and metaphor, televisual astronauts of course floated free of narrow national readings. _Apollo VIII_'s picture of a distant, fragile Earth energized a dawning transatlantic radical ecology movement, while the Anglo-American feminist Mary Ellman, in 1968, wrote of the astronaut's space-suited body—awkward and encumbered "as the body of a pregnant woman"—revealing man's physical strength to be "gratuitous."[12] For some, man's triumphal conquest of space exposed his analogous inability to conquer poverty, injustice, and social inequality at home on Earth. Sammy Davis, in the Moon-landing night debate, gave merely a faint echo of Black Power's much more radical take on warped American priorities.

In fact, the euphoric excitement of the moment produced quite quickly, in Britain, a backwash of sometimes sour reflections about what it revealed about the special relationship. In November, veteran journalist William Hardcastle, in an article in the BBC's _The Listener_ entitled "Mid-Atlantic," mused whether "[in] one sense . . . this [the broadcast of Americans on the Moon] is a propaganda exercise, a commercial for America's overweening technological expertise." Hardcastle was expressing less provocatively what the technophobic countercultural press in both the United States and Britain was already saying. In the August/September issue of the underground monthly _OZ_, Bob Hughes had written that the _Apollo_ landing had been "the greatest and most expensive public relations exercise in the history of man," one that was, he thought, saturated with religious parody and obsolete symbols of nationalism and patriotism.[13]

Readings of the Moon landing as emblematic of a future of technological progress clashed from the start with contrasting readings that dwelt on the irony of American modernity in space and American atavism in Vietnam and in its burning ghettos, the contrast of power and impotence, the contradictions between a NASA-inspired future techno-utopia and a descent into a domestic dystopia of assassination, race-war, and anarchy. The summer of the Moon landing news from the United States was full of Black Power anger, a radical Women's Liberation movement, and the explosion of the Stonewall Riot and Gay Lib demos in New York City, while in Chicago Judge Hoffmann was preparing a media-circus show trial for the Chicago Eight. For many observers, the decade's close suggested that the conquest of the Moon might be an end rather than a beginning, the concluding chapter of an era defined by Kennedy-optimism and the missionary project of American-style modernization. Considered thusly, the failure of the internal power at Saarinen's modernist embassy on this night of all nights was as symbolic as that of the embattled defense of the modern high-rise embassy in Saigon during Tet.

Christopher Booker, in his 1969 diatribe against the "gigantic 'vitality-fantasy'" of "swinging London" and countercultural revolution, *The Neophiliacs*, anticipated the exhaustion of what he called the twentieth century's "American dream . . . the most powerful 'vitality image' in the world." The novelist J. G. Ballard, in an interview six years later, echoed more sympathetically this sense of closure in his own recollections of 1969: "Armstrong landing on the moon. That was a stupendous event. I thought the psychological reverberations would be enormous . . . . In fact it was almost nil . . . . Clearly the Space Age is over." The Moon landing, viewed from Trafalgar Square, is then a moment that can be unpacked in a number of different ways. Most obviously it made a graphic statement about a common humanity—but also about a shrinking Atlantic and American technological hegemony. If Anglo-American viewing was coparticipation, as in so much else it was the British receiving and the Americans giving. It was an event that celebrated, if in those flat American tones, the common language of a medium that made each accessible to the other as never before, and yet it highlighted difference. As the first lines of a British novel published shortly after the landing put it, "In the same year that Man first flew to the moon and the last American soldier left Vietnam there were still corners of England where lived men and women who had never travelled more than fifteen miles from their own homes."[14]

Special Relations

Introduction

THE ISSUES

Much has been written in the past twenty years or so about the so-called special relationship between Britain and the United States.[1] Most of this literature has been concerned with diplomacy and politics, and with the ways in which these may have been, in the post–Second World War, influenced by the transatlantic connections of each country's elite professional classes, public and private institutions that facilitate exchange, and the ever more intricately enmeshed and globalized realms of media, commerce, and finance. This study—more a series of explorations than an attempt at an all-inclusive narrative—examines a more demotic field.

Viewing the special relationship as popular culture involves potentially a vast area of study, and begs large issues embedded in what are now long-standing debates over how "culture" operates across national boundaries—in this case quite specifically across the north Atlantic among English-speaking peoples—and its relationship to both public policy and private subjectivity. It means explicit or implicit engagement with the vast scholarly literature on "cultural imperialism" generally and "Americanization" specifically, on "globalization" and the presumed polarities of hegemonic production and local reception. While this study has, I hope, something to say about these large framing issues, it is not a sustained exercise in postmodern or post-postmodern argument so much as a highly selective excursion. As such boundaries had to be established.

This is largely a study of one side of the "relationship," Britain, chiefly in the metropolis of London within the twenty years or so from the mid-fifties to the mid-seventies, and mostly among the (largely considered) middle class. Though admitting, in fact insisting upon, a certain circularity of cultural influence, we are not especially concerned with the ways in which Americans might have absorbed aspects of Britishness, except, as in the seventies, when this seems to have had a rebounding influence in Britain. This book is concerned with Britain's reaction to American popular culture, as transmitted through the vast increase in contact in this period—through tourist and professional cross-traffic and in the unparalleled growth in the density of transatlantic media. The one was facilitated by a great surge in relatively cheap and rapid air-travel; the latter, by radio, phonograph, and television. The period, the two decades, roughly, between the Suez Crisis in 1956 and the American Bicentennial and British fiscal crisis of 1976 encompasses the era when personal and media connection most thickened. Phenomena of special postwar cultural relations that this study will spotlight include the prospect of the Manhattanization of the London cityscape in the late fifties, anti-American protest in the sixties, Anglo-American Pop, rock, and utopian counterculture, the radical politics of liberation in the late sixties and early seventies, and the transatlantic construction of "heritage Britain" in the decade that followed.

White admittedly there are many Britains, the focus here is unapologetically on London, not only because it is more central to national life and culture than any other major city in the United Kingdom can be, and because pragmatically to include provincial life in this study would have risked spinning the narrative out of control, but also because it is necessary to contest a trend in cultural studies that has focused on the eccentricities of local reception while losing sight of the big picture—that is, of the force, persistence, and depth of the transatlantic influences that are most pronounced in the capital. It was in London that the special cultural relationship was most tangibly—though of course not, in the modern media-drenched world, exclusively—available, where the actual presence of American tourists, American residents, and American students was densest, and where the mid-Atlantic financial, commercial, and entertainment institutions were most available.

Finally, some will feel that this study's focus on America-in-London overstates the influence of but one of a multitude of postwar social factors. Its intention, however, is not to offer a complete explanation for cultural change, but rather to undo neglect, and its rationale lies precisely in the blindness of much of the current scholarly literature to the American presence and its influence. A repeated coda of British responses to implications of American influence throughout the period has been a defensive insistence on the "authenticity" of British (or English) form and content in just those genres where the transatlantic contexts are most obvious—commercial architecture and urban design, protest folk music and jazz, Pop art and psychedelic rock, the counterculture's alternative press, or the radical late-sixties liberationisms of race, gender, and sexuality. This is to privilege and exaggerate local difference in ways that serve to deny, displace, or trivialize what had once been no doubt too easily assumed—the hegemonic reality of the postwar American cultural presence. It was, and is, a defensiveness that says more about British anxieties over identity generally in the post-Suez era than about how their culture actually operated to absorb and adapt.

One might observe that postwar London did not, as is sometime suggested in postcolonial, postmodern studies, transit from Imperial Metropolis directly to "a globalized and transcultural 'world city'" of decolonized migrants and London-born transnational communities.[2] Mixed into the "transitional and conflicted environment" where models of national identity were challenged and re-examined was not only postcolonial migration but also a quite different presence—that of middle-class American sojourners in the capital, and the technology-driven, consumerist, media-inscribed culture associated with them. This was a diaspora with a difference. It was by and large temporary, often in pursuit of leisure, usually white (though black America left a pronounced mark on race relations and black self-identity in Britain), and generally wealthy enough to pursue habits of conspicuous consumption—a community diffused throughout the capital though occupying most densely certain colonized areas.

The volume of Americans entering Britain in any year after the early sixties is much greater than the annual influx of New Commonwealth immigrants, a fact that has been largely ignored because their migration was, as individuals, a generally transitory one and largely white at a time when popular discourse centered race in the challenge to British identity; for all the anxious talk of Americanization the American presence was more likely to produce sarcasm than fear and hatred. And yet . . . one might argue that the Anglo-American nexus this influx promoted actually did more to subvert traditional British mentality, class relations, and cultural style than did the first and second generations of postcolonial peoples. American presence was more subtly penetrative—exposed only momentarily and episodically, as when Conrad Hilton's hotel shot above the tree-line at Hyde Park.

Americanization as Cultural Imperialism?[3]

In the postwar era America's political and military leadership of "the free world," the dollar's dominance in the world financial system, its robust and globally expansionist commercial operations, and the rapid global proliferation of its media, especially television, generated journalism and scholarship that was generally, if not always, critical of Americanization-as-cultural-imperialism. European intellectuals were inevitably more concerned about the "challenge" of "Coca-Colonization" and "admass" culture than apparently were the eager consumers of American commodities and American style.[4] In Britain, though traditionalists (and some voices on the left) might rail at American vulgarity, intellectual objections were perhaps more muted than those in, say, France, where Servan-Schreiber's mid-sixties warning in *Le Defi Americaine* struck chords of apprehension that had long resonated there.[5] American influence was, however, much more pervasive—and more familiar—in Britain than in the rest of Europe, and Americanization, as threat or reality, became a cliché of popular British discourse by the fifties. A common language provided easier access, Anglo-American cross-traffic was of longer standing, American commercial, industrial, and financial penetration was deeper and earlier, and Cold War "American Studies" programs (significantly complicit "in the process of Americanization," according to one critic) were more extensively entrenched in British universities than elsewhere in Europe.[6]

There was an overheated tone to much of the "threat of Americanization" literature in Britain as elsewhere, moral panics that reflected often a more general unease over modernization, mass "leveling-down" culture, and consumerism, for which America served as both convenient symbol and presumed agent. Even a scholarly exploration like C. W. E. Bigsby's 1975 collection, *Superculture: American Popular Culture and Europe*, had a breathless character in its enumeration of ways in which "American values, ideals, myths and ideas penetrate the consciousness of a world for whom the modern experience is coeval with the American experience."[7] Correspondingly there was often a general neglect of just how, at the ground level, Americanization worked, what were the significant cultural boundaries, and what kind of dialogue actually occurred across them. The term itself was loaded with generally negative, defensive connotations, characterized by tropes of invasion in a binary cultural world of (threatening, mobile) America and (stationary, passive) target peoples. If the issue passed from excited journalism to a more serious, reflective scholarship in the seventies,[8] it continued often to be dominated by relatively crude assumptions about the coercive agency (of American institutions and practices)—as in, notably, media studies, a critical discipline in the seventies and eighties for issues of Americanization and cultural imperialism. At the same time from other quarters there was an increasingly skeptical questioning of the very concept of a unique and unitary "American" cultural presence and of its efficacy in asserting itself as a model for the world. As Richard Rose wrote in 1974, "What is often called Americanization may be no more than a set of experiences common to all (or most) Western industrial societies." There followed a scholarly debate, appropriate perhaps to the dystopian seventies, about, not the potency of America as cultural and economic invader, but its limitations and the way the "American model" was rarely simply transferred to other societies but twisted and reformed and hybridized to "fit."[9]

Although some on the left persisted in an understanding of Americanization as cultural imperialism, and, more eccentrically, some on the right continued to engage in a robust defense of Americanization as a modernizing, democratizing positive force, by the eighties and nineties these fell outside what quickly became the revisionist mainstream.[10] Much of this revisionism has, like the work of Richard Pells, emphasized the "relatively brief" nature of American cultural ascendancy in the fifties and, more important, the circularity (cross-fertilization) and fluidity of cultural contact as well as critical issues of contestation and "reception."[11] The emerging discipline of Cultural Studies re-examined consumption as "social process," emphasizing specific social geographies and the ways in which the use of imports—of, especially, American commodities, idiom, and style—is locally negotiated, creating variety rather than a homogenized "flattening out" of global culture. As two practitioners have recently claimed, "[It] has become increasingly apparent that British consumers' reactions to 'Americanization' are in fact locally variable and specific."[12]

Conceptually valuable as this perspective has been, as an interpretive orthodoxy it threatens, by privileging models of transmutation and adaptation in a pick-and-choose world of cultural choice, to substitute for a crude idea of invasion and coercion an equally simplistic one of easy self-agency. Such anthropology-driven approaches favored by a highly localized cultural studies project have not been wrong in focusing on difference and hybridity,[13] quite the contrary, but they have—in collaboration with more traditional defensive assertions of the "authenticity" of the national or local—had the effect of shifting scholarly interest away from the underlying reality—namely, that American popular culture was a transformative engine of great power, and away from just how and through what kinds of agents it operated.

Richard Pells argued, surely too categorically, that "the 'Americanization' of Europe is a myth," or at least "mainly symbolic."[14] This of course is to beg the understanding of what Americanization (or modernization or globalization) might mean—concepts not as obvious as many sometimes assume. Hybridity and adaptation aside, the centrality of American influence can hardly be denied in either the form or content of European, and especially British, cultural practice, though no one today would argue that this influence resulted in cookie-cutter duplication. Finally, for our purposes here many such studies of Europe and the United States seem to overstretch to apply to Britain generalizations more congenial to language cultures other than English, and so fail to engage very convincingly just the degree—for Americanization implies degree—to which influence has or has not taken root. In this sense, Britain is a quite special case.[15]

This book does not attempt to replow already well-tilled ground—in the subcultural exploration, say, of the use of American rock'n'roll and American style to focus teenage rebellion, the hegemony of Hollywood in British cinema, or the familiar debate over advertising and the importation of American values along with its cornflakes. Structural changes in the media are largely beyond our scope as well. Nor does this study have much to say about another enduring, usually negative topic from the fifties on—the "corruption" of the vocabulary and pronunciation of British English.[16] What it does offer is a thick description and analysis of the transatlantic character of a number of metropolitan locations and "moments" over a critical twenty-year period, with the object of repositioning American culture and its agents as central to any narrative of Britain in this era—and beyond.

Whose Culture?

London was the most important postwar locus for British modernity, as the northern industrial cities had been in the previous century.[17] Central to the re-shaping of the subjectivities of mid- and late-twentieth-century urban life, and for much of the postpermissive, postmodern critique of this reshaping, it was also the site of greatest American cultural and physical penetration. With the important exception of the impact of American race relations on black Londoners, this study keeps its focus by and large on the capital's middle class rather than cosmopolitan or traditionalist Establishment elites or (especially teenage fractions of) the working class, where much subcultural sociology and culture studies anthropology has concentrated its exploration. American influence is of course to be found there, but the experience of cultural contact, beyond the bricolage of commodified style, is likely to be subjectively more profound among an educated, individuated middling sort in search of a role, a minority of the nation, but a large, growing, consuming, minority that was, culturally, strategically located.

This brings us to a contested issue of some importance for any historical study of popular culture that attempts to revisit the sixties—namely, whether any narrative of such flamboyant times risks overstating the cultural changes that are so firmly lodged in generational memory. Clearly one cannot take the rhetoric of euphoric countercultural and liberationist self-discovery at face value, nor assume that the majority of the nation, of any class or generation, embraced "permissiveness" and rock-driven rebellion. But to assume therefore that a radical minority culture is aberrant and marginal to the conservative majority and therefore dismissible, as was common among much postparty commentary at the end of the era and among much scholarly revisionism since, begs large issues of historical narrative and how over time change occurs. Majorities are generally conservative, viewed through opinion polls and quotidian practice.

The rewriting of the era was under way—among participants as well as of course those reactionary voices who had never regarded (often American-inspired) generational change as either desirable or inevitable—already before the seventies malaise encouraged a sense of failure and dissipation. In Britain Christopher Booker and Bernard Levin got their cynical demystifying shafts in early. In the United States, William O'Neill's history of the sixties, *Coming Apart* (1971), sounded something of the same disillusion ("I wanted to call this book *Good Riddance*, and the galley proofs bore that title"). Since then scholarship has been torn between two poles—those who, often survivors of a radical left tradition, argue defensively for a continuity of sorts from the paradigm break experienced by the generation of '68, and those who take a more skeptical view that contemporary rhetoric and popular memory greatly exaggerate and mischaracterize the real legacies—for good or ill—of the times. By the eighties and nineties the negative critique of the sixties in the United States, either at the hands of liberals or culture warriors on the right, clearly had the better running. Subsequently less polemical scholarship, like that of Doug Rossinow, tended to abandon the larger question of legacy for narrower examinations of countercultural communities as localized subcultures.[18]

In Britain, the seventies and after saw, on the sociological left, an investment in concepts of working-class subcultures that denigrated the fashionable "middle-class hippy culture" imported from the States, while arguing with some force that the majority of working-class youth, both black and white, though employing the signs of rebellion as style, stayed well within the rules of a reciprocal game that ensured their "outsider" mentality and social exclusion. The main thrust of centrist historical sociology has meanwhile been to emphasize the conservatism of both the large majority of youth of whatever class and the general population. This scholarship, often based on conclusions drawn from somewhat tendentious polling techniques, has greatly informed the general narratives of the postwar period that have proliferated since the beginning of this century. So much so that a new orthodoxy has tended to replace the undoubtedly overblown exaggerations of the sixties "revolution" with a flattened out nonhistory of cultural stasis.[19]

When the late Arthur Marwick published his massive history of the sixties in 1998 he was attacked for its conceptual weaknesses (its empiricism), his own liberal animus against both Marxism and much postmodern scholarship, and his persistence in regarding the era of his own generation as culturally revolutionary and its consequences as enduring. Though committed, as he said, to "what happens to majorities, rather than minorities," his concluding judgment was that "permissive attitudes and permissive behavior continued to spread at accelerating rates [after the sixties] .... The cultural revolution, in short, had continuous, uninterrupted, and lasting consequences."[20] Such a judgment was certainly open to criticism from those who argued against a radical shift in popular attitudes and that "permissiveness" per se had a much longer history. Less persuasive, however, is the countervailing assumption that no enduring cultural shift in values and mentality occurred at all, that the kinds of cultural change that the flower power children seemed to be importing wholesale from the States were entirely superficial and transitory. These scholars, such as the historian of postwar Britain currently prominent on BBC documentaries, Dominic Sandbrook, prefer to take their cue from Anthony Sampson's view, in his 1971 edition of the *Anatomy of Britain*, that, rather than drugs, sex, and rock and roll, a "broad picture unfolds of the British living a withdrawn and inarticulate life ... mowing lawns and painting walls, pampering pets, listening to music, knitting and watching television."[21] Such assumptions can lead to truisms of little interpretive value ("During the supposedly radical sixties, the majority of Britain's fifty million people led quiet and somewhat dull sex lives. ...),[22] while submerging, as Sandbrook often does, important agents of change in a welter of misleading rhetorical contrasts: "With more than seventeen million sales worldwide by 1975, *The Sound of Music* easily outdistanced the Beatles' leading album, *Abbey Road*, which sold just nine million"; or "[A]lthough many historians of the sixties pay a great deal of attention to the International Poetry Festival ... it was ... considerably smaller than the typical crowd for a Second Division football match."[23]

By the late sixties, however, mass music festivals, if not poetry readings, were much larger than the largest football crowd, and, as James Jupp observed in 1969, the quarter of a million youth who gathered in Hyde Park that summer were, "Unlike a Cup Final Crowd," a self-conscious and organized "culture," while the vicarious participation of millions more in the Pop and rock music scene suggested a mass phenomenon that at least "rivalled" football's television fandom.[24] He might have added what Sandbrook suppresses, the fact that football, the Beatles, and even poetry, were not necessarily mutually exclusive interests.

CROSS-TRAFFIC

Underpinning this exploration of the special nature of Anglo-American cultural relations from the fifties to the seventies is the fact that the density of transatlantic contact increased significantly in this era and shifted critically from the episodic and casual to the continual and routine, at least in the capital. Contact proliferated in three critical areas: the volume of short-stay and long-stay tourism, the back-and-forth of professional (commercial, financial, and academic) travel—often involving significant periods of residency, and virtual connection through transatlantic media, especially television.

Sightseers

Tourism—and especially dollar-rich American tourism—as a growth industry held out a promise of significant economic advantage to every British government anxious about the country's perennial balance of payments difficulty since the war. The encouragement of tourism became national policy—sometimes in the face of local concerns over traffic congestion, hotel development in residential areas and competition generally for reasonably priced accommodation, swarms of young people sleeping rough in parks (especially a concern in the late sixties), the overcrowding and endangering of historic sites by package tour groups, and an annoyance generally at being "colonized"—that is, losing a sense of local ownership and belonging.[25]

Attlee's government established a British Tourist and Holidays Board in January of 1947, and the next year Board of Trade officials presided over an interdepartmental committee on tourism. By January of 1951 the government was sponsoring an official advertising blitz in popular U.S. journals and newspapers. Meanwhile in the private sector, the Travel Association had been concentrating its own publicity resources on the potential American market as well. In an era when austerity kept the British at home, affluent Americans were bringing an increasing number of dollars into the country.[26]

According to the *International Tourism Quarterly* in 1971, the golden American core of the general increase in tourism into the U.K. had grown inexorably between 1964 and 1970 (nearly tripling to 1,400,000).[27] Labour under Wilson had moved to encourage this money-spinner by subsidizing tourist hotel development, and in 1969 a Development of Tourism Act established the British Tourist Authority to promote tourist attractions and funnel further financial assistance toward the construction and renovation of tourist hotels. Though some thought much more might have been done, perhaps the creation of a Ministry for Tourism, it is clear, however, that the real driving force lay less in British efforts to advertise and increase hotel capacity than in the phenomenal prosperity and mobility of Americans, the increased speed (commercial transatlantic jet travel began in 1958) and progressive cheapening of travel (through charter flights or Icelandic Air's low fares), and, generally, a "democratization of leisure" in the sixties. All in fact that the British had to do was to lie back and think of the balance of payments. The devaluation of the pound in 1967 served further to attract foreign consumers.[28]

Britain's earnings from tourism nearly doubled during the third Wilson government's period in office, with consistent increases of 20 percent or so a year. The enormous increase in visitors at the end of the decade, and some panic over yet further projected increases, prompted the GLC to generate its own "urgently needed" plans for "management" of the tourist "industry" at the local level. If the rate of growth in fact slackened somewhat after 1971, the numbers of tourists generally, and in particular American tourists, continued to increase as wide-bodied Boeing 747 "jumbo jets" (beginning in 1970 on the New York–London route) significantly increased capacity. "On a typical day," Alisdair Fairley informed the readers of *The Listener* in March 1973, six thousand Americans arrive in Britain.[29] Though the 1973 energy crisis stalled growth for a couple of years, after 1975 the trend continued upward. As C. W. E. Bigsby colorfully put it, "Almost certainly, more Americans will visit Europe between the years 1974 and 1980 than Europeans emigrated to the United States in the one hundred and fifty years between 1820 and 1970."[30]

Just how the great influx of American visitors was regarded by most British, and what role they might have played in Anglo-American cultural relations, is, of course, less certain than the numbers. As there was a general rise in tourism from other parts of the world as well, English-speaking American "cousins" could often be regarded as less awkward guests, though their affluence, accents, and uninformed naivety inevitably made them the humorous butt of jokes and cartoons. Whether this comic stereotyping reflects a deeper anti-Americanism in the post-Suez world depends probably on class and perhaps locale. In 1967 Piri Halasz, in her *Swingers' Guide to London*, offered advice to the more sophisticated of her American readers on "How Not to Look Like a Tourist" and "How Not to Act Like a Tourist."[31]

Certainly one does not have to look hard to find annoyance and ill-will among at least some of the literary elite and social Establishment, however much the Duke of Bedford might have profited from playing host to coach-loads of Texans at Woburn Abbey. The *Economist* reported that there were "rumblings of British resentment" especially after the leap in the volume of tourism after 1969 (in London some of this seemed fueled—it was not a new sentiment—by the fear that local residents were being squeezed out by the Labour-promoted development of luxury hotels).[32] In the summer of 1971 V. S. Pritchett grew sarcastic in a broadcast on Radio 4 about how "startling" it had become "to hear an English voice in the centre of London, which was simply taken over" by tourists who regarded the native inhabitants as "a curiosity," "simply picturesque." They represented, he thought, a kind of "offensive private colonialism." "The tourist is not rare. He Swarms. He is an example of mass human pollution."[33]

> [T]he summer 'American season' is ending. Knapsacked, Fanon-reading students are returning to strikes and confrontation at Berkeley and Ohio State.[34]

Antitourism as one form of anti-Americanism had long been a familiar discourse. What was new in the sixties and early seventies was a particular distaste for a striking change in the demographic of tourism in Britain, not just the increase in the more modest, less sophisticated middle-American families, but a surge in the proportion that were unattached youth—less interested in the packaged rituals of the tourism industry than, in the free-wheeling, backpacking style of the era, having a good time. Sixties youth tourists were seen not only as a social problem that raised concerns about care and housing but also as conduits of drug-culture radicalism spreading from a dystopian America. By the end of the decade it was estimated that something like a third of all tourists were "young visitors." In 1972 the journalist Morrison Halcrow told *Daily Telegraph* readers that the tourist "invasion" had become even more tiresome for many with the advent of the youthful tourist "doing the trip on a shoestring," even if the countercultural "hordes of penniless young overseas visitors, 'sleeping rough,'" had proved a temporary problem (though even well-heeled Americans gave cause for irritation, as they put up the price of antiques, theater tickets, and "flats in Belgravia"). The next year Alfred Sherman, a political journalist who had migrated from the Marxist left to the Conservative Party, informed the same audience that "the lower down the [social] scale one goes"—to students and "hippies"—the less the country got out of Labour's rush "into the scramble for tourists," and the more they caused Londoners "a loss of amenity and self-respect."[35]

Although some unease over the great influx was widespread, especially severe views seem to be, if not eccentric, at least not widely expressed beyond certain predictably prickly Tory and Establishment circles drawing on their own long traditions of anti-Americanism. Moreover, what anti-Americanism there was was often, it would seem, drawn as much from a familiar "discourse" that had been in place since at least the Second World War and the years immediately following as from actual contact. If one compares, for instance, the views British people expressed to Mass Observation during the war or those recorded in a survey of 1952 (Americans as friendly, generous, and cheerful, though boastful, immature, ostentatious, noisy, and materialistic) with a survey of British university students more than a decade later (who regarded Americans as dynamic, vigorous, and friendly, though vulgar, adolescent, materialistic, shallow, and noisy), the sense is of an ambivalence that was learned and rehearsed. What did arguably change in the sixties was perhaps the large proportion that had believed in 1952 that "the British could withstand any possible ill-effects of American influence."[36]

Nevertheless, the image of the American did acquire a deeper experiential context through the sixties and early seventies as tourism became thickly commonplace (and not only in the summer months), rather than exceptional. There was also an emerging infrastructure, at least in London, that serviced American taste as well as Britons in search of American style. This raised the issue of how a host country might expect to attract tourists, not by "being themselves" but by offering an urban environment attractive to tourists who might want to see the iconic sights but expected the comforts of home. Inevitably it led to a sometimes painful discussion of how the growing number of Americans as visitors and residents might come to exert an influence in reshaping the urban landscape and its amenities—toward on the one hand a modern American consumerism that would subsequently see McDonald's replace Coca-Cola as symbolic of intrusion, and on the other the Disneyfied faux heritage realm of the London Dungeon (1976) or public houses named or renamed to suit American expectations.[37]

The irony of a Britain in need of (American-style) modernization grounding its search for American dollars in its "quaint" historical character was available throughout our period. In 1959 Colin MacInnes had a character in his novel *Absolute Beginners* observe of Belgravia, site of wealthy American migration:

> I see it as an Olde Englishe product like Changing the Guard, or Saville row suits, or Stilton cheese in big brown china jars, or any of those things they advertise in *Esquire* to make the Americans want to visit picturesque Great Britain.[38]

This had become a more tangible issue by the seventies because of the vogue for nostalgia, heritage, and preservationism—itself related to the thickening cross-traffic of Americans. In 1971 the *Economist*, a British journal increasingly dependent on a transatlantic readership, observed, only somewhat tongue-in-cheek, that "the Royals are worth subsidising simply as a lure for foreign visitors." And more seriously, that while "[h]istory, pageantry, and high quality shopping are

Britain's main draws," tourists made "an essential contribution to the preservation of . . . British heritage. Many historic houses, villages, old churches and so on could not be kept in a proper state of repair without the tourists' money."[39]

A much larger and less certain area of speculation is the degree to which tourism might have become a factor in the Americanization of Britain, not through commercial institutions that offered American commodities to both tourists and local residents but at the level of interpersonal experience and connection. Tourism by definition is transitory, and the industry at least at the lower end tends to be organized in ways that probably work to isolate rather than to encourage communication between host and visitor. This may have been less true earlier when many American visitors even in London would have stayed in modest bed-and-breakfast hotels, but by the seventies the majority probably stayed in the large hotels, newly built or rebuilt to cater for a mass market. These proliferated especially during the development boom of 1970–73, when the number of large hotels in central London doubled.[40]

The growth in short-stay tourism between the mid-fifties and the mid-seventies certainly left its mark on British attitudes about Americans. As a GLC steering group on tourism observed somewhat anxiously in 1971, "Walk along Whitehall on a summer's afternoon and the chances are that over half the people you pass will not be Londoners."[41] Many of these of course would not have been from the States, but North America provided by far the largest category of foreign visitor.[42] The longer-staying among them, like their counterparts among the British professionals, students, and academics who increasingly expected to spend time in the States, matter more for our purposes. Like holiday tourism, this was a demographic that increased very significantly in this era but involved a deeper transatlantic engagement and exchange.

Changing Places

Muriel Beadle traveled from southern California to take up residence for a year in late-fifties Oxford with her husband (a visiting lecturer at Balliol) and son. She later recalled, in a much-republished memoir of her experiences, her embarrassed reluctance to strike up conversations with other Americans when shopping in London: "My own accent would have equated me with them—and they're *tourists*. I'm not. I *live* here." This desire on the part of longer-stay visitors from the States to blend in, to adopt a kind of protective coloration, is familiar throughout our period, though perhaps sharper in the earlier years and in Establishment environments where, as Beadle claims, "class stratifications" made her "uncomfortable." Beadle's account affords a nice view, from an American perspective, of a world of transatlantic experience that would shift in some respects, like British society itself, fairly radically over the next twenty years, and in others remain familiar and constant. Social formality, dress protocol, the exclusion of women from college social life, the difficulty in picking up class-specific differences in accent ("I never mastered the art"), the apparent indifference of the English to "comforts" Americans took for granted were no doubt especially reflective of the time and milieu, as was the unexpected drabness of their lodgings, the lack of central heating, lousy telephone service, and the common expectation that "Americans are supposed to complain about something." On the other hand, Beadle's Anglophilic expectations of "mannered civility" in an England that was a "cultural homeland" endured and indeed, as we shall see, enjoyed a special revival in the "heritage" obsessed seventies.[43]

Among the increasing number of academic migrants, social isolation and the difficulties of household management would no doubt have been most pronounced among wives, though single women without family or "introductions," especially in the fifties and early sixties, could feel pretty firmly closed out from even the casual rituals of social life. With the increased migration of professional women later in the period, and the loosening of social restraints generally, things no doubt eased considerably. In the seventies Brenda Maddox, an American journalist for the *Economist* based in London who constantly flew back and forth between Britain and the United States, was perhaps representative of a new generation of professional women who managed successful transatlantic careers. Nevertheless, though married to an English academic, she continued to experience "[her] own transatlantic imbalance." Another professional woman, Susan Marling, came to Britain in 1973 and developed there a career in journalism and broadcasting. She often commuted to the United States, not always for her work in the media but sometimes simply "for sharp talk, power showers and the guiltless pleasure of valet parking."[44]

Though the long-staying American visitor, or indeed, intermarrying permanent resident, was distinguished from the mere tourist by his or her attempted participation in British life, it may be doubted whether these became in our period exactly a "cosmopolitan" class floating easily among the "locals" as one scholar has suggested. Transnational occupations—in academia, the media, commerce and finance, the arts—are not necessarily transnational "cultures." If there was a cosmopolitan class of Americans in London, they were more likely to be "swinging" media celebrities (especially in the sixties) or, as Alistair Cooke suggested (in his Rede Lecture at Cambridge University in 1975), the wealthy retired who "flocked to live in London on the claim that it was the last civilized city."[45]

By the sixties it was likely, thanks to a network of public and private international programs, that those of the professional and political classes in each country would have had some transatlantic experience—as a student or young careerist. Well before the war, Rhodes scholarships, the Commonwealth Fund (the "Harkness Fellowships," from 1925), the Rockefeller and Guggenheim foundations, the Carnegie Endowment for International Peace or the American Council of Learned Societies operated to encourage Americans to study in Europe and British scholars and preprofessionals to have some experience in the States. After the war there was the Cold War–driven Fulbright program (1946) and the State Department's own Foreign Leader Program (after the passage of the Smith-Mundt Act in 1948), while the Ford Foundation invested substantially in the fifties in schemes for youth and leadership exchange. In 1967, Margaret Thatcher, like many young Atlanticists on the right of the Labour Party, spent several weeks visiting America on the State Department program: "The excitement which I felt has never really subsided."[46]

The vagaries of the visa system and migration-counting make it impossible to gauge with any precision either the actual number of professional or academic visitors from the mass of sightseeing tourists. It is reasonable to assume, however, that they increased significantly in this period. GLC surveys estimated that by the early seventies some 11 or 12 percent of short-stayers came to Britain for the purposes of education and "business"—including conferences and conventions (the American Bar Association met in London in 1971)—and that the number of foreign (mostly American) business visitors' bed-nights would grow (from roughly 4.4 million in 1967 to 15 million by 1980).[47] Transatlantic networks in many fields—academia, the arts, the media—were encouraging transatlantic traffic. In that of British historical studies, say, the period saw the growth of Anglo-American connections in a context of increasing scholarship support for postgraduate travel and research and less expensive, easier access to Britain. The North American Conference on British Studies, which was founded in 1950, had established by the sixties a close relationship with the Institute for Historical Research and the Royal Historical Society.

At the same time, visiting positions at British universities (and especially at the newer postwar universities) proliferated, both in expanding American Studies programs and generally, leading to fear that the "inbred" American practice, complained of by Kingsley Amis and others, of novelists and poets with academic posts churning out promotion-generating books would spread to Britain as well. Amis in characteristically grumpy form claimed, in 1969, that the literary "culture" in Britain was becoming Americanized: "[D]ifferences get ironed out . . . as Kent becomes more and more like California," a sentiment that resonated closely with V. S. Pritchett's despairing observation that "it is going the same way with us as America . . . . [A] great many of us have been to America, and, although we enjoy ourselves, we are not altogether happy about culture as industry."[48]

Fears of the Americanization of the British academic and literary worlds, through of the influx of American writers and academics as well as the (American) consolidation of the publishing industry, often reflect the ruffled annoyance of an older generation like Pritchett and Amis at the tendency of many younger British writers to disparage "British" traditions and look, instead, to New York, Chicago, and San Francisco. But the visibility of American writers and scholars in Britain did rise precipitously from the mid-fifties to the early seventies, a phenomenon that can be tracked through the pages of the *Times Literary Supplement*. The *TLS* had sporadically covered American literature since the end of the First World War, but in the mid-fifties began to devote more sustained, regular attention to new American work. New American publications regularly found reviewers, American publishers ran full-page advertisements, and the paper itself solicited new American poetry. This was aimed not only at the British market but also increasingly at achieving significant sales in the United States—something it was apparently successful at until the *New York Review of Books*, itself modeled on the *TLS*, cut into the American market from the mid-sixties.[49]

Visibility also drew in part from the fact that American literary visitors on holiday or promoting their books—like Norman Mailer, John Updike, or Saul Bellow—were commonly available to the British media for radio and television interviews, as were the growing community of Americans resident in Britain—often visiting lecturers like the poet Robert Lowell—in the late sixties and early seventies, for topics ranging from their special areas of concern to the widest observations on American modernity, the counterculture, feminism, race relations, the war in Vietnam, and the anarchy in American universities. Moreover, younger staff at the BBC were increasingly likely to have visited the States, and their enthusiasm for America was often resented by older managers.[50]

While the cross-traffic in the other direction was also significant, these British scholars-in-residence, though they might be lionized on campus, were not of much interest to the American media—which was rather less curious about Britain than their counterparts in British radio and television were, obsessively some thought, about the States. British academics who spent time in the United States—and by the end of our period it can seem as though nearly everyone on the make or of some eminence did so—were however important transatlantic cultural conduits. Their own research and writing was often informed, positively or negatively, by their American excursions, and back in Britain they were often courted, as were Americans in London, by the media for panel discussions and commentary on the American scene. This was especially true of those British academics in the expanding fields of American Studies and the sociology of race relations, but the media was also interested in the wide range of academic fields— English Literature especially (including the many British novelists who took up visiting posts at American colleges and universities), but also sociologists of crime and youth culture, historians, architectural critics, and psychologists.

Along with the growing academic cross-traffic, there was a growing American presence in London drawn from the arts, in an era when transatlantic communication flourished in the world of theater—both directors and actors, especially in alternative experimental theater—and in music and the plastic arts (with

American exhibitors becoming common in the major private and public British galleries). The most prominent celebrity chef and propagandist of serious cuisine in sixties London, Robert Carrier (MacMahon), came from New York (in 1959), as "camp outsider," and did, as one obituarist thought, more to broaden the "appeal of fancy food and cookery" than Elizabeth David, "as radical, perhaps, for British mores as the contraceptive pill or the Beatles."[51] Arguably, the most prominent film director in London was the American ex-pat Stanley Kubrick (most British directors of note having gone in the other direction).

The snobbery that the American presence in London often provoked in the earlier period had been largely an elite phenomenon, tinged no doubt with an element of envy in a postimperial, post-Suez world. It often dwelt, as did Nancy Mitford in *Noblesse Oblige*, on the presumed crass materialism of the American-as-overpaid-consumer: "Americans relate all effort, all work and all of life to the dollar. Their talk is nothing but dollars. The English seldom sit happily chatting for hours on end about pounds."[52] Such views did not disappear; indeed they, or some version of them, entered popular culture as American tourists in the sixties became ever more numerous and more visible throughout the year. But it did become more difficult to sustain without contradiction and complication the simple anti-Americanism of the past in a social environment where a much larger number of middle- and upper-middle-class British people had personal knowledge of American friends and associates, and an ever-thickening exposure to American life on television that, as Daniel Snowman observed in 1977 in his extended essay on *Britain and America*, offered "ordinary people" the opportunity "for the widening of their direct and indirect experiences of other times, places, and people." Not that this impressed V. S. Pritchett, who found that "[p]eople whose blood boiled about foreigners once in a lifetime can bring it to a boil every night by looking at television."[53]

The most memorable chronicler of the phenomenon of "Changing Places" in the academic transatlantic world, the novelist David Lodge, famously offered in 1975 a satirical picture of Anglo-American difference that is not free of the snobbery of the earlier era, though of a self-deprecating kind. His contrasting characters—the American English lit. scholar from Berkeley ("thrusting, ambitious, caustic, Jewish") and his meek counterpart from Birmingham ("diffident, amateurish, decent, white Anglo-Saxon protestant")—are drawn from familiar stereotypes, though informed by Lodge's own transatlantic experience (as a Harkness fellow at Brown University in 1964–65 and as a visiting professor at Berkeley in 1969).[54] Whether they successfully offered, as he intended, types that were "a quintessential representation of each country" depends on whether national character is to be viewed as essential, unitary, and "authentic," or, as this study suggests, malleable, plural, and increasingly transatlantic.

Transatlantic Television

There has been some debate over the past twenty years or so about exactly how the content of American television programming in a globally expanding marketplace might actually be received locally—that is, how the overt and subtextual messages of its entertainments and its advertising might be "read" by diverse communities. What is not debatable, however, is the fact that American television programming in the fifties and sixties, in spite of attempts at quotas,[55] saturated British viewing, and American televisual techniques and American genre (crime and police shows, soaps or quiz programs) significantly influenced domestic production.

By the year of the Suez Crisis, the public broadcaster, the BBC, and its recently established commercial rival, ITV, were already providing a wide range of American viewing—from *Amos n' Andy, Burns and Allen, Jack Benny,* and *The Life of Riley* on BBC to *The Bob Cummings Show, My Little Margie, Topper, Father Knows Best, I Love Lucy, Dragnet,* and *Gunsmoke* on ITV. By the end of the decade there was more comedy, the *Bob Hope Show* or *Phil Silvers,* more heart-warming American domestic drama (*Lassie*), and more Westerns (*The Roy Rogers Show, Wells Fargo, Laramie*). These were sometimes promoted by bringing the actors themselves to London: Roy Rogers rode "Trigger" from his hotel to the Leicester Square Odeon.[56]

Asa Briggs, the authorized historian of the BBC, cautions somewhat defensively that nonetheless "British television . . . remained essentially British, not American or Americanized." This assertion begs a number of questions about the medium generally and what "essentially British" might mean over time. While the top ratings may have gone to especially popular domestic offerings, American fare was widespread through the schedule and targeted a wide audience of adults, young people, and children. ITV, challenged to fill its schedule without the production backup that the BBC enjoyed, especially relied on relatively cheap imported American filler—and quickly came to seize a commanding lead in audience share—at a time when watching the telly was rapidly becoming "the core evening leisure activity of the home-centred society," at what Stuart Laing has called "a specific transitional moment in the country's sense of its own identity."[57]

Criticism of a feared Americanization of British television was certainly common in, for instance, the pages of the BBC house journal, *The Listener*: "[T]hey export an awful lot to us," the British author Gillian Freeman observed in 1969. "We may well end up peeling the protective foil from a TV dinner as we watch a re-run of a re-run of *Those Were the Days* which weren't even our days in the first place." Raymond Williams complained that "American jokes [on television] were incomprehensible," while William Hardcastle was repeatedly sarcastic about what he called "mid-Atlantic television" and Philip Whitehead attacked the obsession, as he saw it, of British television news with the United States and its problems. On the other hand it is probably true that the critics overstated any general unease about Americanization. As Alan Howden observed, "I don't think there is any particular pro- or anti-American attitude in regard to imports. If the British public like a programme, they will like it; if they don't they will call it 'American rubbish.'"[58]

If Americanization implies a wholesale and uncritical appropriation of American style and mentality, then the British were not, exactly, Americanized in this twenty-year period of greatly thickening contact. British people, like others, picked out what appealed to them according, no doubt, to personal class and circumstance. But if Americanization implies a continuous "presence" of the United States in the public consciousness, whether offering hope, mere diversion, or threat (anti-Americanism is itself evidence of presence), then Britain was significantly Americanized in this era. What American television had to offer, like American cinema before it and the easier transatlantic travel of the postwar world, was often, whether the images were of New York's skyscrapers or the streets of San Francisco, a classless realm of flat-accented celebrities, modes of pleasurable consumption, and, above all, a sense of "modernity."

PART I

Mayfair Modern

————•◆•————

The 15 April 1966 issue of the popular American weekly news magazine *Time*, anticipating the arrival of the summer tourist season, and echoing the lyrics of country singer Roger Miller's hit of the previous year ("England swings like a pendulum do") informed its middle-American readership that London, "the Swinging City," was the place to be. It was the decade's world city, like tough guy New York or L.A. had been in the forties or Rome of *la dolce vita* in the fifties. For those who could jet there—or indeed for the thousands of "South Ken Yanks" already in residence—the capital boasted a unique frisson of Pop art modernism in a milieu of staid tradition; miniskirts, bell-bottoms, and velvet jackets among the derby-hatted, brolly-carrying pin-striped City gents; and a horizontal "sedate" cityscape of literary imagination erupting, here and there, with skyscrapers: "London, a city steeped in tradition, seized by change .... Ancient elegance and new opulence."[1]

If London also offered a respite from the rage of Vietnam protest and racial confrontation—other lead stories in this issue—it was a world that was not altogether unfamiliar, increasingly marked as it was by an especially fashionable mid-Atlantic hybridity. The "scenes" that Mayfair, Chelsea, or South Kensington (the epicenters of the swinging phenomenon) had to offer—the casinos, art galleries, boutiques, antiques markets, clubs and plush venues for private parties from Park Lane to Sloane Square and the King's Road—were all sites, the editors of *Time* suggested, marked by a "cool" combination of contemporary American and traditional English influences. "Shot through with skyscrapers, including the 30-story London Hilton," the new West End was, as Soho with its jazz and blues clubs had been in the fifties, a geography with a transatlantic character: "[T]he center, the heart of London, has gravitated slowly westward to the haunts of the city's new elite ... somewhere in Mayfair." Moreover, the magazine informed its readers, the swinging areas farther west, Chelsea, Earl's Court, and South Kensington, were being transformed (in part, they might have noted, through the agency of American migration there) into a kind of Upper East Side.[2]

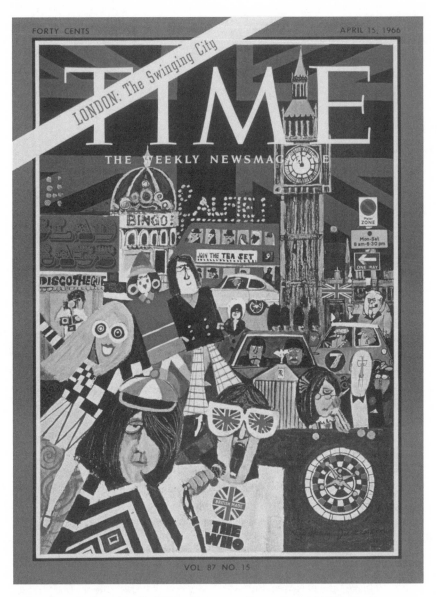

1. "London, the Swinging City." *Time* cover, 15 April 1966. From TIME, 15 April 1966 ©1966 TIME, Inc. All rights reserved. Used by permission and protected by the Copyright Laws of the United States. The printing, copying, redistribution, or retransmission of the Material without express written permission is prohibited.

The iconic cover of this issue of *Time*, a collage of brightly colored cartoon images—Big Ben, a discotheque and a bingo hall, the Who in Union flag–decorated glasses, miniskirted young women and dinner-jacketed casino gamblers—was produced by a British artist, but British Pop art and commercial design, at the heart of the reimaging of London in the early sixties, owed a large debt to American influence, as in the exuberant use of the Union flag in commercial design to decorate everything from Morris minis to underwear. This desacralization of the national emblem, its "tension between patriotic sign and its decontextualised, transgressive identity," and its implied challenge to correct behavior, can be traced directly to American Pop artists' ironic use of the Stars and Stripes in the fifties, and to Jasper Johns's "ambivalent paintings."[3]

If British Pop art in the sixties paralleled as well as imitated the trajectory of, say, Andy Warhol in New York, and if its mature forms worked their own significant influence on American popular design, its origins lay firmly among the young London avant-garde (Eduardo Paolozzi and Richard Hamilton, especially), who, fascinated by American advertising, technology, and media, formed the Independent Group in 1952 and expressed what David Mellor has called a "provocatively unparochial embrace of a dominant, American-based popular culture and its imagination." At the more commercial level, American influence was also loudly influential. Alan Aldridge, art director for Penguin Press in the sixties who "dragged paperback cover designs into the twentieth century, . . . took his cue from American advertising" and sought "to become a sort of Anglicized Andy Warhol." While the London fashion scene may have drawn inspiration from the modernist boutiques of Paris or Milan, many of that scene's artists and photographers, those who laid the "foundations for the visual mythology of 'Swinging London,'" were captivated by New York (many went to see for themselves). Their model "of a highly coloured, brightly animated city of youthful sub-cultures" was the New York evoked by the production of Bernstein's *West Side Story* that opened in December 1958 at Her Majesty's Theatre and by snappy-suited Madison Avenue businessmen and smartly dressed gangsters. This was a vigorous, virile metropolitan America that could offer more of "a corrective to English conservatism of habit" than, perhaps, effete Continental fashion. When the Austin Reed department store in Regent Street, with its distinctly unmodern frontage and somewhat stuffy sartorial tradition, decided to try to attract a younger clientele they hired the RCA artist Robyn Denny to paint an entrance mural. Denny (who would himself exhibit in New York two years later) produced a striking pre-Pop design informed by brash American advertising art that, in David Mellor's view, "epitomises the euphoria of London in the process of re-development—at the height of the office-building explosion which had begun the previous year" and exemplifies the way the relocation of the myth of New York as locus of cool to the London scene served as "prelude to an epic of 'swinging London.'" Three years later Denny's store-front served as a stage-set for one of the Beatles' first publicity photo shoots.[4]

When *Time*'s publisher Bernard Auer asked one of the researchers for the Swinging London story, British-born Mary McConachie, who had joined the New York staff in 1964, why she intended to stay in America, she said "I like swinging New York." Even at the height of the London Pop art world's self-consciousness of its own export success, of having shifted world attention to English chic, there remained often a need to compare, measure against, reference the Big Apple. Robert Fraser, Warhol's dealer in London, whose gallery in Duke Street was at the center of the swinging art world scene, spent his early twenties in New York City. In 1966 he rather waspishly told Piri Halasz, "Right now, London has something that New York used to have: everybody wants to be there."[5]

The New York art, media, and advertising worlds radiated an ethos of mon-eyed chic and democratic savvy that was attractive to many young British avant-gardists—like Richard Smith, another RCA painter in his twenties, who, when he returned in 1961 from a Harkness Fellowship in the United States (where he had met Jasper Johns), moved into a postindustrial loft space in the East End; his subsequent career sent him shuttling back and forth across the Atlantic for exhibitions and college teaching. If, as Simon Rycroft has rightly observed, there was not "a simple appropriation of American ideological or aesthetic freight," the deep cultural politics of the swinging world of London modernism clearly employed an American-inspired democratization of style (and of the marketing of style) in its challenge to the codes and hierarchical values of traditionally class-conscious Britain. It both offered and, sometimes, satirized an art-as-advertising, media-promulgated vision of a "classless" consumer society, to be led by a new British elite of the self-made, talented, and urbane in a milieu of libertarian per-missiveness. This ethos flourished in a jet-set world of businessmen, professionals, entertainers, artists, admen, TV executives, and leisured flaneurs heading east to Mayfair and South Kensington or west to New York and L.A. It is hardly coinci-dental that the important sites of Swinging London were also mostly within the geographic ambit of West-End American tourism and residence or that the aspi-rational mental world of those new-generation British who were on the make was often enmeshed directly or at one remove in American commercial, advertising, and media interests. As Tom Wolfe observed in his contemporary essay on Mid-Atlantic Man, "The Englishman today goes American, becomes a Mid-Atlantic Man, to . . . get out from under the domination of the English upper classes by . . . going classless."[6]

Mid-Atlantic, Mayfair-Modern Man (or woman) represents, however, a quite different version of the classlessness of the self-made social climber than that of-fered by the "Angry" writers of the fifties and early sixties. Though also informed by a reading of the modern world as one defined by American-style individualism and opportunism, their antiheroes struggled out of the subordinate confines of "authentic" communities via hypergamy and a cynical aping of the social norms of the traditional elite to which they aspired. The Angry model is one of a deracinated self within a decaying but tenacious social order; the sixties Pop model is one of a new very fluid elite that relishes elements of the old order, as style, but floats free from it in its essentially narcissistic self-regard. Its proper home is Mayfair or South Kensington, not the brash provincial North; its milieu the chic gallery, jazz club, or swank casino rather than the boardroom—more Anthony Armstrong-Jones than Joe Lambton. It was not marked, among its most flamboyant avatars, by a calculating cynicism so much as a self-justifying exuberance, a shifting multiplicity of self, and a repudiation of suburban middle-class disciplines. If this ethos was embraced as well by significant youthful elements of the traditional class, it was an elite that found in international-set leisure and casual moneyed self-indulgence, an identity unmoored from much sense of historic location.

A striking example of the sixties class-surfing outsider can be seen in the career of Emilio (Mim) Scala. Son of an Italian immigrant father made unexpectedly wealthy by lottery winnings, Scala grew up in the Fulham and Chelsea area of West London working behind the counter of the family's ice-cream parlor—"the next best thing to an American drug-store"—while reveling in American rock'n'roll recordings, Soho jazz clubs, and Teddy Boy style. By 1960 he had left home, sharing a place with, among others, a young American writer (heir to another ice-cream fortune). He drifted in and out of a number of marginal enterprises—organizing private gambling parties and an abortive provincial jazz club—while experimenting with an ever-widening (often American-inspired) variety of substances, from "purple hearts" to hash and LSD. An early fan of American TV, theater, and film, he finally settled into a job as a theatrical agent, and in 1964 formed his own agency in Soho.[7]

The world of the theatrical agent in London was a liminal one of connections and behind-the-scenes influence and, like the world of film-making generally, characterized by a New World informality, especially a New York or L.A. style of wheeling, dealing, and schmoozing. Young, clever, stylish, and fast-talking, Mim Scala prospered, and his company (partners were brought in to form the Confederates Agency) netted James Brown as its first big-name client. Business was done as often over drinks or at lavish parties as in an office; the world of the theatrical agency with a transatlantic clientele and aspirations throve on the hedonism of a Mayfair of scotch-fueled Hilton Hotel receptions and Playboy Club soirees. On the one hand there was his very useful association with Victor Lowndes, an American partner of Hugh Heffner's with "loads of money." His parties were events where Scala and other hopefuls in the industry could meet the glitterati of American show-biz, their agents and hangers-on. On the other,

Scala also cultivated a close relationship with useful elements of the traditional, if young and swinging, British upper class. Sir William Pigott-Brown, dissipated scion of the county gentry, had cash for timely investment as well as the kind of social éclat in town and country to draw in just that kind of American impressed by aristocratic panache *and* libertine abandon: "Promiscuity was king, and [at Pigott-Brown's Berkshire estate Orchard House] everybody got laid, stoned and drunk in the highest possible fashion."[8]

The three chapters of this section will examine, first, American architectural modernism in London through two additions that drew significant media attention, contestation, and public awareness—the Hilton Hotel on Park Lane and the American embassy in Grosvenor Square; second, the ways in which these sites, as visual referents and stage-sets, offer symbolic targets for the developing anti-Americanism of the mid-sixties, while tracing the ways in which antiwar marches, radical theater, and student rebellion ironically owed much, not only to American models of protest but also to personal contact with Americans. That is, it explores ways in which reactions against Americanization themselves illustrate the circularity and permeation that defines modern Anglo-American transatlanticism. Much of what follows rests on two assumptions. The first is that London itself, in the postwar world, became even more central to British life than it had been at any time since the Industrial Revolution shifted attention to the pushing, modern-defining North and Midlands. This "recapitalization" of London as focus and emblem of national life in the postwar period has gone on pretty much unabated since the fifties.[9] The second is that contemporary visual changes to the British urban environment, both planned and haphazard, the motorway schemes and parking garages, the new town centers and shopping malls, and especially the mushrooming of nodes of high-rise office development, were popularly read in the fifties and sixties as a cultural Americanization, however much the planners, architects, and professional critics might insist that modernism in Britain was "international" or Continental or, indeed, sometimes uniquely domestic in inspiration, design, scale, and placement.

In fact, the best-known example of postwar *British* modernism in London signally failed to establish the basis for a widening popular awareness of a nativist modernism or commitment to its urban planning regime. The 1951 Festival of Britain briefly offered a vision of the possibilities of an aesthetically democratic London breaking free of tradition in a socialist-designed scientific future that would be given concrete form through new British architecture and new British design. Moreover, it was hoped that the festival, by showcasing Britain's recovery as a reinvented "modern" nation, would prove especially attractive to tourist dollars: "More than ever we must convince America that our eyes are on the future, for any conscious, 'half-timbered' appeal will only prove a boomerang."[10] The festival, however, was a short-term, limited gesture, more a symbolic end than a beginning, more evocative of wartime planning of the forties than the often helter-skelter commercial modernism of the fifties. If there had been a "collective project of imagining," of a future characterized by a modern living environment, it quickly passed. In the Tory years that followed the nostalgic Britishness of Coronation Day celebration, the public were presented with, on the one hand, the refurbishing of churches, royal palaces, and Victorian monuments and, on the other, largely un-planned, episodic development, new commercial construction that would more often suggest American capitalism (without American scale) than the domestic (if Scandinavian-inflected) social democracy of the South Bank Festival.[11]

When, at the end of the sixties, Christopher Booker published what proved to be the first shot in a long-sustained literary and political assault on the inau-thenticity and emptiness of Swinging London's decade, he did so by drawing attention to its transatlantic character. Imagining a Londoner of a decade earlier transported to 1965, he followed a visual route marked by disturbing signs:

> First, perhaps, as he sped along the curving M4 motorway from London Airport below the unfamiliar howl of jet airliners, would have been the soaring new glass and concrete blocks breaking the skyline . . . . They were by no means a forest, as in New York, and certainly not as tall as the skyscrapers of Manhattan—but enough to alter the scale of central London.

Booker's distaste for the era is characteristic of a dystopian discourse common in the seventies—one that often explicitly traces the loss of "British values" to postwar "'Americanisation'—a brash, standardised mass-culture, centred on the enormously increased influence of television and advertising."[12]

Much the same presentation of the modern in Britain as a kind of American colonialism can be found, if less sourly expressed, in David Lodge's mid-seven-ties comic treatment of a similar theme. His visitor driving through the modern cityscape is not an Englishman of the past transported through time to gape at a disturbing alien world but an American academic who finds amid British differ-ence an emerging and comforting similarity:

> Driving back to the University, Morris took the newly opened section of [Birmingham's] Inner Ring, an exhilarating complex of tunnels and flyovers . . . an oddly stirring sight, for the city that was springing up was unmistakably American in style—indeed that was what the local blimps were always beefing about—and he had the strange feeling of having stumbled upon a new American frontier.[13]

This study begins with a consideration of some key sites of modern architec-ture in the fifties and early sixties, and what they may say—in their design, the business of their construction and their popular reception—about transatlantic relations. The focus is on plausible connections between London's new-built envi-ronment, American culture generally, and aspects of Anglo-American cross-traf-fic (including, not insignificantly, the cross-traffic of architects and developers).

We are not concerned with debates about varieties of modernism*s*, about the ways in which particular styles of the modern are inflected, as they are, by local vision and creativity, or even with the question of how "American" and how "British" the new construction in London might be regarded by historians of architecture and design. Indeed, the defensiveness of some in insisting on the authenticity of a particularly British modernism in architectural design, on its autonomy and indigenous creativity, is remarkably similar to parallel discourses in other cultural areas.

These buildings and the reactions to them focus in a particular way "the extraordinary contradictory impulses toward the modern"[14] in British society at the time. The new-built environment suggested to many minds the kind of progressive, secular, consumerist future for which urban America was the best available model. The popular revulsion *against* modern architecture by the end of the sixties reflects more than specific disenchantment with failed realizations, aesthetic or functional, and the social dysfunction they may have encouraged. Historians looking to explain the faltering of modernism's popular appeal have stressed the domestic failures of the Wilson government to live up to its rhetoric, and the failure of the continuous economic progress that modernism presupposed. But to the extent that a positive identification, perhaps internalization, of the *modern* meant a positive reading of *American*, the media-images of crisis across the Atlantic ultimately also powerfully contributed to an anxious confusion about modernity—in an era that saw men on the moon but also the assassination of Robert Kennedy and Martin Luther King, Jr., the Mai Lai massacre, Berkeley and Columbia universities in anarchic turmoil, and burning ghettos from Watts to Detroit.

CHAPTER 1

London, USA?

The long decade from the late fifties to the early seventies saw significant changes to parts of the cityscape in inner London. If well short of wholesale reconstruction, there was a visible "modernization" of some key areas as not only bomb sites but also streets of surviving Victorian and Georgian buildings were swept away for new traffic schemes, office building slabs, and the odd high-rise tower. Though there were areas where the changes were dramatic—London Wall near Moorgate in the City, the London County Council's own Elephant and Castle redevelopment south of the River, along Victoria Street in Westminster or north of the Euston Road—the result was by and large a scattered and episodic modernism, and the visual "destruction of the familiar" was not nearly as extensive or as shocking in the sprawling immensity of London as in some provincial city centers gutted for parking garages and shopping precincts. While there was some resistance to many of these projects as they went up—from preservationists, those whom the schemes displaced, and those who resented the lack of local consultation—developers rarely had much difficulty in winning over council officials and Whitehall with their modern aesthetic and its promise of economic regeneration.

Thrusting modernism—its scale, the anonymity of its design, and, especially, its verticality[1]—had long been popularly associated with American culture. Among those who opposed such changes, a rhetoric of invasion and resistance could draw upon a more general unease over American commercial and military supremacy and the loss of national autonomy in the post-Suez era. Such connections were ideologically weighted—on the right, among the suburban middle-class for whom the nostalgic idea, massaged by Betjeman and Larkin, of "village London" versus an American-styled urban modernism had one set of meanings, and on the left where commercial development meant speculative build-it-quick American-style capitalism and the destruction of local working-class communities.

Reaction to modernism and the international style as un-English and threatening national decadence and decline can be commonly found in the interwar period. The influential architect Sir Reginald Blomfield associated it with Continental, often German, émigrés—that is, with authoritarianism and ideologies at odds with "English pragmatism" and traditional values. There was a shift, however, in the popular reading of "foreign" modernism the decade or so following the Second World War, when the best-available association was with the cultural and commercial exporting prowess of the United States rather than the Continental avant-garde, just as, Serge Guilbaut has argued, in the art world the postwar rise of an *American* abstract expressionist avant-garde "succeeded in shifting the cultural center of the West from Paris to New York." As Britain struggled to reconstruct, "the expansive image of America" not only offered expanded possibilities of urban pleasure, design, and convenience but also, to a different audience, focused "the fears of a social and cultural order that felt itself under siege."[2]

Responses to modernism in the fifties and sixties cannot, however, be seen simply in the terms of a straight-forward dialectic between the defensive domestic and the invasive foreign. One unexplored aspect, for instance, of the intertwining of popular cultures and the reciprocity of their causes and effects is the connection between the nostalgic expectations of ever more frequent American visitors and the marked turn in domestic taste in early seventies Britain toward a nativist subjectivity that on some level was constructed as riposte to the modern *American* world, but on another was complicit with it (and the American media) in constructing an antimodern reading of "real" British culture. Whatever role a mutually reinforcing, growing synchronicity of Anglo-American imagination and longing might play in the shifting of attitudes, any such process developed over some time and at a pace set by a host of cultural factors well beyond the physical spread of a modernist architectural aesthetic. One must be cautious of projecting backward what later came to seem a popular consensus against the arrogance, uniformity, and alienating scale of much modernist reconstruction of key sites. Moreover, background and social class are probably critically important factors in responses of different parts of the London population to the world about them (the architecture *and* the tourists) as it changed.

In contrast to the public discourse of the arts and architecture professionals and of the protest and preservationist pressure groups, it is difficult to recover popular, in-the-street reactions of inner-London people going about their daily lives. However unappealing some of these prominent, badly aging urban designs might have later seemed, often from mismanagement and neglected upkeep, one can imagine a variety of reactions at the time, from dislike at the loss of the familiar, through casual indifference, to enthusiasm for at least the conveniences modernism often brought in the form of new shops, cinemas, and supermarkets. There was, in fact, at the level of popular experience, a quite complex interaction over time with these sites. We should also remember that buildings do not go up overnight. Their emergence was a process—often a lengthier process in London than in the States where shopping malls and office blocks seemed to mushroom. In Britain there were planning permissions to be gained, a variety of fora for debate and challenge, and the sometimes impeding nature of British labor relations. Locals might live for some time with the destructive clearance of familiar sites, the blockage of roads and pavements, the hoardings-enclosed spaces like oversized postwar bombsites, then years of construction as fifties and sixties modern grew above the Georgian roof line.

POSTWAR CONSTRUCTION, THE PROMISE
OF MODERNISM, AND THE URBAN AESTHETIC

Although the "international style" often favored by fashionable British architects and builders in the decade or so from the mid-fifties was derived directly and self-consciously from the prewar European avant-garde modernism of Le Corbusier, Mies van der Rohe, or Walter Gropius, its visible aesthetic would often have been read by many beyond the academic and architectural community as a characteristically *American* import. This is so not only because the skyscraper revolution happened first there and the world had long looked to Chicago or New York for the most dramatic realizations of large-scale, grid-patterned, skyscraper-canyoned urban modernism. The American association also derived powerfully and more generally from the twentieth century's fascination with metropolitan America itself as symbolically "modern." And thanks to the war and to the magnetism of American money and academic opportunity, often the European originators themselves were now American residents who, though belonging "to the whole world," as Herbert Read said of Walter Gropius, were more specifically citizens of Massachusetts, Illinois, or California. It was also a style that was associated with the commercially driven boom in London's speculative building sector following the lifting of postwar controls by the Tory governments of the 1950s, with, that is, helter-skelter building regimes more familiar to American capitalism than to the urban planning traditions central to much of European modernism.

Through the fifties and into the early sixties there was little government control—at either the local or national level—over the commercial-modern schemes favored by many property developers. As Harold Macmillan, then Minister for Housing and Local Government, said when he introduced the Town and County Planning Bill in December of 1952, "The people whom the Government must help are those who do things: the developers, the people who create wealth."[3] The following year building licenses (introduced during the war to ration building resources) were abandoned, and controls on the construction of office blocks lapsed at both the national and local level. Speculative building, already given a boost by the abandonment of the "development charge," was further encouraged by the fact that local authorities' plans were sharply inhibited by strict controls on their ability to borrow and, after 1959, by their obligation to pay full market value (rather than "use value") for any land they might wish to acquire for public development. While its own schemes faltered, the London County Council approved millions of square feet of privately developed new office space.[4]

A modern style—if not the "Modern Movement"—had modestly come to commercial London in the twenties and early thirties, for instance in the "jazz modern" of the Daily Telegraph Building in Fleet Street (1928) or in the odd, chunky, "almost New York" look of the riverfront of the Shell-Mex House (1931). The first significant piece of academic modernism was, appropriately, introduced by that emblem of contemporary American commercial practice, a progressive advertising agency (Crawford's), which hired Frederick Etchells to design an office building, influenced by Mies van der Rohe, in Holborn in 1930. For the most part, however, these remained relatively idiosyncratic intrusions into the Victorian and Edwardian fabric of the city, isolated buildings that usually did not offer to subvert culturally important locations and, like the *moderne* growths of bypass strip development beyond the heart of the capital, were not particularly challenging to a local sense of ownership and belonging.[5]

Though the war and its destruction seemed to offer the opportunity for a wholesale re-envisioning of the capital, London—pockmarked rather than razed to the ground—had in fact not been badly damaged in its traditional core. While there were plans for significant reconstruction in the City, where 9 million square feet of office space had been destroyed, elsewhere the prospect of radical redesign, planned by public authorities, faded rapidly. Housing beyond inner London was the great need, and the postwar Labour government concentrated on this rather than redeveloping the city center. In the late fifties and sixties, belated but massive projects of high-rise council-flat development rose, usually on the periphery. These were perhaps *not* characterized as peculiarly American (though public housing projects in the United States were in fact sometimes referenced as models[6]). The rapidly proliferating public and private "slab-on-a-podium" office building projects of central London, however, *were* associated with American modern—inspired as they often were by Skidmore, Owings and Merrill's Lever House in New York—and inevitably raised the issue of the "Manhattanization" of the capital's skyline.[7]

By the time taste and the economy changed in the early seventies, this had hardly happened; the footprint left by large vertical or horizontal glass and concrete boxes was strategically limited rather than defining. And as tastes changed, the aesthetic "failure" of the largest redevelopments—the sterility of Victoria Street, the destruction of Notting Hill Gate, the scatter of undistinguished large government office-blocks like the three immense slabs in Marsham Street (1963–71), or the commercial rebuilding of Paternoster Square to the north of St. Paul's Cathedral (1961–67)—became visible confirmation for many of a threat halted if not averted. Some sites, such as London Wall or the Westway motorway flyover, were frozen in time as uncompleted reminders. These highly visible points of deformation became useful as an architectural cautionary just as American political leadership of the "Free World" ran into a dead-end in Southeast Asia and American technological modernism at home collapsed into social malaise and self-doubt.

THE HILTON HOTEL AND THE THREAT OF MANHATTANIZATION

[S]eated in the grill-room of the London Hilton, [Morris Zapp] sank his teeth luxuriously into the first respectable-looking steak he had had since arriving in England.

The Hilton was a damned expensive hotel, but Morris reckoned that he owed himself some indulgence after three weeks in Rummidge and in any case he was making sure that he got full value out of his occupation of the warm, sound-proofed and sleekly-furnished room on the sixteenth floor.[8]

If any single modernist intrusion commanded an iconic status in popular discussion of what appeared to be American-driven change in London in the sixties, it was the Hilton Hotel in Park Lane, proposed in 1957 and finally completed in a somewhat reduced form in 1963 after an extended process of public inquiry and debate, appeals, and redesigns. It was not the first tower in London—before the war there had been the London Transport building in Broadway and the Senate House in Bloomsbury. But these were relatively earth-bound in comparison with the Hilton, the first structure in the city to rise above the dome of St. Paul's Cathedral. On the eastern edge of Hyde Park, it both visually intruded into residential Mayfair and ruined, it was claimed, the *rus-in-urbe* illusion that the park provided—being when completed the only building clearly visible above the tree-line. Moreover, its top floors offered its patrons—wealthy American businessmen and tourists—a vulgar view, it was said, into the private gardens of Buckingham Palace.

The Hilton was commonly regarded as a harbinger of a vertical revolution, and sparked considerable apprehensive discussion. J. M. Richards, an influential modernist and architectural critic for *The Times*, warned in 1958 (in the American journal *Architectural Review*) that, though more high buildings in London were "bound to come" and in a way expressed the city's "vitality," "even a few buildings" of great height around Hyde Park would "seriously disturb" the illusion of "rurality" that such spaces provided—an "awful warning of what to avoid is offered by Central Park in New York." Richards was not opposed to high buildings in London per se—he approved the plans for the Millbank tower as a kind of "vertical punctuation mark" needed "to stop the long, dull horizontal line . . . seen from Westminster Bridge"—and thought they would commonly not be as tall as "skyscrapers on the American scale," but worried about their quality (slabs, not airy glass towers), the traffic congestion they would cause, and their diminishing

2. The Mayfair Hilton. Author's photograph.

of historic buildings. If built in numbers, though "unspectacular . . . by American standards," they would be "foreign to London tradition" and as mere monuments to individual profit, of little "civic significance."[9]

By the end of the sixties there were, Pevsner counted, seven buildings taller than St. Paul's—and work had begun on another, the National Westminster Bank in the City, which would be taller than any of them. In his influential guide to the architecture of Westminster and the City, first published by Penguin Press in 1957 and in two further editions in 1962 and 1973, Pevsner, the doyen of architectural critics of the time, was like Richards, characteristically of two minds. He was famously an early advocate of good modernism and deplored the persistence of conventional neo-Georgian as "hopelessly out of touch." The prospect, however, of an Americanized cityscape led him to warn in 1962 (when the Hilton tower was nearing completion) that planning authorities "had to be careful" of creating an American jungle, though he then believed that "so far nothing is lost yet" and much could be gained by the "judicious siting" of future towers. A decade later, however, he was in a despair tinged with nostalgia (an ethos that grew rapidly as the seventies evolved) about the drastic alteration to the skyline, "wholly to the detriment of London . . . the greatest and the saddest change."

> These skyscrapers are not as high as those of America and they rarely come in clusters. So the result is not dramatic; it does not remind one of New York or Chicago but of some medium-sized city of the Middle West.

Ironically, Pevsner suggested, London was getting a modernism that was more "American" than cosmopolitan New York—the thin, scattered and unimaginative cookie-cutter modernism of the provincial United States. Similarly, his final judgment on the Hilton tower was that it was second rate even by Hilton's standards. Elsewhere, in Istanbul ("outstanding") and Berlin ("clean and sleek"), they had built good, interesting hotels, but not in London: "It is all a great pity."[10]

Second only, perhaps, to the Coca Cola trademark, the Hilton Hotel chain became a charged motif of spreading American influence and presence abroad and, specifically in the left's critique, of a commercially driven cultural imperialism in the early Cold War era. It represented by the early sixties—to both Americans and Europeans—an example of vigorous, opportunity-grabbing, aggressive American enterprise that was—like the red-and-white Coke ads flashed in bright lights above Piccadilly Circus—highly visible. The only way one could avoid seeing the Hilton tower in West London, the quip ran, was actually to stay in the hotel itself. The Hilton chain had a further meaning. While Coke represented the export of a product that offered to conquer popular taste, the Hilton represented the export of Americans themselves, the tourists in their thousands, the longed-for bringers of American dollars to some, to others a rude invasion.

Hilton's anticipation of success in Europe was built on shrewd predictions of the expanding and expandable market for accommodation from tourists and business travelers. There was a demonstrable lack of provision in London (as elsewhere in Europe) for the sector that promised to grow most—those who could not afford to stay in the Dorchester, and would have been uneasy there in any case, but who wanted something more than a B-and-B in Gower Street that could provide only narrow beds, damp rooms, shilling-slot gas fires, and cold toast. The promise lay in an "industry" that would grow if it could provide what many middle-class Americans wanted most—a taste of foreign experience while staying in the safe, familiar, and comfortable, hotels that were themselves American-owned or at least American-styled and that served scotch "on the rocks," iced tea, and soft toilet paper. By 1970 more than a million and a half Americans a year made their way through London's hotels—many owned and operated by American firms. By 1975 C. W. E. Bigsby could write of the physical domination in Europe generally of American-owned hotel chains in central locations—Hilton International (by then a subsidiary of Trans World Airlines), Holiday Inn, Sheraton, Intercontinental (owned by Pan American Airways), and Loews—as emblematic of the American "penetration" of Europe.[11]

It was the lack of suitable provision in London for this anticipated expansion of the American tourist market that was used in the fifties and early sixties to rationalize the relaxation of planning controls that might have inhibited the building of large-scale hotels in the culturally important central and west London boroughs. Such encouragement was in any event congenial to Tory conceptions of free enterprise, though the Labour-dominated LCC and Wilson's national government after 1964 were also eager to attract as large a flow of U.S. dollars as possible. Some Tory traditionalists might fear the vulgarization of the stuccoed Georgian serenity and late-imperial grandeur of West London's squares by high-rises and traffic, but they fought a by and large rear-guard resistance in a party that nationally was committed to the encouragement of the commercial development of central London as a riposte to socialist planning.

Under the Conservative governments, the Board of Trade was determined to do what it could to support commercial reconstruction in a number of strategic areas well beyond the modernist revolution already under way in the City (London Wall): Paddington, the north side of Hyde Park, and Park Lane were places where tourists would be likely to want to stay. Those on local councils and the LCC who wished to preserve the horizontal aesthetic of "traditional" West London could no longer count on the 80-foot elevation clause introduced into London bylaws in the late nineteenth century, and could only prevent government ministers from overriding their refusal of permission by the most vigorous mobilization of public opinion—and then, as in the case of the Hilton Hotel, securing only modest modifications to a well-financed, well-connected, and forcefully argued project.

The Marshall Plan was launched in June of 1947, followed two years later by the creation of the North Atlantic Treaty Organization. The same year, 1949, Conrad Hilton—later claiming that the State and Commerce departments had urged him to do so in the interest of "international good will" and the need to inject U.S. dollars into the economies of countries "needing help"—turned to international expansion through a subsidiary, Hilton International Inc. Beginning in the American dependency of Puerto Rico, he quickly moved on to Madrid, Istanbul (only "Thirty miles from the Iron Curtain" Hilton would boast), and West Berlin—which offered not only a tabula rasa for modernist architecture but also a highly politicized Cold War locus. Conrad Hilton himself insisted that his expansion into Europe was as much an act of enlightened anticommunism as a money-making proposition, a "practical idealism."[12] He aimed to serve the needs of the kind of official and private Americans flooding into postwar western Europe—the host of government advisors, commercial agents, top- and middle-level business executives—as well as the upper end of the developing middle-class tourism market. Affordable luxury for those who still saw a European holiday as a once-in-a-lifetime experience, as well as the more seasoned luxury-liner-soon-to-be-jet set. Hilton International Inc. aimed to create an advertising-enabled lock on international style through brand-recognition ("Take me to the Hilton") across Europe in a way that left the established upper-class hotels in London and elsewhere seeming local and mired in a stuffy traditionalism.

London was always a promising target, though unlike Berlin the opportunities were hedged around with the difficulties of finding a site in a part of the capital not already cleared by bombing and characterized by a complicated (by American standards) real property market and redundant levels of planning bureaucracy. In fact, Hilton had probably been sniffing around for a London property since a trip to the city shortly after the war, when he was impressed not only with a tradition of exceptional service (he stayed at the Dorchester) but also with the generally "poor condition" of British hotels and the lack of what he called "American business methods."[13] Having, famously, bought the Waldorf-Astoria in New York in 1949, he set his sights in the next few years on the prestigious Grosvenor House Hotel in Park Lane.

In London Hilton formed an association with the rising property speculator Charles Clore to pursue a deal for the Grosvenor House. Clore was one of a breed of London financial deal-makers, often Jewish, who had been able to build property, retail, and financial empires in the volatile markets of the postwar period. In the absence of capital gains tax (until 1962) and with often cozy relationships with local officialdom and supported by sweet credit deals with the clearing banks and insurance companies, they built fortunes from next to nothing. By the sixties powerful deal-makers like Clore, Harold Samuel, Jack Cotton, Joe Levy, and Harry Hyams had come to represent the kind of aggressive business methods that were invariably associated with New York property tycoons like Big Bill Zeckendorf.

Not only were the methods "American"—aggressive, contested take-over bids, the conglomeration of diverse unconnected enterprises, and rather loose account-ing practices—but there were personal connections and a shared entrepreneurial culture as well. When New York builder and developer Erwin Wolfson met Jack Cotton at his country house on the Thames in 1959 (to discuss plans for what would become the Pan-Am Building), he later recalled, "I was worried that I would meet some forbidding, stiff-collar Englishman. Instead Jack might have been a warm-hearted American Jew."[14] Clore and Cotton made frequent trips to New York in the fifties, and their financial interests extended to development projects on both sides of the Atlantic. During the postwar boom in urban develop-ment there was significant British interest in North America; Cotton was able to draw in British bankers for a significant piece of the development capital for the Pan-Am building, another British group invested heavily in Boston development, while Second Covent Garden Properties was persuaded by Zeckendorf to bail out his enterprises in 1960–61 (he had lost heavily in hotel investments). British investors were not always adept at judging the market in the United States and, like the Second Covent Garden group, could find themselves coming in at the end of a boom and losing heavily. Nevertheless, investment traffic was increasingly significant in both directions.[15]

It is unclear who approached whom, but by 1954 Clore had an understanding with Hilton that, if his own investment company could acquire the Grosvenor House, he would lease it to Hilton International in a profit-sharing arrange-ment.

Clore was riding high, having in 1953 successfully completed the hugely profit-able acquisition of J. Sears and Co., a British shoe retailing firm that had hundreds of other assets, and was involved in an ultimately unsuccessful (though profitable) attempt, with Harold Samuel, to gain controlling interest in the Savoy Group (a high-prestige company that owned a cluster of prominent London hotels—the Savoy, Claridge's, the Connaught). Since the war the running of hotels itself had not been a high rate of return business in London, but for a man like Clore the attractiveness of this market lay in the fact that hotels were therefore underval-ued—often with assets that could be stripped off and sold and standing on real property that had development potential. When the Grosvenor House board re-fused his embrace, he offered stockholders nearly twice the going share price in a contested take-over bid (very much Clore's style), but the attempt failed—per-haps because Hilton withdrew.[16]

It may be that Hilton had already decided on a new "international style" hotel in London rather than an arrangement to run a traditional, established property. Within a year of the collapse of the Grosvenor deal, Clore was searching for a prestigious Mayfair site and in 1956 bought properties at the end of Park Lane, facing Hyde Park, for half a million pounds. Whether this was at Hilton's bidding or on spec, within months he had closed a deal with Hilton International. Clore would keep the freehold, find financing, and build a hotel—to Hilton specifications and leased to the American corporation. Negotiations were vigorous, with Hilton himself coming over to London, and stringent conditions were imposed committing Clore to building the hotel as quickly as possible in order to catch a surging American summer tourist trade. For Clore's part there were tangible and intangible advantages: he would later use the hotel as an important asset in negotiating with Prudential Assurance for long-term development finance for his City and Central Investments Company. Less tangibly, if importantly, was the useful "social lustre" of an association with Conrad Hilton, the anticommunist American Catholic, in the same way his well-advertised hosting of a party for the Duchess of Kent had earlier served his on-the-make interests in a world where connection and appearance meant much.

At a time when Clore's enterprises were expanding in many directions (he wanted to add Selfridge's to his empire, but, rebuffed in the early fifties, he quietly bought shares until he could exercise his controlling interest in 1965), the association with Hilton brought prominence of a kind—a public mark of his growing importance in the world of property development (Clore's City and Central property company was quoted on the stock exchange in 1959) but also of his American associations. Clore's personal reputation drew heavily on his perceived American connections. When, a few months after the completion of the Park Lane Hilton, he attended Cotton's annual gala luncheon at the Dorchester, Clore took a place at the high table next to E. A. Kekich, the commercial attaché from the American embassy in Grosvenor Square.[17]

This had both positive and negative resonances. In the sixties Clore became the most visible exemplar in Britain of the New York style in financial dealing (he died in 1979 with assets valued at around £123 million). However, he and the other Jewish entrepreneurs of the boom years of property development also became the butt of a pretty sharp anti-Semitism at a time when his methods of property acquisition and conglomeration attracted the ire of both those concerned about the vulgarization and Americanization of London's architectural heritage and the anticapitalist left. The New Left, though often embracing a *public* modernism expressed in new council housing estates, the Post Office Tower, and even "the great sculptural beauty" of the motorways, had little use for Clore's aggressive tactics of self-advertisement, conglomeration, and asset-stripping. In Edward Thompson's 1960 collection of New Left essays, *Out of Apathy*, the young Raphael Samuel singled out Clore as an exemplar of "bastard capitalism," a parvenu whose "business palatinate" and connections within the Establishment typified a new ruling elite where status anxieties on the American model have joined the traditional divisions of the English class system, giving to society a tone more blatantly snobbish and vulgarly commercial than would have seemed possible in 1945.[18]

The popular press, however, could portray—at least while the property boom lasted—the "Men Worth Millions" (the *Sunday Express*) in a more positive light, as heroic, or at least successful, individualists able to stand on equal terms with American entrepreneurs. The *Sunday Times* saw in Clore's partnership with Hilton evidence of Clore's "courage" and "resources," and offered the skyline-altering hotel itself as "a characteristic memorial to his own energy and enterprise" (though there might have been a certain archness in that "characteristic"). By and large such new Americanized capitalists were necessary in a post-Suez world, not of empire builders and explorers, but of "the innovators and iconoclasts who are required, from time to time, in any society, if it is not to sink into stagnation."[19]

Clore's usefulness to Hilton extended not only to the successful search for a prominent site on Park Lane for the new hotel but also to the lengthy business of finding financial underwriters and builders as well as threading Hilton's way through the planning permission tangle for what would be one of the most expensive Hilton projects of the decade. The choice of a London-based architectural firm, with whom Clore had a close association (Lewis Solomon, Son and Joseph), and a London-based construction company would also serve to soften the opposition of those who might resent the kind of American economic penetration that Hilton International symbolized. The hotel plans—a £4 million (rising to £6 million) scheme for a 35-story, 400-foot tower and 700 bedrooms "to overlook the park"—were announced in July of 1957 when they were presented to Westminster Council. Clore had purchased the properties without prior planning permission but apparently with some inside assurance that—except for the issue of the final height of the tower—this would not be a problem.[20] Whatever misgivings the Conservative-dominated council may have had about American intrusion, it was eager to advance property development generally, including *high-rise* development. Before the end of the decade, it approved both the Millbank Tower in Chelsea and New Zealand House in Haymarket. There were also hopes for development in the Paddington area and, especially, along the northern side of Hyde Park—in higher flights of commercial fancy there was a vision of a British Central Park fronted by a line of modernist skyscrapers. In the late fifties highrise schemes could pretty much count on the approval of the national government, which, *The Times* reported, "supports the general idea of large hotels in the area."[21]

As ambitious property developers do, the Hilton-Clore team promoted the scheme with optimistic projections of what a colossal hotel on the posh Park Lane site would bring to the city: a turnover for the hotel owners of $10 million a year (half from room rents and half from food and entertainment) would generate $30 million a year "to this country" by attracting larger numbers of well-heeled American tourists prepared to spend big, while the hotel project would employ hundreds locally in construction jobs and, once the hotel was finished and operating, as many as 700 management and staff positions. Such claims were standard fare for Hilton, who insisted that his enterprise in Europe was not a matter of "invaders intent upon siphoning back all profits to the United States" (though stockholders expected to make money), but a patriotic extension of U.S. foreign aid in the worldwide struggle against communism in which the United States had to "exercise our great strength and power for good against evil."[22]

Hilton International was sensitive about "selling" its projects locally. By the late summer when the scheme reached the next level, the Labour-controlled London County Council, an awkward opposition had emerged among Labour councillors, spurred by some public indignation and increasing attention from the London press. By the time such resistance had secured a public inquiry in November, Hilton was prepared further to inflate its estimate of the dollars that would pour into the economy from the United States. As Richards tartly observed, all the arguments put forward at the inquiry in favor of construction were "commercial arguments," and any objections were likely to be overruled by "a Government in need of dollars." William Richard Irwin, vice president of Hilton International and their front-man in Britain, now testified that he anticipated $36 million generated annually as a result of Hilton's being able to meet the "urgent need for luxury-class accommodation in London."[23]

The public inquiry that accompanied the government's decision to call in the planning application from the LCC was a familiar device to vent the steam of objection; there was little doubt that the minister of Housing and Local Government, Henry Brooke, would ultimately approve some version of the tower once the formality of the open forum had been gone through. Irwin and his lawyers were forced, however, on the defensive by criticism from local residents, commercial interests, and planning and preservation "experts" who attacked the height of the tower. Irwin, for his part, played an uncompromising role, no doubt certain of higher-up support generally for American investment in Britain, but risking the appearance of know-it-all American arrogance: "My principal criticism of Londoners is that they low-rate their city."[24]

The inquiry received some press coverage, and, in the year following the Suez Crisis, this served to draw attention as a matter not just of the modern versus traditionalist debate familiar during the postwar reconstruction era, but of the power of U.S. dollars and values. As one spokesman for local residents put it, "If this building is allowed, it will represent hereafter a symbol of the supremacy in 1957 of a dollar-earning machine over values of far greater importance and lasting quality.[25]

Although the lawyer for Hilton dismissed this as "just sentimentality," in May, when the minister approved the scheme, the tower was marginally reduced (to

33 stories) as a gesture to opposition that would allow the government to register concern "about congestion and the Park." The LCC was dragged along—Brooke told them that the hotel was vital for increasing American tourist earnings—but by the time the Hilton tower was topped out in July of 1962 its planning committee was calling again for stricter rules for tower construction. In fact, though several tower approvals quickly followed the Hilton permission, dense high-rise development along the northern side of the park never materialized.[26]

As the Hilton tower slowly rose above the roof line of Park Lane it drew more attention in the press, and there were increasingly barbed judgments from professional critics. Such presence as it achieved in public consciousness increased as in the later stages of its construction the tower became obvious to casual users of the park. By the time it was topped out in July of 1962, Richards (both architectural correspondent for *The Times* and editor of the *Architectural Review*, "mouthpiece of modernism in England") was prepared to declare the y-shaped monolith with a curved front (to maximize the number of rooms with views of the park) to be "of very poor quality aesthetically." He later called it "brash and commonplace," mandarin language that invoked American social qualities that had long been a cliché of Establishment condescension. Much of the popular apprehension and discussion of the structure beyond the persistent criticism of academics and expert professionals (in 1983 Jones and Woodward dismissed it as a "particularly inept building") stemmed from the expectation that the Hilton tower was a portent of things to come. But a fuller "Manhattanization" failed to develop. With the single exception of Basil Spence's Household Cavalry Barracks to the south of the park in Knightsbridge (1967–69, another structure unloved by the critics), the Hilton tower remained the only modern building clearly and prominently visible from much of Hyde Park, and so was more singularly in the public's eye than most of the visually numbing slew of modernist constructions that went up elsewhere in the city in the sixties.[27]

When the London Hilton was opened in the spring of 1963 in a ceremony attended by British dignitaries, Conrad Hilton and the Hollywood stars that he counted upon to secure useful publicity,[28] it joined twenty-one other Hiltons operating abroad with a gross revenue that year of more than $215 million and a net profit of some $6 million from operations. Debate about dollar imperialism was not merely a matter of profit however. Hilton's system involved what was sometimes called "instant America," not only the provision of American plumbing, soap, soft toilet paper, and familiar American food, but the introduction of American managers and the training of an Americanized domestic staff—some of whom were taken to the United States for six-month courses in hotel service and management. As Conrad Hilton's hagiographer Mildred Comfort summed up in 1964, "In addition to working capital, Hilton provides concepts of architectural design, efficiency of operation, managerial controls and techniques, extensive world-wide advertising, sales promotion and publicity programs." It also provided a Bible and a copy of Conrad Hilton's *Be My Guest* in each room.[29]

Much has been written of late about the empowering gaze of the flaneur/tourist. Whether Americans staying in the upper floors of the Park Lane Hilton feel particularly empowered with their commanding view of the capital, or whether it actually annoys many Londoners to think they are looked down upon from a great height by the rich, brash, and commonplace, *viewing* (views of, views from the tower) is central to whatever symbolic power the Hotel had in sixties popular discourse about the Americanization of British space and culture. In his memoir of the world of finance and property development in the early sixties, Charles Gordon later recalled some of the frisson the Hilton evoked: "Mayfair then, before the casinos arrived, the most relaxed urban village in the world, was quiet and restrained. The Hilton's arrogant tower smirked as if it was signalling to us from Clore."[30]

Air conditioned throughout, with five bars, fast lifts, and ice water on tap, the Hilton attracted throughout the sixties comment and some condescension from those, like Hunter Davies, who in 1966 found its service "undistinguished" and its food "pretentious" and preferred the Mayfair—though the Mayfair's own introduction of a Polynesian restaurant with a tropical thunderstorm every half-hour was itself evidence of what Davies decried, the Hilton's "attempt to Americanize the London hotel scene." Like the Mayfair, the older Dorchester also moved with the times and sported, by the mid-sixties, an American bar with "Harvard-crimson curtains and a plaster Great American eagle almost as big as the one on the U.S. Embassy in Grosvenor Square."[31]

If other American-owned hotels soon appeared—notably the Carlton Tower in Belgravia, begun before the Hilton was finished by the Hotel Corporation of America, with an "American-style Rib Room" restaurant—where American tourists could go, as Halasz said of the Hilton, to "sleep in American beds, eat American food, get typically lousy American service, and mingle with hordes of other Americans,"[32] the Park Lane Hilton was the first tall building to provide its clientele, not all of them Americans, to be sure, with a restaurant and bar at the top of its tower, a feature that was becoming a worldwide cliché of sixties urban amenity. The Hilton's claim to provide the highest, if not the best, dining experience in London lasted three years.[33] The first prominent advertisements for the Hilton (in *The Times* and *The Daily Telegraph*) featured a full-page sketch of its tower viewed from the Serpentine in mid–Hyde Park, looming above the trees (surely a playful if provocative response to the recent charges that the hotel would destroy the park's special idyllic illusion), with the invitation that "the London Hilton will be proud to welcome you in international style." The telephone number was "Hyde Park 8000."[34]

Cities are born horizontal—as places where people can walk about their
business from one port of call to another. Whether they die vertical is
something we have yet to discover—although the moment of truth seems
very close in New York.
                                                —David Crawford, 1976[35]

In the sixties a high-rise project—sometime several—of note and visibility
was finished each year, continually through the decade. If it is not quite true that
"London's face changed," there was enough robust construction and such a variety
of new views and alterations to familiar local streets that many Londoners from
Shepherd's Bush to the City would have had a sense of living through a period
of radical, if episodic, change, and there was anticipation—were the pace to continue—of a general transformation. The Hilton did not usher in an era of clus-
tered skyscrapers, the "jungle" Pevsner warned of in 1962, but it was followed for a
decade by eye-arresting structures visible from most parts of the inner city—and
also by a growing density of traffic and schemes to deal with their consequences.
When Park Lane itself was turned into a "divided highway" to ease congestion,
Alistair Cooke—who had witnessed Robert Moses's highways rip through New
York City—complained bitterly that "I am sorry to see this old-fashioned, and
fatal solution being attempted in Hyde Park.... You will soon have less park, more
noise, more carbon-monoxide—and what is much worse—more traffic."[36]

Basil Spence and Partners' Thorn House in Upper St. Martin's Lane (16 stories,
180 feet) was the first high-rise (completed 1959) in central London, the harbinger, many thought, of a massive development scheme there. Richards had, the
previous year, observed that the commercial redevelopment of the "seedy" area
of Seven Dials was inevitable, though a cluster of Thorn House structures would,
he thought, raise issues of "light and air." One prize-winning plan would have
buried the Victorian stretch from Trafalgar Square through Seven Dials to St.
Giles under the kind of elevated dual carriageway Robert ("Cities are for traffic")
Moses was imposing on Manhattan, and Soho Square would have disappeared
under a huge parking garage. Along the river (and thus more widely visible) were
the Shell Centre on the South Bank (26 stories, 338 feet) and the Vickers tower at
Millbank near the Tate in Chelsea (thirty-two stories, 387 feet), both of which were
finished the same year as the Hilton. The Millbank tower was especially prominent
visually and also raised criticism for replacing, not derelict properties, but sound
Victorian housing in good condition. Also completed that year was the Skidmore,
Owings and Merrill–influenced nineteen-story New Zealand House that rose 225
feet above Haymarket, dwarfing Nash's Theatre Royal across the street. It was
also, as Richards complained, visible from St. James's Park, where, he thought, it
broke "the classical skyline presented by the two blocks of Carlton House Terrace
flanking the Duke of York's column." Elsewhere, Westminster City Hall (19 sto-

ries, begun in 1960) announced a general rebuilding of much of Victoria Street from Whitehall to Victoria Station, while the Economist Building Group added a tower (15 stories, completed in 1964) to the area of St. James's. In the City both the Barbican complex and London Wall added pieces of interest to the skyline north of St. Paul's throughout the decade—especially Britannic House at London Wall, topped out at 35 stories (395 feet) in 1967, the same year that Seifert's notorious Centre Point (also 35 stories, and a much more generally visible 398 feet) was completed at St. Giles Circus at the top of Charing Cross Road. It faced competition in central London only with the Post Office Tower (finished the year before), a techno-spire that trumped all other projects at an eye-catching 580 feet.[37]

The Post Office Tower was the most striking—and the most "modern" looking in its functional-industrial appearance—of the tall constructions of the decade, and much was made of its innovative combination of function (as a mast for the new microwave communications technology) and amenity (with its revolving restaurant and observation deck near its top). It became, in a way, a positive icon of sixties modernism in contrast to the corporate intrusion of the Hilton tower, and glimpses of its thrusting finger are typically backgrounded in contemporary TV and film as part of the stage-set of Swinging London (as in Desmond Davis's and George Melly's 1967 comedy film *Smashing Time*) just as, only a few years later, it is often elided from the London landscape in seventies "heritage" TV and film. At the public opening on 19 May 1966, Anthony Wedgwood Benn, then Postmaster General, claimed it symbolized the kind of forward-looking twentieth-century Britain that the Labour government intended to promote (though the Tories initiated the project in 1961). The microwave communications technology of the tower, of course, was developed in North America, and it serviced not only the main microwave paths from London to other parts of Britain and the Continent but also the satellite ground station that brought direct access to U.S. telecommunications. That same year as the moon landing it provided the symbolic starting point for an air race to the Empire State Building and back to celebrate the fiftieth anniversary of the first transatlantic flight.[38]

While the commencement of new buildings tapered off, there were seven or eight major projects still in process of erection so that there was actually a flurry of topping-out ceremonies toward the end of our period: at the top of Tottenham Court Road the Euston Centre (with American-international style glass-walled towers) added a construction of 408 feet, the Commercial Union heaved its massive bulk (28 stories, 387 feet) over Leadenhall Street in the City, and Spence's Knightsbridge barracks finally joined the Hilton along the periphery of Hyde Park in 1969.

Though sixties modernism was not a monolithic phenomenon, and some of these structures displayed styles—like the Shell Centre with its smooth stone cladding and small fenestration or the "new Brutalism" of, say, the Barbican towers—that were not merely replicating American-international style, it has been argued here that the person in the street in postwar Britain would have been powerfully inclined to see even these structures as Americanization rather than, say, Continentalization. The postwar generation of modernist architects themselves (like the major property developers) were much more likely to have academic, commercial, professional, (and sometimes domestic) connections across the Atlantic than across the Channel, while the list of young architects lured to the United States by the chance of studying under the Modern Movement exiles there is also extensive. Some developed transatlantic commercial careers, attracted by not only the chance to study under notable names but also the likelier prospect of actually being able to build international style designs.[39]

In December of 1964 Susan Sontag interviewed the modernist architect Philip Johnson on American TV. He spoke of the need to learn to live up to the ideals of the new-built environment, to learn to appreciate the clean-lined and uncluttered interiors, in effect the need to "adapt to a house." The interview was picked up and broadcast by the BBC's "Monitor" program and reviewed by the novelist Anthony Burgess. "There's something repellent," he observed, "about the exaltation of a building above its inhabitants, and I fear the arrogance which must, logically, sooner or later purge a useful art of its usefulness." The next month, in a radio broadcast on the BBC's Third Programme, the British architect Sir Basil Spence, renowned for his Coventry Cathedral and engaged in a well-publicized project for the new Sussex University, claimed that he saw architecture as "a humble art." Talk turned to comparison of American and British construction, and Spence attempted to create an apologia for British architecture that drew a not entirely convincing distinction between American technological prowess, enormous bulk, and rapid mass production (he didn't like the Pan-Am Building, but it had gone up in only twenty months) with the finer British "sense of scale" and "sense of quality"—a version of the familiar "Britain's Greece to America's Rome."[40]

Much mainstream modernism—good, bad, and indifferent—continued to be built in London well into the early seventies. Spence's attempt to tease out a meaningful distinctiveness rings hollow, as these projects were often simply modeled—and in a degraded form—on well-publicized American designs. There was of course a ferment from early in the decade within the British architectural profession. The New Brutalism, though theorized in London, was, however, strongly Americanophilic, deeply influenced by the later American work of Mies van der Rohe, and could involve direct quotation of American buildings (the Birmingham City Library was modeled closely on the new Boston City Hall).[41]

At the same time, the postmodern assault on architectural modernism (and indeed on the New Brutalism) in Britain in the sixties and early seventies also owed much to American critics like Robert Venturi (whose *Complexity and Construction in Architecture* became influential well before semiotics were imported from

France at the end of the decade), the writings of Christopher Alexander (*Notes on the Synthesis of Form*), or the lectures of the visiting American scholar David Gebhard. Reyner Banham's assault on the modernism of his teacher Pevsner was deeply informed by his own reading of domestic architecture in a mobile, informal America. Like so many of the young British postwar academics, Banham did a stint of teaching in America. Touring the western United States, he found in Las Vegas strip-development and, especially, in Los Angeles, his own vision of the future and the kind of excitement others had found a generation earlier in New York City or Chicago.[42]

Commercial and governmental modernism peaked in 1962 but continued to be built throughout the decade. In 1964, George Brown, then Secretary of State for Economic Affairs, halted further construction of office blocks in London, a ban that initially delayed many schemes, though any serious check to development was undermined by Labour's encouragement of further hotel construction and the London County Council/Greater London Council's ambitious plans for new roads in London (which saw relaxed planning controls on contiguous land). While the ban was driven in part by the scandal as many saw it of the profiteering by speculative developers during the Tory boom years, Labour proved as open as the Conservatives to the need to encourage the growth of the American tourist economy. It granted in fact a new subsidy of £1,000 per room to hotel developers, while the new Greater London Council exercised little of its enhanced planning authority over hotel development throughout the city. Another large hotel with a restaurant-topped tower, the London Inter-Continental, was approved in 1965 at Hyde Park Gate, where its construction meant the destruction of a row of historic houses (and an even better view, when it was opened in 1975, into the Buckingham Palace Gardens). Labour's controls on new development, such as they were, and the reintroduction of the betterment levy in 1967, drove up rents and increased profits for existing owners. This regime was, in any event, relaxed—at least in the City and central London—by the Tories after 1970 under pressure from the City. The second property boom that followed saw a new flood of planning approvals until, with the onset of recession in 1973 and the growth of a more sharply focused opposition to the scandal of speculative building and to threats to local environment, all further office development was halted.[43]

Although concerns were expressed about the impact of high-rise modernism well before the completion of the Hilton tower, that event helped to generate a discourse of concern that gathered power with the completion of each major project throughout the period. Jack Cotton's Piccadilly scheme of 1959 would have been built, however bad the design, had it not been for his rash premature flaunting of his anticipated success in getting planning permission. When Joe Levy's Euston Centre project, with its cluster of towers, sought planning permission in the mid-sixties, it was objected to by the Royal Fine Arts Commission on the same

3. The Euston Centre from Regent's Park. Author's photograph.

grounds they used to oppose the Hilton—it would overlook a royal park (Regent's Park). Levy got to build his office blocks and tall tower but had to reorient and reduce the height of his scheme.[44] Economic downturn of course played a major role in the delay and cancellation of commercial and governmental projects, as did popular protest and a shift in popular sentiment toward an idealization of "village London." In 1967 the Civic Amenities Trust introduced the idea of the conservation area—taken up with some enthusiasm by London boroughs in the next four or five years and used to toughen the planning application process. More public local consultation was strongly recommended in the Skeffington Report of 1969, and this also "changed the environment" by encouraging less secrecy in the approval of development schemes.[45] The Piccadilly Circus towers design of 1972, a much better design than Cotton's, stood no chance.

The decision, finally, to abort plans to redevelop the Covent Garden area in the mid-seventies is often taken as the critical turning point when an invigorated public protest defeated the planners. But the modernist ideal was already long on the defensive. Though in the City construction of the National Westminster Bank tower and the Barbican project carried on through the decade, the ambitious plans for London Wall were frozen in place, the pedestrian walkways high above the traffic leading nowhere. To the west high-rise modernism faltered in the wake of public debate over Centre Point, completed in 1967 but left vacant for years. Three high-rise towers proposed in 1973 to overlook St. James's Park and the Abbey were not built. While arguments against these projects emphasized the problems of scale and visual aesthetic, as well as issues of traffic and congestion, it is clear that the opposition to them, like that to the Covent Garden scheme, exploited at some level a powerful concern that the modernism of Anglo-American speculative developers was un-English, the loss of the familiar built environment—this was especially true of the skyscraper plans for Piccadilly Circus—read as the loss of national identity in historic storied locations. That such a reading might be a recently learned response, grounded as much in the commercial culture of the tourist brochure, Hollywood film, and heritage TV as in an "authentic" sense of self and tradition may beg of course large issues of the shifting construction of British identity generally.

CHAPTER 2

The Embassy and the Crowd

While Charles Clore was negotiating a Park Lane site for Conrad Hilton's modern monument to the "practical idealism" of postwar American commercial expansion, the London press announced the choice in Washington of the modernist Finno-American architect Eero Saarinen to design a new American embassy for the entire west side of Grosvenor Square—a megastructure in the heart of Georgian/Victorian Mayfair, on a site paid for entirely by outstanding war credits, that would symbolize for many the tangible reality of the Cold War American imperium.[1] Later that year, as buildings were being demolished to clear the site, President Eisenhower—whose bronze uniformed image now stares out confidently over the square—effectively brought a halt to Britain's Suez adventure, and so precipitated a crisis of national identity and a foregrounding of the problematic of the Anglo-American relationship that reverberated through the next two decades.

Embassy-building itself was a significant American Cold War strategy to project the image of a newly self-conscious world hegemon. Congress voted tens of millions in the fifties and sixties for the construction of large, centrally located structures that—in their size and their modernity—reflected a much larger American presence (as the number of consular, defense, and intelligence staff grew dramatically) and, generally, the modernity, prosperity, and self-confidence of the American way. In the fifties modernism was the preferred style for new embassies endorsed by the U.S. government's Foreign Buildings Operations (F.B.O.), a style that it consciously linked to the idea of freedom—in contrast to the heavy, classically detailed Soviet style.

Although architects and designs were approved by a committee led by the Italian émigré dean of architecture at MIT, Pietro Belluschi, Saarinen was chosen for London uniquely by juried competition. Other commissions were announced that year for Athens (Walter Gropius), Stockholm, New Delhi, Riyadh, and Oslo (another Saarinen design). The London project, however, was to be the largest and most expensive of these, and members of the F.B.O.'s advisory committee were concerned that the scale and quality reflect not only American modernity but also a restraint and harmony appropriate to Britain, an opinion endorsed by the then ambassador in London, Winthrop W. Aldrich—who in fact seems to have had, like the tourists thronging for a glimpse of the "changing of the guard," a sharper sense than the British themselves of their essentialized "traditional" character. Another visitor, from the F.B.O. advisory committee, agreed and consequently Saarinen's commission required that his design "create good will by intelligent appreciation" of its site. Loosely interpreted, and Saarinen would interpret it very loosely, this meant, not necessarily the heavy neo-Georgian favored by the Grosvenor Estate (and despised by many British modernist architects and critics), but some respect for the prevailing height, mass, and classical formality of the rest of the square.[2]

SAARINEN'S EAGLE

When the first sketches were published, there was at first some critical approval in the London press for a design that would introduce the "vitality and self-assurance of American architecture." The embassy was to be 330 feet long and 71 feet high, faced in the Portland stone Saarinen had admired on his whirlwind trip to reconnoiter London in 1955, with a checkerboard fenestration intended to be allusive of traditional Georgian style. Later responding (in his diary) to criticisms that, allusive or not, the building did not after all seem very appreciative of the site, he claimed that the original intention had been to create a "landmark" that would lead to the evolution of the site toward a "future square" rather than the re-creation of a literal Georgian aesthetic. Perhaps inevitably, Saarinen would "confuse intention with achievement." Most observers were not persuaded that the overblown behemoth of a building that rose on the west side of the square in the three years following the Suez Crisis preserved any sense of a Georgian aesthetic or indeed the idea of a square itself. The result was a kind of cuckoo's egg, especially as the Grosvenor Estate continued to develop the rest of the square in neo-Georgian Corinthian.[3]

As completion—delayed for a year—neared in the spring and summer of 1960, the shortcomings of the new embassy became a talking point in the architectural and popular press. The building in fact became a kind of lightning rod for a mild anti-Americanism, and could represent "American vulgarity" either because it was not modern enough or because it was too modern. One critic asserted that the building exported "prestige in the form of 'glamour,'" language that drew on associations with Hollywood America. What seized public attention more than anything else was the anodized aluminum American eagle, 8 feet tall with a 35-foot wingspan, that was raised to the top as the building neared completion. Designed by the Polish-American sculptor Theodore Roszak, it had been substituted for a stone cartouche of the Great Seal of the United States in the original plans. It was, Saarinen said, used "freely and symbolically," and he regretted that it was not

4. The U.S. Embassy in Grosvenor Square. Author's photograph.

larger still. As with the Hilton, the embassy drew fire from the Labour left—this time for its flaunting of a national emblem of a "monstrous" size, an "architectural eyesore," a "blatant monstrosity."[4]

Led by Richards in *The Times*, critical assessment of Saarinen's accomplishment when complete was swift, and nearly universally negative. As modernism it lacked "integrity," it was not the kind of "good modern" needed in London, and relied for its effect on the tawdry "artifice" of gilded aluminum beam ends and window reveals, its "trickiness" hiding the "underlying bones" of its structure. British modernist voices in the American journal *Architectural Forum* in March generally regarded the embassy as not American enough. Peter Smithson complained that it was surprisingly unrevolutionary: "[We] are puzzled why you . . . should accept such frozen and pompous forms as the true expression of a generous egalitarian society." R. Furneaux Jordan wrote of the building's diplomatic delicacy and false humility, and Reyner Banham worried that it abandoned "muscularity" in favor of "ballet-school" architecture. Later Pevsner's judgment would follow much the same line: a "decidedly embarrassing building" that was surprisingly conventional in its "effort to be in tune with the London tradition."[5]

Architectural comment tended to dwell on the technical problems, the failure to complete the square on the west side, the "thin and tawdry" gilded aluminum trim, the mannerist affectation of its broken facade and fenestration, and the raising of the building above the ground floor in a way that created a kind of moated base. Popular reaction dwelt on the arrogance of the eagle (though Richards perversely argued that it was not big enough or stylized enough to be interesting) and on a reading of the building that suggested the reification of an American cultural as well as political suzerainty. Its colonizing size alone, and the way it stood fortresslike, independent of the rest of the square, its announcement of its own importance seemed to some at odds with the somewhat boring nature of its overall aesthetic—reminding one, appropriately perhaps, of a giant department store (as a later guide to London architecture observed) rather than the civic "stateliness and formality" that had been the architect's objective. Just before his premature death in 1961, Saarinen reached his own conclusion about the negativity of the British response: "In my mind, the building is much better than the English think—but not as good as I wished it to be."[6]

However Saarinen's embassy may have been regarded architecturally, it commands this largest of Mayfair squares, and American tourists are prone to mistake the Grosvenor Square gardens for the embassy's "grounds." These had been rearranged after the war along formal lines with a south-to-north avenue, making the Roosevelt memorial of 1948 the principal focus. The bulk of the new embassy building, however, reoriented this focal line again from east to west—that is, away from Roosevelt's helping hand to Saarinen's emblem of dominance. As the New England novelist John Updike commented when he visited London in 1969, "[T]he great glass box on Grosvenor Square" was one of the most obvious "outcroppings of American power" in London, and one "which turned out to need its moat."[7]

President Kennedy visited the new embassy on 5 June 1961, greeted by a crowd of children from the American schools at Bushey Park and Prince's Gate. His new ambassador was the well-liked, well-spoken, and well-connected career diplomat David Bruce, who would later be contrasted mercilessly by the press with Nixon's awkward, gauche millionaire Walter Annenberg. Kennedy himself was popular in Britain, and mourned. In 1965 a modest bust was unveiled by his brothers Robert and Edward near Park Crescent. Though in a somewhat casual position beside the Marylebone Road pavement, it was, in our period at least, reverentially treated: "[T]here is always a fresh wreath," Updike observed, and concluded that such tokens were evidence "of America's unique, inescapable scope in the world." The flowers, which have long since ceased to appear at this small shrine, may of course have been laid by American residents as well as British admirers. By the sixties there were tens of thousands of American professionals and businessmen and women and their families living in the capital, and by 1968 also a population of the unattached: the backpackers, countercultural itinerants, draft-dodgers, and hash-heads. They were not Americans likely to be invited to the elegant drink soirees hosted at the embassy by the Cultural Secretary, or attracted to the "events" sponsored there.[8]

The new embassy had space (thanks to Saarinen's load-bearing walls) and resources for entertainments that advanced the Kennedy era's commitment to project "international style" with an American flavor. The Cornell University Glee Club, en route home from Russia, provided the first evening concert, and the next year Roberta Peters, Metropolitan Opera diva, gave a recital in the small embassy theater. The standard cultural fare focused, however, like the building itself, on American modern: American abstract painting, concerts of twentieth-century American music, American modern dance. Or there were more didactic occasions. The embassy offered free lectures (often by notable British and U.S. academics, or visitors from the American art, literature, or music scene like Leonard Bernstein) on Tuesdays and films on Wednesdays. While the arts were favored topics, another purpose was served, no doubt, by the screening at the embassy of U.S. Atomic Energy Commission films (which could also be borrowed) on nuclear physics and the positive uses of radiation.[9]

PROTEST

Only a half-dozen years after completion of the new American embassy, Grosvenor Square became the well-photographed and televised site for the most dramatic anti-American protests ever seen in London. Whatever its architectural statement, the embassy would have been the obvious target as passions mounted over the war in Southeast Asia. But Saarinen's assertive structure and its crowning eagle was for many richly symbolic. They changed the square's iconic status from one that, with the memorials to Roosevelt and the "Eagle Squadrons," had signified Allied collaboration, to one of intrusion and domination. If it seems ironic that a decade of significantly thickening cultural relations between Britain and the United States should also see the sharpest demonstration of anti-American protest, that is only a seeming contradiction. The ethos of the late sixties generation—the Underground and antiwar cultures—radiated outward from the States and underpinned an international style of protest. By 1968 anti-Americanism, like the counterculture, had become an American export phenomenon.

On Battle of Britain Day (17 September) 1961, the Committee of 100, a militant outgrowth of the pacifist Campaign for Nuclear Disarmament (CND), organized a march of celebrities, intellectuals, and students to Trafalgar Square, where antinuclear speeches were made. Then, in what was to become a familiar continuation of protest, the group moved on to Grosvenor Square for a ritual act of civil disobedience. Confronted by police, they sat down in the street and there were "noisy exchanges." Before this, spin-off factions from the annual (since 1958)

Easter march from Aldermaston to Trafalgar Square, like the Anti-Polaris Group in April of that year, were already accustomed to head also for the embassy, where they were met by police standing "shoulder to shoulder." But the Committee of 100 now began organizing year-round events aimed also at the Russian embassy near Kensington Gardens. There were "mothers' marches" with prams, "protests of silence," and sit-down protests—with an increasing number of arrests (31 in April of 1961, 138 in April of 1962, 126 in October). In March of 1962 a protestor managed to deface one of the abstract paintings in an embassy exhibition with the CND peace symbol.[10]

During the tense October days of the Cuban Missile Crisis, there were further scenes in front of Saarinen's new embassy, where pacifist antinuclear campaigners jostled with more militant anti-American leftists in presenting demands that the United States step back from the brink of war. After the Cuban crisis, and as U.S. military involvement deepened in Vietnam, the peace movement largely dropped its interest in the Russians and concentrated on Grosvenor Square. Though the East Anglian USAF bases—especially Lakenheath—remained available as loci for relatively low key demonstrations, Grosvenor Square was *the* site, a stage-set for a visual manifestation of the solidarity of dissent that promised certain confrontation with police, probable arrests, possible violence, and newspaper photo-journalism and perhaps television coverage. In March of 1965 a group of six men and one woman chained themselves to the embassy railings and to door-handles inside the building. In April students down from Oxford—including the president of the Oxford Union, Tariq Ali—were arrested at the embassy and remanded on bail. In October there were a two-day nonstop demonstration and seventy-eight arrests.[11]

There was an element of anti-Americanism embedded in the antinuclear lobby from the outset of the Cold War when fear of becoming a target for Soviet nuclear weapons first surfaced over Britain's support for NATO and the Korean War and later when U.S. bases in Britain converted to nuclear. As Canon Collins put it, "[T]oday we are an American satellite . . . a forward base for rocket-firing on Russia." In 1957, in the warm afterglow of Britain's own hydrogen bomb test at Christmas Island, the antinuclear movement aimed first to secure a British renunciation of nuclear weapons, assuming that Britain—as A. J. P. Taylor later recalled—"was still a great power whose example would affect the rest of the world." As reality sank in, in the years after Suez, as the inability of any British government to resist pressure from Washington became clear, as even the Labour leadership rejected unilateralism, the U.S. government became the main target and the locus of protest shifted from the Ministry of Defence—the object of the Committee of 100's first sit-down demo (in February 1961)—to Grosvenor Square (in September).[12]

And yet, the (transatlantic) story of the antinuclear movement's anti-

Americanism is more complicated than it might seem. The formation of CND in February 1958 was anticipated a few months earlier by the National Committee for a Sane Nuclear Policy (SANE) in New York. CND of course drew directly and powerfully from older pacifist traditions in Britain and deployed in its well-pub-licized Aldermaston marches a mass protest ritual already familiar to interwar England, but there had long been significant Anglo-American "circularity" in the peace movement. Most obviously there was the transatlantic Quaker com-munity, its idea of "public witness," and the institutional ties of the British and American Friends Service organizations, just as there had through much of the twentieth century been a degree of transatlantic pacifist solidarity on the socialist and Marxist left. By the late fifties, in Britain as in America, the antibomb cause attracted celebrities from the entertainment industry as well as university stu-dents, and the British New Left's pacifism, Raphael Samuel recalls, found a special resonance in Stanley Kubrick's 1957 film, *Paths of Glory*.[13]

George Kennan, former American ambassador to the Soviet Union, provided an immediate catalyst for the formation of CND. In November 1957 he delivered the annual Reith Lectures on BBC radio, attacking Dulles's hard anticommunist line and the danger of nuclear war that it seemed to encourage. American influ-ence of another kind is pronounced among those militants who wanted to take the CND beyond marching and into direct action. The developing American civil rights movement provided contemporary examples of peaceful protest—espe-cially the sit-in or sit-down that became a common Committee of 100 tactic by 1960–61. The black American campaigner for civil rights Bayard Rustin was an active member of the CND Direct Action Committee from 1958 (he would help organize the "March of 100,000" on Washington, DC, in 1963). Later sponsors of the DAC included Americans Ammon Hennacy, Homer Jack, A. J. Muste, and Linus Pauling. Directly and indirectly, the American example helped to galvanize a larger, more diverse movement in Britain. As Sheila Rowbotham, for whom CND was a first entry into radical politics, recalls, "The combination of the Civil Rights movement in the United States and the opposition to nuclear weapons in Britain meant that direct action was no longer confined to the tiny anarchist groups."[14]

Just how widely the appeal of such tactics of protest may have reached, from the radical left into a broader generation of sixties youth, can certainly be debated. It promised more than it delivered, and its visibility in the memory of the times may belie its failure to mobilize a sustained mass movement outside the universi-ties. Nevertheless, the deflationary cynicism offered by revisionists like Dominic Sandbrook risks losing sight of the special location of moments that disrupt and challenge and voices from outside the majority. Otherwise one is left with a history of flattened landscapes and the quotidian interests of "most ordinary people" who had "a lot of better things to worry about."[15]

From the winter of 1958–59 there were frequent demonstrations at air bases in

East Anglia where the British were moving to construct missile sites and nuclear storage areas for the U.S. Air Force. Within the CND, a younger, more militant faction organized a Direct Action Committee that espoused a more distinctly anti-American line. One later survey indicates that younger CND members—those who joined in their teens or twenties—were nearly three times as likely as older members to cite "overdependence on the U.S." among their reasons for joining the movement. And yet, they were also much more likely to be followers of American popular culture—in their love of protest folk music and jeans—than the older activists. Later, Jeff Nuttall observed, "[T]owards the end of the great days of Aldermaston, . . . certain of the whackier and younger CND followers . . . formed a cultural nucleus that looked mainly towards America and the Beats for its model." When, in the mid-sixties, George Clark, CND and Committee of 100 member, imported the idea of "Campaign Caravans" into the London struggle for housing reform, he was borrowing directly from similar antipoverty projects in the United States.[16]

Finally, there is the debatable influence of Ralph Schoenman, a postgraduate from Yale who came to the London School of Economics (L.S.E.) in 1958, became active in the CND—he wasn't the only American student to do so, though Tariq Ali calls him "a rare breed"—and espoused what some found a shockingly deep hatred for the United States. A leading voice for direct action—mass demonstration, confrontation, and civil disobedience—and for the creation of the more militant Committee of 100, his influence on Bertrand Russell, whose secretary (some said puppet-master) he became, was resented, and his revolutionary anarchism (he urged, for instance, the disruption of the State Opening of Parliament) older members feared would bring the movement into disrepute. During the 1961 Easter demonstration, it was Schoenman who, against Canon Collins's wishes, led some 600 marchers on from Trafalgar Square to the American embassy. The same year he was imprisoned for two months and narrowly escaped revocation of his visa. Schoenman himself, not given to modesty, claimed that "every major political initiative that has borne the name of Bertrand Russell since 1960 has been my work in thought and deed."[17]

Schoenman, with his stridency, intemperance, and anger, was for a few years the most visible face and loudest voice of American anti-Americanism in Britain—though also something of an embarrassment. When he was excluded from the Committee of 100 in 1963 his influence in the movement "evaporated," and by the next year Christopher Driver could observe, "Nowadays a faint chill tends to come over the conversation of nuclear disarmers when Schoenman's name is mentioned." He remained secretary of the Bertrand Russell Peace Foundation (and of the "Who Killed Kennedy Committee"), and was in and out of London for several years. Arrested again at one of the Grosvenor Square demos in 1966, he was finally deported when attempting to re-enter Britain in 1968.[18]

CND itself exerted some influence across the Atlantic. A nascent American antiwar movement, as it mobilized on hundreds of college campuses, and as it merged the antinuclear into the anti–Vietnam War movements, adopted the famous CND peace symbol. There is a circularity here. Protest returned to Britain enhanced with countercultural weight, crossing an ocean made significantly smaller by charter flights, and transmitted by a broadcast medium that itself dissolved distance. Like the counterculture in which it was in part embedded, the anti–Vietnam War movement on both sides of the Atlantic shared rhetoric, tactics, organization, and a style of agit-prop art—street theater, posters, Underground press—that was a reflection not only of the immediacy of media communication but also the back and forth mobility of individuals.

By 1965 Tom Hayden's and Carl Oglesby's Students for a Democratic Society moved from civil rights to antiwar activism, organized a march on Washington, DC, and began knitting college campuses together across the country in opposition to the conscription-fed escalation of the ground war. While in Britain the organization of radical militancy had its own Trotskyite and New Left sources, the direct action campaign of the Vietnam Solidarity Committee (VSC) organized in 1966 and the Radical Students' Alliance resonated closely with the tactics of the SDS across the Atlantic and attracted a significant number of radical young Americans studying in London. In February one of the first Vietnam demonstrations in Britain, organized by radical antiwar protesters based in Oxford, paraded before the American embassy in Grosvenor Square with a banner (and chant, to the tune of Pete Seeger's antiwar protest song "Where have all the flowers gone") asking "Where has Harold Wilson gone? Crawling to the Pentagon!" "Teach-ins," starting on the Berkeley campus, spread to other American universities, and to Britain, as did some of the leaders of the American movement who advocated such tactics: in 1965 Carl Oglesby met Tariq Ali in Croyden. In the spring of 1966, in the aftermath of the customary Easter demonstration at the U.S. embassy, those arrested—including Ralph Schoenman—sang what had become "the CND anthem," *We Shall Overcome,* at the Marlborough Street Magistrates' Court.[19]

On 13 December 1966, the Americans bombed a suburb of Hanoi. After a pause the war continued to intensify in the next year, with the center of Hanoi bombed in May. By the end of the summer the number of U.S. forces in Southeast Asia exceeded half a million and resistance to the war intensified as well. Demonstrators marched on the Defense Department in Washington. In London antiwar militancy, both organized and random (graffiti was transatlantic: Berkeley and Notting Hill saw walls daubed with the same slogans—often inspired by Blake) proliferated in harmony with the American movement. In London as in the States, the summer of 1967, "like lightning crackling behind the sunshine of the psychedelic movement," signaled a turn in the counterculture from free love and flower power toward confrontation and militant struggle. In Grosvenor Square, bullets were fired through windows of the American embassy. A "Revolutionary Solidarity Movement" left behind a screed denouncing Yankee fascism and racism and calling for the liberation of "American negroes." On the night of 2 September, two young men (age twenty and eighteen) protesting the Vietnam War broke into the embassy and were seized by U.S. marines. And in March the next year a bomb exploded in the American Officers' Club at Lancaster Gate.[20]

On both sides of the Atlantic, October 1967 was a critical threshold. On the 17th seven young American men, mostly postgrads from the L.S.E., handed in their draft cards at the embassy after a march around Grosvenor Square by the "Stop It" committee (a group of Americans against the war). The first major demonstration, coinciding with a mass march on the Pentagon in Washington, D.C. (and more than 400 arrests), was organized by the VSC on the 22nd. What *The Times* called an "Anti-War Riot" began in Trafalgar Square and proceeded to the embassy where flour bombs were thrown at the police and mounted police were used to herd demonstrators out of the Square toward Oxford Street. There were forty-four arrests. The police were apparently caught off guard, and had the organizers themselves been prepared for the turnout and the relative lightness of the police presence, they might, Tariq Ali claims, have occupied the embassy building, and Saarinen's eagle would undoubtedly have been draped with the red and blue flag of the Vietnamese People's Liberation Army.[21]

17 MARCH 1968

The year 1968 began with the Vietcong's massive, and wholly unanticipated, Tet offensive, coinciding with the Vietnamese lunar new year celebrations that began on 30 January. Hue was overrun, and a six-hour battle for the American embassy in Saigon (a modern six-story tower completed in 1967) was seen on American and British television. Tet had a galvanizing effect on the transatlantic antiwar movement. As student protest deepened and widened throughout the States, the VSC made coordinated plans for further direct action in London. On 14 March protestors disrupted performances at twenty West End theaters, climbed onto the stages, and attempted to "educate" audiences about the war. Sometime before this, Tariq Ali had telephoned Vanessa Redgrave in Paris where she was opening in *Camelot* on the 13th, urging her to perform wearing a white headband—signifying Vietnamese mourning. Redgrave refused, but agreed to march at the head of a VSC protest in Trafalgar Square and at the American embassy that was planned for the 17th. Ali and the VSC council had decided to attempt to occupy the embassy, though she may not have known this.[22]

By 1968 Redgrave's career was more advanced than that of Jane Fonda, as were her politics. Her increasing militancy made her a vocal and bitter critic of U.S. foreign policy and capitalist exploitation, though as with many in CND this drew some inspiration from the American left: "[It] was thanks to Paul Robeson that the

anti-communist witch-hunting of the Eisenhower years failed to brainwash me .
. . . I found all of Robeson's songs, and played them over and over again." She was
also, like many British actors, increasingly enmeshed in a dense web of personal
and professional cross-Atlantic connections; these came into play in the antiwar
movement in circular and mutually reinforcing ways. Fonda's committed antiwar
activism was apparently inspired to some extent by Redgrave's own highly public
voice. They first met in Hollywood in the summer of 1965 at a fund-raiser for the
Student Nonviolent Coordinating Committee's effort to register black voters in
Mississippi; in September 1968, Fonda named her daughter Vanessa, "because she
is strong and sure of herself and was the only actress I knew who was a political
activist"; and by October 1968 the two were in regular communication. Inspired by
reports of Fonda's antiwar work aimed at U.S. conscripts, Redgrave "decided [that
she] must initiate a similar campaign"; she began to contact GIs at Mildenhall and
elsewhere, helped organize a GI antiwar newspaper, participated in leafleting the
USAF bases in Britain, and organized entertainments and benefits for those who
responded. At a benefit at the Lyceum in London that Redgrave helped organize
in 1971, Jane Fonda sent a message of encouragement on tape, and U.S. servicemen came on stage to speak. That summer a number of U.S. airmen presented a
petition at the embassy calling for an end to the war.[23]

When Redgrave appeared at Trafalgar Square on 17 March 1968 to call for victory for the Vietcong, she was wearing the white headband and brought greetings
from actors and film directors. The turnout was large—estimates run from 10,000
to 25,000, with more joining as the crowd surged along Oxford Street, where
department stores had prudently boarded up their ground-floor windows. The
crowd that funneled into Grosvenor Square was composed of radical students,
pacifists, anarchists, Marxist revolutionaries, and no doubt a fair number of sympathizers and spectators curious to see what would happen. There were rhythmic
chants of "Ho, Ho, Ho Chi Minh," "Hey, hey, LBJ, how many kids you kill today?"
and other slogans familiar from American demos. The march had been well publicized, and there was what Mick Farren calls "an anticipatory hysteria mounting
in the media." Thousands had come into London from provincial cities, including many American students, research academics, and faculty, and more would
have come had buses not been stopped by police on highways beyond the capital.
In the melee that followed, the press and television had a field day as confrontation turned to violence. Thwarted demonstrators, stopped at the street before
the embassy, threw clods of earth, stones, and coins at the windows—a dozen or
so were broken—and at the police. There were smoke bombs, firecrackers, and,
ultimately, police charges that injured scores of demonstrators and a number of
police (unlike such confrontations in the United States or Europe, the Met did
not use either tear gas or water canon). Of the thirty or so police horses, one was
injured—an event covered in sympathetic detail by the press. In the aftermath,

fragments of the crowd swirled around to attack the windows of the new Europa Hotel on the north side of the square (some claimed wealthy businessmen and tourists had booked champagne lunches and a view there to watch the action). About fifty went on to attempt to get into the Dorchester, where more windows were broken before they were dispersed by the police. Later there was a concerted effort by militants (reports ranged from 100 to 1,500) to force their way into the Hilton Hotel, but police were already there in force, and protestors had to be content with shouting, "Yanks Go Home!"[24]

In the days that followed, as several hundred demonstrators appeared before magistrates, the press echoed M.P.s in parliament in denouncing violence that was often presented as having been orchestrated by "foreigners." While Pakistan-born Tariq Ali himself was the object of some of this, the German contingent and a variety of Continental anarchists were singled out, as were activist Americans who were identified in the crowd. One American student from Essex University was fined £10 for shouting "Burn the Embassy," and Callaghan, the Home Secretary, moved to ensure that Ralph Schoenman would not be allowed back in the country. The Conservative deputy leader, Reginald Maudling, called, as did other opposition M.P.s, for the deportation of foreign student demonstrators who "stirred up violence."[25]

The day after the riot, *The Times* published a range of photos—of workmen cleaning the square of litter (no doubt including copies of the leaflets the VSC handed out with Gerald Scarfe's cartoon of Harold Wilson preparing to lick LBJ's arse), of the injured horse, of course, and of a "US Out" graffito daubed onto the Roosevelt Memorial. The event had been broadcast on evening news throughout the U.K., and, as Farren, no special friend of Ali et al., later claimed, "[T]elevision was the key . . . the revolution *had* to be televised . . . a lavish VSC commercial." The fighting had lasted almost two hours, and, as Ali later recalled, "We got close to the imperial fortress, but by 7 pm we decided to evacuate the square . . . . The coverage on the television news [of the poor horses] gave me an idea of what to expect from Fleet Street the next morning." Certainly the television coverage—in color for those who could receive it—was dramatic, but one wonders whether Ali was amused when a couple of years later the BBC made use of its archive footage of the Grosvenor Square melee to illustrate a program on Marx and the Hyde Park Riot of 1866. The drama of confrontation that he hoped would be a beginning was here framed by the past and turned into heritage TV in a program that, as Raymond Williams sighed, paid more attention to Marx's boils than to his ideas.[26]

Events in Paris soon eclipsed the relatively contained protest movement in Britain. In France there were peculiar conditions favoring a more robust, deeper, and more widespread revolt—Parisian habits of direct action, the uncertain tenure of a ten-year-old Fifth Republic and its aging leader, and an albeit tempo-

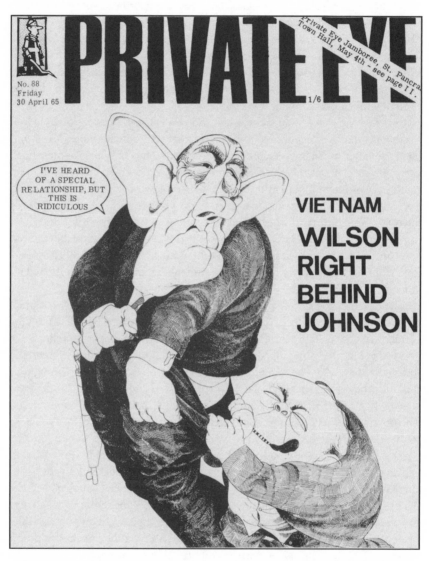

5. "Wilson Right behind Johnson." Gerald Scarfe cartoon from the cover of *Private Eye*, 30 April 1965.

rary coherence of some of the intellectual left, the generational rebellion, and the Marxist-dominated labor movement. In contrast, and in retrospect, the British antiwar movement seemed shallow, ephemeral, imitative, and lacking in much ability to reach out to ordinary people in their daily lives. It was not, many claimed then and subsequently, in tune with the deeper conservatism of the British system and dramatically underrated its toughness and tenacity (much the same was said about the American revolt once the student antiwar fervor had subsided). Moreover, in Britain the old and much of the New Left were deeply suspicious about the ideology of the antiwar-*cum*-counterculture movement; the press managed both to sensationalize and to trivialize it, the trade unions were largely uninterested, Wilson's government, while paying some lip-service to Johnson's war did not after all lend British military assistance, and British youth were not being conscripted to fight in Southeast Asia.

The course of the American descent into violence, mass confrontation, and assassination in the spring and summer was followed closely by the British media—first Martin Luther King's assassination in April (his killer, James Earl Ray, was captured in Britain), followed two months later by the assassination of Robert Kennedy (the embassy, now not a site for protest but for the long queue of some 5,000 who signed books of condolence), and then the dramatic televised scenes at the Democratic convention in Chicago in August. In London there were gestures from a variety of dissident groups, anarchists, militant students, and Underground fringe elements: in July the Hilton Hotel suffered a further £4,000 damage, a stone was thrown through a window of the Playboy Club, and police battled rioters at Hyde Park Corner where students dragged barricades across the road. But such skirmishing was episodic and relatively unorganized. The VSC held off, gathered its resources, and prepared for another mass demonstration in early autumn.[27]

The march of 27 October was meant to counter the negative reporting of the 17 March confrontation by encouraging peaceful protest, abdicating any designs to occupy the embassy, and concentrating on the ritual airing of grievances at Trafalgar Square, Downing Street, and Hyde Park. One of the largest mass demonstrations in Britain since Chartism ran more or less according to plan. But Tariq Ali's handing in at Downing Street of a petition signed by 75,000 failed to seize the media attention that had marked the drama on 17 March, and praise from the Home Secretary, James Callaghan, of their "self-control" further underlined, as it was meant to do, a reading of the event as uniquely British, unthreatening, and ultimately dismissible.

The October demonstration—tactical success and strategic failure—is nevertheless of interest. Inevitably, the British antiwar movement attracted the attention of academic sociologists: the extensively prepared and publicized October demonstration offered an opportunity to "study" the phenomenon of mass protest. Three scholars with an interest in "pop" culture and "alternative value systems," and associated with a new media Centre for Mass Communications Research that had been established as student militancy was gathering steam in 1966, worked out in advance an arrangement with the BBC, ITN, the *Daily Mirror,* and the *Guardian* to subject the event as it developed to analysis. Such projects had their counterpart in many American universities by the late sixties, as sociologists seized on the youth culture and generational revolt phenomenon.[28]

By 1966 and 1967 accounts in *The Times* reiterated the theme that those arrested were "young persons" and dwelt on their obscene language and rude behavior in the face of magistrates: in Britain, as in the United States, the Dr. Spock generation. A week after the October 1968 march, the newly founded *New Society* reported on the youthfulness of the protestors, estimating that 64 percent were under twenty-five years old (as were 78 percent of those arrested), and about half were students. The *New Society* study (by sociologists, two of whom were from the L.S.E.) attempted to counter the right-wing "myth" that the October 1968 march involved "a mass of overseas activists," but their own survey confirmed that about one in six antiwar protestors was in fact "non-British"—a figure that rose to more than a quarter of the older (over twenty-five) participants and begged the question, of course, of just what constitutes a significant minority—as well as "foreign." Although Germans, especially, had appeared early on in the CND movement, and there were other Continental (often anarchist) and Commonwealth students, the majority of these foreigners were probably American, if participation in radical university politics at the time is any indication. The reiterated chant of "Ho, Ho, Ho Chi Minh" was, the *New Society* piece observed, rather "like a US cheer-leader's call."[29]

While the VSC and the International Marxist Group hoped to build on the perceived success of 17 March—as a media event if nothing else—and on the promisingly larger turnout of 27 October, a year later it was clear to most that 1968 in Britain had been the apogee of protest-as-direct-action rather than the beginning of a radicalizing avalanche. While there was some activity in Grosvenor Square in sympathy with the October 1969 Vietnam moratorium called in the United States (where millions took to the streets in the largest protest ever witnessed there), it seems to have been a largely low-key, and mostly American undertaking.[30] The next year saw the last significant march against the war, during the Cambodia incursion. After the National Guard killed a number of students at Kent State on 4 May 1970 there was a demo in Grosvenor Square, and later a couple of gasoline bombs were thrown at the embassy. In December "Group 68" (an antiwar organization for Americans in Britain) presented a giant Christmas card addressed to those imprisoned in the United States for draft resistance. Though an overtly radical American presence remained in the universities and in the British Underground keeping open conduits back to the Chicago conspiracy trials and the fringe violence of the Weather Underground, the majority of young backpackers pouring in seemed more interested in enjoying themselves than in confrontation.[31]

Seventies and eighties revisionism often represented the phenomenon of the late sixties as a kind of ephemeral frenzy of a generation warped by permissiveness, a decade characterized by the sudden collapse of the wildly optimistic political and social agendas of a minority counterculture in the following "hangover" or "morning-after" years. Subsequently, popular historians like Dominic Sandbrook have sustained a dismissive, and often contemptuous, consensus that characterizes late-sixties radical protest in Britain as the "fashionable" emulation of what might have been a genuine social phenomenon in the States but in Britain was inevitably "trite and incongruous," and evaporated with hardly a trace when "revolution went out of fashion" among the metropolitan elite, while "most people" simply never much cared.[32] It is one purpose of the following chapters of this study to offer an alternative view, not to deny that the specific utopianism of the late sixties and early seventies failed or that it was located largely in a minority, but to re-establish its at least momentary depth and longer-term, at some level, transformative significance. The period was a kind of cultural tsunami for many of the younger generation; this wave was supported by an underlying swell that had been building since the Second World War, a surge that moved from West to East. The protesters in Grosvenor Square may have been confronting U.S. power and capitalism, but at the same time they themselves reflected the extending global influence of American popular culture. Counterculture and protest culture in Britain did not involve a severing, or even a questioning, of *these* transatlantic cords but rather signified their tenacity and multiplication.

CHAPTER 3

US/Us: The Left's Special Relationship

———•◆•———

> No socialist today would dream of doubting the client status of
> this country *vis-à-vis* the United States.
>
> —Perry Anderson, 1968[1]

For much of the British left, the United States as the citadel of capitalism had long supplanted Britain itself, birthplace of the Industrial Revolution and worldwide colonial exploitation but since at least the 1920s financial, commercial, and industrial second fiddle to the land of Fordism and Taylorism, Pittsburgh, Wall Street, and Madison Avenue. The staggering industrial output of the United States during the Second World War, the juxtaposition of British austerity and U.S. prosperity in the years following, and the focused and sustained American financial and military presence in Europe in the early years of the Cold War put the seal on the idea that the twentieth century was America's century and that the economic system of the "Free World" was defined by, based on, and sustained through American capitalism.

The postwar generation on the left, like many among the Oxford *Universities and Left Review* group, did not, unlike the older, prewar *New Reasoner* cohort, have much embarrassing "ideological ballast" to get rid of post-1956. Few could seriously contemplate the sclerotic Soviet system as any kind of alternative model, however useful it might have been in checking American hegemony worldwide. There was the possibility of course of a reformed socialism in Eastern Europe somehow emerging, but what enthusiasm there was for socialist alternatives to the American way was increasingly reserved for, on the one hand, a liberated Third World in Africa and Asia, and on the other, a cultural transformation from below in the West, and a hope, among some, that the antinuclear, civil rights, and anti-Vietnam movements were green shoots of a generational challenge within the citadel itself.

In light of the near-collapse of intellectual Marxism in fifties America, the view of American capitalism familiar to the British New Left in the fifties and early sixties drew heavily on American liberal critique of the social and economic system there—on David Riesman's or William Whyte's exposés of the sterility and conformity of suburban life and Vance Packard's or John Kenneth Galbraith's explorations of corporate America and its advertising-led commodity culture. It was also informed by the maverick American Marxist sociologist C. Wright Mills—Raphael Samuel later claimed that Mill's *Power Elite* was especially influential among the *ULR* crowd—and democratic socialist Michael Harrington. As Norman Birnbaum, an American sociologist from Harvard then teaching at the L.S.E., cofounder of the *New Left Review* and general editor of New Left Books, ironically observed in 1960, "We have been enjoined to celebrate Britain's tin-plate version of the affluent society at the same moment as well-paid professors at Harvard turn against their own."[2]

Galbraith's *Affluent Society* was "incomparably the most influential popular work" of the era on American capitalism—on both the puritanical and "vestigial Marxist" left and on the modernizing revisionist Labour right.[3] Reflecting on the failure of the British Left in the fifties, Perry Anderson observed in 1965 that it was Galbraith who offered "a frontal attack on the social priorities of capitalism" that was, in the context of the "anguished, parched" British terrain, "fresh and radical." "Harvard liberalism" may have provided the Labour left with rhetorical ammunition in its warning against, as Nye Bevan said, becoming "thoroughly Americanised," of becoming a "rootless, acquisitive, shoddy and processed version of capitalist America." But it also, and more deeply, informed the significant players on the "Atlanticist" Labour right—Denis Healey, Tony Crosland, Roy Jenkins, and Hugh Gaitskell, and their younger followers like Roy Hattersley—where some accommodation with the reality of relative affluence for much of the working class by the end of the fifties at least promised an escape from left ideological rigidity and a way constructively to engage the Tories' monopoly of the "You Never Had It So Good" advantage. The Labour right were, moreover, much more likely than the radical left to have personal experience lecturing and networking in the United States with the lights of the Democratic Party and academic liberal Establishment. As Hattersley would recall, "We felt at home in America."[4]

Both the New Left and the Atlanticist right listened closely to voices from the American academy and progressive American journalism, by the sixties often heard directly from the United States itself as radio and television connection thickened. The British left became obsessed with "reading" America, and much of their analysis of their own contemporary condition rested on an understanding of technology-driven *American* society as both alienating future and instructive source of the "structural contradictions" that might lead in Britain to a crisis-inspired recovery of community. The surprising explosion of radical revolutionary politics among white, middle-class American university students in the mid-sixties presented an acute problem, however, that divided the left between those who reluctantly admitted that contemporary radical politics in the United States, as Terry Eagleton and Brian Wicker wrote in March of 1968, "is in many ways a model, and perhaps a foretaste, of what is in store for everyone in the western social tradition," and those who dismissed the counterculture as the lifestyle radicalism of bourgeois anarchists.[5]

In the United States, liberal critique of the alienating *conformity* of capitalist modernity, especially the supposed sterility of middle-class professional and suburban life and its commodity culture, led, as Marshall Berman has argued, to the rediscovery of a romantic radical individualism among the younger of the New Left. As expressed in the SDS Manifesto, the 1962 Port Huron Statement (a document much studied by some of the younger left in Britain), there was a need for the kind of radical social change that would free all to seek their own "self-cultivation, self-direction, self-understanding and creativity," to find a "meaning in life that is personally authentic." It was a message, imbued with the "vocabulary of existentialism," that propelled many young radicals on both sides of the Atlantic to a spiritual break with the crude-seeming Marxist materialism of their elders.[6]

The argument here is not that the British intellectual left necessarily looked more to the United States than to Europe, but that some, especially younger postwar-generation British Marxists, found American contributions in, especially, sociology to be compelling because of the theoretical poverty of British work; many, like Stuart Hall, were prepared to argue, reluctantly and with qualifications, that in the field of *praxis*, if not theory, U.S. campus radicalism offered a challenge to the "ideological rigidity and traditionalism" of the European left.[7] Even among those intellectuals most resistant to Americanization and suspicious of the American counterculture's existential project of *personal* liberation, there was a preoccupation with the American threat that itself tended to reproduce its supposed domination.

THE BRITISH LEFT AND AMERICA IN THE SIXTIES

In 1967 Raymond Williams, E. P. Thompson, and Stuart Hall published an extended essay as a *New Left May Day Manifesto*. This was a collaborative effort by a cross-generational committee—many of whom were associated with the *New Left Review* (Hall was its first editor)—that had been formed in 1966 with the intention of setting out an apologia and program. The context was the fragmentation of the left since 1956 and disenchantment with an Atlanticist Labour Party that in government seemed to be promoting, through modernization ("the theology of the new capitalism"), American capital and American imperialism:

> Our practical dependence on the United States, expressed in political and military alliances, locked in financial arrangements and the penetration of our economy by United States capital, and supported, as a planned operation, by many kinds of cultural and educational colonisation, makes any attempt at disengagement a fight from the beginning.[8]

The pamphlet was expanded into a book and reissued by Penguin Press (under Williams's name) the following year when the events of April in London and, especially, May in Paris perhaps gave these academic socialist musings some unexpectedly sharp pertinence, though, riven as they were by internal disagreements over strategy and overtaken by events, they do not much engage the then current crisis. Some sections deal directly with American themes—its political economy, its "drive outward," its shaping of the technological age—and there are references throughout to the United States as now the home base of capitalism and the need to understand the particular character of its influence. The British fiscal crisis was but one sign of the subordination of British capitalism, ironically by the very means it had achieved its own supremacy in the nineteenth century—laissez-faire imposed by the strongest. From the first rank, Britain was downgraded to, at best, that of the leader of the client states; in a sense Britain itself had been colonized—a trope Williams had explored in *Culture and Society* (1958) and developed in his writing on the influence of American television in the early sixties. As with other colonial peoples, resistance meant reconnecting with their own sources of "democratic practice."[9]

In Williams's 1968 *Manifesto* such reconnecting, however, had little directly to do with the romantic utopianism of the *American* "new left," or with the countercultural anarchism of much of the anti–Vietnam War movement there and in Britain. Though the *New Left Review* had a few months earlier published an interview with Herbert Marcuse, there is little here that affirms or even acknowledges the cultural rebellion going on in the United States and Britain. That which does, does so in a somewhat distant, if not condescending way. There is a nod to "the new young Left," the "newly active generation" in the United States, but the collective essay of the previous year had been rather more enthusiastic:

> Few events in the past years have given us greater cause for encouragement than the rebirth, on the campuses and in the squares of the great cities of the United States, of a movement for peace and against imperialism which works toward the same internationalist objective as our own. The élan and courage of this young movement of American people presents an urgent claim upon us for our solidarity.[10]

While this language was stripped out of the 1968 *Manifesto*, its affirmation of American student radicalism did find expression in articles in the *May Day Manifesto Bulletin*, a typewritten monthly "internal document" edited by and circulated among the younger of the New Left from January 1968. An organ for "exploring differences," its pages often indicate the generational tensions and ideological fracture lines in the movement between "freelance freebooters of the underground left" with their "poetry of revolution" and those who were more patiently committed to the democratic initiatives and community organizing that would make the antiwar cause, for example, "understandable and relevant to the people at large in the country."[11]

The old New Left had in any event been in some confusion since 1961 when Perry Anderson displaced Stuart Hall as editor of the *NLR*. By 1964 Anderson himself wrote of a fault-line between the weak "ethical" socialism like that of Williams that evacuated the concept of conflict and one that was concerned (like Anderson) with a "structural" analysis of British society, while Peter Sedgwick followed a rather different analysis. He regarded the movement as having irretrievably broken (he himself had drifted to the Trotskyite International Socialists) into "the Two New Lefts"—one, following C. Wright Mills's repudiation of "the labour metaphysic" (the working class as necessary agent of change) and committed to radicalizing middle-class youth, the other preoccupied with "purism and scholarship," a socialism that "organizes no party, supports no strikes, rallies no class, carries no banner, articulates no ideology."[12]

For the confirmed left of whatever faction and especially those who were middle-aged, 1968 certainly came as something of a surprise, and, for all the claims of solidarity, many viewed student upheaval on American campuses as ideologically suspect. Perhaps significantly, Williams (who was forty-seven in 1968, and University Reader in Drama at Cambridge 1967–74) was absent from the Manifesto group conference called in April at University College, London (UCL), when militants—some of whom were committed to an "anti-university," communes, and direct action—resolved to embrace a new militancy that would reject parliamentary socialism altogether. Williams remained cautiously on the fringe of the Anglo-American student rebellions—committed as he was to a careful "reasoning, describing, persuading." Three years earlier he had argued (hopefully) that the New Left was not so much a political party with an activist agenda as a "group of writers and political thinkers" hoping to exert suasion within the Labour Party through "moral critique" rather than "dogmatism." Though he did not attend the UCL conference, he did march, as usual, to Trafalgar Square for the annual CND Easter demonstration—as he had done for the past decade to protest nuclear weapons—only a couple of weeks after the melee at the U.S. embassy. In a BBC Third Programme radio broadcast a few days later he attempted a justification of ritual demonstration, as opposed to violent confrontation by "a small minority." Characteristically, he located the modern protest march in its (British) historical context—as a revival of the mass Chartist demonstrations of the previous century—and stressed the necessity for visible protest in an era dominated and controlled by a commercial mass media that was inherently undemocratic (he had demonstrated against the German Springer Press following the shooting of Rudi Dutschke). This is an essentially liberal view of protest-as-communication ("soberly and quietly") rather than protest-as-provocation ("Need demonstrations be violent?").[13]

If Williams had misgivings about the "libertarian" new New Left characterized by American university militants, neither did Eric Hobsbawm (four years older) or Edward Thompson (three years younger than Williams) have much positive to say about radical American counterculture. In March 1968, Thompson wrote to Sheila Rowbotham, "grizzling about the introspective druggy youth culture" as a form of "psychic self-mutilation . . . self-absorbed, self-inflating and self-dramatizing. *Very* like Methodist revivalism." Though he had an American mother, visited the States after the war and frequently thereafter, admired the "internationalism" of the American academic left, and was especially close to C. Wright Mills, Thompson harbored deep misgivings about the malign effect of U.S. cultural hegemony generally. In 1951 he had written (in a Communist Party of Great Britain [CPGB] tract on *The American Threat to British Culture*), "The 'American dream' really is . . . childish . . . debased . . . and its poison can be found in every field of American life." Though Thompson would protest, "I do not think I can be accused of being anti-American," he disliked the commercialism of American popular culture generally and distrusted the politics of "gesture and style" of young countercultural radicals. "Youth if left to its own devices, tends to become hairy, to lie in bed till lunch-time, to miss seminars, to be more concerned with style rather than consequences of actions."[14]

Eric Hobsbawm (fifty-one in 1968) had an abiding love for American jazz and had spent a summer on the U.S. West Coast (at Stanford University), but he had even less interest than Thompson in the American generational rebellion. The beginning of the spread of the civil rights movement into universities and the sharp radicalization of students at Berkeley across the Bay go unmentioned in his memoir, and he recalls only the boring "nowhere space" of suburban Palo Alto. Nor is he, by the end of the decade, especially interested in the counterculture that, unlike the blues and jazz derived from oppressed African Americans, sprang from an essentially middle-class white youth—and was exported to Britain like commercialized American mass culture generally. In his widely read 1968 economic history text *Industry and Empire*, he echoed Raymond Williams's lament that the media that shaped and communicated popular culture in Britain—cinema, television, and "the arts of popular entertainment"—were "dominated, as they have been ever since the triumph of the mass market, by the USA." Hobsbawm later complained that *his* intellectual generation had lived in two countries—their own and France, not, as with the current generation, their own and the United States. The "ultras of 1968," like the Situationists in France, more inchoate Bakunin anarchists than real Marxists, were, he felt, mere protestors in a stable and prosperous society, not revolutionaries. Communist intellectuals of his time had not been, in any event, *cultural* dissidents—"[T]he major divide was not, as in the era of rock music, between generations":

> For middle-aged leftwingers like me, May 1968 and indeed the 1960s as a whole were both enormously welcome and enormously puzzling . . . . [It] was not a botched attempt at one kind of revolution, but the effective ratification of another: the one that abolished traditional politics, and in the end the politics of the traditional left, by the slogan "the personal is political."[15]

On the whole, the younger left responded differently, though not Perry Anderson, who was only cautiously prepared to believe in 1968 that, though British culture, especially the "reactionary and mystifying culture inculcated in universities and colleges," was a stifling force, the student struggle in Britain might yet emerge—as it had done in the States and elsewhere in the industrial world—as the "initial form" of revolutionary practice. Other young, or relatively young, academics and postgraduate students associated with *The New Left Review* (Robin Blackburn, Alexander Cockburn, Gareth Stedman Jones, Tom Nairn), or with the Marxist-Catholic Slant Group (Terry Eagleton, Brian Wicker) were, like David [John] Caute or Sheila Rowbotham, more enthusiastic about "student power" not only in France but also across the Atlantic. For some this may testify to increasing transatlantic contact at the personal level. Caute, for instance, spent a year at Harvard on a Henry Fellowship in 1961–62, returned to America in 1966–67 as a visiting professor at New York University and Columbia University, lectured on the West Coast at Berkeley in 1974, and published a book four years later on American anticommunism.[16]

At school in North Yorkshire, Rowbotham had read the American Beats and the *Evergreen Review* and laughed at Tom Lehrer and Lenny Bruce and came to feel, through the "wild extremity" of her CND commitment, herself also to be "a kind of collective outsider now" as well. In Paris for a year abroad before Oxford she found the French "less susceptible to American youth culture" than she and her British friends; her own experience at Oxford and in London was marked by close and important American influences. Hobsbawm no doubt had Rowbotham—whose doctoral dissertation he supervised—and those like her in mind when he observed that her generation lived in Britain *and* America. By the mid-sixties she was living with Bob Rowthorn (a member of the editorial committee of the *NLR* in 1968), who had been at Berkeley in the early 1960s when it was "just beginning to stir with the first signs of student radicalism," and who was himself radicalized by Bob Scheer, graduate student in economics at Berkeley and left-wing journalist. Later two "bronzed and skinny" American friends, Nancy and Frank Bardacke (who were also part of the Berkeley student movement—Frank was arrested in 1967 as one of the "Oakland Seven" conspirators) stayed with them in London. "They were my introduction to the new American radicalism, the first friends to connect me to an international left politics." By the time Rowbotham committed herself to the anti-Vietnam movement in 1965, the United States had come to mean the Berkeley of her friends but also Malcolm X, Michael Harrington, and Woody Guthrie:

> I seized on these insights from across the Atlantic because they illuminated the daily evidence of race and class inequality surrounding me in Hackney. . . . I read everything I could find: Jack London, Upton Sinclair, John Dos Passos, Frank Norris and many more.[17]

For many of the younger activists, the Vietnam War made the "generalised peace politics of CND" seem increasingly irrelevant. By 1966 Bob Rowthorn was planning a Berkeley-style "teach-in" at Cambridge, and, Rowbotham later recalled, "[We] began to look outwards towards . . . the new community politics, influenced by the American New Left"—and, increasingly, by the "transformatory vision" of the American counterculture, first by its utopianist enthusiasms and the "psychic discovery" offered by its "heady mixture of music, drugs, art, and underground papers," and latterly by its anger. By 1967 she was working with Tariq Ali on the radical Underground paper *The Black Dwarf*, where visiting American militants were often to be found exchanging experiences—like the SDS woman Ali recalls who wanted, after Tet, "to emulate the NFL guerrillas" through a campaign of bombings in the United States itself. It was a radical American friend, Henry Wortis (then a postdoc fellow in genetics from Stanford), and his wife, Shelley, who helped Rowbotham recognize and understand the "male chauvinism" she experienced within the antiwar and countercultural left generally (and in particular at *The Black Dwarf*) and to encourage her own turn toward a politics of Women's Liberation.[18]

Though the *New Left Review* may not have been especially committed to the counterculture and its doubtful Marxism, the lives and work of the contributors to Williams's *Manifesto* are thick with American connection. Raymond Williams was deeply interested in cultural meanings embedded in the Anglo-American mass media, and especially in television. Like Richard Hoggart, he despaired of American media influence, even—or especially—when expressed as democratization:

> At certain levels, we are culturally an American colony. But of course it is not the best American culture that we are getting . . . . To go pseudo-American is a way out of the English complex of class and culture, but of course it solves nothing; it merely ritualizes the emptiness and despair.

Nevertheless, he was often tasked (1968–72) with reviewing American-made television shows for the BBC's *The Listener*, and published in 1974 a study of *Television, Technology and Cultural Form* that drew not only on this work but on a year-long stay at Stanford University's Department of Communications (the book was written in California). The expansion of the American communications system was, he argued, not just filling a vacuum but had become *the* determining factor in the development of media technologies and style in Britain and indeed in "the whole non-communist world." He was, however, happy to find contradictions: "In the young radical underground, and even more in the young cultural underground, there is . . . an eager sense of experiment and practice."[19]

Jamaican-born radical sociologist Stuart Hall was thirty-six in 1968 and a resident fellow and deputy-director at the Centre for Contemporary Cultural Studies at Birmingham. He was the first editor of the *New Left Review* where, before Anderson's coup, there had developed "differences of emphasis and style" between the editorial board and a "working editorial group" that included the New Yorker Norm Fruchter, also a founding figure of the American New Left Group at Oxford, which served to channel Anderson and younger new New Left figures into the increasingly fractured "movement." Hall, like others, regarded American corporate capitalism as at the center of the postwar socialist problematic, and derided Labour's modernist version of "an Americanized Britain"—"hamburger stores at every intersection, and the open, unfenced reaches of new-town suburbia stretching into infinity." As a sociologist, however, he was drawn to American scholarship, to the work of Becker and Matza on deviance and to Michael Harrington, Norman Mailer, and C. Wright Mills, whom he had published in the *NLR*. At a conference in 1967 organized by the Slant Group he took the middle ground on the authenticity and usefulness of the American radical student movement but was willing to argue that, in spite of its populist nativism and its manifold "polarities and contradictions," it pointed to "the vigour, variety, courage and revolutionary thrust which has decisively broken through the American consensus." Unlike many of the older New Left, he also took the American hippy phenomenon seriously, and argued after the "Summer of Love" in 1967 that theirs was a genuinely revolutionary project, albeit one located mostly among the American middle class.[20]

Of the other, younger, contributors, Bob (Robert Eric) Rowthorn, who was twenty-nine and an assistant lecturer in economics at King's College, Cambridge, in 1968, had, as we have seen, also spent significant time on the West Coast at Berkeley. Terry Eagleton, who studied under Raymond Williams at Cambridge, was twenty-five and a fellow at Jesus College in 1968, when, in March, he and Brian Wicker were prepared to find much of interest in the "radical re-casting of revolution [in America] into the language of existential projects, personal liberation and life-style, cultural and psychological experience." Eagleton later would spend time as a visiting scholar on the West Coast at San Diego where he lectured "sun-dazed, slit-eyed" young people who seemed "to have just wandered in off the beach."[21] And finally, two of the contributors to Williams's *Manifesto*, Richard Parker and Sean Gervasi, were themselves Americans. Parker, twenty-two in 1968, came to Oxford from Dartmouth College to study economics and subsequently became also an editor of *Ramparts* and a founder of the radical West Coast journal *Mother Jones Magazine*. Gervasi, an economist and political activist, came to Cambridge in the sixties and played a role in the inauguration of the British anti–Vietnam War movement. In 1966, the L.S.E.'s refusal to renew his assistant lectureship helped to spark the student rebellion there.

THE VIETNAM WAR AND TRANSATLANTIC ALTERNATIVE THEATER

Many of the New Left on both sides of the Atlantic were concerned not merely to be a protest lobby within the political Establishment but, improbably, a vanguard of the common people. Like the old left before them, however, they were also acutely aware of the class distance between themselves and those they hoped to persuade. The problem was particularly acute in the antinuclear and antiwar movements, where neither in the United States nor in Britain did the industrial working and lower middle classes seem much interested. After 1961 some like Perry Anderson were less troubled by problems of popular mobilization and looked to concentrate on "intellectual transformation."[22] But for others the energizing of student politics opened an interesting—if somewhat faute de mieux—avenue. The more sanguine came to believe (or hope) that the significant expansion of higher education in the sixties in both countries and the student rebellion that seemed to follow from this indicated that students themselves might constitute a new alienated class that could take their own disaffection to the people in some romantic reprise of the nineteenth-century Russian *Narodniks*. The New Left looked to means of reaching out, not only to their students but also to a postwar public that was more defined by its consumerism than by shop floor comradeship. In the words of the *New Left May Day Manifesto*, there was "a need to win back the cultural control exercised by film and broadcasting," to resist "cultural and educational colonisation."[23] This was in line with the location of the left's leadership in the universities, polytechnics, and art colleges, and with the resonance radicals achieved within at least some sectors of the performing arts, among avant-garde directors like Peter Brook or young playwrights like Howard Brenton or David Hare. In this, the generation of 1968 rediscovered the agit-prop techniques of the twenties and thirties, the theater of Brecht and the cartoons of Grosz, just as the sexual politics of the counterculture was to some evocative of Weimar decadence—and led to a rush of undergraduate enthusiasm for Isherwood's Berlin Stories (Herr Issyvoo himself had long been a resident of Southern California).

Alternative theater in the service of the antiwar student movement flourished in the major metropolitan areas of the States—beginning on the coasts, especially San Francisco and New York, but spreading to even provincial, mid-Western university towns by the late sixties. Experimental theater techniques—confrontation with and involvement of the audience, shocking, often obscene language and themes, the idea of "disposable art" (much of this had been of course the stock-in-trade of the Beat movement of the fifties)—not only informed Underground drama collectives in Berkeley and Greenwich Village but seeped into mainstream theater as well. In spite of the obvious contemporary European influences, in Britain experimental theater was, according to Marwick, popularly regarded as "an invention of the Americans."[24]

Peter Brook's coming to New York in 1965–66 to direct the transfer of *Marat/ Sade* confirmed his dedication to the antiwar movement. His own "Manifesto of the Sixties" was an affirmation of an art that changed things, socially *engaged* theater at a time when "all theatrical conventions are being challenged and rules no longer exist," a time when one had to "question all accepted forms."[25] A somewhat aging enfant terrible, forty years old in 1965 when he received a C.B.E., Brook is characteristic of those in the world of the arts in the sixties who had active careers on both sides of the Atlantic. Beginning in 1953 when still in his twenties he had mounted productions every couple of years or so in New York. Often, as with *Marat/Sade*, these were transferred from famously successful West End productions in London.[26]

In the interwar years most fashionable popular theatrical artists were expected to play at least New York, and perhaps Boston. Moreover, as British players, directors, and writers moved into film they found themselves increasingly drawn to the American West Coast as well, into the Los Angeles colonies of ex-pats who came regularly to move back and forth between the United States and Europe and between the world of stage and screen. After the war, an increasingly interconnected English-speaking entertainment world was further facilitated by air travel and the complicated commercial intertwining of American money and British talent in the film, television, and theatrical industries. A well-known "star" performer like Sir John Gielgud would as a matter of course have agents on both sides of the Atlantic.[27] By the sixties it was not just "names" who did this kind of commuting; younger actors and directors just beginning or in midcareer could often manage to find engagements in the United States—though Actors' Equity might make for difficulties. It was the money of course but also the exposure, the possibilities of tapping into a much richer entertainment world than the West End offered, and often the lure of the possibility of crossing the line from theater to a much better paying Hollywood. From the late fifties there had also been some considerable interest in Britain, especially among the coming generation of young actors, in the ideas behind Lee Strasberg's Actors' Studio, a New York workshop that famously promoted Stanislavsky's "method acting" techniques. Marlon Brando's screen success spoke to those like Michael Caine or Julie Christie who were interested in looking beyond the traditional stage training of the Royal Academy of Dramatic Art (RADA) with an eye to crossing over into Hollywood film. Both occasionally attended classes at the Chelsea Actors' Workshop, in studios in the King's Road—an ephemeral early-sixties attempt to emulate in London Strasberg's methods.[28]

Cross-Atlantic traffic was not all in one direction. In 1956 Charles Marowitz, the young lower East Side actor, director, and theater critic for the new *Village Voice*, "stultifying in New York," moved to London where he established himself in Fitzrovia, got a job as critic for the influential new wave magazine *Encore* (while continuing to write pieces for the *Voice*), and, beginning with his "In-Stage" rooftop theater in Fitzroy Square in 1958, promoted the developing fringe movement in London throughout the sixties. In 1962 Brook invited him to assist with the Royal Shakespeare Company (RSC) production of Scofield's *King Lear*; Marowitz remained for some years involved in Brook's work, helping to run the auditions for his Artaudian "Theatre of Cruelty" season in 1964. In February of 1970 his own experimental theater "The Open Space" was raided by police for showing Warhol's *Flesh*; the prosecution in this twilight period of censorship was dropped, and the film played to full houses.[29]

American actors might also aspire to the London stage, but their accents were an issue unless performing in American roles (British accents, on the other hand, were often an asset in the States), and the trade union problem was a significant obstacle. Marowitz's Texan friend David Healey, however, managed to "hammer his way" in from a beginning in the USAF's "On Target" company, an information and education program run for NATO bases in Britain. Lavish American musical theater productions—if rarely their actors—often crossed the Atlantic in the sixties and seventies, often drawing large audiences; by the seventies concern deepened that there was a skewing of commercial theater offerings as splashy Broadway shows in London were coming to depend ironically on *American* audiences—as did, at the other end of the theatrical spectrum, reiterated runs of familiar classics of "official culture," what Howard Brenton called "the corpses on our backs"—to the detriment of new work by contemporary dramatists.[30]

On 26 September 1968, one day after the abolition of theater censorship in Britain and a month before the largest of the antiwar marches to the American embassy, Rado's and Ragni's *Hair* opened at the Shaftesbury Theater, bringing to mainstream Britain the hippy counterculture of the East Village. Billed as "an American tribal love-rock musical" it either, depending on one's perspective, creatively subverted the familiar formulas of Broadway or was a landmark in the commodification of a debased and popularized radical counterculture. Three versions had previously been denied a license from the Lord Chamberlain's office for being "dangerously permissive." The chief examiner found its attack on patriotism, its advocacy of free love of all kinds, and the obscenity of its language offensive (though he admitted to not understanding the meaning of "freaked them out"). It was, in the event, a popular success, and drew, especially, a younger audience, often students who came down to London from university to experience "the age of Aquarius": nudity, drug-taking, antiwar protest, and the desecration of the American flag.[31]

Two years earlier Peter Brook's own ambitious anti–Vietnam War drama had opened at the Aldwych Theater. *US* was not a musical celebration of the counterculture but a grim, experimental, collaborative "investigation" of U.S. atrocities in Vietnam. It was informed by the Brechtian techniques of the Berliner Ensemble, Antonin Artaud's "Theater of Cruelty," and the collaborative and improvisational approach of Joan Littlewood's Theatre Workshop in east London, but also by the visits to London of American fringe groups like the Living Theater and the contemporary explosion of American radical guerrilla street theater, with its unannounced public "happenings." Happenings had come to Britain in 1963 when

Mark Boyle (who would later specialize in psychedelic light shows) collaborated with an American, Ken Dewey, at the Edinburgh Festival and then in a series of events in London. Subsequently, Jeff Nuttall devised his own at the Beat bookshop in Charing Cross Road, Better Books, after meeting the American theater director Herb Balu, "who told me what was happening on the West Coast."[32]

US was intended to be a disturbing, provocative happening that drew its audience into a confrontation with the "cruelty and madness" of the Vietnam holocaust, while exposing issues of guilt and complicity—expressed in the ambiguity of the title's double entendre. Brook protested, not perhaps entirely convincingly, that the play was not anti-American ("[T]he word stings me") because the United States ("which I visit and love") "was part of us, her atrocities are committed in both our names," and those of "us" who remain silent on both sides of the Atlantic shared in the crimes of torture and genocide; *US* was meant to "zap" their conscience.[33] Brook himself had been involved with the American theatrical scene since the early fifties and was working on the transfer of *Marat/Sade* to the New York stage, and later its film version (released in 1967), while evolving the improvised structure for *US*.

The script for *US* was a complicated affair, evolving over a period of several months and based on the efforts of a team of authors, notably Denis Cannan and Michael Kustow, who trawled through newspapers and published documents for the story of America in Vietnam. "Saturated" by newsreels and the American television reportage of the "horrors" of the war, they were also concerned with how to compete with "real images" on television.[34] There were discussions in London and New York. The American composer Richard Peaslee, who had done the score for *Marat/Sade*, was drawn in for the music (lyrics were by British poet Adrian Mitchell, who had also worked on *Marat/Sade*), and the final script was shaped by a process of trial and improvisation involving twenty-five actors and workshops presided over by Joe Chaikin (American director of the New York–based, off-Broadway "Open Theater," whose own *America Hurrah* would be produced at the Royal Court in London the next year) and the Polish director Jerzy Grotowski (whose "Labortorium" in Wroclaw emphasized stripped down sets and intense confrontation between actor and audience).

Back in Britain there were experiments in drawing the audience into performances that included game-playing with art college students from Bradford. Brook intended "a theatre of confrontation" in line with the sensational productions the Royal Shakespeare Company had been mounting since it moved to the Aldwych under Peter Hall's general direction. RSC rehearsals began in July of 1966. There were long discussion sessions on issues such as "violence in America." The intention was to shock "with the immediacy of a Happening" and through "naturalistic improvisations": "Those who had been to America continued to invent ordinary scenes . . . [but] quickly revealed to the actors how little they really knew about life in America."[35] The process was itself a learning experience.

The play divided into two acts. The first was an exploration of American life and myths, and threw together reportage, readings from Ginsberg and Warhol, improvisations from American movies, advertisements and Marvel comics, satirical music ("Zapping the Cong"), and Mitchell's coruscating poetry. The second—which caused some sharp differences among the team—was more didactic, involving a dialogue between a young Englishman determined to burn himself on the steps of the American embassy in Grosvenor Square and Glenda Jackson's dissuading, questioning young woman. A self-critical dialogue targeted American consumerism ("'American'—what do you see? . . . A big car, long—as a house"), the Anglo-American relationship ("They're buying everything . . . Antiques. Drugs. Pictures. Love"), and the ambiguities of being anti-American while enjoying the money and safety that would be lost "[if] we kicked out the Americans." The increasing academic cross-traffic came in for biting sarcasm in a song, "Any Complaints?":

> My girl Kate's teaching in the States,
> Lecturing from town to town.
> Pays her bills, gets her thrills by
> Studying the influence of Yeats on Yeats.

It ended with a coup de théâtre that some found disturbing. Live butterflies were released, but one (possibly artificial) was kept and set alight. Actors blindly groped about with bags on their heads and then sat in a long-sustained silence, "a confrontation between the United States and us, Vietnam and London" and "reopening the question, each night, for all of us, of where we stand." The production lasted about three hours.[36]

There were, over a six-month run, fifty performances at the Aldwych, with the house always full. Brook took the entire cast to Grosvenor Square before the show opened to protest the war, and opening night, with David Frost, a TV crew, and various demonstrators outside the doors, drew considerable coverage. The play had narrowly avoided drastic censorship or refusal of license. Lord Cobbold, the Lord Chamberlain, thought the script was "bestial, anti-American and communist." Concerned discussion with the Foreign Office and George Brown, now Foreign Secretary, drew in both the British ambassador to the United States, Ormsby-Gore, and the American ambassador Bruce. Chief examiner Heriot, who "loathed the script," objected that "[t]he attitude [of *US*] to America seems to me to be dangerous and insulting to an ally" and recommended refusing a license. Though Brown also found the play revolting, the government (and he in particular) was under fire for its support for the American bombing campaign, and censorship would certainly provoke further outcry. Unsubtle hints however were dropped that the RSC might be risking its Arts Council subsidy when Hall,

Brook, and George Farmer (chairman of the RSC's finance subcommittee) met with Cobbold. Eventually the play was allowed—with some cuts in language either obscene or insulting to LBJ (or both).[37]

A joint parliamentary committee was sitting to consider the ending of censorship of plays, and this may have tempered Cobbold's stubbornness, though he was also advised (by Sir Tim Nugent, a former comptroller) that the play would in his view be preaching to the converted—"the same, very left-wing beardies" who usually made up RSC audiences—and "I doubt if many recruits would be won for the Anti-Americans . . . . I think this could probably be explained to that nice and very sensible US ambassador." They need not, perhaps, have worried on Bruce's account. The urbane ambassador and his wife took an interest in the arts, including fringe theater. In 1967 they met the American expatriate, alternative theater director, and cofounder of the Underground paper *IT* at his new Arts Lab in Covent Garden. Jim Haynes was not only asked to come lecture to embassy wives on the London theater scene but also was recruited to take one of President Johnson's daughters to the theater.[38]

In the event, Cobbold himself wrote before the play opened to reassure Bruce, though he admitted there was "a risk that some people may see an anti-American slant in it." Following the well-trailed opening, reviews were mixed—not because of its "anti-Americanism" but for what some regarded as the boring intellectual guilt of Hampstead socialists (whom Dennis Potter would later call "Tea-bag Rebels"); others, because it lacked solutions. Tariq Ali, who reviewed the play negatively, was among those who were annoyed that it stopped well short of any program of radical action and proceeded, with the support of Adrian Mitchell and Clive Goodwin, to launch his own revolutionary paper, *Black Dwarf*. Charles Marowitz reviewed the play for the first issue of the new counterculture magazine *International Times*, and found it "pretentious" and clichéd. Reprinted in the United States in the influential *Tulane Drama Review*, the review caused a serious rift in his relations with Brook. Peter Hall, while admitting that the play "succeeded in its aim of stirring up feeling about an escalating war which, as yet, had not registered with the British public" and had been a "savage, ferocious piece," felt that it was too eccentric to be called a theatrical triumph—puzzling and irritating, angering and embarrassing audiences in equal measure. On opening night, breaking the long silence at the end of the performance, the theater critic Kenneth Tynan shouted from the stalls, "Excuse me, but are we keeping you waiting or are you keeping us waiting?"[39]

When Brook's film of parts of *US* combined with scenes of 1967 London was released (as *Tell Me Lies—A Film about London*) in the United States in February of 1968 it caused considerable outcry. In the film, the protagonist encounters protest marchers, an Angry Arts festival, fund-raising tea-parties in Hampstead, direct action in Grosvenor Square, and, finally, Black Power activist Stokely Carmichael.

The *Christian Science Monitor* found it to be "Bad taste amounting to obscenity." Brook himself went to the United States to do the talk shows and fend off the inevitably angry reactions and apprehension at the effect it might have on the unstable universities—the president of the University of Michigan asked for it to be withdrawn there.[40]

The explosion of alternative theater in the sixties often drew on Continental—especially French—inspiration, but was also strongly influenced not only by knowledge of the New York scene but directly by American expatriates like Marowitz and Haynes or, latterly, Dan Crawford, who, at age twenty-seven, founded the London fringe venue the King's Head, where he mounted productions that "reminded me of things I'd seen in Greenwich Village." Also influential were frequent visitors from off-Broadway such as the Living Theater, the Open Theater, and the Café La Mamma company. In 1969 there was a twenty-day festival at the Royal Court (where David Hare was literary manager). Called "Come Together," the most outré kinds of actor/audience relationship were encouraged: vomiting on stage, chocolate cake smeared in laps. By 1970 there were altogether around thirty-two fringe group venues in the capital, as well as those that emerged in the late sixties in many of the universities (like the University of Bradford Drama Group, which mounted two of Brenton's early works) or traveling companies like David Hare's and Tony Bicat's Portable Theatre.[41]

Much British experimentation, especially on the radical left, was influenced by the innovative productions of the Living Theater—a communal workshop, "a family," as Nuttall says, "of disaffected youngsters living in the theatre where they worked." Peter Brook had been impressed by Living Theater's New York production of Jack Gelber's *The Connection* as early as 1960. Thrown out of their home in New York in 1963 (they had been ejected from several locations), they became nomads in Europe, "messengers and reluctant evangelists of an attitude and a way of life," and their founder Julian Beck became a familiar presence in the sixties Underground in London. When he left the United States in 1964, Chaikin, who had been a principal actor for Living Theater, stayed in New York to work with the Open Theater, a "very American" loose association of actors, directors, playwrights, and critics with Chaikin's own laboratory at its center. Brook saw his work in New York and had been impressed by his interpretation of Artaudian ideas. Following Chaikin's work with Brook on *US* the Open Theater was involved in its own anti-Vietnam effort—performing a benefit at Madison Square Garden for SANE in December of 1966 and joining the "Angry Artists against the War in Vietnam" benefit in February of 1967. They followed Living Theater to Britain for *American Hurrah* later in 1967 and, though Beck's troupe returned to the United States in 1968 for a cycle of radical political plays, Open Theater continued to bounce back and forth across the Atlantic for four European tours between 1968 and 1973.[42]

Those interested in the radical, antiwar, anticommercial arts also had access to the "raw and direct" work of American Underground filmmakers, screened at the Institute of Contemporary Arts (ICA) or the London Film-makers' Co-op at Better Books or at the Roundhouse Midnight film series, and distributed by agit-prop collectives such as Cinema Action (a workshop founded in 1968 that also did its own mobile-camera productions), Politkino, and the Angry Arts Film Society in northwest London. The Angry Arts offerings included, for instance, *No Game*, a film on the Pentagon demonstrations of 1967, *Garbage*, on the New York rich, and a "haunting" film about *The Columbia Revolt*—which came available just as the British student rebellion gathered steam.[43]

THE "TIDAL WAVE OF STUDENT REVOLUTION"[44]

"[O]ur will to change the world was turned into a theatrical event."
—Students and staff of the Hornsey College of Art[45]

On 19 November 1969, David Caute's play *The Demonstration* opened at the Nottingham Playhouse. It was ironic and comic, informed by both the American campus revolts and the British form of "student power" that followed. Student militancy turned from protest to rebellion—sit-ins and occupations—and swept through many British universities, polytechnics, and colleges in the spring and summer of 1968. That at the Hornsey College of Art in north London became a kind of media event. Michael Kustow offered space at the ICA for the students to put on an exhibition-protest, "Hornsey Strikes Again," while a Movement for Rethinking Art & Design Education held a conference of sympathizers at the popular countercultural venue, the Roundhouse. Hornsey became a paradigm of student revolution because of the length of the occupation (May and June), the anarchic attempts at participatory democracy, and its suppression through the closing of the college by its governors and subsequent purging of staff and students when it reopened in November. It also had an articulate explicator and defender in one of the college's instructors, Tom Nairn.[46]

Caute had participated in teach-ins at Oxford in 1965, was a contributor to the New Left *Manifesto* and its monthly *Bulletin*, and, after his return to Britain from Columbia University in the autumn of 1967, was active in the attempt to set up an "anti-university" in London following similar experiments on the American East and West coasts. The rallying cry "student power" was itself an American invention.[47] Borrowed from the militant civil rights movement's call for "black power" ("Are students niggers?"), it had originated during the 1966 Berkeley student strike. Though the British student movement was delayed, less pervasive, and less sustained than the American experience, the disruption of higher education when it came was if anything more shocking to mainstream sensibilities. Student rebellion—its demands, rhetoric, disruptions, and, some would say, posturing—would in one form or another continue to bedevil especially provincial university life well into the seventies. By late 1969 however the main eruption, with its collaborative energies and excitement of purpose, was already subsiding into a kind of residual culture, the rhetoric and rituals of dissidence; and dissection and explanation were well under way.

University students in the fifties and early sixties had been widely regarded as for the most part remarkably conventional and conformist, their essentially liberal goals of self-improvement seemingly advanced by the expansion of access. Though this was more extensive in the United States (where by the 1960s a significantly larger proportion of youth attended some form of college or university than in Britain),[48] the creation and expansion of new institutions of higher learning in the late fifties and sixties, potentially at least challenging the elitism of the Oxbridge system, was perhaps more striking in Britain. The new universities and polytechnics were marked—in their architectural style as in their curriculum—by a modernism that promised American-style informality and access.

Sir Basil Spence designed much of the new campus for Sussex University, creating as other modernists did at Leicester or Warwick an appearance of functional modernity to house, often, expanded sciences and social sciences—especially sociology, a growth industry in the sixties.[49] The contemporaneity that defined the new provincial campuses presumed a student body who would repay public investment by applying themselves to socially, technologically, and economically useful skills in an age in which success was to be measured in terms of (American-style) professionalism and specialization. The sixties also saw the foundation of the first British business schools on the model of those at Harvard or the University of Pennsylvania. Warwick University, which began taking undergraduates in 1965 as its physical form—"a utilitarian social environment"—was still in early stages of construction on its ample site near Coventry, was initially inspired by the Massachusetts Institute of Technology, offered "Business Studies" on the American model, and was significantly underwritten by corporate initiative and donations—especially from Rootes Motors, Ltd., a Coventry auto manufacturer acquired by Chrysler International in the late sixties. The dangers, as seen by the left, of an Americanized approach to higher education in Britain had been spelled out by Raphael Samuel at the beginning of the decade:

> Sociologists act as advisers to market research companies; historians are commissioned to write official histories of the major corporations; economists act as advisers to investment houses . . . . [T]he trend is in that direction.

When Edward Thompson, director of the University's Centre for the Study of Social History since 1965, was finally drawn into the student revolt at Warwick in 1970, he excoriated "a mid-Atlantic business school" with a "brave new discipline," commercial sponsorship, and administrators who were drawn from the world of finance and industry. A benefactor concerned to promote "Anglo-American understanding" had provided the resources for a large hall of residence that was opened in 1968 by the U.S. ambassador, provoking the first student antiwar protest there—and the bringing of police onto the campus.[50]

Warwick, like Sussex, established an exchange program for American students; there were also faculty exchanges, something that became increasingly common at British provincial universities throughout the decade. The first professor of English at Sussex, David Daiches, crossed the Atlantic on several occasions in the sixties to lecture at McMaster University in Canada, Wesleyan in Ohio, and the University of Minnesota. The years 1966–67 found him on the West Coast at U.C.L.A. At Sussex (where the new library adopted the Library of Congress classification system) the English school was combined with American Studies, and students in this discipline were expected to develop some knowledge of the culture and literature of both Britain and the United States. At the same time a number of American universities began to develop "study abroad" programs for their undergraduates. Some of the fruit of this cross-traffic was no doubt unanticipated, as the antiwar movement heated up in the United States. When a teach-in on Vietnam in February of 1968 led to paint-throwing and flag-burning at Sussex an American student, Michael Klein, was expelled, leading to further disturbances.[51]

In the early and mid-sixties, while student unrest began to manifest itself on American campuses, sociological and political surveys in Britain consistently relayed a message of British (in)difference, of the essential quiescent and conservative nature of British youth. In 1964 the sociologists Philip Abrams and Alan Little made much of the low political temperature of youth, whose identity within a new "youth culture" seemed if anything to "de-politicize" them. Those very few who had voted in the recent general election "vote in the same way, for the same reasons and on the basis of similar political attitudes, as *the old.*" The same year, Frank Musgrove published his findings on "young people" in the north of England. Arguing against the common late-fifties, early-sixties view that generational hostility had significantly increased, he claimed that in Britain (where university students appeared to be less "extroverted" than American students), those who were prepared actively to challenge the social order were a small minority—found chiefly at the "lower levels" among juvenile delinquents and at the "higher levels" among Beats and CND supporters. Noting that the 15,000 who attended the Aldermaston march of 1958 numbered "less than a quarter of a good football match attendance," he concluded, "There is no immediate prospect of any massive rebellion by the young against their condition and the dominant customs, trends and institutions of our society." The year before, another survey in Britain of more than 200 third-year university students confirmed, it was argued, that at both an elite institution (Oxford) and a major provincial university (Manchester) undergraduates were hard-working, conventionally aspiring, and performing young men (women were excluded from the survey). If anything, the researchers regretted a supposed "loss of spontaneity, bohemian colour and lightness" they apparently thought had characterized prewar student life at Oxford and Cambridge, though they did not regret the fact that there was little evidence of the "angry young men" they expected from the expansion of access.[52]

The commonplace observation that, during the turmoil of the sixties and early seventies, "most" of the university population in both the States and Britain remained more conventional and immune to countercultural liberationist values than the contemporary media representation would suggest was, of course, a theme of the conservative right during the turmoil—somewhat contradictorily, since the right also emphasized the danger of extremism on campus. In Britain the Labour government itself conducted a survey in February 1969 that seemed to confirm its view (and hope) that the disruptions were a brief, dissolving episode that did not touch most students.[53] This has since become the motif of much revisionist sociological and historical scholarship, right and left. And yet interpretation of the "evidence" is not as straightforward as it may seem. Assumptions rest often on crude survey analyses that are prone to embrace categories like "conventional" as static and unhistorical, and advance a blinkered, unnuanced majoritarian reading of popular culture. At the very least this underrates the role of minority movements in redefining and evolving subjectivities and generally moving history along. Moreover, it is by no means clear that the evidence does allow us to draw a clear and unambiguous distinction between the many and the few. Surveys such as the ones cited above commonly have their own agendas, nor can their findings be easily projected beyond a narrow point of entry. They are insufficient reason to jettison out of hand the alternative view of many contemporary, engaged scholars "on the ground."[54]

> To hear some students talk, one would have thought that the battle of Vietnam was being won on the playing fields of Houghton Street, that Black Power and student power were all of a piece. [David Martin, reader in Sociology, L.S.E.][55]

The student revolt in Britain began in 1966 in an institution with a significant American presence, the London School of Economics. American faculty like the distinguished University of Chicago sociologist Edward Shils—himself a sort of paragon of transatlantic movement[56]—had long been associated with the school, and it was especially attractive to postwar generations of American graduate students and, latterly, undergraduates doing a year abroad. Robin Blackburn, who was dismissed from his teaching position for supporting the militants, later observed "that it was American students who were very often the ones who knew how to stand up to authority . . . . There's a sort of arrogance and complacency about power in Britain which these Americans were beautifully able to puncture."[57]

Though in October 1966 student leaders seized upon the appointment of a new director from white Rhodesia, confrontation had already begun to escalate in September when the president of the L.S.E. student union, South African–born sociology student David Adelstein, violated the administration's ban on political discussion at union meetings. Issues included the National Union of Students' participation in the International Students' Conference (in March the next year a bombshell article in *Ramparts* would expose C.I.A. funding for the ISC), the failure of an American assistant economics lecturer and anti–Vietnam War activist, Sean Gervasi, to have his contract renewed, and student demands to share in university governance. On 17 October Adelstein wrote to the Chairman of the Governors denouncing the appointment of Walter Adams as the next director of the L.S.E. and followed this with a letter to *The Times*.

Growing student protest at the L.S.E. in the winter of 1966–67 was the first evidence that the issues of student "free speech" and academic governance had crossed the Atlantic into an environment that was if anything even more hostile than that in America. When the president of the L.S.E. Graduate Students' Association, Marshall Bloom, an American who had been involved in the U.S. civil rights movement, also insisted on holding meetings and taking votes in the face of the administration's explicit ban, disciplinary proceedings were begun against him as well as Adelstein, who had been briefly suspended in January. Both were suspended in March (loss of student status threatened Bloom with the U.S. draft). From November 1966, when the university began to move against Adelstein, L.S.E. students responded with sit-ins and class boycotts—and ultimately an occupation in March 1967, actions that resonated closely with student tactics in the United States.[58]

The student rebellion was of course self-consciously acting in parallel with American events and their songs (inevitably "We Shall Overcome") and banners suggested as much: "Berkeley 1964, L.S.E. 1966: We'll bring THIS School to a halt too." The issue of just how central an actual American presence was to the "trouble at LSE" and elsewhere was raised by university administrators and the press and in Parliament; the Labour government kept a close eye on American students in Britain throughout the late sixties.[59] About 400 of the just under 3,000 full-time students at the L.S.E. were American, and some, like Bloom, maintained close ties with the radical movement in the United States and with the U.S. student media (he was correspondent for the Collegiate Press Service). Among the students' supporters in the faculty were American scholars as well, and Adelstein chose one of these, Lee Albert, as his counsel during the disciplinary proceedings. When disciplinary action was taken against Adelstein and Bloom in March, the Director, Sir Sydney Caine, was asked whether American students were "at the bottom of the trouble." He equivocated but allowed that the American student rebellion "might have provided something of a model." B. C. Roberts, a professor of industrial relations, added more robustly that some of the American students, "prominent in demonstration at home," had taken up the Adams agitation "within a few weeks of their arrival in this country" and were, he suggested, among "a hard core of militants who are against any form of authority." American students generally were regarded by administrators like Henry Kidd, Secretary of the L.S.E., as sometimes awkward about substandard facilities and amenities (in comparison with back home), and presumably were—whether radical or not—less likely to accept received rituals of authority or be diffident about complaining than their British-born peers. Kidd himself clearly believed that the significant increase (25 percent over the past year) in Americans—due, he suggested, to the U.S. military draft—lay behind the rebellion. This was a view widely shared beyond the university. One MP noted that, when the L.S.E. union debated the sit-in, most of the speakers "seemed to have an American accent." They were "fluent users of the jargon of protest," Kidd claimed.[60]

When Americans Paul Hoch and Vic Schoenbach arrived "fresh from our recent radicalization at Brown and Columbia," they found an already fermenting scene. "Campus radicalism," according to Tariq Ali, "had spread to Britain from the United States," and Hoch himself played a role in the student occupation in March of 1967. By the summer of 1968 militants at the L.S.E.—where in June Lewis Cole of the Columbia SDS spoke on shutting down war research—were in close collaboration with Ali's Vietnam Solidarity Committee, and more than 2,000 of the marchers in the demonstration of 27 October spent the night in once-again occupied L.S.E. buildings.[61]

The renewed L.S.E. occupation was part of a more general surge of university confrontation, often inspired by those who were organizing contingents for the anti-Vietnam protests of March and October, but also by the radical agenda adumbrated the year before on many American campuses: ending university collaboration with the "military industrial complex," demands for curricular relevance, advocacy of university democracy—that is, the inclusion of student representatives in university decision-making (including the hiring and firing of faculty), and the need to reach out to oppressed communities beyond the university. In the spring and summer of 1968 there were outbreaks of student militancy at Essex (where a demonstration was sparked by the arrival of a British military spokesman from Porton Down and a talk by a U.S. embassy spokesman was canceled because "his safety could not be guaranteed"), Sussex (where 50 students burned the Stars and Stripes and threw paint on a visiting U.S. official), Leeds (where there was a sit-in to protest the disciplining of protestors), Hull (where 500 students occupied the administration building), Oxford (where students occupying the Clarendon Building compelled proctors to rescind regulations forbidding the distribution of leaflets), Cambridge (where Defence Secretary Dennis Healey's car was surrounded by angry student demonstrators), and Leicester, as well as the prolonged trouble at Hornsey. The L.S.E. would be the site for yet another occupation in 1969. As David Triesman, a radical undergraduate sociology student at Essex, boasted: "We are a post-CND generation, taught our final lessons in Grosvenor Square."[62]

At Oxford, Tariq Ali, elected president of the Union in 1965, had attempted to push forward a radical agenda (there was a Vietnam War "teach-in" organized with David Caute), but generally the revolt at Oxbridge was less dramatic than in some of the provincial universities. Nevertheless, by the time Terry Eagleton arrived as a tutorial fellow at Wadham in 1969 he found student militancy "in full swing": there were candlelight seminars in the student-occupied Schools building, "codes, signals, combat jackets, passwords, pseudonyms, all the panoply of a guerrilla army . . . . Students agitated for reform to the English Literature syllabus to chants of 'Remember Che!'"[63]

This is the scene that David Caute satirized the same year in the play he produced at Nottingham, *The Demonstration*. An older professor of drama, "an intellectual of the Old Left," at a British university in the throes of a student take-over, is pitted against a humorless "New Left" political scientist, a militant with posters of Lenin, Trotsky, and Che on his office walls, who, ten years younger, has spent time at an American university. The drama offers a satirical and ironic, if quasi-sympathetic, reading of the demands, sit-ins, and take-overs that had boiled up first on American campuses, then spread with dramatic effect to France and to Britain. Caute's play is built around the alternatives of violence and dogmatism on the one hand and a more humane, but more passive, cultural politics, and is full of allusions to issues then tearing the academic left apart in the United States—where was the connection between theory and practice, between the academy and the street?[64]

At the center of *The Demonstration* is an American student, "Shane," who advances the countercultural ideal of revolution-by-lifestyle. Shane, "the American leader of the Anti-University," is Edward Thompson's "self-absorbed," "self-dramatizing" youth, Hobsbawm's middle-class *cultural* dissident for whom sexual liberation and the personal were all: "[Shane:] People who formulate never copulate . . . . We have to be—spontaneous." His reply to "propaganda by deed" is "propaganda by seed." Though there are overtones of the kind of Apocalypse we get in Lindsay Anderson's *If*, the machine-gun fire is only for humorous effect. The play ends with two columns of students converging—those carrying SDS, Resistance Movement, and Peace and Freedom banners, and those who had earlier stripped naked and covered themselves with "luminous paint, tattoos and that sort of thing," the (Americanized) "hippies." Caute's irony suggests that neither can much speak to social victims outside the university or advance real social solutions. Black militants briefly appear and students vow to support them—by protesting "outside the American embassy." Workers appear, but students want to discuss racism and the war, "Alienation . . . Apartheid . . . Vietnam . . . Dehumanization," not "work."[65]

The themes running through Caute's work reflect more than his own personal experiences at Columbia. The culture of student rebellion in Britain was by the middle and late sixties saturated with the very special (cultural) relations with the United States that obtained in some British universities. When serious confrontation and student occupation finally arrived in the winter of 1970 at Warwick, it was at a university with a "mid-Atlantic" style of business-oriented administration and benefactors eager to promote Anglo-American "understanding." Edward Thompson, though wary of the American-inspired campus radicalism—he told Peter Linebaugh, then an American postgraduate, that as a teacher he resented the anti-authoritarian posing of "snotty-nosed 18-year-olds"—was drawn in when confidential files made public during the sit-in at the administration building revealed that university officials had been secretly collecting reports on the political activities of both students and staff, including especially the visiting American labor historian (David Montgomery) at Thompson's Centre. What came together at "Warwick University Ltd." (in Thompson's evocative phrase) was both aspects of Americanization: the culture of student rebellion—antiwar protest, the occupation of administrative offices, the publication of confidential documents, the charges of university connivance with defense contractors—and the Americanization of at least one institution of higher education.[66]

In Britain, the ferment in higher education was greatly facilitated by direct Anglo-American exchange. This was more important than in the student movements elsewhere—in France, Italy, Germany, or Latin America—because of shared language and the density of personal relations. Though ostensibly part of a radical student *internationale*, the British student rebellion owed more to the looser, more romantically utopian movement in the States than it did to the tighter Marxism of the French or German movements in the dissemination of a radical culture beyond a small intellectual minority. This was true of the *forms* as well as content of radical action: confrontation strategies, agendas for radical university reform, and methods of breaking down the wall between university and the wider community—the occupations, the "trashing" of administrative offices, the threatening harassment of officials, the flag-burnings and paint-throwings replicated exactly the violent turn in forms of protest in the United States. While some of the British student leadership personally experienced the American movement by attending State-side SDS conventions, listening and participating in its debates, and reading its propaganda on student power, most learned of American campus experiments simply from the visiting Americans among them and from the transatlantic media—both commercial and alternative. The Oxford "teach-in" of 1965 was directly inspired by events on the American West Coast, publicized in Britain by both the older radical pacifist organs like *Peace News* and the newly developing Underground press, and was followed by a wave of teach-ins elsewhere.[67]

Also American in origin was the idea of an alternative "free school," or "anti-university," whereby faculty and students would offer lectures or discussions free or for a modest fee, erasing hierarchic distinctions between teacher and student as well as "artificial splits and divisions between discipline and art forms and between theory and action." It was brought to London by Allen Krebs, who had founded a Free School in New York City, the New York psychiatrist Joseph Berke, motivated by Alexander Trocchi's American Beat–inspired ideas of a "Spontaneous university," and young British academics like Peter Jenner, "who had gone off to America and came back with a whole load of new ideas." The first experiment, the Free School in Notting Hill, attracted the support of John "Hoppy" Hopkins and the American Joe Boyd, both of whom were in the vanguard of a developing London counterculture, and quickly came to offer in its psychedelically painted basement in Powis Terrace not so much free further education for the underprivileged as a drugs-and-rock commune that also attracted the notice of the police.[68]

After 1968 the free school idea spread to the British university left, sometimes as a spin-off from confrontation and occupation—as at Warwick. After the earlier experiment with a Free School in Notting Hill, the "Anti-university of London" in Shoreditch was set in motion, largely as a result of the efforts of Joe Berke and the Philadelphia Foundation's Institute of Phenomenological Studies—which had organized the Dialectics of Liberation conference at the Roundhouse the year before. Berke had become a leading "exponent of 'Counter-Culture'" in Britain and was a close follower of the teachings of R. D. Laing: "[He] arrived with an enthusiastic retinue, mustered a pretty glamorous anti-faculty, and commenced business on 12 February at 49 Rivington Street, EC2" (the premises had previously housed Schoenman's Bertrand Russell Peace Foundation). There were to be talks by Ginsberg and Burroughs and courses on the pharmacology of psychotropic drugs, the sociology of guerrilla warfare, and comic books. It was meant, in the words of the *May Day Manifesto Bulletin*, to be "an ongoing experiment in the development of consciousness ... related to other revolutionary experiments in universities, communities, communes and direct action now taking place in Europe and America." For its brief existence it was supported by R. D. Laing, David Caute, and alternative arts promoters like Michael Kustow.[69]

Communication and exchange of radical rhetoric and radical form, like the self-discovery and commitment that marked the era generally, was greatly facilitated by a transatlantic popular culture (shared vicariously via recordings in the cannabis-smoke of the student flat or the student union, or directly at the Albert Hall), but also by direct personal relations with visiting American faculty, postgraduate students, and undergraduates. By the end of the decade few if any British higher educational institutions of any size were free of an American presence, as at the L.S.E., and few of the events of student rebellion lacked American participation—if, as at the Hornsey sit-in, only in the form of "Mel, an American whose energy for washing up and mopping floors seemed insatiable," or the American exchange students who joined in the antiwar demonstrations at Warwick, or the "innovative Americans" in the Stop It Committee who planned to drop the slogan "Oxbridge paddles while Vietnam burns" over a bridge during the televised Oxford and Cambridge boat race.[70]

This presentation has focused—against the grain of much continuing scholarship on "the global disruption of 1968"[71]—on the density of actual Anglo-American connections. In this sense the dominant contemporary media representation of the "anarchy" in British universities as derivative was correct, though insensitive usually to the ways in which the British version of the American crisis was distinguished by differences in class relations, traditions of academic access, methods of teaching, and relationships with the surrounding society. The contemporary critique of the student rebellion—in the British press, on radio and TV, and in the minor academic industry that grew up to analyze what had happened—itself offers another aspect of contemporary preoccupation with Anglo-American special relations, one that takes us toward the dystopian reading of the seventies that was also obsessively concerned with American cultural influence. By tracing the British rebellion back to American roots, by saturating TV screens with representations of the dramatic events on the American East and West coasts, media commentary entrenched and confirmed expectations (and fears) of Anglo-American closeness. This apprehension was now of a different order of magnitude from the threat in the fifties of American jazz, rock'n'roll, and rebellion without a cause. While there are still presumptions of deep and historically determined cultural difference, enhanced by the exotic nature of the turmoil in the States, the contradictory message was that that distance was fast eroding and that the U.S. was indeed becoming "us."

Media coverage treated the Continental dimension of the student revolt lightly as the movement spread through British institutions,[72] in part because the unrest more easily melded with the larger, voyeuristic representation of "drugs, youth and counterculture" in the United States. These connections were encouraged by programs such as that arranged by Alasdair Clayre for BBC Radio 3 in March of 1969 that brought Chomsky, Marcuse, SDS leaders from Berkeley and Columbia, Underground journalists, and other activists together in the same studio for "a distillation of rebel opinion in America."[73] The BBC gave some radio and TV time to those, like Tom Nairn—then a recently expelled lecturer at the Hornsey School of Art—who presented the case for "subversiveness," and to the sympathetic analysis of some New Left critics like Robin Blackburn. But by and large an unsympathetic, not to say contemptuous, academic Establishment (often with a special animus against American style and standards) had the better running on air and in the press—most notably John Sparrow, Warden of All Souls, Oxford, who wrote and spoke of "revolting students" and their challenge to "civilisation," or John Carey, fellow of St. John's and a former Pro-Proctor of Oxford, who

poured scorn on upper-middle-class militants pretending to be workers and posing as revolutionaries.[74]

Sparrow had been in the line of fire when 200 students "swarmed" into the
Clarendon Building on Whit-Monday and occupied the office of the proctors:
"Well, it has happened here; on a small scale, but with ugly enough results." Like
most administrators he blamed a small minority of radical students ("Most students in this country find such an anarchic and patently impractical gospel difficult to swallow") who, as part of an American-inspired counterculture, were
committed to anti-intellectualism as they were to "anti-art," and to an assault
on conventional respectability: "[T]he shaggy hair, the dirty jeans, the bare feet
on the pavements, the sluts, male and female, making love (if that is the word
for it) in the streets, the drugs, the pills, the whole apparatus of Dirt for Dirt's
sake movement." Such views resonated with a more widely heard reading of the
American scene. Alistair Cooke's *Letter from America* presented middle England
with his own superficial analysis of the crisis there on campus, embracing as
usual the moderate right, liberal-conservative, commonsense views of the upper-
middle-class and wealthy Americans with whom he played golf and felt most in
tune. "SS and SDS" was the title *The Listener* gave to his *Letter* of early May 1969
on the explosion of student rebellion across the United States: "An old fashioned
libertarian," he found it all too distressingly reminiscent of the student fanatics
in late Weimar Germany.[75]

When Richard Hoggart came, at the end of the seventies, to reflect on the student rebellions of the previous decade, he—like many in the less contemplative
mass media—also found them un-British, "in short, not sufficiently rooted in
the soil of British experience. It was not only intellectually but imaginatively too
derivative."

Hoggart was fifty in 1968, and headed the Centre for Contemporary Cultural
Studies (then lodged within the English Faculty at the University of Birmingham),
which he had helped establish four years earlier—though day-to-day control was
already in the hands of Stuart Hall. Like Williams, he was more interested in authentic, local working-class culture, under threat from, on the one hand, media-
driven American mass culture—the Hollywood, "candyfloss" world he regretted
in *The Uses of Literacy*—and, on the other, the conflicted class loyalties of working-class scholarship boys like himself. The rebellious counterculture disrupting
British universities in the late sixties was a middle-class American import and in
its libertarian hedonism offensive to the essentially conservative domesticity of
provincial British working-class life. In Hoggart's view, the student power movement—though showing a "gentleness" rarely found outside Britain—threatened to destroy the very institutions that advanced the postwar socialist dream
of working-class self-improvement by denigrating high curricular standards:
"[R]elevance is a confidence trick if it is bought at the expense of our right . . . to
grapple with the hardest".[76]

When the *Political Quarterly*, deprecatingly self-described as stolidly progressive "fossils of Social Democracy," offered their own "Special Issue on Protest and Discontent" in the autumn of 1969, the editor echoed much of the academic Establishment in his call for a "Time for Reason" and a return to "practical" political means. He also reproduced the media's characterization of British "difference": "[In] Britain we now have a very low tolerance of disorder and public violence compared to our eighteenth-century ancestors (or, for that matter, to modern Americans)." Similar concerns on the centrist left were expressed by Colin Crouch (who had been an activist sociology student at the L.S.E. in the late sixties) and Stephen Mennell in a 1972 Fabian Society pamphlet that warned against the student power agenda on the grounds that political engagement would endanger university freedom "as has happened to the University of California at Berkeley." Moreover, as Kingsley Amis had observed, students were simply not in a position to be able to judge what should be taught or who might be qualified to teach them. Over all, "any prospect of student *power* in academic issues must be viewed with caution." In the light of the much-publicized influence of American advocates of student power in British universities, their recommendation that a more restrictive policy for admitting overseas students was worth exploring, presumably in order to maximize places for deserving British students, might have had an unarticulated motive.[77]

That the revolt and its agenda threatened educational standards and consequently the value of a university degree was understandably the most common charge leveled by the challenged educational Establishment (outside the sociology departments). However justified this fear may have been, and the naive demands of student enthusiasts made them easy targets, the authorities and the press conspired to keep the issues of curriculum and scholarship more visible than the much less defensible matter of the privileges and closeted authority of the dons. Moreover, the rhetoric of "university standards in danger" allowed (both subtextually and overtly) two familiar postwar prejudices to resonate together—that the American system of higher education lacked academic rigor, at least at the undergraduate level, and that a democratic expansion of access to higher education would, by bringing in less well prepared lower-class students, lower academic standards in Britain.

Though some on the left, like Richard Hoggart, were also deeply disturbed by the threatened collapse of "standards," the rhetoric of "British universities in danger" appealed more deeply to many on the right who detested Americanization and the loss of a British difference that enshrined quality and elitism. Leading figures in the Labour government, many of whom were Atlanticist by inclination, played down the university crisis—in part because, as David Fowler has argued,[78] they felt the protests were more controllable in Britain where students were dependent on grants and were in any event not concentrated in large megauniversities like Berkeley, but also because they did not want, by admitting danger, to give the right a stick with which to beat the government and its own educational reforms.

In 1969 and 1970 a series of pamphlets assaulting both liberal and radical educational reform, *The Black Papers*, provoked much public discussion in the run-up to the general election. They plowed just these themes of the "perniciousness" (Kingsley Amis) of student demands for participation, as a "Berkeley fashion" (G. F. Hudson), and the sloppily romantic Blakean "Sleep of Reason" that underlay them (A. E. Dyson): "Student power has come to us from America and in this country owed its initial impetus to American graduate students working—or not working—here."[79]

In 1969, while campus rebellions were still unfolding in both the United States and Britain, two much-discussed books appeared, one American, one British, that tried sympathetically to make sense of the phenomenon from a left point of view: Theodore Roszak's *The Making of a Counter Culture* and the collection of essays edited for the *New Left Review* by Alexander Cockburn and Robin Blackburn, *Student Power*. Roszak, who had spent some years in Britain editing *Peace News*, taught at a university in California and had previously edited *The Dissenting Academy*, an angry collection of essays that charged intellectuals in American universities with being either apologists for the regime ("henchmen") or ineffectual recluses. To the extent that Roszak was himself close to the action at Berkeley, *The Making of a Counter Culture* was an insider's account, though from the standpoint of a social psychologist and historian. Its focus was on the presumedly alienating effect upon youth of the modern technological and bureaucratic society for which universities were meant to prepare the coming generation.[80] The British collection published by Penguin, with its New Left editors and its militant secondary title ("Problems, Diagnosis, Action"), was meant to present a case for the student rebellion from a more or less Marxist point of view. Taking the same title as a Monday Club tract of the year before (which had deflated the radical movement as an American graduate student–inspired "pale imitation" of the violence at Columbia and Berkeley), it domesticated the revolt by engaging issues of class while attempting to defuse antistudent rhetoric in the media and among the political right. In his introduction Cockburn genuflected toward the movement across the Atlantic ("No survey of student insurgency could be complete without acknowledgment to the students of the United States") and the collection concluded with a lengthy end-piece account of the Berkeley student strike of December 1966 by Carl Davidson, but the main argument lay in Stedman Jones's analysis, an essay that maintained an orthodox, and rather unconvincing, class reading of the rebellion in Britain.[81]

The Anglo-American connections of the student revolt—among many British students there was a sense, not simply of emulation, but of a shared participation—may of course disguise significant differences of class, precedent, emphasis, degree, and perhaps persistence (not least because British students were in no danger of personally being called upon to serve in Southeast Asia). Socialist organization, rhetoric, and ideology were already familiar and available to many British university students (more so than in the States) before the wave of American-style utopianism and libertarian leftism washed over them in the middle and late sixties. Nevertheless it is clear that 1968 in British universities was inspired less by the orthodox left (established campus Marxist groups by and large held back) or, indeed, by the events in Paris than by a transatlantic consciousness that extended in some form well beyond the most activist cadres. This fact allows us to approach the question of depth and legacy with perhaps more generosity than those who have seen the student revolt as a marginal, alien affair that accomplished little. It was, arguably, a symptomatic, if brief, eruption of something larger and more pervasive. In this sense, the naive radical moment at university, like the utopian counterculture it drew from or the "minority identity" liberationisms that followed, may have had a more complicated significance than is often acknowledged in either a dismissive revisionism or the elegiac nostalgia of that generation's memoirs. Quite plausibly, though perhaps not exactly in the way the organizers of the Hornsey revolt intended, the events for those who participated did signify "the profoundest educative experience" that taught them "about themselves."[82]

There is, finally, another level of Anglo-American connection—to be found in the ways institutions responded to challenge and disruption. There had been a postwar growth in the provision of psychiatric counseling as a "student service"—more common at first on American campuses, but expanding in Britain, "following the American example" in the sixties, especially at the new universities with their increased intake from the "less assured" classes. On both sides of the Atlantic, a developing profession of university counselors responded to the challenge of student rebellion with predictable theories and individualizing remedies couched in shared assumptions about the inherent instability of late adolescence or (especially in Britain) the psychosociology of alienated students recruited from outside the traditional university-bound caste. That many militants embraced the "anti-psychiatry" criticisms of R. D. Laing, and came to regard counseling as a "management instrument," no doubt added some fire to the determination of many university psychiatrists to emphasize the problematic emotional context of the politics of liberation. Practitioners on the ground did find themselves swamped with the detritus of the counterculture—especially psychotropic drug overdosing—and their responses inevitably encouraged a reading of the phenomenon in the United States and Britain as a disorder that was symptomatic of personal maladjustment.[83]

In Britain, Anthony Ryle, in charge of the Student Health Service at the University of Sussex, published his analysis of the student rebellion the same year the same publisher, Penguin Press, brought out Cockburn's and Blackburn's

Student Power. Student Casualties offered a sharply different picture, however, of the upheaval at Sussex and elsewhere in 1968. Admitting that the newspaper representation of the modern student as a long-haired, pot-smoking, promiscuous protestor was a "distortion," and claiming that one had to resist the temptation to "explain away" student revolt through psychiatric factors, he nevertheless did just that. Student militants suffered from "affective psychosis." He located the current phenomenon in a problematic context—the "instability of the modern world"— which enhanced alienation and thus served to deepen the characteristic crisis of the adolescent's "search for personal identity." Admitting that drop-out rates were higher in the United States than Britain, Ryle argued that the consequences were more severe in Britain, where students had less chance of readmission and where, in addition to the destructive nature of student drug use and promiscuity, there was the further complication of the recent increase in students from the nonestablishment classes (less likely to abide by codes of behavior) taking courses in fields (politics, sociology, psychology) that led them to question "social assumptions." As with the *critics* of psychiatric "management," much of Ryle's analysis as well was derived from American sources.[84]

The next year, Dr. Myre Sim, then a lecturer in psychiatry at Birmingham University, published a new edition of his 1966 compendium of advice to tutors about the psychiatric health of their students. The intervening four years had seen tangible increase in university drug use, "promiscuity," and violence—all of which had "psychiatric factors in their origins." His rather odd take on the rise in student violence ("The high point of student violence in Great Britain was the Grosvenor Square demonstration but this differed from other demonstrations only in degree") was to focus on what he regarded as its buried psychological meaning—that students really sought to have violence done to them, "rough handling or by getting their heads in the way of police batons." This, Sim believed, indicated sexual guilt and a desire for punishment.

> Many are perpetual protestors . . . . Many are from the more bohemian elements of the student population whose moral standards in sex are more "permissive." Many are drug takers as well and have generally renounced the morality of our society. Could these attitudes provide a clue?

Indeed, they did. Sim was obsessed with student sexual hedonism, which he regarded as a kind of incest, reactivating taboos and leading to the aberrant behavior of the militant radicals. Again, American sources, like M. Schofield's *The Sexual Behaviour of Young People* (1965), are cited. Sim, who published two major textbooks on psychiatry for the Anglo-American market in the sixties, emigrated a few years later across the Atlantic, and ended his career as a distinguished academic in Vancouver.[85]

PART II

The Counterculture

The student rebellion provided "an entirely new career course" for the psychedelic rock band the Social Deviants. Organized by Mick Farren, "rock and roll revolution" editor and contributor for the London Underground paper *IT* (*International Times*), the group had played at the UFO Club in April of 1967 before leading off the "14-Hour Technicolour Dream" forty-band rock concert at the Alexandra Palace later that month—the "apogee of underground activity" produced by the eccentric Oklahoma expatriate Jack Henry Moore, who became Farren's own "new music mentor." Their style a conscious borrowing from Warhol's Velvet Underground ("[A]rtistically we robbed them blind"), the Deviants had already booked a gig at Essex when student rebels occupied the university and, living on smuggled sausage rolls and jam tarts, urged the band to come help celebrate the revolution there in an act of solidarity. Other such venues followed, and the next year Farren and the Deviants departed for a North American tour, to "the place I'd always wanted to be."[1]

The student rebellion in Britain may have been galvanized by the events of May in France, but its form and culture were dictated more by Berkeley than Nanterre (and by Berkeley through Nanterre). "America" had long been "symbolic of pleasure," as Simon Frith has observed, and the sixties counterculture, "one of the most obvious clusters of cultural moments and movements to spring to mind when thinking of Americanization as constituting a discourse of liberation," was a self-conscious embodiment of this idea.[2] The radical *style* that expressed its generational separateness was largely an American export—the tie-dye t-shirts and jeans, the marijuana, rock music, and 'fro hairstyles, the Underground papers, comix, and posters, the natural foods, granny glasses, and sandals, all the wide range of hippy paraphernalia of the alternative society that brought San Francisco or the East Village via Portobello Road to Hornsey, Hull, Sussex, Essex, and the L.S.E. When student radicals spoke of the need for a cultural as well as political revolution, it was more often this flower power mélange than the communitarian culture of an idealized industrial working class that they had in mind as an alternative to the dehumanization, sterility, and one-dimensionality of late-twentieth-century capitalism.

The counterculture was not exactly an internationally "spontaneous" artifact of the Cold War and the threat of nuclear holocaust, as Jeff Nuttall suggested in that critical year 1968 in his well-known essay *Bomb Culture*. His view suggests his own generational location (the glory days of CND and the Beats) and an understandable wish to represent British antiestablishment creativity as sui generis and authentic. If it is true, as David Mellor has argued, that the British counterculture, its psychedelic designs, performances, and metropolitan locus, saw a significant cross-over of individuals, institutions, and styles from the Pop art scene to the Underground and that it "found its roots deep within the swinging scene," as Simon Rycroft had observed, Swinging London was itself well anchored in a certain transatlanticism, as we have seen. This further complicates the ways we can read what Rycroft calls the "interrelated discourses of Modernity, technology, [cultural] hegemony and counter-hegemony." Nuttall's own enthusiasm for bizarre "happenings," for the confrontational art that characterized British Pop, was directly inspired by New York beat artists and performers like Yvonne Rainer and Robert Morris.[3]

British Pop borrowed from New York a fascination with the modern, with its technologies and its metropolitan consumerist ad-world. The counterculture as well—though often antimodern and anticonsumerist in its rhetoric—depended on new-world technologies for its distinctive style, its light-shows, monster amps, and the dense, exploding feedback textures of its electric guitars, while its own commodities, its papers, posters, and comix, depended on colored reproduction techniques and styles that drew from an American-led art and commerce world, from Roy Lichtenstein, Warhol, or Marvel Comics. Admittedly, Anglo-American psychedelism was also influenced by a distinctive British visual and musical style, a manifestation of not only cultural circularity and hybridity but also what Rycroft has called the "localization" and "re-tribalization" that often occurred within the (American-led) global, electronic media–enabled, countercultural consciousness. Valuable recent scholarly work has explored ways in which British "difference," drawing on local resources and perspectives, informed the development of an international youth culture in the sixties. The 1968 Underground was indeed shaped by the back-and-forth of transatlantic influence in specific contexts—and not simply in different national contexts, but in the uniquely local areas of Notting Hill, Dam Square, Christiania, or Kreuzberg. But it was in all of these places first and foremost driven forward by penetrative, media-amplified American cultural hegemony and, indeed, often diffused directly by American agents, a youth diaspora, to the rest of the world.[4]

The counterculture can be considered as a system of aesthetics the central purpose of which was the destruction of boundaries and conventions, of the distinction between art and life, viewing and performing, work and play. It also eroded the boundaries between formal art and amateur craft in its valorizing of the self-made, between the hippy desire to shock the bourgeoisie and the avant-garde search for anti-art, between the demotic world of the graffiti "artist" and the elitist world of the New York gallery. In the visual arts, transatlantic connections were dense and sustained wherever there was a significant cross-over between the worlds of the avant-garde and the counterculture: in painting, conceptual exhibition, photography, and experimental film-making. Marshall Berman has emphasized ways in which the critique of the failure of the modern vision is itself part of a continual dialogue (of "perpetual disintegration and renewal") from within modernism. In this sense, the counterculture represents not so much a break with hegemonic postwar American modernity but its continuation.[5]

The three chapters in this section will closely consider the counterculture of the mid- and late-sixties as a transatlantic generational phenomenon, with particular attention to both its American agents in Britain and the metropolitan sites where it was played out locally. We begin with one of two iconic events, the Beat-inspired international poetry happening at the Royal Albert Hall in 1965, and conclude with another, the Dialectics of Liberation conference at the Roundhouse two years later. While one must admit important elements of circularity in the development of a transatlantic generational counterculture, and pay witness to the uniqueness of its local contexts, the British counterculture was in essentials derivative, though it is necessary to deny the negative, trivializing implications usually attached to that term. This section will also look closely at key examples of its institutionalization and proliferation—in the Underground press and the large-venue rock concert.

CHAPTER 4

From the Albert Hall
to a British Counterculture

The American underground seemed to be the real thing, the
original expression . . . . They had a spark for which we were
very grateful.

—Robin Blackburn[1]

Recently Barry Miles, who probably had more of a hand than anyone in the
promotion of a British Underground in the sixties, has argued that those who
emphasize the derivative nature of British counterculture are insensitive to real
differences in its origins, cultural context, and nature. If the counterculture can be
represented as a generational revolt in the United States against the consumer culture of the prosperous fifties, in Britain (where many fewer people owned cars or
lived in the suburbs) it was, he asserts, grounded in a quite different generational
need to break out from a world of postwar austerity "controlled by old people."[2]
This contrast is unconvincing. Austerity was well in the past, and revolt in Britain
was, if anything, a rebellion against the cozy security of the Welfare State by youth
with money to spend on clothes, radios, and record-players; if, as he points out,
American youth had *more* money to spend than their British counterparts, nevertheless by the early sixties British youth were more affluent than they ever had
been. This is especially true of lower-middle and middle-class youth who came
from families that *did* often live in the suburbs, have cars, and were increasingly
likely to attend university.

More particularly, Miles claims that the counterculture in Britain was far less
commercially organized and based than that in entrepreneurial America. With
its roots in the art schools and avant-garde bookshops, in an amateur, relatively
small-scale scene where there were few independent recording labels and few
large commercial venues and promoter-managers, the British movement looked
to benefactors and modest grants for support rather than to commercial enterprise, and had, he claims, a limited sense of the generationwide possibilities:
"The Americans thought they could change the world, the sky was the limit;

in England the horizon was very low indeed." Again, the contrast is overdrawn and Miles overly defensive—itself perhaps significant—about the authenticity and autonomy of a *British* counterculture. The contrasting picture of successful American commercial ambition (and its hippy capitalism) and British diffidence and amateurishness exaggerates the commercial success of the counterculture in the States (where, apart from a few promoters like Bill Graham, there was plenty of amateurism and failure) and underrates the extent to which the British scene was lubricated by a very similar speculative opportunism (in the proliferation of club venues or the commercially organized Pop festivals). On occasion there was a risible incompetence that suggests naivety, and it is tempting to see this as culturally British (the 14-Hour Technicolour Dream was intended to raise substantial cash for *IT,* but the ticket-takers ran away with most of the takings). But without denying significant differences in commercial culture generally, and especially in the arts, the fact remains that attempts to turn the counterculture to profit were often strikingly similar on both sides of the Atlantic—not least because the organization of the various institutions of the British Underground was itself heavily dependent on young American entrepreneurs, something Miles's own various projects demonstrate: "I enjoyed having so many Americans involved with *IT*—they didn't have the 'mustn't grumble' mentality."[3]

Significant differences *can* be found in the contrasting physical environments. In fact, crowded London was not as well provided as the major American cities with their less cramped, more plentiful performance-auditoria. For modestly popular events, London could offer venues like the Hammersmith Odeon, where in June 1964 Joe Boyd, newly arrived from the States, saw the Newcastle band the Animals, the Nashville Teens (from Weybridge, Surrey), and the Swinging Blue Jeans (Liverpool) play with Chuck Berry and rockabilly pioneer Carl Perkins.[4] Or the London Palladium, early venue for Sunday night televised Pop. There were a few larger sites—the Royal Festival Hall and the Royal Albert Hall, venues that proved inadequate for the Beatles and the Stones, or the Alexandra Palace and the Olympia's vast, sound-swallowing interiors—while, at the other end, the basements and temporary, shared locations in central London's bust-prone club scene, though offering close intimacy, had difficulty both accommodating the ever-growing numbers and avoiding trouble with police and landlords.

It was that icon of British modernism erected on the South Bank in 1951 for the people's Festival of Britain, the Royal Festival Hall, that hosted Bob Dylan and a capacity crowd that included the Beatles on 17 May 1965 (John Lennon would later claim that it was hearing Dylan that turned him from mere professional song-writing to the kind of interior subjectivity that marked the hippy counterculture: "I started being me about the songs"). Dylan had first played the Festival Hall in May of 1964, a sellout, and since then had climbed in the U.K. charts, displacing the Beatles and the Stones at No. 1 by the time of the 1965 tour.

The Royal Festival Hall would host both American and domestic folk, Pop, and rock when its classical schedule allowed, but for the really popular performers it provided inadequate seating (about 3,000). When Dylan returned to London in June, he twice played the Royal Albert Hall (whose echoing Victorian interior could accommodate 7,000), and again at the conclusion of his last major British tour in May 1966.[5]

WHOLLY COMMUNION AT THE ROYAL ALBERT HALL: THE POETRY INTERNATIONAL, 1965

The Royal Albert Hall in South Kensington, built from the proceeds of the Great Exhibition, opened by Queen Victoria in 1871 and dedicated like the rest of the Albertopolis of museums and educational institutions to the improvement of the people, holds a position of some importance in the iconography of postwar British identity. After 1941 (when the Queen's Hall was destroyed by German bombers), "the nation's village hall" became the site of the annual summer Proms. Ironically, while the Proms evolved to include, with the standard classical repertoire, more modern elements—jazz, gospel, and even, in 1970, the rock band Soft Machine—the enormously popular "Last Night," with its over-the-top patriotism, its flag-waving mass-singing of *Land of Hope and Glory* and *Jerusalem* (broadcast to the nation by the BBC), became increasingly a national ritual celebrating a nostalgic, heritage-inflected, white, middle-class, middle-aged, suburban Britishness.

From the late fifties the Albert Hall schedule reflects a growing demand for youth-oriented popular events. It was the venue for a live-broadcast BBC-sponsored Jazz 'n' Pop Festival in 1963 that defined Beatlemania when, introduced by George Melly, the group played to a sellout crowd of screaming teens. And it was here two years later, in the summer of 1965, that an Anglo-American affair unfolded that marks the Beat Underground–inspired beginning of the counterculture in Britain.

A poetry reading and happening, not for a few Beat literati and their admirers in a smoky Soho coffeehouse, the crowded basement of a hip bookstore, or the avant-garde ICA, but for thousands in a concert venue, was the impromptu idea of Barbara Rubin, experimental filmmaker from New York and close friend of Allen Ginsberg. Ginsberg had arrived in England in early May at the conclusion of a world tour that had taken him to India, Cuba, and Eastern Europe. After a few days giving small readings outside London he came to stay with Barry Miles, twenty-two-year-old former CNDer and manager of the avant-garde bookshop in Charing Cross Road, Better Books, where a public reading was quickly arranged. Better Books had been managed by a gay American poet from Montana before Miles took it over in January. Miles himself was an art college student in Cheltenham when he met John "Hoppy" Hopkins, a photographer who supplemented his income by selling marijuana. Hopkins provided Miles with an introduction to the "American London" parts of the West End, where he socialized with wealthy young Americans like Christie Johnson, whose father was a well-known screenwriter and director (with two large apartments in Grosvenor Square that were "like being transported back to California"). He also met a seventeen-year-old there whom he married in 1963—Sue Crane, who wore cowboy boots and, though English, had been educated in California and New York and spoke with an American accent.[6]

The Better Books reading, attended by Warhol and Donovan, then regarded as the coming British answer to Dylan, was a crowded success with an audience that spilled out onto the pavement. This suggested there might be enough interest for a more ambitious event in a larger venue. Lawrence Ferlinghetti was due to arrive in London in a few days, and Gregory Corso and William Burroughs were in Paris and presumably available. So the idea of an international (though largely Anglo-American) poetry reading emerged from a casual discussion among a small group that included Ginsberg and Rubin, Miles, an experimental filmmaker and poet from New Zealand (John Esam), and Dan Richter, another American expatriate living in London. Esam was also an "evangelical" proselytizer of acid, provided by an American friend. Richter was a young actor from Connecticut who had toured with the American Mime Theater, married an English girl, and founded the contemporary poetry review *Residu*. The next year he would be engaged by another expatriate American, film director Stanley Kubrick, to mime the part of the bone-tossing ape-man in *2001*.[7]

As they considered ideas for a possible location, Rubin asked what the largest venue in central London might be, went to the phone, and booked the Albert Hall on the spot. As Miles later commented, "It needed American chutzpah and know-how to think that big." Richter's mother-in-law put up the deposit, and an ambitious scheme was drafted for an international spectacle that would reach across Cold War lines (in the event, the three communist poets Andrei Voznesensky, Pablo Neruda, and Pablo Fernandez refused to read). Michael Horovitz, who had founded *New Departures* as a vehicle for the Beats and who saw Ginsberg as inheritor of Blake's visionary project, played a leading role in setting up the program, and Alexander Trocchi, who had returned to Britain with Ginsberg and Burroughs in 1963, agreed to serve as compere. A week before, a photo-shoot gathering on the steps of the Albert Memorial was held for the press to raise media interest, and that evening at Trocchi's flat in Notting Hill a "collaborative poem" was created (mostly by Ginsberg) as a "spontaneous invocation" for the event. It began with Blake's "England! awake! awake! awake!/ Jerusalem thy Sister calls!" The same summer in L.A. Jim Morrison and Ray Manzarek would find in Blake the name for their acid rock band, The Doors [of perception].[8]

The Poetry International, or "Wholly Communion" as it came to be known, was "a magnificent shambles." There was a capacity crowd of nearly 7,000 on 11 June, and many were turned away. "Hippy chicks" (and Barbara Rubin) in psychedelic face paint handed out flowers as people entered. What followed was as much performance art and alternative theater as poetry. Ginsberg opened with a Tibetan mantra to the accompaniment of his finger-cymbals. The audience, or rather the different audiences, variously listened, danced, smoked pot, threw flowers, or intoned their own mantras; "uneasy attendants and police hovered at entrances, deprecating drugs and fourletter words"; there were flowers thrown at the stage, "weird papier-mâché creatures" in the aisles, guitar-playing, hecklers, and "a girl in a white dress danced under the pall of potsmoke with distant gestures of dream." R. D. Laing "brought along some of his patients, who danced and blew bubbles to music heard only in their heads." For Nuttall, who stripped naked and painted himself green, it was an opportunity for a gloriously uninhibited happening. As Alexis Lykiard observed, "Artaud, who understood the sanity of madness, would have relished it." It was not all hippy play and art-school madness. The British poet Adrian Mitchell "probably got the most concerted audience response" for two pieces he read on (anti)American political themes—racism and the Vietnam War (one of which he contributed to Peter Brook's *US*).[9]

The poetic performances both on and off stage provided a rich field for alternative filmmakers like Rubin, though the best documentary was produced by a young British film artist from the Slade School, Peter Whitehead. *Wholly Communion*, a thirty-three-minute film in the handheld camera, cinema verité style launched his career, attracting the attention of the Rolling Stones' manager,[10] who commissioned him to do a film of the group's first tour of Ireland the same year (*Charlie Is My Darling*). He followed this with an hour-long documentary, *Benefit of the Doubt*, on the making of Peter Brook's anti–Vietnam War play *US*. Drawn to the unfolding drama in the United States itself, he traveled to New York and produced, in 1968, what he regards as his most important film, *The Fall*, a "behind the barricades" documentary of the student rebellion at Columbia University.[11]

The Albert Hall happening has been rightly regarded as a defining moment, the much reported and talked about sign that the bohemian Underground of coffeehouse poetry readings was evolving into—perhaps absorbed into—a "continuous event," a spontaneous, above-ground counterculture and generational style. Charles Marowitz, though skeptical about the depth and authenticity of the counterculture, observed that the Albert Hall poetry spectacle at least made those who attended aware that there were people from all over Britain and beyond who shared their enthusiasm for subversive, participatory carnival, that there was a popular base that extended well beyond the metropolitan aesthetic *provocateurs* "who began brandishing paint, flashing lights, tossing textures, orchestrating sounds and juxtaposing texts for the greater glory of counterculture." For Miles as well it signaled the arrival of "a new constituency of youth . . . seeing each other for the first time *en masse*." For some others, however, like Trocchi, who had come back from the United States as a missionary for the "coherent, subversive doctrine" of the Beats, the new counterculture threatened to submerge the older avant-garde in an unfocused psychedelic revolution. In some sense this was fifties Greenwich Village Underground—and its heroin—versus a California dreaming counterculture—and its pot and LSD. Ferlinghetti's contribution served as a bridge. "To Fuck Is to Love Again" evoked the new locus: "Dreaming of utopias/where everyone's a lover/I see San Francisco from my window." Trocchi attempted to build his own bridges to other coming groups in London, especially Joe Berke, R. D. Laing, and the antipsychiatry and free university movements, but felt just generationally outside the times and became disillusioned. By the end of the sixties he had withdrawn to a penthouse in Kensington where troubled youth drifted in and out—police discovered £2,000 worth of jewelry in his study, stolen by a house guest from a room in the Hilton Hotel.[12]

Miles, however, claimed that the summer of 1965 "determined the direction my life was to take, and acted as a catalyst for many other people in London at this time." Like Michael Horovitz, he was attracted to the subversive and artistic possibilities of a fusion of the Beat and countercultures. He and Hopkins immediately set up a (short-lived) magazine, *Long Hair* (the title was suggested by Ginsberg), to maintain the "North Atlantic turn-on"—that is: "the *Poetry* revolution, the *Prose* revolution, the *Clothes* revolution, the *Jazz* revolution, the *Pop* revolution, the *Sexual* revolution, the revolution of the mind, free thought and action, and *Love*." Published by "Lovebooks" in Fitzroy Square, with editorial offices in New York, it would speak for those who after the Albert Hall readings looked to "the founding fathers of this new spirit in poetry." The first issue contained pieces by Ginsberg and Ferlinghetti, Horovitz and Nuttall.[13]

CIRCULARITY: AN ANGLO-AMERICAN COUNTERCULTURE

The transatlantic nature of British counterculture is hardly in doubt and most scholars, like Elizabeth Nelson,[14] have acknowledged the obvious—that, in an increasingly media-driven youth culture, American, especially West Coast, influences dictated much of its form and content. Just why British middle-class youth, who seemed more prone than their working-class counterparts to "California dreamin,'" might be vulnerable to a romantic Americanization puzzled many denigrators of the phenomenon at the time and in the following decade. Answers were found in the faddishness and superficiality of a postwar youth culture that rested on the increased affluence and independence of lower-middle and middle-class youth whose university grants meant they could delay entering the adult world of work, and in the decadence of a "permissive society" rotting from the top down without any sense of a postwar, postimperial, post-Christian purpose. In much of this self-examination, little close attention was paid to the special synchronicity and circularity of the Anglo-American countercultural moment, the late-sixties density of media connection, or, especially, the significantly increased personal cross-Atlantic traffic that marks the era.

What had come by the late sixties to be called "the" counterculture by both its more self-conscious practitioners and the press was anarchic and fissiparous by definition. A quasi-sociological term, "counter culture" assumed a wider, more generationally inclusive meaning than the other somewhat earlier American coinage, "the Underground," derived from the New York Beat scene of Zen, drugs, and poetry. Regarded only as an artifact of its time, sustainable only in a period of economic surplus, the counterculture in historical perspective is diminished and trivialized in the often humorous form promoted by nostalgic color supplements and encapsulating, "the way we were," television programs. And yet, to be young and active in those years was for many to have shared a generalized feeling of excitement, energized creativity, and mutuality, of optimism as well as anger, and a powerful sense of personal liberation. The rapid decay of the counterculture, celebrated by the right in the seventies but also admitted and regretted by more sympathetic observers, works to prevent a serious understanding of any deeper legacy, as does the easy sociological dismissal of its style and content as yet another version of family-escaping youth revolt. It may be, however, that the American youth-inspired moment unraveled something in the fabric of British culture that was not simply rewoven in the reactionary seventies and eighties. As George McKay has argued, the sixties were in important ways "a beginning not an end."[15]

Tariq Ali has reminded us that to retrieve the counterculture as simply or mainly a personalized "happy mysticism" of acid trips, free love, and far-out music risks washing out its political ideology, the intimate connections between the personal and the political. While it may have quickly faded at its broad margins into a readily commercializable style devoid of a very focused set of radical values, there was an aggressive radicalism at its core—of course a minority—for whom values, style, music, and practice cohered into something that was not only a subcultural identity but also an evangelizing way of life, some diluted form of which reached well beyond the introspective hippy communes in Notting Hill. In Britain at least the radical counterculture generated and nourished a maturing nucleus of continuing radical activism in the seventies and into the eighties. Often denigrated for being merely middle class, it was a powerful fact that it *was* middle class, rather than yet another postwar working-class or ethnic youth subcultural style. It bit into the conventional, established society in both the United States and Britain in ways that beg comparison with the evangelical awakening of the eighteenth century, and while much of its radical vision (its "utopianism") was unsustainable, it left a legible imprint, shifting cultural paradigms and subjectivities in ways that are often unappreciated because now so familiar. As Bernice Martin observed in 1981, "[W]hat was striking in 1968 is often too commonplace today to require comment."[16]

The United States, with its complex mix of ethnicities and its frontier libertarianism, has long been a land of cultural contestation; Britain, with a historically unitary, Establishment culture, less so. Consequently, and ironically, the counterculture, though arguably more marginal in Britain than in war-torn America, may have been uniquely unsettling there in a class-bound country with a postwar identity crisis. Hence the chorus of criticism, understandably on the traditionalist right, but also among elements of the left who regarded imported American-style hippy anarchy as less "authentic" than a historically and locally based culture of working-class resistance.

In fact, of course, cultural traffic was not in one direction only. London was already the site of a heady fermentation of subversive Pop style, borrowed from New York perhaps, but given a London art-school flavor and sent back to the States in, especially, mid-sixties English rock music. Any of the several successful "British invasion" bands—like the Dave Clark Five, more popular in the States perhaps than in Britain[17]—can serve to establish the circularity of Anglo-American exchange in the sixties. But countercultural circularity has its most complicated exemplar in the Beatles.

Promoted in the media as a British answer to American domination of Pop music, and as an authentic expression of Northern "honesty, dynamism and authenticity" at the end of an era of moth-eaten Conservative decline, the Liverpool Four brought to an essentially American form something local—though this was, in the beginning at least, well short of what William Mann, music critic for *The Times*, enthusiastically claimed to be "a general revival of native British musical traditions" in the face of Americanization.[18] Though Beatlemania was an exploding British phenomenon before it crossed the Atlantic, it was the astounding force (and profits) of their *transatlantic* success that enabled the band to evolve and explore where others had been trapped in the industry.

Though much has been written about the Beatles' uniquely British elements—the art-school, music hall, or South Asian influences—what they had become by the time of *Sgt. Pepper's* illustrated strongly a continuing Anglo-American dialogue (as did their private lives). While moving beyond their early fascination with Elvis Presley, Little Richard, Buddy Holly, and Chuck Berry, their mid-to-late-sixties evolution, as Jonathan Gould has vividly reconstructed, continued to be influenced by the American musical and countercultural scenes—and especially Dylan's own evolution. By 1967 the Beatles' work and appearance more overtly referenced the West Coast psychedelic scene, Timothy Leary's acid-evangelism, and the Asian mysticism closely associated with psychotropic experience—drawing from Aldous Huxley's West Coast experiments and Ginsberg's tantric performances, but also reflecting or at least presented as their own uniquely post-Raj "British" cultural affinities.[19]

Barry Miles, who connected in his own enterprises the American Beat and London Pop-art scenes, the bookshops, galleries, and rock venues of countercultural London, and its Underground press, has revealed how close Paul McCartney was to this world from the summer of 1965, before either George Harrison or John Lennon (who did not read Leary's *The Psychedelic Experience* until 1966) had much interest in the avant-garde or the hippy scene. By the release of *Sgt. Pepper's* in 1967 the group had been drawn, largely through McCartney's efforts, into the London world of happenings and anarchistic experimental theater and Pop art—what Ian Macdonald oddly calls the "mélange of local influences from the English fringe arts and the Anglo-European counterculture" in his effort to distinguish an English Pop-scene and its art-school-informed audience as "fundamentally different from America." This is an exceptionally misleading characterization of what was clearly a "high modernist moment" in *transatlantic* popular culture. The Pop art, the Happenings, the alternative theater that informed their psychedelic turn can hardly be considered "local" phenomena.[20]

Nevertheless, it is true that the Beatles transmuted this borrowing and were, especially in the case of *Sgt. Pepper's*, enormously influential back across the Atlantic: "Virtually all the West Coast psychedelic bands cite it as a milestone in their development." San Francisco hippydom in fact owed other debts to British culture: its fascination with Lewis Carroll's *Alice in Wonderland* and its supposed invocation of the mysteries of psychotropic chemicals, or the American counterculture's discovery of the works of J. R. R. Tolkien, fantasies that resonated with its self-representation as Hobbit-brothers fighting the military-industrial complex. If there was no British counterpart (until 1969) to the Tolkien Society of America, formed after the release in the United States of a cheap paperback edition of *The Lord of the Rings* in 1965, the "Frodo Lives" buttons proliferated on the streets of San Francisco while Muz Murray's mystical Underground magazine (and shop, tearoom, and commune) *Gandalf's Garden* flourished in South Kensington and the psychedelic rock venue "Middle Earth" opened in a basement near Covent Garden. Middle Earth's inaugural guest of honor was Chet Helms, manager of San Francisco's Avalon Ballroom, who also ran the Family Dog, a druggy community of musicians whose stated intention, oddly enough, was to transform San Francisco into "America's Liverpool."[21]

In 1969 Ian Birchall published an influential essay lamenting the decline of "an authentic British style of rhythm and blues" that had both created a worldwide audience for British rock music in the early sixties and had been able, in a language borrowed from the frustration and oppression of American blacks, to reach and speak to white British working-class youth. He believed that the Beatles in particular had from 1966 "renounced" what he regarded as a uniquely British style in their experiments with a countercultural surrealism that embraced drug-induced fantasy and private escape and consequently lost much ability to speak to working-class British youth. Similarly, Eric Burdon, whose band the Animals had earlier used gritty American blues and rock material to give their music, Birchall claimed, "an authentic feel of Newcastle," had also "fallen prey to the cult of San Francisco." The consequence had been a shift back to "American hegemony" in the British charts; by 1968, half the records in *NME*'s "Top Thirty" were by American artists. Though the overall picture of a loss of market in the United States *and* the U.K. for British bands after 1966 may be accurate enough, from the perspective of the cultural hybridity that defines the entire period, Birchall's analysis is unconvincing. It may well be, as Joe Boyd, who moved to Britain in the mid-sixties to search for recording talent, would later observe, that "the best [British] groups, the most influential, the most powerful and the ones that did best in America were the ones that were quite unafraid to be English" and were therefore "more relaxed" about "shopping in different cultures." Nevertheless, it is unclear exactly how an "authentic" (whatever that may mean) British version of the American rhythm and blues tradition might have, in fact, spoken more directly to Newcastle working-class youth than, say, had the American models popular in Britain before 1963. While granting the domestic and export success of the early-sixties British bands, and a degree of local, domestic inflection, by any objective standard British rhythm and blues remained very closely derivative, in its sound, and in the affected American accents of the British singers, to its transatlantic origins. There is some irony of course in the fact that it was British bands in the sixties that "taught white Americans how to love their native music," but, as Joe Boyd trenchantly observed, "[T]his was enough for most black audiences to decide it was time to move on"—to Motown and soul.[22]

Clearly, both the British rhythm and blues tradition that Birchall laments and the psychedelic phenomenon were closely related to American models. Depending on one's interpretive perspective, this can suggest either circularity and hybridity or cultural hegemony and imitation. By the sixties, however, this problematic of how local "authenticity" might be expressed in the face of a musical export culture from the United States was already a familiar issue bedeviling two popular genres—jazz (whether dance band, Dixieland revival, or "trad") and the folk revival.

The complex business of reading American Jazz—already a mixed-race hybrid—in its British contexts, of finding an indigenous (or global, postimperial) voice in an American form, has been masterfully explored by George McKay in his study of the "attitudinal culture of [British] jazz," *Circular Breathing*.[23] It was a culture that was obsessed with the authentic, the original, with, that is, the problem of inauthenticity and unoriginality. Though commonly associated with the left in the fifties and especially with CND as music of the outsider, the rebel, and the bohemian, in its revivalist, retro, academic form, especially perhaps in the sixties, it could appeal also to nostalgic Tories like the poet (and jazz critic) Philip Larkin looking for a comfortable refuge from the counterculture.

Another genre that provoked issues of authenticity and imitation was the folk revival, also closely associated with the left in the fifties. By definition, "folk music," on both sides of the Atlantic was more self-consciously local, more insistently situated historically and ethnically than rock (despite the black American origins of rhythm and blues). Much of American folk music, in its heartland of Appalachia, may have been distantly derived from English, Scottish, and Irish sources, but it spoke directly to themes of American rural and labor experience. This was especially true of the "retrieved" protest folk that was nurtured by the American left from the thirties to the fifties and, especially, of Alan Lomax's New Deal–inspired project of collection and collation. In Britain A. L. "Bert" Lloyd and Ewan MacColl, in spite of their large debt to Lomax, were concerned about, as MacColl later said, a "whole generation becoming quasi-Americans" and resisting "American cultural imperialism" through the rediscovery of native folk traditions, emphasizing British folk's "indigenous and industrial working class origins." Moreover the popularity, by the early sixties, of American *commercial* folk and its imitators in Britain added substantially to this sense of grievance among the purists—an issue addressed by Bert Loyd in 1967 when he published his own anthology of *Folk Song in England.* Such protests themselves confirm how common was the experience recalled by Michael Brocken about his youth: "I was first drawn towards folk music by Americans."[24]

As elements of the purist traditional revival, protest folk, and contemporary folk movements merged, they reached a larger and younger popular audience. By the early sixties there were, like the jazz clubs before them, folk clubs in Soho—Les Cousins or the Scots Hoose—that hosted visiting American performers and gave a kick-start to the careers of a new generation of sixties British performers who had grown up on American rock'n'roll and skiffle, heard visiting Americans like Muddy Waters, Big Bill Broonzy, Josh White, Brownie McGee, and Jessie Fuller, and bought recordings available from imported American independent labels.[25]

Among the wider audience, the most popular "folk singers" in Britain, the performers who could fill large venues, were not the purists. The most popular domestic folk group in the sixties was a Liverpool quartet, the Spinners, whose approach was eclectic and included American and West Indian material as well as "British" songs and whose vocalist, Cliff Hall, was a black Jamaican who came to Britain during the war, "got hooked" on the American Forces Network, and taught himself to play and sing like Jimmy Rogers and Hank Williams: "The music of Jamaica was all but forgotten, he immersed himself in becoming country and westernized." Nor were the most celebrated folk artists in Britain British. In the early sixties American protest folk from the Cambridge, Massachusetts, coffeehouses—the more lyrical sound of Joan Baez (closer perhaps to the nostalgic European tradition) and the harsh, cynical, less romantic sound of Bob Dylan—crossed over into the mass medium of Pop and found a huge following in the British radical and protohippy scene, inspiring imitators like Donovan Leitch and reaching its apotheosis in Dylan's 1965 London concerts and appearances on British television.[26]

However much the traditional folk, contemporary folk, and folk rock scenes draw upon and express a kind of transatlanticism, there may have been, as Simon Frith has argued, marked differences in audience reception: he has claimed that in Britain folk often appealed, at least in mainstream England if not in the Celtic borderlands, to a sense of regret, a nostalgia that was "fearful of the urban proletariat and its music," whereas in the United States radical folk ideology by the fifties often offered not regret for the passing of organic communities of the past but "a source of inspiration, a way of countering the debilitating effects of the mass media and imbuing the working class with 'folk consciousness.'" This distinction can be overdrawn, no doubt. Audience response is probably more complicated on both sides of the Atlantic; also, distinct resonances in the local contexts of the fifties may have quite quickly softened and melded into the more globalized sixties and seventies. Certainly this seems true of the messages and techniques of the performers themselves. By the sixties lines of distinction were rapidly eroding, not only by the merging of generational style in Anglo-American student protest but also by the easy circulation and mass marketing of the transatlantic recording industry. The English folk singer Cyril Tawney was inspired specifically by the traditional music of the English (or Cornish) west country and its association with the sea, and was a familiar nativist voice on British radio and television in the sixties. One of his most popular songs, "Sally Free and Easy," was recorded by Dylan (among many others), while Tawney's own style of singing and guitar playing had been formed expressly on recordings of the American Pop folk artist Burl Ives.[27]

Finally, though British traditional folk—the performers and their audience— may have been "narrow-minded," defensive about preserving an acoustic sound in pub-and-coffeehouse venues, and deeply suspicious of the lack of a focused left-protest message in much of the popular transatlantic rock scene, it was not immune to some of the same influences. Before 1954 MacColl had been closely involved with his first wife's (Joan Littlewood's) experimental Theatre Workshop, and when he and Peggy Seeger organized the first annual folk Festival of Fools at "the New Merlin's Cave" in London in 1965 the instruments may have been all acoustic and many of the songs left-didactic, but the production owed much to the techniques of alternative theater and the elaborate happenings that infused the Pop and coming psychedelic scenes as well. The festivals at Merlin's Cave involved three stages for skits, monologues, songs, and readings, and there were sound effects, dances, imaginative lighting, and costumes. In 1967 festival songs included "The Flower People" along with, no doubt ironic, renditions of "Yankee Doodle" and "Home on the Range."[28]

Much as traditionalists might have deplored the fact, folk provided for many throughout the sixties a rather permeable and fluid transatlantic genre, absorbing influences from the Pop scene and lending something of its own character to the developing hippy countercultural assault on commercial modernism. It was precisely the intersection of folk and Pop, and especially folk and psychedelic rock, that Joe Boyd sought to promote and mine with groups like the Incredible String Band. As Brocken has observed, "[T]he work of Donovan, the Incredible String Band and Tyrannosaurus Rex all reflected an acoustic Tolkienesque blend of mystery, English folk lore and children's fairytales. When mingled with American musical influences from the likes of Joni Mitchell, Buffalo Springfield, Love and the Byrds, innocence was elevated as an important market . . . very much part of the hippie aesthetic.[29]

There is substantial transatlantic cross-fertilization in the formative influences surrounding psychedelia and "mind-blowing" rock. Resonating with the drug experiments of Ken Kesey and Timothy Leary, San Francisco rock—the out of control performances as much as the music—fed back into the British scene from 1965. The Beatles introduced psychedelic, drug-allusive elements in their post-1966 albums *Revolver*, *Sgt. Pepper's*, and *Magical Mystery Tour*—visually as well as musically in the Pop-art pastiche of the *Sgt. Pepper's* album cover and in George Dunning's 1968 surreal animated film *Yellow Submarine*—intended largely for the American market by its American producers. By the late sixties psychedelic rock achieved its mature forms in the contrasting sounds of the acid R&B of the Grateful Dead and Jefferson Airplane in San Francisco and in Britain with Soft Machine or Pink Floyd, a band that first came to public attention playing at the American Steve Stollman's "Spontaneous Underground" club in London—a venue that, Miles tells us, had "something of the atmosphere of the Albert Hall reading, except that it was weekly and there was a lot of pot and acid about." Pink Floyd may have had a distinctive, British sound, but their manager, Peter Jenner, an economics teacher who had left the L.S.E. to help found the Notting Hill Free School, recalls that "[we] thought we were doing what was happening on the West Coast, which we'd never heard."[30]

If the explosion of trippy, psychedelic album-cover graphics owed a debt not only to San Francisco light shows, poster-artists, and Underground comix that emerged after 1965 but also to London Pop-art design, this was itself deeply enmeshed in contemporary cross-Atlantic relations. Peter Blake is generally credited with designing the well-known *Sgt. Pepper's* album cover, though his then-wife, the American-born Jann Haworth, was a major contributor to a collaborative effort that included the Beatles themselves. Blake, in any event, was deeply influenced by American fifties and early-sixties Pop art and its collages. An early work, "Self Portrait with Badges" (1961) paraded "provocative affiliations to American popular culture," denims and badges of Elvis. After marrying Haworth in 1963, he went to her hometown Los Angeles for an extended visit to do drawings for the *Sunday Times*. It was, however, Paul McCartney who originated the idea of a photo-collage design and first submitted a list of subjects, many of whom were American; and though the Beatles had toured the United States during the "Beatlemania" of the mid-sixties, it was McCartney's own visit to the West Coast in April of 1967 that sparked a special interest in the psychedelic happenings and his idea for a "Magical Mystery Tour," with its evocation of Ken Kesey's acid tripping Merry Pranksters. From 1968 McCartney's developing relationship with the American photographer Linda Eastman (whom he married the next year) further drew him into American Pop and countercultures, and to New York, especially, where he explored the club scene and Fillmore East, and generally "fell in love" with the city.[31]

The British rock music world of the late sixties and early seventies, in its characteristic forms, in its Avalon Ballroom and Fillmore East and West inspired venues, open air concerts, psychedelic album covers and posters, and organization as a music industry, was instructed and led by the larger American scene and market. All of the hopeful British bands of the era, like Farren's Deviants, were or aspired to be transatlantic. This was so only in part because, as Nik Cohn rather cynically observed, at the peak of the "British invasion" in the United States, "English pop had it fat in there and most everyone cleaned up." The attraction, however, was more than the prospect of big bucks. By the late sixties the counterculture offered antiestablishment radicals in Britain like Farren a wished-for Americanization, an instrument to break up domestic social constraints and conditioning. It was self-consciously and ironically American—grounded as it was in a romantic rejection of American mainstream cultural materialism and American Cold War leadership. It offered British youth an alternative deeply informed by American populism, anarchic libertarianism, and antiestablishment youth style to focus their own cultural and political assault on the British Establishment. Not for the first time, a version of America was *imagined* as an alternative to ossified Britishness.[32]

THE COUNTERCULTURE AND THE MEDIA

The countercultural context of the student rebellion—the drugs and promiscuity and profane insulting of the dominant culture—provided a text for both those of the sympathetic left like Theodore Roszak and for its many denigrators in academia and the mass media. In Britain, however, the issue of "permissiveness," the political debate over Labour's liberalization of the law on abortion, contraception, drugs, divorce, homosexuality, and pornography, and the backlash of suburban moral outrage personified by Mary Whitehouse and the "clean-up TV" campaign of her National Viewers' and Listeners' Association, had been a largely domestic affair, less influenced by apprehension of American cultural influence—though there was finger-pointing at American-style materialism generally and the violence of imported American TV programs in particular. Unlike the fifties, when the presumed importation of a rebellious "juvenile delinquent" street culture via Hollywood films, rock'n'roll, and a tough style of quiffs, jeans, and American motorcycle jackets, the Pop art, libertarian culture of Swinging London was by and large viewed as a home-grown narcissism—its mod affectations and sartorial flamboyance more Oscar Wilde than anything American popular culture had to offer. Moreover, after 1962 the music of the Beatles effected a partial, if temporary, reversal of the cultural domination of American popular music in Britain, and, in the words of one writer for the *New Left Review*, "counter-colonized" American popular culture.[33]

The shift of the rock musical center back to the United States and the darkening sense of domestic economic difficulty encouraged a more pessimistic reading of contemporary popular culture and its transatlantic character in the British media. The spreading of the American youth revolt to British colleges and universities, the appearance of an Underground press in London full of obscenity and radicalism and closely imitative of American models, and American-style rock concerts—with domestic freaks and hippies, runaways and wanderers, bearded and tangled-haired new travelers thumbing rides to the Isle of Wight, Glastonbury, or Phun City—provided ample copy for moral panic about cultural subversion and social disease. As Simon Frith observed, "Every town and province had its hip promoters and pubs, its festivals and head shops." By the end of the decade, when the film *Woodstock* was given an "X" rating by the British film board, and persisting through the early seventies, British mainstream and tabloid media were deeply engaged in voyeuristic analysis (and, for many, a wished-for postmortem) of the counterculture both in its *fons et origo*, California, and on the streets of Britain: "The media interest in the underground was increasing, just as the movement itself set into slow decline."[34]

By 1969 radio and television, as well as the press in Britain, reported from America sensational accounts of the depth and drama of the counterculture there. Alistair Cooke's predictably deep skepticism and misgiving about the whole American decade of domestic violence and rebellion was evident in his weekly BBC broadcasts and in his "Letters from America" in the *Guardian*. Other, younger "our man in the U.S." correspondents contributed their own accounts of the colorful and bizarre, of American social dysfunction, and of generational conflict, as did Cooke's exact contemporary, Alan Pryce-Jones, who, having moved from London where he had been editor of the *Times Literary Supplement* to live permanently in New York City in 1960, served as an occasional reporter on the

American scene for the BBC. ITV followed suit, with Thames and Granada, in particular, committed to a "with it" approach to reporting the youth phenomenon on both sides of the Atlantic. At Granada, John Birt's *World in Action* set out "to plot the key litmus events and movements"—hippies, feminists, and homosexuals—and "made a powerful programme about the trial of the Chicago Eight, that year's *cause celebre* for the alternative society." In November Birt took a team to Washington to film the massive angry and tear-gassed antiwar march. The following year the alternative society came to Granada's ITV sound stage itself when David Frost hosted a "debate on the counter culture" featuring Richard Neville of the London Underground magazine *OZ* and Jerry Rubin and other "Yippies" from the States. Rubin, apparently determined to rival Abbey Hoffman's disruptive exploits on American television, inspired saboteurs in the audience to create "a Yippie riot" on stage in what the *Daily Mirror* called "the Frost Freak-Out." In fact the dramatic nature of events in the United States, and the temptation to cover them with sensational reportage at the expense of European affairs, led Philip Whitehead, TV reviewer for the *Listener*, to complain in 1972 that "British television often seems obsessed with the United States and its problems."[35]

The publication of Roszak's sympathetic analysis of the American counter-culture in a British edition in 1970 produced a spate of, mostly unfriendly, media commentary. Clive James, a young Australian journalist who had stayed in Britain after university, had some personal interest in American popular music and youth culture. But in March he wrote a sharply disapproving review for *New Society* followed by a sarcastic piece in the *Listener* the next month: the "counter culture" was a "poisonous term," and Roszak's "useless analysis" was "shallow without being naive." For James, the whole phenomenon was awash in irrationality, and Roszak's book itself was "a symptom of the American disease." Others in the media were less acerbic. Charles Davis, a former Catholic priest who had married and left the Church, told a Radio 3 audience that the American counterculture was, as Roszak implied, a Romantic reaction against technocracy, "unformed and uninformed." But where James saw only irrationality, Davis found, in spite of the alternative society's fascination with the occult and drug experimentation, a budding spirituality: "[T]he future of religion is bound up, I would argue, with the future of the counter-culture now in the making . . . . [T]he counter-culture of youth is unquestionably religious."[36]

Serious British media coverage of the Underground scene, as opposed to the sensational voyeurism of the popular press, sought to explain to a bemused or threatened older mainstream public—suburban parents seem often the target audience—just what was going on, on the other side of the generation gap. After the universities erupted, there was widespread incomprehension of what could lead youth who were not unemployed troublemakers but the relatively privileged, those who profited from the wider access to university education and student grants, to turn on the system. As radio and TV programmers scrambled to find a way into the counterculture—without abandoning "objectivity" and distance—the result was often a kind of ethnographic expedition into an alien territory marked by the exotic, the irrational, and the perverse. The genre is typified by two radio series commissioned after 1969.

In the summer of 1970 the BBC turned to Wilfred De'Ath to "explain" the countercultural phenomenon in England. De'Ath—whose eclectic interests were those of a freelance opportunist—had no particular connection with the Underground and had never been to the United States, but "Good Time George" Melly, whom he had interviewed for the *Today* program, was a friend. In a series of programs broadcast on Radio 4 in August and September he explored aspects of the English Underground in what he called four "reconnaissances." The series was a pastiche ferreted out from Notting Hill's "crash pads," vegetarian restaurants, resource centers for nomadic youth, interviews with those promoting Underground arts, and the Underground press. Throughout, De'Ath's strategy was to establish the *English* Underground as inherently un-English, an American transplant, in reportage that maintains a constant level of irony and wry humor: "[A] word or phrase may come over from America this month and catch on here next, by which time it will be dead in the states." Portobello Road and the surrounding area were "the nearest London had got, I suppose, to New York's East Village." The first "Underground revolutionary" he came to know—through BIT (the Binary Information Transfer), a counterculture information service that helped newcomers find accommodation in London—was "a sweet-voiced American girl," Jane, a drama student ("theatre for the people") from "the Radical Studies Institute" of Antioch College in Ohio, who ("like so many other young Americans") was in London "to get her head together" and looking for a revolutionary, macrobiotic commune. Over a lunch of brown rice at the vegetarian restaurant Seed, Jane talks loudly and incessantly—she found the English Underground excessively tame by comparison with that in the States—and "I felt for a moment as though I had escorted an exceptionally garrulous American tourist into the tea-room at Fortnum and Mason."[37]

The "English Underground" series was followed by another BBC commission for De'Ath—this time to take his investigation back to the United States in three talks on "Inside, Outside USA," broadcast on Radio 4 in February and March of 1972. His purpose was "to explore the American counter-culture," which he found in seedy decline in San Francisco—the depressing "tired remnants of a Movement"—and a drop-out generation hawking psychedelic rubbish to Middle America in order to support its drug habit. A final report on the counterculture in decline came back to Britain, with a trip around communal living experiments in the countryside and in London, communes that attracted "the best and the worst" and whose future "is uncertain here and in America." The irony of a movement that promised self-discovery and liberation declining into "a sick scene" had become a commonplace of popular journalism on both sides of the Atlantic by the early seventies. In London, Robin Page, writing for the *Daily Telegraph* claimed that the youth-littered beach at Brighton was a site of drug exploitation, seediness, and violence, and drew predictable inferences: "It can only be assumed from this that the alternative society here is being influenced by the violence that has crept into the American movement and shown itself in the 'Weathermen' and the cult surrounding Charles Manson."[38]

While De'Ath was reporting on the decay and disintegration of the Anglo-American Underground on Radio 4, a less anecdotal, more scholarly series on the counterculture was presented on Radio 3 by George Morrison Carstairs, a professor of Psychological Medicine at Edinburgh University, President of the World Federation for Mental Health, and soon to be Vice-Chancellor of the University of York.[39] Though not unsympathetic, his diagnosis was in line with that offered by many within the university health services who sought explanations in a psychological cum sociological reading of the radical movement and its leadership.

Both De'Ath and Carstairs, in their attempts to bring the late-sixties counterculture to the BBC's largely middle class, non-countercultural Radio 3 and 4 audiences, had to shift away from their earlier focus on the problem of disruptive and threatening working-class youth to the now wider generational crisis in the universities, the hippy bohemia of Notting Hill and, indeed, the secondary schools of the middle-class suburbs. For De'Ath there was no easy bridge, and he fell back on an ironic reportage of the ephemerality of an American import. For Carstairs, with his earlier investment in theories of teenage identity crisis and the importance of the parent-child relationship, the "anger and destructiveness," sexual promiscuity, delinquency-as-protest-behavior he found in working-class youth did provide a way into the psychology of the counterculture in an era marked by, he claimed, a general loss of parental authority. Like De'Ath, he also looked to America, not to dismiss the phenomenon but to understand something about both American-led cultural globalization and the critical differences between the counterculture's American and British loci. The goal of his three talks was a better understanding of both the universal and the particular receptivity of modern youth to what he called, in the wake of psychedelic romanticism and student rebellion, the "epidemic of unreason."

Carstairs's story of the "global" rebellion of youth begins with the Berkeley campus in 1964, and the rapid spread of its ferment into countries like Britain—where there was, he argued, a significantly different social and cultural environment. Unlike De'Ath, Carstairs had considerable, if somewhat dated, American experience, having been a Commonwealth Fellow there in 1948–49 and a Rockefeller Research Fellow the following year (he would return as a Woodrow Wilson fellow at the Smithsonian in 1981). His Reith lectures, broadcast in the early sixties, had stressed the influence of a particularly American-styled modernization on British character—the growth of stress in modern life, the decline of the authority of religion and traditional values, the loss of social cohesion, and the stultifying conformity of William Whyte's "Organization Man."[40] But postwar America had also been a country full of self-confidence and optimism—"where everything is thought possible." The *American* youth movement of the sixties consequently was grounded in an impatient, easily frustrated utopian idealism. Britain, on the other hand, presented the coming generation with a sharply different postwar experience, a general postempire re-examination of its institutions and a consequent undermining of "authority" generally and, in the permissive sixties, of the family as a locus of authority. Nevertheless, the British and American countercultures exhibited quite similar psychological responses: disillusion and distrust of authority, an indefinitely prolonged period of adolescent turmoil, the demand for the immediate gratification of desire, and what Bettelheim had identified as the neurotic drives of the student leaders—their "paranoid misperception."

If a serious social demoralization and fears of an insecure future lay behind the global counterculture's epidemic of unreason, Britain seemed, Carstairs thought, more resistant to the "blindly destructive character" of the end-of-the-decade Underground. Like De'Ath, he found confirmation and some satisfaction in the apparent disintegration of the violent, direct-action radicalism of the late sixties, oddly preferring even the "at least purposeful" violence in Ulster to that of the Angry Brigade. In any event it had, he concluded, excited little response in Britain, and many youth seemed more receptive to a kind of sensual passivity, to chords struck by "my fellow Scot" R. D. Laing, who propelled them toward an inner discovery, from doing to feeling.[41]

CHAPTER 5

California Dreamin'

In the summer of 1967, the "summer of love," Peter Stringfellow was managing a provincial soul music nightclub, when

> [w]atching the news at home in Sheffield one afternoon, I saw footage of San Francisco, where there were kids jumping around—some naked, some wearing kaftans—with flowers in their hair. I just thought it was fantastic and brilliant and immediately decided to transform King Mojo from a soul and pop art venue to a hub of the Flower Power movement.[1]

The radical and hippy countercultures—the psychedelic rock venues, Underground press, alternative theater, and agit-prop poster art—in a sense grew out of and remained enmeshed with early-sixties Pop while widening its generational market. If Pop art was part of Britain's high modernist moment, its emergence in London can be dated to the 1956 traveling exhibition from New York's MOMA, "Modern Art in the United States," at the Tate. As we have seen, there was a creative cross-traffic, with American artists exhibiting in London and young British artists and students, like Gerald Laing and Richard Smith, making their way to New York City. British Pop was deeply attuned, like its important London venue in Mayfair, the ICA, to transatlantic rhythms, and its promoters "were positively pro-American."[2]

In the rock music world the British band the Who, especially, employed Pop art design and performance, memorably in their record cover for the album *The Who Sell Out* (December 1967), which featured Warholesque images of giant cans of deodorant and baked beans, and in the happening-like orchestrated smashing of equipment in their on-stage performances or the ritual trashing of their motel rooms. In the most infamous of these incidents in Flint, Michigan, they left a Cadillac submerged in the motel swimming pool—an image reminiscent of the counterculture venue in London, the Roundhouse, where in 1966 "a garish Pop Art Fifties American car stood like a giant junk-shop joke about the hope of modernity."[3]

In the early sixties, exhibitions at the American embassy gallery in London had offered the American avant-garde as symbolic of the United States itself—just as the CIA in the late fifties had promoted abstract expressionism as "symbolic demonstrations of freedom." Another reading, however, was promoted by a 1969 Anglo-American exhibition at the Arts Council, "Pop Art Redefined," which projected Pop as, in the words of its cocurator, "a resistance movement: a classless commando which was directed against the Establishment," or by the opening party at the new ICA in the Mall where, as its director Michael Kustow observed, "[E]veryone—young, old, straight, freaky, stiff-suited or near naked—joined in a Bacchanalian dance to the electronic voodoo of an impassive rock group."[4]

Roy Lichtenstein's comic book graphics (in 1971 Kustow mounted his own exhibition of American comic book art) and Andy Warhol's art and films defined the sixties American Pop scene for their British viewers, and were influential in the counterculture there. Warhol, especially, straddled with his amoral detachment the arts world, the counterculture, Pop, and rock scenes. There was the popularity of his ambiguously erotic alternative films among the student and hippy communities, and the long-running attempt to censor them in Britain, his involvement with the Velvet Underground, or his design of the Rolling Stones' *Sticky Fingers* album cover and sleeve. *US* included readings from Warhol in its pastiche of antiwar Americana; Warhol's *Pork* was performed at the Roundhouse; and the emerging Gay Liberation movement—itself owing much to the dramaturgy of hippy subversiveness—seized upon Warhol's celebrity silk-screen portraits as camp icons.

Psychedelic rock—its sound, its performance, its light-shows, and its poster-art—had a clear affinity with art-school Pop. It was a British artist, Michael Hollingshead, who introduced Timothy Leary to LSD, and returned to London to set up the World Psychedelic Centre in Pont Street in 1965 (where he made abortive plans for a mass LSD turn-on event at the Albert Hall). Other Pop and avant-garde artists in Britain had, like David Hockney, already followed the familiar trail to America—usually California—long marked out by British academics, writers, actors, and directors. Some, like Ron Kitaj, who trained at the Royal College of Art, or Jim Dine, traveled in the other direction as well. Dine, like the somewhat older Claes Oldenburg, was a pioneer of performance art "happenings" in early-sixties New York. Both he and Oldenburg visited and exhibited in London (Dine's installation at Robert Fraser's Gallery in 1965—a graffitied, gift-wrapped penis, his commentary on "Swinging London"—resulted in a police prosecution). Dine moved to London with his family in 1967 and stayed for four years. A year after his solo exhibition at the Museum of Modern Art in New York, Oldenburg mounted a striking and much-reviewed show at the Tate in July of 1970 that featured a giant painted plaster cheeseburger (four years before McDonald's opened its first burger bar in Britain in Woolwich). At the new Hayward Gallery another American Pop conceptual artist, the Californian Newton Harrison, created controversy and media coverage in the autumn of 1971 when his fish tank—where live fish swam before being publicly eaten—was smashed by Spike Milligan and others protesting "art cruelty" (a violent spontaneous event that was, of course, itself a "happening").[5]

Its fusion with the radical counterculture shifted Pop art and "post-Pop" from a somewhat apolitical early-sixties character toward a more overtly political commitment. In 1970 there were simultaneous demonstrations at museums and galleries in New York (at the Metropolitan), London (at the Tate, where British Pop and alternative artists engaged staff and visitors in spontaneous debate), and Amsterdam charging the art world with racism and sexism. Pop art moved from an implied if oblique commentary on modern (that is, modern-as-American) consumer society to, especially in the hands of feminist artists by the early seventies, an explicitly radical, sometimes bitter engagement with the domestic mainstream. Inevitably this meant a more parochial, less transatlantic focus and awareness, and American art and criticism became arguably less important to British artists in the seventies. Nevertheless, the radical Art and Language Group of minimalist and conceptual artists in Britain (from 1968) remained transatlanticist (there was a parallel A&L Foundation in New York), if riven by rivalry and ideological dissention. The transatlantic nature of sixties Pop and countercultural art continued of course at the level of career opportunity and personal movement. In his study of the legacy of Pop and Underground art in the seventies, Edward Lucie-Smith lists 176 artists in a biographical index. Of the 36 who were British, most had exhibited in the United States.[6]

One of the first events at the new ICA in the Mall, a locus for the international Pop art scene from its opening in the spring of 1969, was a group exhibition of contemporary photography. Included were some fifty-four photos entitled "The English Seen" by a young British photographer, Tony Ray-Jones. While Pop art had embraced experimental and montage photography, Ray-Jones's material was in an older, American tradition of deadpan documentary. He dwelt on somewhat seedy scenes not of swinging Chelsea or the rainbow-hued counterculture (a photo of Notting Hill Gate [1967] is of old clothes scattered around a vacant building site), but of a fast-fading ordinary life, catching what an American photographer friend called "the impoverished mentality of a postwar generation": unsmiling, middle-aged men and women with their children, often at tatty seaside resorts; provincial beauty contests; the overdressed, charmless wealthy at tired, washed-out rituals like Wimbledon. Though marked by a self-conscious determination to step away from a style of either commercial fashion photography or Pop experimentalism, they also confirm the transatlanticism of a creator who sought to use techniques learned in America to record an English way of life "before it becomes Americanized."[7]

Ray-Jones, born in 1941 in Somerset, enrolled in a graphic design course at the London School of Printing but left for Yale on a scholarship in 1961. There, and in New York City, he found the inspiration to take his own photographic interest seriously—a genre that was not so highly regarded in Britain. After finishing a Master of Fine Arts in graphic design at Yale in 1964 he spent a year or so with a New York friend, Joel Meyerowitz, photographing scenes of common street life. As Meyerowitz later recalled, Ray-Jones "loved America intensely, and he loved it for its music"—the jazz of Ray Charles and the poetry of Ginsberg: "The country he left behind was still recovering from the second world war, but New York was buzzing with newness," and it "matured his vision." When Ray-Jones returned to London in 1966, it was "with a foreigner's outlook, as well as that of a native," to bring the techniques of a young generation of American photographers to bear on the folklore of a nonswinging, class-and-tradition-bound Britain. This was a world away from the mid-sixties Pop-photo and fashion-mag view of Swinging London, a transatlantic genre characterized by the sexy and elegant work of, say, the American expat Claude Virgin. Like Ray-Jones, Virgin trained in New York, but in a studio-bound modernist aesthetic. In London he established himself in the King's Road and produced work for *Vogue, Town,* and *Queen* that made a transition from the heavily made up studio models of the late fifties to miniskirted Pop. These two photographers, one an American Anglophile who settled in London and enjoyed its clubland and chic Mayfair aesthetic, the other an Englishman who found in American naturalism the means to expose the pretensions of just that world, make for a suggestive contrast in cross-cultural expectation, perception, and motive.[8]

Following the ICA show, Ray-Jones accepted a teaching job at the San Francisco Art Institute (with the intention of moving into cinematography in L.A.). S.F. was the beating heart of the counterculture, and though Ray-Jones's documentary work was hardly psychedelic, his descriptions of his own work reveal perhaps a little of the Underground sensibility of that time and place:

> The situations are sometimes ambiguous and unreal .... This, I hope, helps to create a feeling of fantasy. Photography can be a mirror and reflect life as it is, but I also think that perhaps it is possible to walk, like Alice, through a Looking Glass, and find another world with the camera.[9]

Plans for a West Coast career were tragically cut short, however, by leukemia, and in 1972 Ray-Jones flew back to London three days before he died there at age thirty.

HIPPIES

Ginsberg . . . carrying a flower and wearing a red shirt . . . chants, playing on the squeezebox like a busker. He offers a flower to a blushing police-man . . . . Some smoke defiant joints, some scrape at the flowers painted on their faces, most just gather the vibrations.
—Hyde Park, 16 July 1967

The "hippy"—the word itself was an American Beat coinage—was, as Marwick asserts, "essentially an American phenomenon." Nonetheless, it acclimatized well in certain ecological niches of the metropolis and, as Marwick also suggests, perhaps had a more lasting effect on popular lifestyle and leisure than is often imagined. Domestic hippies of the sixties—unlike the unwashed caravan travelers they subsequently became—were an urban, and especially London, species, whose bare feet, flowing caftans, flower-power mantras, cannabis-masking incense, body-paint and spontaneous "happenings" were as much performance art as subversive protest. London, however, was not Scott McKenzie's golden San Francisco—a detached, floating realm between sea and desert, an alternative capital for the alternative society—and it was central to mainstream national culture in a way no American city could be. Its vastness included and contained the hippy phenomenon, while contributing something of its own art-school Pop-art, avant-garde, permissive-era cool.[10]

The American hippy look and lifestyle unfolded within this special environment—UFO and Middle Earth, Portabello Road, the squats and communes in Notting Hill and Camden Town, and the parks and commons thrown open to concerts and the sleeping-bags of nomadic youth. There was by 1967 a metamorphosis, as Roger Hutchinson observed, "of Mods, art-school Beats, lingering Teds, and even Rockers into the mid-Atlantic clone which became known to outsiders as Hippy."[11] Energizing this change was a factor not addressed in subcultural theorizing about British youth style: the actual presence of a growing number of Americans—in the hippy communities as in the universities, among the psyche-delic club and music festival organizers, and in the offices of the major organs of the Underground press.

Important and highly visible areas of British youth culture were colonized by American countercultural style (though by no means all, as anti-hippy skinheads or West Indian Rastas indicate). Observers then and subsequently echo Simon Frith's view that "Britain's hippie moves were conscious imitations of what was happening in America"—even if, as he also points out, British hippies also owed something to a British art-school sense of aesthetic play, while the shake-up of the U.S. music scene and the widening of the audience beyond teens and into the universities and the suburbs "began with the Beatles."[12]

There was in fact much contradictory representation in the media about the origins of the counterculture, largely because the visible flower-power, psychedelic, drug-enhanced protest style from the States, absorbed, transformed, and recirculated as it had been by the Beatles, intersected with an ongoing domestic British debate over "permissiveness." The text that represented hippies as an essentially American phenomenon in an era when American culture, and particularly American youth culture, was perceived to be increasingly global in its influence, fits into an older and larger discourse about Americanization—a negative or positive discourse depending on one's perspective: either alien and necessary (to counter British cultural conservatism) or alien and dangerous (to British values). On the other hand, those, usually on the antisocialist right, who were already invested in the idea of a progressive postwar British cultural decline and disintegration caused by the collapse of parental, moral, and state authority, tended to see in work-shy, promiscuous flower children—whether American-inspired or home-grown—the inevitable result (and confirmation) of a loss of national character. For them the rot began at home, in "permissiveness" and undisciplined, post–National Service self-indulgence.

In its search for an etiology of domestic hippydom that might harmonize with the common sense of its readers and viewers, media reportage shifted its emphasis, sometimes in the same text, from one side to the other, from the foreign to the domestic locus of the generational crisis, and in the process also tended to blur definitions of just what "hippy" actually might mean. In Britain the texts defining a domestic countercultural ideology came rather late—Richard Neville's *Play Power* or Mick Farren's *Watch Out Kids*, both affirmations of an antiwork ethic and a freak-out lifestyle that gave journalists something clearly subversive to reference. But "hippy style" reached far beyond those who were self-consciously dedicated to its philosophy. The popular press sensationalized but also fudged the meaning in a way to be able to draw in everything that seemed antiestablishment and avant-garde. In 1967 the *Daily Telegraph* threw together under the same rainbow-colored blanket all the "writers, musicians, psychedelic popsters and hippies" who found London to be the "focal city for permissive experiments" in art and life, while by 1969 the *Daily Mail* guessed that there were 60,000 "part-time hippies" in Britain (a figure probably taken from the estimated sales of the Underground press), with a London hard core of some 2,000 "full-time Hippies," whatever that might mean.[13]

What was American, what British? In 1969 the *Guardian* commissioned a collection of essays and interviews on *The Permissive Society* in a paperback with a psychedelic cover that brought together contributors from across the arts, fashion, and journalism, from Mary Quant to Margaret Drabble (on "the sexual revolution"), from the American singer Scott McKenzie ("the voice of Flower Power") to Adrian Mitchell's "Guide to the Underground," Geoffrey Moorhouse on R. D. Laing, Jonathan Miller on censorship, and, on the negative side, Richard Hoggart and Alistair Cooke (recycling a sour Letter from America). In his introduction,

Thomas Harford, a deputy editor at the *Guardian*, presents the aggressive individualism, wild styles, and drug-taking, and the disappearance of taboos of all kinds as based upon and enabled by the dramatic spread of a tolerance that began in Britain in the 1950s with affluence and an ever greater freedom of expression. It is in this context that the powerful American influences poured in—Ginsberg as the "poet-leader" of the flower people, psychedelic drugs, and, latterly, the turn to a newer American-inspired anarchism in "Student Power, Black Power, and the philosophy of violent protest."[14]

The novelist, poet, and playwright Adrian Mitchell, then a freelance journalist in his mid-thirties, jumbled together in his "Guide to the Underground" an Anglo-American host of "Priests and Prophets of Permissiveness": Lenny Bruce ("lay preacher to the Underground"), Dr. Benjamin Spock, Allen Ginsberg, and Bob Dylan, but also Alex Comfort (and his CND protest songs), the Beatles, Jeff Nuttall, Peter Cook, and the *IT* and UFO founder and photographer John "Hoppy" Hopkins, among others. For Mitchell, the British "anti-commercial, anti-war, anti-police" aesthetic counterculture lacked an "American sense of daring," and America's "strong influence on the British Underground should be welcomed." It was, of course, American influence of this kind ("outlandish forms of hippiedom")—enhanced and made accessible by the Anglo-American media—that Alistair Cooke admitted but deplored: "[British youth] can simply see a Californian smoking pot on the telly, rush out into a Wimbledon backyard, grab a handful of the stuff, and do the same." For Cooke, much of the media, and mainstream middle-class British generally, the hippy phenomenon, defined by permissiveness (not "tolerance"), meant drugs, promiscuous sex, ear-shattering music, and a general jettisoning of personal responsibility. The danger of its "infecting" ever younger youth—an issue brought into focus by the prosecution of *OZ* for its pornographic schoolboy issue in 1971 and by reports of middle-class runaways and wild times at sprawling music festivals—was encouraged by its close association with the virus of American cultural invasion generally.[15]

The hippy sexual revolution came to a London already liberated—at least the swinging beautiful people were. Nevertheless, the unapologetic sexual promiscuity that hippydom endorsed came to have special American connotations, as did the uninhibited sexual enjoyment endorsed, indeed demanded, by the liberation movements for women and gays—both characterized in part, and with reason, as American imports. American stereotypes—the oversexed GI, the domineering American female—were already well established, and much as the right blamed a socialist government for permissive legislation, American associations also provided some underpinning for a 1970s dystopian reading of a Britain degraded by American cultural colonization. In reality, of course, the sexual counterculture (or countercultures), however transatlantic in rhetoric and imagery, engaged subtle and not-so-subtle differences in the deep cultural conditioning of class, ethnicity, and national character. San Francisco had long been a wide-open city; London much less self-consciously so. When Dave Burke came to London from California in 1970, he told the Underground paper *Gay Sunshine* that the London scene was unwelcoming for gay "heads" like himself.[16] Change, however, was in the air.

Notting Hill in the mid-sixties was a run-down, mixed race area marked with the hoardings and construction sites of Jack Cotton's new Notting Hill Gate at its southern edge, the straggling second-hand, antiques, and fruit and veg flea-market of Portobello Road to the west, and on the north the chaos of the emerging Westway fly-over that was dissecting the working-class Irish and West Indian populations scattered there in dilapidated, cheaply subdivided housing. In the fifties and sixties, areas of the city like Notting Hill that escaped the rampant property boom were sought out by the art students and artist-Bohemians whose world merged with that of the dropout counterculture after 1965. Though hippy squats could be found anywhere in the less-fashionable parts of the capital, Notting Hill became the epicenter of the British counterculture. It was here, in what he sarcastically called London's "East Village," that Wilfred De'Ath, like other journalist flaneurs of the time, naturally began his "reconnaissance" into the hippy nether world.

Pop-art had already discovered the eclectic Victorian look provided by the second-hand clothing stalls of Portobello Road, the velvets, military jackets, and beady paraphernalia of the Beatles' slide into psychedelia. The hippy community embraced the second-hand markets and charity shops as both a ready source of cheap goods and a means of rejecting the world of commercial commodity and style. Nearby streets, like those around Coleville Terrace or to the west in Ladbroke Grove, became sites for movable communes of "heads" and "freaks" with a street culture of cannabis, LSD, itinerant music, and a graffiti art that saw Blake ("The Tigers of Wrath are Wiser than the Horses of Instruction") circulate from Berkeley to hoardings at Notting Hill Gate. Networks of Underground word-of-mouth communication, BIT, the alternative press, Tony Elliot's *Time Out* (from 1968), and, from 1970, Nicholas Saunders's *Alternative London* manuals sign-posted this expanding world of free-thinking, sexually liberated, and casually employed youth for newcomers like "Judy," an American girl interviewed by Richard Mills for a characteristic quasi-sociological "study of alternative communities" in 1970. Judy, like De'Ath's Jane from Ohio, was one of the nomadic tribe of American dropouts who were outriders for the London hippy scene as they were for the student rebellions. Notting Hill hippy living arrangements might mean no more than the temporary crash pad in a nameless squat, but many in the late sixties were drawn together in a search for communal living with a specific political, musical, artistic, or dietary-cum-religious purpose (or any combination of these). Jane searched for a radical macrobiotic community; by the turn of the decade others looked to find lifestyles defined by sexuality or sisterhood.[17]

Clem Gorman arrived in Notting Hill in 1970 to create a communal theatrical troop. Though, like Richard Neville, he came from Sydney, he was inspired by the hippy commune scene in northern California, in particular the San Francisco Diggers—a group in the Haight Ashbury district who scrounged free food from restaurants and free clothing to help young dropouts. This and other "digger" groups in the United States took their name from the radical egalitarian English Civil War sect; in 1967 the digger movement returned home when Sid Rawles, a self-appointed hippy spokesman, established a London community (the Hyde Park Diggers). While the radical commune movement in Britain could draw on historical domestic inspiration, the immediate impulse came from Timothy Leary's and Richard Alpert's "colonies for transcendental living" in Massachusetts and New York, and the explosion of communal experimentation in California. The transatlantic Underground press encouraged and enabled the spread of alternative living groups by reporting on experiments in the United States and through the free ads placed in papers like *Frendz*—a London spin-off of San Francisco's *Rolling Stone* magazine; life on the Coast informed life in Notting Hill.[18]

Varieties of vegetarian idealism characterized many of these radical living groups, and when Gorman launched a cheaply reproduced typescript *Guide to Making Communes* in 1971, he advised that the best place to get information on communal living in London was the Ceres Grain Shop in Portobello Road.[19] Ceres and the Harmony Foods (now Whole Earth) business that followed were successful examples of what came to be called hippy capitalism. They sold whole grain and "natural" food to the expanding, Zen-influenced counterculture, but managed to survive quite comfortably after the alternative society began to age and dissipate, as Notting Hill itself morphed into a chic locale for the liberal, professional upper middle classes in the late seventies. They were founded by a young, long-haired American entrepreneur, Craig Sams, and his brother Greg.

As a student Craig Sams had converted to macrobiotics—with its Buddhist yin and yang and its rejection of the mainstream commercial food industry, "the Hippy diet" of the most evangelical element in the counterculture—and moved to the East Village, where he found "the first macrobiotic restaurant in the U.S.," the Paradox. In October of 1966 he moved on to London with the intention of establishing a macrobiotic community as well as opening a restaurant of his own like the Paradox: "[We] formed a group who promoted these ideas at the UFO club and other gatherings." A tentative venture in a basement in Airlie Gardens south of Notting Hill Gate found a following that expanded when he moved to the Gloucester Hotel in Westbourne Terrace. With his brother Gregory's help, "Seed" opened in 1968—no reservations, "no exclusivity," and a tape recorder belting out psychedelic rock and the blues. It became a favorite locus for the Underground (and those who wanted to catch a glimpse of John and Yoko) and inevitably became "a tourist thing," as it was listed in all the alternative culture guidebooks and magazines. The difficult business of getting steady supplies of natural foods (vegetables, whole grains, tamari, miso, and so forth) led to the American brothers opening their own whole foods shop, Ceres, in 1969: "It was an instant success," and spawned a host of imitators—shops like Infinity, Arjuna, Community, Harvest, Acorn, Sesame, and On the Eighth Day. In 1970 the Sams brothers began to cater for the proliferating rock festivals, including the Isle of Wight and the Plumpton festivals, and the next year had the concession to provide all the food at Glastonbury, while also handing out free food for Sid Rawles of the Diggers to distribute.[20]

American entrepreneurs were common in the London counterculture. There was, for instance, Joe Boyd, "a very tall and somewhat aloof American expatriate whose roots were in the East coast folk-music scene" who teamed up with Hoppy Hopkins to found one of the first and best-known of the psychedelic music venues, the UFO (for Unidentified Flying Object—or Underground Freak Out) in the basement of an Irish social club in Tottenham Court Road. Or the young American Steve Stollman, who arrived in London in 1966, at age twenty-three, in search of music for his brother Bernie's record label in New York and soon established another club in Wardour Street in Soho, Spontaneous Underground, that became a "village pump" for the psychedelic rock crowd. The Sams brothers themselves attracted American friends, many from Boston, who established themselves in and around Notting Hill and Ladbroke Grove—a kind of macrobiotic American mafia that spread from cooking classes into New Age journalism and shiatsu instruction, while by the early seventies opportunities for taking the British whole food business beyond the fading hippy community in Notting Hill and out of the hands of entrepreneurial believers like the Sams brothers attracted the interest of other, more deeply capitalized Americans looking to expand their profits overseas.[21]

The best-known Underground institutions—*IT*, *OZ*, UFO, Spontaneous Underground, Middle Earth, the Sams brothers' Ceres Grain Shop, or Indica Books and Gallery—were all anchored in central and west London, where the density of both the dropout generation and American colonization encouraged entrepreneurship. American-style hippydom was a London village phenomenon, its most committed members a small minority, and its tenure uncertain—facts that were often emphasized by journalists: "They are not to be found in suburban London or in the typical provincial small town. Nor may the new tolerance be taken for granted . . . . [T]he new climate is far from stable." For Richard Hoggart the view from the provinces, at least from the cultural studies offices at Birmingham University, cautioned that there were many youth subcultures populating a varied provincial as well as metropolitan urban environment, and London—and at that only a small part of London—was "a small stage-set, an amorphous sink, with a floating population, most of whom change daily." What seemed to be a dominant youth culture, he suggested, was merely the result of "the new travelling student population," and in part an "illusion" shared by "courtesy Londoners" who came to participate in its "rootless license." Roger Hutchinson, writing twenty years on in his elegiac homage to *The High Sixties*, echoes—though more positively—some of the same themes: "Only there [in London] . . . did the fantasy truly flourish . . . congealed from many single sunburnt afternoons." Some enthusiastic participants like Mick Farren would agree, not because it was all a mirage, but because he believed that the radical hippy moment, so essentially American in its anarchic subversiveness, could never have originated or been long sustained in culturally conservative, elitist Britain. Others like Charles Marowitz, who though an American emissary for the Beat generation was never really comfortably inside the later counterculture, reiterates the charge that it was in its essentials unsustainably alien: "The convulsions produced by the counter-culture and its youthful insurrections were, morally, politically, culturally, and quintessentially un-British." Frith and Horne conclude that, though Britain did have an authentic countercultural movement, it lacked depth; for all its happenings and Underground press and far-out graphics, "it was never based on a *community* of artists as in San Francisco."[22]

And yet there is ambiguity in such analyses. Britishness is hardly fixed or essential, and many, like Marowitz, seem unsure whether American-imported hippy radicalism "masked" or engaged and challenged "deep-rooted British hang-ups" and middle-class "suburbanity." Cultural historians have yet fully to engage meanings that the countercultural project carried into populations where elements were adopted as fashion and recreation rather than a way of life. It is probably not the case, as some subculturalist students of semiotics have suggested, that all signification was stripped away in the adoption of a sub-hippy bricolage. Marowitz's now commonplace claim that the utopian challenge was doomed to end in farce and disillusion harmonizes with Farren's own "goodbye to all that" (he married an American and immigrated to America in 1981). But such cynicism is often compounded of a bitter and nostalgic personal sense of loss interwoven with aging.

Flower-power hippies were certainly already passé as the decade ended, and the mainstream community celebrated their demise. For Alistair Cooke and his suburban audience, they had been a disturbing aberration from the beginning ("[As] many as 60 per cent are seriously sick, mostly with schizophrenia"). Media analysis, however, was often contradictory—sometimes within the same text. At the height of the hippy craze there had been a tendency to exaggerate it as a generational phenomenon, one that was spreading through the universities and down into the schools, from London to Birmingham and Liverpool, from Notting Hill to Croyden and Surbiton. At the same time, and especially after the hippy fashion began to wane, it could be dismissed with relief (or regret) as marginal and ephemeral, an alien presence infecting a minority of mostly respectable youth. This was to avoid a deeper exploration. The question posed by the *Guardian* enquiry of 1969 remains worth considering, though it was quickly shifted into irrelevance by those who were defeated, disillusioned, or triumphant: "It was wonderful. But . . . was it superficial, a passing phase? Or has it given us something enduring and important? Are people better because of it? more open-minded, generous, tolerant of the other man's point of view and way of life?"[23]

THE UNDERGROUND PRESS

In his last "reconnaissance" into the English Underground, Wilfred De'Ath described an image that would have been familiar to his London listeners in early autumn of 1970—a barefoot girl on the Portobello Road, perhaps a runaway teen, offering passers-by multicolored copies of the countercultural press—*IT, OZ, Friendz,* or *Gandolf's Garden*—a medium the disdainful, center-left *New Statesman* dismissed as "American, anti-socialist, beatnikery." In what Elizabeth Nelson calls the "great days" of the English counterculture, the girl would have been one of scores, perhaps hundreds, of freelance street sellers who picked up their bundles at the offices of a dozen or so alternative press publishers to hawk "among the tourist strips and through the major hippy enclaves."[24]

IT (or *International Times,* as it was before the Thompson Group threatened legal action) began publication in October of 1966; Richard Neville's *OZ,* in January of 1967. Countercultural best-sellers, at their peak they moved something like 40,000 copies a week and 20,000 copies a month, respectively. But there were many more ephemeral, haphazardly appearing imitators. Perhaps a thousand alternative magazines were launched between 1965 and 1974, from *Idiot Unternational* or *Ink* to local alternative papers like *Brixton's Own Boss* or the radical Christian *Catonsville Roadrunner.* There was even a brief effort by dissident BBC staff called *The Brutish Empire.* Then there was the Underground-influenced rock music press: Jan Werner's *Rolling Stone,* imported from San Francisco from 1967 (a regional office was opened in London in 1969 to produce a British edition), led the way away from the chart-listing teen magazines to a more serious, somewhat older readership. It was popular on both sides of the Atlantic counterculture, though the British editors fell out with the San Francisco main office and broke away to form their own Underground paper, *Friends* (later *Friendz,* then *Frendz*). London's own large-circulation *New Music Express* felt the heat and finally reorganized in 1972 with a new team of writers recruited from *IT, OZ, Frendz,* and *Cream.* Though generally with a duller layout, the radical anarchist and Marxist Underground papers dedicated to revolution rather than hippy play also mirrored some of the countercultural style in their cartoons and graphics: Tariq Ali's *Black Dwarf* (followed by his *Red Mole* when he left *Black Dwarf*), *Red Notes,* a *Manual of the Urban Guerrilla,* the anarchist papers *Freedom* and *Anarchy,* and a host of other local and ephemeral partisan publications hawked, often, around the colleges and universities. By the early seventies the American Underground genre also sharply influenced the style and rhetoric of the black, feminist, and gay liberationist press in London.[25]

The American origins and character of the British Underground press in the late sixties and early seventies are hardly in doubt, and were made much of by their political and cultural enemies. Peregrine Worsthorne appeared on BBC2's "Man Alive" program to attack the "low intellectual quality" of *IT*, as well as the dangerous foreign influence it disseminated: "[T]he middle-aged suspect, not unreasonably, that these American-style papers may corrupt their children, damage community relations, reduce British cities to New York level, or pollute the public mind."[26] If it is true that the lively counterculture in, say, Amsterdam or Copenhagen had some influence in London, this was, as in the case of the Dutch monthly *Provo* (1965–67), American influence at one remove. These transatlantic connections can be addressed on three levels: in the direct personal contacts that existed between American and British entrepreneurs, the substantial American content of the papers, and the form in which this material was conveyed.

The Underground press in London was at its inception deeply indebted to the personal influence of what Nuttall called "an army of expatriate Americans wandering, active" throughout Western Europe in the early and mid sixties. As Andrea Adam, *Time Magazine*'s inside reporter on the London Underground scene, later observed of the imported counterculture generally, "The Americans and Australians who came to London had so great an effect because we were un-fettered, we weren't encumbered by the culture or by the place we lived." Young Australians in the British Underground—Richard Neville, Germaine Greer, Clem Gorman—often found the repressive elitism and politeness of British life annoying, and were likely to feel that their own Ozzie culture was "a half-way market between England and America," as Neville has remarked.[27]

IT began as a self-proclaimed British version of the *East Village Other*, whose editor, John Wilcock had founded "the progenitor of modern subversive journalism," the *Village Voice* in the fifties. Wilcock was a Yorkshireman who had migrated to the New York Beat scene and become a major player in the Underground press there and, in 1966, on the West Coast, where he edited the *LA Free Press* before returning to Britain. The idea for a major British Underground paper grew out of discussions between Hoppy Hopkins (who had photographed Ginsberg's London visit), Barry Miles (who now ran Indica Books and was the London correspondent for the *EVO*), and Jim Haynes. Haynes was a "long-haired American" and "libertarian anarchist" from Louisiana who had been posted to an American airbase near Edinburgh in the late fifties and stayed on after discharge, opening an avant-garde bookshop—where he first met Miles—and then, in 1963, founding the successful and influential Traverse Theatre company. Plans to bring the Traverse to

London for a 1966 season (with the help of Charles Marowitz) brought Haynes to town, and planning for an Underground paper progressed rapidly. Haynes, who was interested in "a *Village Voice* type paper" chiefly for theatrical advertising, insisted that his friend and a director for Traverse, Jack Henry Moore, a flamboyantly gay Oklahoman, be included (after the first editor suddenly departed, Moore edited a number of issues of *IT* before another expatriate, Brooklyn-born Bill Levy, took over). By summer of 1966 they were ready to go. Start-up capital of £500 was borrowed from American financier Victor Herbert who lived in Paris and L.A. and who also helped fund Julien Beck's Living Theater. Haynes announced the Underground press's arrival in Britain on the BBC's *Late Night Line-Up* chat show, and helped distribute copies of the first issue, a run of 10,000, outside the Aldwych Theatre where Peter Brook's *US* was playing.[28]

John Wilcock, whose stories in *IT* from New York had ensured a "tilt towards the United States," also exerted some influence on the evolution the next year of Richard Neville's *OZ*. Neville, an arts student at the University of New South Wales in the early sixties, where he founded a first version of the magazine, had been an admirer of the antiestablishment humor of Lenny Bruce and American hip culture. In 1966 he came to London and re-established *OZ* three months after the inauguration of *IT*. By its third and fourth issues the monthly had taken on a psychedelic look, and in August Neville asked Wilcock to guest-edit the sixth issue, confirming *OZ*'s turn toward a vividly countercultural look and tone. Like many in the Underground, Neville would personally explore the New York countercultural scene; in April of 1968 he flew to the United States on a cheap charter flight, stayed in Greenwich Village with John Wilcock, met Andy Warhol, and saw a production of *Hair*.[29]

Though direct American control of the Underground press declined toward the end of the decade, Americans continued to be in evidence among the sponsors and editorial board members well into the early seventies, when the genre began to fade. Without denying that the British Underground evolved in its local context with a late infusion of local talent, it is hard to credit claims that this in a significant way displaces the reality of American cultural hegemony or establishes the primacy of "the local" over "the global." Even without the close personal involvement of American advisors, sponsors, and editors, the *content* of the alternative press continued to proclaim its nature as a satellite of the American East and West coasts. When Wilfred De'Ath interviewed him in early September 1970, Richard Neville told him, "We print what we feel is relevant to our time, our society." But the example he gave was the paper's coverage of the People's Park brouhaha in Berkeley, California: "[We] got a news-sheet from them of which, within three days, we had printed over thirty thousand copies as an insert for a new issue of *OZ*."[30]

The first *IT* editor, Tom McGrath, a heroin-addicted Scot who had edited the pacifist journal, *Peace News*, claimed that London was not ready for a fully psychedelic paper on the emerging West Coast model, and both McGrath then and Miles subsequently were sensitive about charges that its content was U.S. dominated. In March 1967 McGrath asserted that its primary focus was England and that "Britain has come up with a new spiritual movement," while Miles has recently protested that *IT* was "not an imitation American" paper. In fact, though *IT* did not adopt the psychedelic look of the monthly *OZ*, Miles admits that the two papers were "complementary" and he wrote for both. There were important differences between the kind of community news *IT* provided and the hippy graphics of *OZ* and some of the other London Underground, but ultimately protests about originality are unconvincing. Miles himself told Jonathan Green that "it was very much the Lower East Side drug scene that we were emulating." The main fare they offered their readership—in line no doubt with what that readership wanted to read—was dominated by American style and, often, American content well before Miles traveled to New York "to get to know the people at the *East Village Other*." *IT*'s first editor, McGrath, had been close to Theodor Roszak when they both worked for *Peace News*, and at *IT* he was assisted by David Mairowitz, a New Yorker who had been involved in the Berkeley Free Speech movement. David Robins, who started working for *IT* shortly after the American Bill Levy took over as editor in 1967, recalled twenty years later that "[t]he extent to which the Americans dominated the scene was substantial. But I liked them, cos after all that was what we all wanted: to be American, to go there and live there."[31]

IT in fact annoyed many within the radical political Underground with what appeared to be a lack of interest in the *domestic* political and social struggle. In October of 1969 the London Street Commune (members of which would later "trash" the *IT* offices) published an "Open Letter" in which they claimed that the Underground was lost in "a stifling haze of hashsmoke and American hipkultur." In spite of criticism, however, the paper continued until its demise to rely substantially on American content. Issue number 138, as late as 18 September 1972, contained only 5 (out of 24) pages devoted to original articles on events and topics in Britain (there were 9 pages of U.S. reprints and 5 pages of other articles dealing with American topics). American hippy culture was even more in evidence in the material offered by Neville's *OZ*, which played more to the freaks and heads with wild graphics and comix and had little pretension to literary hipness. Its first issue contained more than three pages on the United States, its last (in 1973) an interview with Timothy Leary; most issues dealt with various aspects of the American countercultural scene in articles and graphics. Much of the alternative press not only commonly included news and commentary from the American counterculture, and especially the San Francisco rock music scene, but, like *OZ*, often filled pages with material copied directly from, say, the *Los Angeles Free Press* or the *Berkeley Barb*.[32]

Tying the Anglo-American Underground media together in content and style, an Underground Press Syndicate (created in the United States in 1967)—and later a Liberation News Service (founded by Marshall Bloom)—facilitated the distribution of transatlantic countercultural material among what was by 1969 a wide network of alternative papers, some in continuous publication and many as ephemeral as mushrooms, across the United States (from Cambridge, Mass., and New York to Los Angeles and the Bay Area) and in London. That the Underground press in Britain was, like the hippy and psychedelic culture it replicated, largely a projection of an American genre was something its critics were eager to exploit. When, in 1971, Richard Neville and two other *OZ* staff members were prosecuted under the Obscene Publications Act of 1959, the defense brought in as witness a professor of jurisprudence from Oxford (an American trained at Harvard Law School). Professor Ronald Dworkin, who was often to be heard on BBC radio and TV talk shows commenting on the dramatic American antiradical trials of the period, observed that the prosecution of *OZ* on grounds that it was likely to deprave and corrupt would be unconstitutional in the States. The prosecution replied: "That may be. But we are not, as yet, an adjunct of the United States."[33]

Finally, it is the *form* of the Underground press in Britain, its visual character, that proclaimed as much as its promoters and its content its closeness to the trend-setting American models it emulated: the in-your-face psychedelic colors and screaming titles, the amateur layout, and, perhaps more than anything else, the cartoons, strip-comics, and cover illustrations. It was British Pop art meets (and is superseded by) San Francisco design. *IT*, as David Huxley has shown, began by using mostly British comic material (like Jeff Nuttall's cartoons), but from 1968 on increasingly replaced this with reprints of West Coast "comix." These came to dominate the magazine by 1969. The cover of *IT* number 74 (26 February 1970) was wholly devoted to a Gilbert Shelton's "Furry Freak Brothers" strip.[34]

The mainstream press in Britain drew of course on a long journalistic tradition of social and political cartooning, though by the sixties the humor offered in *Punch* had come to look a lot like that found in the *New Yorker* (though admittedly the more scathing satire of Searle seems uniquely British). The British Underground press commonly simply reproduced American countercultural comix in their pages in part because they were free—thanks to the Underground Press Syndicate and the lack of copyright. When they finally emerged at the end of the decade, *British* comix, publications such as *Cyclops, Cozmic Comics, Street Comix,* or *Nasty Tales,* though domestic products, were unashamedly derivative of the keep-on-truckin' style of Roger Crumb (in San Francisco's *Zap Comix*) or Gilbert Shelton (*The Fabulous Furry Freak Brothers*). Comix-influenced illustration and cover design characterized most of the British Underground press as a graphic representation of the hippy subversiveness of "play." The mix of multicolored illustration and writing—the Blakelike merging of image and word—typified the style of the Anglo-American Underground press generally. Though the *San Francisco Oracle,* with its offset-produced rainbow colors, was especially influential, it may be, as David Mellor has suggested, that the British version of the "transgressive antics" of countercultural graphics often added something—an "English sensibility of bizarre whimsy"—but it is hard to see this, if true, as more than minor, if interesting, local variation on an essentially derived form, and not, as Mellor claimed, "the major structuring device" of British comic-strip Pop art.[35]

By 1968–69 *IT* was running a two-page comix section, mostly reproduced American strips, and in 1970 began publishing a separate comix anthology (*Nasty Tales*) as a money-making venture (following the lead perhaps of the *East Village Other,* which also started its own monthly comix magazine, *Gothic Blimp Works*). It brought the trend-setting American illustrators Crumb, Shelton, Greg Irons, Spain Rodriguez (*EVO* and *Zap Comix*), and Rick Griffin together with British imitators like Chris Welch, Brian Boland, and Edward Barker. *IT* was followed by *OZ,* which funded *Cozmic Comics* in 1972. Like *IT, OZ* had been giving ever more space to reproductions of American comix strips; when the *OZ* editors were prosecuted in 1971, their trial appeal t-shirt logo featured Crumb's heroine Honeybunch (while friends of *OZ* demonstrated outside the court with a 12-foot high papier mâché model of the same). Two years later *Nasty Tales* also drew the Metropolitan Police to the *IT* offices to seize copies of allegedly obscene issues—and prosecution for corrupting children (on the spurious grounds that comics were by definition created for children). The trial received wide publicity—George Melly and Germaine Greer were witnesses for the defense. The American comix reproduced in *Nasty Tales,* and Crumb's work, especially, were singled out by the prosecution. Though *IT* won, the judge refused to award costs, hastening the end for an already faltering icon of sixties counterculture.[36]

The visual side of hippy "play power" entered the radical, marxisant political Underground as well, though satirical San Francisco–inspired comix illustration might sit uncomfortably with heroic socialist realism. Tariq Ali's *Black Dwarf* employed "a young hippy" graphics and cartoon designer who also worked for *OZ.* It was the center-spread he created for a special issue in 1969 devoted to women's issues that provoked Sheila Rowbotham's despair at the chauvinism of the radical counterculture: a Crumb-inspired figure of a large woman with naked breasts, where she had wanted a female Latin American freedom-fighter. What Rowbotham read, reasonably, as pornographic sexist ridicule the designer no doubt meant as a subversive obscenity that, like Crumb's design for Janis Joplin's classic 1968 album *Cheap Thrills,* used pneumatic-breasted women to assert an equality of sexual exuberance—much as Crumb also subverted racist stereotypes of black women. If radical feminists in the United States as well attacked what they saw as the prurient and violent misogyny of the Underground comix genre, by the early seventies there were feminist cartoonists in both America and Britain who inverted sexist ridicule and violence in their own *Wimmen's Comix* or *Tits and Clits.*[37]

As with the Underground press as a whole, the comix genre in Britain was either a wholly American import ("almost totally derivative" according to one observer) or at least closely derivative of the work of the most popular American artists. This can reasonably be portrayed as evidence of American cultural (or countercultural) hegemony, and of the commercial power of American style in the youth marketplace. Britain lacked its own adult strip-comic tradition (it was a medium "at the bottom of the cultural pyramid"), and those who attempted to create an indigenous comix art-form faced both this challenge but also, coming often out of a more elitist art-school tradition than their American counterparts, were perhaps less able to tap into whatever street-scene, gritty material may have been locally available. They certainly found it more difficult to attune themselves to a noninsider, popular readership—using references familiar, it has been claimed, not in the street, but to other art-school graduates. Those that were most successful were those who imitated the American style most exactly.[38]

Part of the popularity of this aspect of the American counterculture lay in its enhanced subversive nature in class-bound Britain, where its flaunted obscenity, vulgar scatology, and trashy disposability had more capacity to disturb and ran more roughly against the grain of polite society than, perhaps, in its country of origin. The revolution in mainstream satire that *did* occur in sixties Britain—from the Goon Show, Beyond the Fringe, and That Was the Week That Was to *Private Eye*—was largely, like Peter Cook and Dudley Moore's sketches of soft-capped Pete and Dud, a product written by and for university graduates. For its relatively brief period, the Underground press and Underground comix ranged more widely and deeply. Though suppressed by censorship as the political tide turned in the early seventies, they also left perhaps more of a legacy than has been appreciated. Certainly mainstream design, in advertising, publishing, and the media, drew on (or co-opted) much from the counterculture—sometimes taking on design artists who had worked for the Underground press before it began to collapse in the early seventies.

In some ways the great success story of British comic satire in the coming decade, *Monty Python's Flying Circus*, can be said to be a kind of hybrid of sixties British university humor and the counterculture. Its cut-out animation and rainbow-colored graphics directly borrowed from the psychedelic and erotic themes of the Underground media. *Python*'s animation was, in fact, designed largely by Terry Gilliam—the *American* Python who had worked in New York for Harvey Kurtzman's *Help!* magazine in the early sixties, as did his friends Robert Crumb and Gilbert Shelton. The Python team's American connections were in fact dense and of long standing (John Cleese and Graham Chapman took their Footlights review to Broadway and onto the Sullivan Show in 1964; Cleese stayed and met Connie Booth, whom he married in 1968). The Python theme song, chosen by Gilliam and Palin in the BBC studios the same day (24 July 1969) they watched the return of Apollo XI, was of course a Souza march. By the end of the decade, it was the American Victor Lowndes who convinced Cleese, over drinks at the Mayfair Playboy Club, that the team could market their routines in the United States and raised the possibility of selling a script for a film to Hugh Heffner, though Gilliam says, "We always had the idea of trying to break into North America."[39]

The Underground press phenomenon flourished in London for only a relatively brief few years before a quite rapid decay and collapse, like the counterculture as a whole that sustained it. Serious retrospective assessment has stressed either its period utopianism and naive lack of commercial nous or its "unEnglish" roots in a nihilistic style of anarchistic American "psychedelic glowering," as David Widgery complained—with an "imported" rhetoric ("Off the pigs!") that raised issues that sounded "flimsy" in a British context. As a Marxist, Widgery had in any event remained suspicious of a movement that seemed more located in the aesthetics of cultural revolt than in the quotidian struggles of labor in the sweated workplace. There was, in fact, plenty of intermingling, as an examination of those who wrote articles for, say, Tariq Ali's *Black Dwarf* would show, or, indeed, as David Widgery's own wide-ranging interests and radical journalism suggest.[40]

It may be that some of the American countercultural promoters and entrepreneurs were personally uninterested in a radical politics of domestic confrontation—in the spring of 1968 Joe Boyd was off arranging concert venues in San Francisco while Ali was marching into Grosvenor Square. But this attitude was hardly exclusive to the Americans in the Underground. Mick Farren, for all his radical "white panther" posturing, his Afro, and his contempt for the British class system, was little more likely than Boyd to find himself on the barricades, and Nigel Fountain has observed that the Yorkshireman John Wilcock thoroughly "echoed in his concern with cultural anarchy rather than political action the preoccupations of the American expatriates in London." Finally, one might observe that Widgery, for all that he decried the bad fit between British context and the "imported" problems of American society, had himself made "the almost obligatory trip" to the United States in 1965, and admitted that the racial explosions in Watts, the violence of American cops (he was beaten in Miami), and his socializing with the "dope-smoking radicals" of the SDS had been "my [radicalizing] education."[41]

Fountain (whose important history of the Underground press is informed by his personal experiences within it) has raised another issue of the timing of the entry and departure of the Americans. While admitting that the movement was clearly deeply indebted to an Anglo-American fusion that "powered" papers like *IT* in the beginning and through the first year and a half, he believes that the withdrawal of direct American influence signaled a shift toward a domestic resurgence that further accelerated the American exodus.[42] But the moving on of the entrepreneurial Americans can as reasonably be a signal that the genre as a whole was played out. The withdrawal of the Americans coincided not so much with the liberation and flourishing of a native creativity as with the waning of the radical moment and the inevitable domestic taming of its utopianism by commercial forces.

Inevitably, but more rapidly than in the United States where the radicalism of the counterculture was better protected by the First Amendment and where, as in San Francisco or L.A., it may have been more deeply rooted in the community, the Underground press in London declined in the early seventies because of the waning of the youth culture that supported it, aggressive and expensive prosecutions by the authorities, and the commercial co-optation of the more viable elements by corporate publishing. By the early seventies what remained had come to represent, not so much a general counterculture as a politically radical subculture, a pattern than an American sociologist found identical in Britain, Canada, and the United States.[43]

CHAPTER 6

Venues of Liberation

UFO was a commercial venture launched in December 1966 by "Hoppy" Hopkins and Joe Boyd to bring in a little revenue for the cash-strapped Underground paper *IT*. It was, Farren claims, modeled on San Francisco's Avalon Ballroom (security was provided by "a strange American," Norman, who "looked fresh out of some Vietnam rice paddy"). It quickly became the most important of the new countercultural music venues for its brief existence: *IT* and *OZ* and "all the American imports" were distributed there; there were dancing, macrobiotic food, movies, and light shows. By the summer of 1967 "kaftans and beads were everywhere and UFO was swamped by tourists and weekend hippies."[1]

As with *IT*, Miles is dismissive of "the public memory" that the UFO club and the London Underground in general were closely imitative of the San Francisco model ("[T]here was in reality very little connection between the two"). But his protest turns on the narrow ground that San Francisco bands were not widely heard in London until after UFO closed. The London scene was in fact closely attuned to the West Coast rock world through the Underground press and word of mouth. In Nuttall's words, UFO presided over a "fad for freakouts on a San Francisco scale" that it helped to organize at the Roundhouse and the Alexandra Palace—where in the spring of 1967 the psychedelic "14-Hour Technicolour Dream" followed both an American multiband model and the hippy capitalism surrounding Fillmore West—the sale of advertising posters, silk-screened t-shirts, and Underground papers.[2]

When the psychedelic revolution arrived in Britain, techniques of performance demanded the kind of indoor venues UFO or Stollman's Spontaneous Underground club could provide, but also what many regarded as a characteristically American technology of massive sound systems, powerful lighting, strobes, and innovative projection apparatus. It was an American couple from Timothy Leary's Millbrook, Joel and Toni Brown, who brought the first elaborate light-shows with their water-slide projectors to the London Free School in Notting Hill and inspired Pink Floyd to hire their own "lighting director."[3] The Underground clubs and pubs—and indeed even the largest of the indoor venues like the Ally Pally—were inadequate, however, for the late-sixties demand for rock-as-mass-experience, and the characteristic countercultural phenomenon of the closing of the era was the outdoor concert, another form that both had its roots in earlier British (jazz concert) practice but was more immediately derivative of American entrepreneurship. But however important listening as participation-performance may have become by 1969 at the Hyde Park or Isle of Wight concerts, the largest audiences of all remained those who simply tuned in to hear American-style disc jockeys play the newest bands. Radio and the phonograph made home itself the most democratic countercultural venue.

POP AND THE MEDIA: AMERICAN ENTERPRISE, THE PIRATE ERA, AND RADIO WONDERFUL

Radio had brought American performance and American disc jockey style and accent to Britain since the war, when American Forces Network broadcasting had made popular American music accessible to many. In the fifties the powerful transmitters of Radio Luxembourg, run by four American companies, brought rock'n'roll to eager teens at a time when the BBC's monopoly sharply restricted Pop playing time. With the American-run or at least -inspired pirate stations in the mid-sixties, and the availability of cheap portable phonographs, transistor radios, and Top of the Pops television programming on both ITV and BBC, the majority of homes were exposed to Pop listening culture. This facilitated the rapid spread of counterculture rock beyond the minority who could frequent the clubs and other indoor venues.

In 1952, the same year that Radio Luxembourg began to broadcast in the commercial American format whereby DJs were handed playlists from record companies who paid for air time, the weekly *New Music Express* in London positioned itself to attract the burgeoning teen market by patterning its format on American chart-topper publications. Thanks in part to the rise of the Beatles, it had a circulation of around 300,000 by the early sixties. The older popular music magazine *Melody Maker* followed suit with its "Pop 50" and "Top Ten USA" charts and its coverage of Radio Luxembourg and the pirate stations. By the mid-sixties it had a weekly column called "Dateline USA," "Music Scene USA," or "US News."[4]

By the late fifties *British* DJs on Radio Luxembourg were not only playing a lot of American rock'n'roll but also managing, like the British rock'n'roll musicians, to sound American. This was not limited to DJs, Pop singers, and teenage argot generally, though these especially were the subject of sharp anti-American criticism in the fifties. As Raymond Williams observed in 1962, the Pop singer was "now flanked by . . . quiz-masters and sports commentators, whose 'Americanism' is in fact more acceptable, in many contexts, to a majority British audience, than the traditional class accent which once monopolized the BBC." This could seem odd, however, even annoying, to Americans visiting Britain in search of romanticized difference: John Updike complained while in London that "the music is all sung in an American accent. What does Dusty Springfield know about a 'preacher man'?" Not all singers and DJs, of course, put on, like Tony Blackburn, an exaggerated American drawl. The most influential of the countercultural rock DJs, John Peel, who had significant experience in the United States, managed to retain in his own voice an essential, unhyped, provincial Englishness. But more typical was Tommy Vance, who like Peel also had some experience in the States at Pop radio stations. Back in Britain at Radio Caroline, Radio Luxembourg, and Radio London he directly modeled his delivery "on the 'speak fast and modulate slow' style of Big Dan Ingram at WABC New York."[5]

The pirate era began on Easter Sunday, 1964, with Radio Caroline's first broadcast from the North Sea, just a few months after ITV pioneered its top-of-the-pops chart-defined television program, *Ready, Steady, Go!* Caroline was the invention of Ronan O'Rahilly, a young Irish entrepreneur with an American mother. He had come to London in the late fifties, moving around the same Soho and Chelsea set as Mim Scala; his first venture was a rhythm and blues club in Soho (Ray Charles "was his hero"), and then, with a partner, the Stanislavsky-inspired Chelsea Actors' Workshop in the King's Road. When that failed he turned to radio (inspiration for off-shore broadcasting came from information at the U.S. embassy in Grosvenor Square about the *Voice of America*, then being broadcast from a U.S. ship operating in the North Sea). After some fund-raising in the States, he had a ship refitted in Ireland and named for the recently assassinated U.S. president's daughter.[6]

Others scrambled to get a piece of the action, and Caroline was soon followed by American (Texan)-financed Radio London, broadcasting from a U.S. minesweeper. It was the most popular of the pirates before this novel way of getting around the BBC's monopoly was closed down by parliamentary act in 1967. Both Caroline and London were set up as "all day music stations" defined by American-style DJ banter and format. Of the two, Radio London, with about 10 million weekly listeners, was the more overtly American. Its jingles were made in Dallas and its model was the Dallas station KLIP. Caroline, though its play list always included American labels—especially American soul music—was regarded as somewhat more of a home product. DJs from both stations and the other pirate ships drifted however to the British mainland and to BBC after the passage of the Marine Broadcasting Act in 1967.

From the early sixties the pirate DJs, though "brashly commercial," came to reflect, in Nuttall's words, "exactly the speed, rhythm and flavour of the maturing alternative culture," without, it must be said, much of its subversive revolutionary radicalism. It was precisely, however, the shock of their American-inspired "demotic style ... after the buttoned-up diction and 'wall to wall Mantovani' heard on the BBC" that made them "trend setters, known and reputed as such, appointed by the public." In 1967, the BBC moved to co-opt this audience and set up its own Pop, top forty style national station, Radio 1, making use of the pool of DJ talent the government was setting about making unemployed. The BBC's Director of Sound Broadcasting, Frank Gillard, had been determined to keep the American threat at bay by resisting legalization of the pirates, but he was also interested in their formulas for success—and in the American culture of popular radio generally (in 1954 when on a visit to the States he had been impressed with the "informality" of American local stations).[7]

> He [Morris Zapp] had a brief honeymoon with Radio One . . . what he took, at the time, to be a very funny parody of the worst kind of American AM radio . . . . Instead of advertising products, the disc jockey advertised *himself* . . . . [It] was only after four successive programmes of almost exactly the same formula—DJs narcissistic gabble, lists of names and addresses, meaningless anti-jingles—that the awful truth dawned on him: *Radio One was like this all the time.*[8]

The BBC's grudging move to disc jockeyed, American-formatted, morning, day, and night Pop radio programming in 1967 created at a stroke the most important generational "venue" for those British listeners who wanted to hear and share the kind of American and British rock music that had defining currency. There remained the distant commercial competitor, Radio Luxembourg, but until the liberalization of the radio broadcasting monopoly in the early seventies within Britain "Radio Wonderful" (a phrase from Radio 1's "jingle") reigned supreme. Many of the more flamboyant DJ "announcers" themselves brought a fan base from their work on the pirate stations and quickly became national celebrities. Though mostly British, young (typically in their early to mid-twenties), and often from modest provincial backgrounds, their American connections as well as on-air American affectations were part of the self-advertising of their coolness. Dave Cash, for instance, was born in Britain but moved to Canada as a child where he did work in advertising and as a local DJ before moving to U.S. stations in Seattle, Dallas, and New York, and then back to Britain to join Radio London to do the popular "Kenny and Cash show" with Kenny Everett. His style was exaggerated transatlantic—as the fanzine BBC publication of 1969 (*The DeeJay Book*) put it, he enjoyed "those knock-out Hawaiian drinks concocted in Trader Vic's at the London Hilton, where he holds court during press interviews." With an "American-based and dry off-set" humor, his catch-phrase was "Groovy Baby!"[9]

The star presenters had distinct styles and drawls, often modeled on L.A., Dallas, or New York DJs and different modes of serious or flippant approach in playing what was hot from the charts or, for the more serious listener aficionados, offering their own selections of unknown, little heard material from hopefuls. This was the choice between, say, the cheeky-cheerful, American-caricatured performance of Tony Blackburn (on his morning Pop program) and the more serious John Peel (late nights and Sunday afternoons for the counterculture). Radio

1 in fact did offer a difference, pace David Lodge, from the commercial American model. It self-consciously presented a smorgasbord of different styles and play menus in order to build, as Simon Frith has observed, a heterogeneous audience through "an oddly eclectic sound" unfamiliar to the American top forty chart programs. This made British DJs arguably more important than their counterparts were in the States generally, where sales alone tended to dictate what was played and what was excluded, though some rock cognoscenti like Nik Cohn claimed to prefer the "real thing": "British jockeys have never been in the same class [with American DJs]."[10]

If DJs promoted a "simultaneity of listening" among British youth,[11] it was also a transatlantic simultaneity; Jan Werner's attempt to import into Britain the influential American rock magazine *Rolling Stone* was based on just such a presumption. Whether this actually encouraged a tighter weaving of Anglo-American identities may depend on the nature of the listening; consumption of Pop was relatively casual. Countercultural listening, however, had a deeper, "lifestyle" reach. To the extent that Radio 1 offered the more serious listening of the counterculture, it was not the populist Blackburn, favorite of housewives and teens who "told bad jokes and stuck rigorously to the station playlist," whom they tuned into, but Peel and his *Perfumed Garden* (while at London Radio), *Top Gear*, and *Night Ride* programs, where they found an eclectic offering of whatever British and American new music that drew Peel's uncommercial interest.

Peel, who made no effort to sound American, had in fact the most extensive American experience of any of the Radio 1 DJs. Born John Ravenscroft in 1939 in Burton, near Liverpool, he was in the familiar way of his generation swept up as a teen by an enthusiasm for American rock'n'roll and blues through his listening to the American Forces Network ("meat and drink to a music-hungry schoolboy desperate to hear Chicago blues") and the BBC Light Programme's *Two-Way Family Favourites*: "I've always described the moment in which I first heard Elvis on the radio as being the defining moment in my life." Shrewsbury School, followed by National Service, left him at loose ends when in 1960 his father, a cotton broker, sent him to Houston to get work experience—variously serving as office boy, selling crop insurance in west Texas, and finally (he stayed in the States for seven years) DJ-ing for radio stations in Dallas, Oklahoma, and California. He had had absolutely no idea what to expect: "[My] understanding of American life was cobbled together from reading the *National Geographic*, cheap adventure magazines, *Jazz Journal* and *Jazz Monthly*, and from listening to Lonnie Donegan's cover versions of Leadbelly and Woody Guthrie songs." What he found was that Americans wanted to hear an English (preferably Liverpudlian) voice explaining the English invasion. Playing up to the role, he found that his public school accent morphed into the Liverpool tones of his childhood—in an odd reversal, it might be noted, of what had happened to Alistair Cooke in the United States, whose own provincial Lancashire voice, already perhaps an embarrassment at Cambridge, became ever more upper-class in line with his near-caricatured image as the engaging (to Americans) face of Old England. Neither of these are especially cynical transformations, but do indicate how identities may be fluid and determined by context and performance.[12]

Peel followed a somewhat nomadic existence from Texas to Oklahoma to California, picking up a fifteen-year-old American wife en route and a serious interest in a radio career. In March 1967 he returned to Britain and secured on the basis of his American experience a DJ job at Radio London (where his name was changed from Ravenscroft to Peel). It was at Big L that he became a media guru to the counterculture through his short-lived program *The Perfumed Garden* ("a sacred little corner of hippydom magically unsullied by commercial forces" that, according to Mick Farren, "came as close to magic as a radio show can"). He played non-top-forty music, read poetry and articles from the Underground press, and mused about radical politics. Sporting a caftan and shoulder-length hair, he had a part that summer at the 14-Hour Technicolour Dream before moving to Radio 1. By 1968 Peel, who introduced the musical tributes to Martin Luther King at the memorial service in St. Paul's, was in demand as rock compere at Middle Earth, UFO, and the Roundhouse (where he introduced the Doors), and regularly wrote pieces for the Underground press (as he later put it, "writing serious crap for [the] range of hippy papers").[13]

ROCK CONCERTS AND FESTIVALS

It is hard to describe how exciting this moment was, we had only heard [Jefferson Airplane] on tiny transistor radios . . . . [To] hear this live at such volume and relatively close quarters was absolutely mind blowing. The revolution was here at Godshill!

Radio aside, of all the chaotic popular aspects of the counterculture, it is probably the rock concert that was most successful in both reaching a mass audience and creating a sense of mass participation that—though the bands themselves may have been predominantly male and middle-class—could cut across gender, class, and nationality (if less successfully race) and establish at least a temporary generational sense of community, almost a religious community where the ecstasy of loud music combined with the sexual resonance of closely packed bodies and marijuana-induced euphoria. Evolving through ever-larger indoor venues in Britain, in the United States the rock concert tapped into a yet larger market with the Beatles and Stones leading the way in sports stadia and convention centers. By the end of the decade the outdoor festival emerged as a generational experience shared, not by the thousands who could crowd into the Albert Hall, but by hundreds of thousands.[14]

The large open-air rock concert arrived in Britain at Woburn, the Isle of Wight, and Hyde Park in 1968; that given by the Stones in July the next year drew the largest crowd of the decade for any metropolitan event (from a quarter to half a million). Filmed by Granada TV and policed by Hell's Angels, it was "a gigantic London version of the free concerts that were a hallmark of the rock scene in San Francisco." Such concerts were regarded with deep suspicion by "almost every group normally associated with the Establishment," and media coverage dwelt on promiscuity, drug-taking, and disorder. ITV's John Birt and his American wife drove to the 1970 Isle of Wight festival in his Ford Mustang and reported on the invasion of the restricted area by free-festival radical freaks led from an overlooking hill they named "Desolation Row" by Mick Farren and his "White Panther" friends."[15]

In retrospect the unprecedentedly large crowds of youth looking to be "hippies for a weekend" were reasonably well behaved in the face of the inconveniences of poor organization, English weather, and police harassment. The moral outrage generated by the press coverage, the ire of local councillors in often Tory rural areas, and the change in the national political environment after the election of 1970 meant, however, the imposition of a regulatory regime that brought the rock festival moment—at least the festival at the Isle of Wight—to a close after only three years. It may be, as Bernice Martin argued in 1981, that there was in this 1970s retreat an inevitable disintegration of the rock community back into its constituent class- and age-homogeneous elements. In the few years of their florescence, however, the mass festivals, as a "search for shared freedom and community," touched hundreds of thousands of youth.[16]

By the end of the decade the mass outdoor concert in both the States and in Britain was the site where the special (countercultural) relationship was most strikingly on display. It is true that by the end of the sixties, with the Beatles no longer performing live, the British invasion had considerably ebbed, and it was home-grown American bands that dominated the sound stages (though the Rolling Stones and the Who could continue to find mass audiences) at the U.S. festivals and often at British events as well. Richie Havens, for instance, the black American folk and Gospel singer whose ad-libbed number "Freedom" became iconic of Woodstock, would play at the Isle of Wight and Glastonbury festivals (and drew a crowd of 15,000 to the Crystal Palace Bowl in 1972).[17]

The open-air festival in Britain may have had its own domestic roots—in folk and jazz festivals in the fifties (the commercial jazz festival at Beaulieu drew some 4,000 in 1958 and as many as 10,000, with attendant problems of disorder, in 1960)—though these too followed an American model, the Newport and Monterrey Jazz festivals, and featured many of the same performers. By the mid-sixties the British "jazz festivals" at Richmond Park (33,000 to hear the Yardbirds at the last of these in 1965) had evolved, again following an American model (and using American electric guitar and amplification technology), into super-loud rock concerts. In 1968 Jefferson Airplane brought their own huge light show screens, liquid projection, an entourage of lighting technicians, and a giant sound system when they played the first of the Isle of Wight outdoor festivals. Inevitably, the countercultural rock festival, like the indoor rock concert, was transformed into an elaborately produced event. When Nikki Farr organized the third, and largest, of the Isle of Wight festivals in 1970, his model was Woodstock, and intended similarly to cash in on peripherals (there were eight film crews under the supervision of an American producer, Murray Lerner).[18]

A catalogue of American rock bands who toured Britain in the late sixties and early seventies for concerts and festivals would reveal a significant traffic from West to East.[19] *Every* British band of any ambition, however, aspired to American tours. In part because that was where the money was, where the market was larger, and where the variety and deep pockets of the U.S. recording industry and the promotional media offered more opportunity to break into the big time than monolithic EMI and BBC. But it was also because rock in Britain engaged a smaller, sometimes more fickle, audience. Even bands that succeeded in achieving a break-through in Britain, like, say, the Moody Blues with their first album in 1967, immediately looked to confirm their success in America (the Moody Blues toured the United States in October of 1968).

> If we had stayed in England we would have broken up because all it did was sap our confidence and all America does is build up our confidence . . . . We are getting some respect now . . . . I get depressed when I go home, it's not dead, it's still.[20]

British rock musicians often seemed to have regarded the home scene as not only insufficiently rewarding but thinly derivative of that in the United States; serious rock musicians were drawn to the sources of inspiration and to "where it was happening." Born in 1945 of an English mother and a Canadian airman father, Eric Clapton, like much of his generation, listened to American rock'n'roll and rhythm and blues on the radio from the age of ten or eleven—and his first album was Buddy Holly's *The Chirping Crickets*. At school he became "obsessed" with a book on the United States he won as a prize and, hearing and seeing American folk, jazz, and rock'n'roll musicians on TV, was "driven by the thought of becoming . . . Buddy Holly, Jerry Lee Lewis, Little Richard and Gene Vincent." A brief and unsuccessful stint at the Kingston College of Art was followed by attachment to the blues scene in the coffeehouses of Soho in the early sixties. Buying an American electric guitar on the hire-purchase plan in 1963 he joined his first band, Rhode Island and the Roosters, before moving on to the emerging Yardbirds. Playing with Sonny Boy Williamson, however (the Yardbirds were his backing group), Clapton was swept away by the demanding and disciplined Chicago blues tradition and had to "almost relearn how to play."[21]

The Yardbirds were promoted by the proprietor of a club in Richmond, Giorgio Gomelski, who was also involved in promoting American blues. The genre was popular in the early sixties, and a young musician forming his own style could experience the sound in a variety of venues: there was an American Blues Festival in Croydon in 1963 or a Rhythm and Blues Festival in Birmingham and a fourth annual National Jazz and Blues Festival at Richmond the next year. Planning a U.S. tour, the Yardbirds signed with Columbia Records in December of 1964, but Clapton, ever a purist, left them to escape what he regarded as their increasingly commercial character. And so on to the influential band Cream in 1966, by which time he was living with three American girls in Ladbroke Square and driving a 1938 Cadillac Fleetwood. In 1966 he heard Hendrix play in London and jammed with him: he "totally blew me away." Now sporting a Hendrix Afro, for Clapton, the "big goal of course was to line up a visit to the United States."[22]

Eric Clapton was of course uniquely qualified to succeed in the transatlantic scrum of would-be musical stars surfing the narrowing distance between London and the American East and West coasts. Many others tried. Noel Redding, for instance, was born the same year as Clapton in Folkstone, Kent, listened to American music on Radio Luxemburg ("[T]his changed my world"), and formed his own band while at art school, touring American G.I. bases in Germany at age sixteen. He also heard Hendrix in 1966. The Experience was formed that year, Redding joined as a bass player, and they toured the United States, playing at the Monterrey Pop Festival and at Fillmore West. San Francisco was a revelation—the atmosphere was so much less "boxed-in" than in Britain, though back in Britain they were lionized after the release of the classic Hendrix album *Are You Experienced*, "a watershed of psychedelic rock." There were appearances on the BBC—the Top of the Pops, the David Frost show, and a jamming session with Stevie Wonder, by which time Redding himself was, like Clapton and Mick Farren, sporting an extreme afro. In 1969, however, increasingly overshadowed by Hendrix's pyrotechnics, Redding left The Experience and thereafter wandered with diminishing success through a number of other bands.[23]

Jimi Hendrix played at the third Isle of Wight festival in 1970 just weeks before he died in London. His "arrival" in the emerging psychedelic rock scene in London had been sudden and compelling: "Jimi played that night [25 November 1966] what everybody wanted to play [and] looked that night the way everybody wanted to look. His performance was to have a huge effect on the whole London scene." Paul Gilroy has observed that in Britain "Hendrix was reinvented as the essential image of what English audiences felt a black American performer should be: wild, sexual, hedonistic, and dangerous," where the frizzy style of his bouffant afro became a symbol of visual revolt among countercultural youth. However much the roots of Anglo-American rock lay in blues and jazz, few of its stars in the United States—and none in Britain except Hendrix—were drawn from, or particularly able to speak to, the African-American/West Indian-British communities. Though Hendrix personally was apolitical, in his appearance and in his subversive assault on the American national anthem (at festivals on both sides of the Atlantic) he was a bridge to another transatlantic traffic that marks the era: the coming to London of black liberation in its American, afro-sporting, leather-gloved Black Power guise.

Joe Boyd, on the other hand, credits "a British tradition of artifice" for Hendrix's guitar-burning antics. For his part, Hendrix was concerned to maintain something of British fusion during his short career: for the iconic "Hendrix at the Fillmore" poster advertising his first appearance in San Francisco, he insisted on London psychedelic vanguard artists David English and Nigel Weymouth, and for his second tour in spring of 1968 he brought along Mark Boyle and Joan Hills to do the light shows.[24]

By the end of the decade, some, most notably the young music critic Nik Cohn in 1969, complained that psychedelic Pop-on-acid had abandoned British Pop's origins in gutsy American rock'n'roll aimed at working-class British teens: "[P]op is all teenage property.... [I]t's about America, its about cities and noise, but right down to it, it's all about Coca Cola." But Cohn's criticism of a counterculture that "wallowed" in art and poetics as insufficiently "real" seems perverse. Mick Farren, whose band explored just those arty elements deplored by Cohn, though in his case borrowed not from British art-school bohemia but from New York, nonetheless echoed some of Cohn's charge a few years later in his influential essay in *NME*, "The Titanic Sails at Dawn," that rock music had to get back to the street. Both would endorse the popular (not entirely convincing) reading of Seventies Punk as an authentic return to rock origins. Unlike Cohn, however, Farren's perspective is from within the Anglo-American radical counterculture and focuses, not on musical style, but on the scale and commercial organization of overproduced stadium rock that turned youth from participants into consumers, and a music that had become isolated from its audience.[25]

That much had been lost in the mass concert's transition away from "spontaneity, sharing and cooperation," that countercultural "style" had become disconnected from countercultural values as an especially American kind of commercial exploitation and media organization co-opted the amateur, participatory, smaller-scale scene, was a common early-seventies complaint. Such a view undervalues the degree to which the large, mass venues of the late sixties and early seventies operated at some level to open out the counterculture of rejectionist, alternative society radicals to something that was accessible to a much larger part of the under-thirty population than those relative few who could squeeze into the funky darkness of UFO. The mass commercial venues in fact retained some participatory meaning, some sense of a self-made new generational subjectivity; something of the radical assault on conventional attitudes toward authority, elitism, and sexual morality was preserved in the celebratory mass gatherings of young people enjoying themselves largely outside the structured, legal inhibitions of straight society. This doing-your-own-thing sense may in fact have been more subversive in Britain than in the States, where middle-class morality had long coexisted with an extreme individualist libertarianism, and where there was hardly any tradition (outside of Boston) of cultural authoritarianism.

Mick Farren and other countercultural idealists misread the depth and endurance of what proved to be a phenomenon in its last stages when he claimed in 1972, in *Watch Out Kids*, that "[r]ock festivals [are] putting down roots and growing into new cities."[26] (Three years later ITV filmed the violent denouement of the third "Free People's Festival" at Windsor as it was closed down by the police; the next year its radical organizer, Ubi Dwyer, and 219 others were arrested.) And yet the larger, less confrontational (or less aggressively policed) commercial festivals—at Reading or Knebworth—continued to draw mass audiences. The view that these events, contained and policed in large parks or commons or in the distant countryside and routinized as summer entertainments, served increasingly as weekend "carnival" that legitimized weekday routines and values, is surely too cynical. In Britain, if not in the States, the festival retained some vigor as a form that possessed the power to contest the prejudices of established society—as the Rock Against Racism concerts at the end of the seventies would demonstrate.

LIBERATION AT THE ROUNDHOUSE

If the British counterculture was born among the regimented seats and aisles of the Royal Albert Hall and, as community, was most widely celebrated in the summer grass and mud of the London parks and rural countryside, another, more modest location in the capital was where it found a kind of institutional home. For some years after 1966 a large, circular, long-disused Victorian railway engine shed at Chalk Farm in north-west London was where the alternative culture came as close to being ritualized in all its anarchic diversity as anywhere, where a liberated recreational hedonism was conjoined with the didactic radicalism and utopianism of Underground theater, film, art, and politics, and where the freaks and heads of the street hippy scene rubbed shoulders with Pop-art celebrities and the "with it" liberal elite of Hampstead and Islington.

Used as a warehouse for gin in the 1950s, the Roundhouse's unconverted, damp, semiderelict interior and its narrow, awkwardly situated street entrance (the wide shed doors looked out onto the railway lines) reduced its speculative value. When in 1964 it was listed as a building of architectural and historic interest (further reducing its commercial potential), the lease-holders offered it to Arnold Wesker's Centre 42, founded in 1960 to encourage working-class and trade union arts. The idea of a kind of people's venue found support from some on the left, but converting the vast Victorian structure to serve Centre 42's purposes entailed significant expense. Wesker's overambitious effort to raise money for this purpose had made slow progress when Jim Haynes called him in late summer 1966 about using the

Roundhouse for an extravagant launch party for the new Underground paper *IT*. Like *Wholly Communion* at the Albert Hall, the *IT* party on 11 October 1966 is one of the defining moments in the history of the British counterculture. Jack Henry Moore helped provide the technical know-how to create the kind of sound and lighting system the psychedelic bands Pink Floyd and Soft Machine needed, and PR was handled by Haynes and Miles (just back from the States). Modestly priced 5s. tickets were sold at Indica bookshop.[27]

In spite of the damp and cold and the lack of adequate toilet facilities, the night was a famous success that, according to Marowitz, left "a sense of the Underground consolidating its power." Perhaps as many as 2,500 exotically dressed people swarmed into the hash-smoke filled vastness to hear three bands playing simultaneously under a dome illuminated by a pulsating psychedelic light-show. There were face-painted hippies and arts glitterati, Marianne Faithful (in a very short nun's habit), Paul McCartney (dressed as an Arab), the film director Antonioni, Peter Brook, and the tripping half-naked who danced around a 1950s Cadillac (from Robert Fraser's gallery) that had been painted in psychedelic stripes by New York interior decorators Binder, Edwards, and Vaughan. Pink Floyd blew the fuses.[28]

Haynes's and Moore's public relations happening was an advertising coup, and the first issue of *IT* quickly sold out its 10,000 copies. The success inspired the *IT* board two months later to establish the UFO club in Tottenham Court Road as a means of perpetuating on a regular basis some of the buzz, extending the possibilities of the commercial exploitation of peripherals, and generally cementing together the Underground press, psychedelic rock, and alternative society communities in London. In the event, the party "did as much to establish the Roundhouse as it did the new paper." If the Roundhouse remained an unsettled locus and idea, much of its attractiveness to the counterculture was precisely its shabby noncommercial feel. It hosted temporary or one-off events for a year or so—UFO moved there for a month after being thrown out of its Tottenham Court Road basement. Drama and large-scale musical productions were, just, possible after the Roundhouse received its theater license late in 1967, and subsequently an enlarged fanlike stage and seating. The first theatrical production was Peter Brook's *Themes on the Tempest* in June 1968, followed by a haphazard mixture of experimental and foreign theater. In the summer of 1969 Julien Beck's Living Theater company from New York brought four productions to the Roundhouse, including a drawn-out, four-hour, evening-long confrontation with the audience, harangued by an abusive black actor. The same month the Royal Shakespeare Company's Children's Workshop brought 140 children to present their own "programme on revolution."[29]

The "alternative" idea was sustained by outré and experimental, often American, productions, well into the early seventies (Warhol's "mind-numbing farrago,"

Pork, full of New York in-jokes incomprehensible to a British audience, or Joe Chaikin's Open Theater), and a number of rock bands used the location for a couple of years after 1968 (the Doors, and Jefferson Airplane on their first U.K. tour). But the helter-skelter, often amateur organization of the original countercultural excitement could hardly have been sustained in the face of the financial necessity to get bookings for a difficult space. A rapidly developing noncommercial "free cinema" came to find in the Roundhouse a more expansive space for screenings of often American countercultural film than the back-rooms and basements of avant-garde bookshops or the Electric Cinema Club in Portobello Road. The 1966 *IT* launch party was followed by a six-hour, all-night film rave arranged by the incipient London Filmmakers' Co-op, formally organized the following Monday at Better Books. Many, perhaps most, of the films shown were the work of New York Underground film-makers.[30]

The London Film-makers' Co-op, though an outgrowth of the Cinema 65 film society that met at Better Books, was closely modeled on the New York Film-makers' Co-operative founded in 1961 as an open-screening, open-distribution collective. In 1964/65 the American alternative film-maker Jonas Mekas, instrumental in organizing the New York group, brought a "New American Cinema" tour to Europe. Not only were these American films influential with the small community of British film-makers, but in fact a number of the alternative, noncommercial film-makers in London at this time were themselves American expatriates or visitors, such as Stephen Dwoskin, Simon Hartog, and Andy Meyer, while others, like the Swiss-born Peter Gidal, had studied in the States. In the beginning the LFMC was practically an extension of the New York movement—though Mekas's bald assertion at the time that "we are opening a branch of the Film-Makers' Co-operative in London" may have annoyed some of the forty or so British filmmakers and alternative film enthusiasts who turned up at the first general meeting. Nevertheless, Dwoskin, who at age twenty-five already had a reputation when he came to London on a Fulbright in 1964 and stayed, can be said to have dominated the group in its first couple of years; the first chairman was the American former-communist expatriate Harvey Matusow, who was also involved in the foundation of the Underground paper *IT*; and the first full-time paid secretary, Carla Liss, had come to Britain with Mekas, bringing with her the core of the LFMC's original film library. She also was an effective go-between in ensuring a continuing supply of new American work by influential film-makers such as Stan Brakhage. Another "New American Cinema" tour organized by P. Adams Sitney in 1967/68 re-enforced the dominance of American influence, as did the fact that as late as 1969, though native British film-makers were beginning to develop their own oeuvre, many of the new "British" films were still being made by Americans.[31]

The LFMC followed the *IT* launch screenings at the Roundhouse with two other "vast and memorable" all-night psychedelic light show-rock-and-film events, at the 14-Hour Technicolour Dream at the Alexandra Palace and a "Christmas on Earth Revisited" night at the Olympia, and with irregular screenings at other countercultural or fringe venues such as the UFO, the Jeannett Cochrane Theatre (for a week-long "Spontaneous Film Festival" from Halloween to Bonfire Night, 1966), and at the Roundhouse, as well as their regular weekly shows at the Electric Cinema or, subsequently, nightly screenings at Jim Haynes's Arts Lab. From the beginning there were close personal links with the other Underground arts: Hoppy Hopkins worked at the LFMC and, in 1970, set up TVX, a pioneer group in the art of music and community video. As in the States, the alternative film movement found in the universities—especially during the ferment of the last years of the decade—a receptive audience for radical productions like the American film-maker Lenny Lipton's *We Shall March Again* (on the confrontation between police and demonstrators at Berkeley) or domestic productions like Pat Holland's *The Hornsey Film*, that closely followed the American "newsreel style." In 1968 the LFMC facilitated the circulation of the New American Cinema exhibition around twelve British provincial universities and acquired many of these films for its archive.[32]

By late 1967, however, a rift began to widen within the LFMC between Dwoskin and his friends on the one hand, often Americans or those most strongly influenced by the American distribution co-operatives, who wished to maintain an emphasis on screening and circulation of domestic and foreign (inevitably often American) noncommercial film, and on the other the increasing number of young hopeful British film-makers, often from the London art schools, who were more concerned to encourage and develop facilities and resources for domestic production. The Arts Lab cinema, run by British film-maker David Curtis, became the focus for discontent. By the summer of 1968 Curtis and Malcolm Le Grice and his students at St. Martin's and Goldsmiths were in the ascendancy. Subsequently this displacement of the American Dwoskin and his friends from the center of the movement, the gradual increase of English film as a proportion of those screened, and the de-emphasizing of distribution and screening in favor of production support would be represented as a victory for a re-invigorated *English* cinema in the face of U.S. cultural domination. In fact it is clear that production itself, though increasingly domestic, remained deeply influenced by the Anglo-American Underground.[33]

David Curtis would later rather unconvincingly claim that "the extent to which American work has been a catalyst to English production tends to be greatly overestimated." In his view, the enduring character of subsequent British film production reflects "original and distinctly English impulses" and was in ferment well before British film-makers had "any direct experience of New American Cinema." Without denying the uniqueness of the British context—the importance of domestic film-making traditions and cultural mentality generally, the distinctly British approach to institutional (especially Arts Council and BFI) funding and perhaps audience expectations—it is clear that on one level at least the insistence on a British cultural autonomy in this aspect of the Anglo-American counterculture is, like the very similar protests in the Underground press and the rock music scene, a defensive reaction against the reality of just the kind of cultural dominance and emulation being denied. Curtis himself admits that domestic film-makers could hardly claim ignorance of the American models: there was a constant stream of American visitors to the co-op, and even if important American film-makers were not screened in Britain they were known. Warhol was "reaching even the Sunday colour magazines by the mid-sixties," and Curtis was "prepared to go to New York to try and see what he was on about." He would in fact return with his bags full of U.S. film prints. Similarly, Malcolm Le Grice, who, like Curtis was a graduate of the Slade School of Art, would claim—though he then taught film at both St. Martins and Goldsmiths—that he knew "nothing" about American Underground film when he joined the Arts Lab in 1968. But even were this (however improbably) so, he admits to American influence from the world of Pop art generally—from Jasper Johns and Robert Rauschenberg—and from American free-form jazz and the music of John Cage.[34]

What is clearly true, as in other areas of the counterculture and avant-garde, is that the seventies would see a drifting apart of the Anglo-American, transatlantic moment. The subsequent reaction against cultural domination heightened sensitivity to the charge of being derivative and imitative of American models, but there is little creditable ground to deny an essential American countercultural hegemony. As late as 1971 the film reviewer for *The Times* could still casually observe that "Stephen Dwoskin is widely regarded as the most significant figure in the British underground cinema (though he himself is American)." In the event, though the LFMC turned toward the promotion of domestic British talent, American influence hardly vanished. Simon Hartog continued to work closely with Le Grice and Curtis to combine the distribution and production objectives of the old and new co-op, and important initial funding (£3,000 to buy processing equipment) came from the same American financier, Victor Herbert, who had provided start-up capital for *IT*.[35]

While the dazzling self-indulgence of the *IT* party may have been far removed from Arnold Wesker's dream of a sober, creative, and communitarian workers' culture, in the following year major events held in what was now a highly symbolic location both refocused attention on the contribution of the arts to the antiwar movement and to radical social reconstruction and endorsed and confirmed a general late-sixties countercultural turn toward militancy and activism. In June of 1967 the Roundhouse hosted an "Angry Arts Week" that brought together protest folk and rock groups, plays, poetry readings, and left-wing, often American, film—in apparent emulation of similarly named events in the United States.

There had been an Angry Arts Week in February at New York University, as part of a "Folk and Rock Marathon." The Roundhouse event, in fact, was organized by the Stop-It Committee of antiwar Americans in London as "a demonstration of the artistic community against American intervention in Vietnam"; there were readings by Harold Pinter, appearances by antiwar actors Paul Scofield and Peggy Ashcroft, and a "confrontation panel" in which Tariq Ali debated Kingsley Amis and Peregrine Worsthorne. The week concluded with a midnight concert by the Yardbirds, Procol Harum, and the Social Deviants.[36]

The next year a major conference at the Roundhouse followed the occupation at Hornsey College of Art in the summer of 1968. The "Movement for Rethinking Art and Design" represented students and faculty from scores of different colleges and endorsed much of the radical Hornsey program. Such events were often accompanied by radical documentary film, either imported from the States or deeply influenced by the American "Newsreel group" work. Following the lead of the LFMC, a number of workshops and collectives sprang up to encourage the distribution of American film and the production of similar material in Britain. Cinema Action, a militant collective that emerged after the events of 1968, attracted David Adelstein and other radicals from the L.S.E. (the L.S.E. rebellion itself was the subject of a film, *Student Power*, directed by an American post-grad student from Cornell, Daniel Schechter; Schechter, like other American antiwar, left-wing militants in London, was a member of the Stop-It Committee, whose Angry Arts Week had been an expensive affair). When Ellen Adams and her husband, Richard Hamerschlag, from Boston, organized an Angry Arts Film Society and Cinema Club in the spring of 1968 to help pay off its debts, the group became the distributors for New York "Newsreel" films in the U.K. and produced a radical film of their own after the last of the great demonstrations at the American embassy—*End of a Tactic?*, an agit-prop documentary with commentary by Henry Wortis. In 1970 the Angry Arts group set up a distribution and production arm on a more permanent basis called Liberation Films.[37]

The most ambitious radical event staged at the Roundhouse was the Dialectics of Liberation—Towards a Demystification of Violence conference held 15–30 July 1967, a countercultural moment that celebrated not only the case for liberated self-expression but also a politics of aggressive engagement with the institutions of destructive twentieth-century capitalist modernism. Organizers were inspired by the radical antipsychiatry of R. D. Laing, the sexual/social repression theories of Herbert Marcuse, and utopian ideas of a free antiuniversity. Laing and his younger colleague David Cooper, and from New York Joseph Berke and Leon Redler, arranged a week of seminars, lectures, and "interactions" that saw Ginsberg back in town, with Julian Beck of the Living Theater, Timothy Leary, Lucien Goldman, Paul Goodman, and Marcuse, who would speak on the repressive tolerance of the bourgeois state and the need for a "revolution in consciousness." Entertainment was organized by a New York conceptual ("happenings") artist and choreographer, Carolee Schneeman. In addition to the professional psychologists, there was, both on the platform and in the audience, a substantial American presence—including nomads like Emmet Grogan, a twenty-five-year-old from Brooklyn, discharged from the U.S. Army for "craziness" before moving to the Haight-Ashbury to join the San Francisco Diggers and the San Francisco Mime Troup (Laing said he wanted to reform the encounter between doctor and patient into "a kind of improvisational theatre"); and the flotsam generally of the countercultural London "tribes" who drifted in "caught on the smoke of rumour." Pot smokers lounged on the upper deck; the Underground press was for sale or free for the taking along with pamphlets by Ginsberg and books by Marcuse and Laing.[38]

Ronnie (named for the Anglo-American actor Ronald Colman) Laing's approach to madness was rooted in American academic and clinical sources. He first visited the States in 1962, and again in 1964 when he renewed his acquaintance with Joe Berke (whom he had met in London), and was introduced to Leon Redler and Allen Ginsberg. A transatlantic network of such associations, and a scatter of expat Americans drawn to Laing in London (such as the author Clancey Sigal, a radical Jew from Chicago who had fled the United States in the fifties and had attached himself to the British New Left) formed the basis for the Philadelphia Association, an instrument for putting into practice Laing's evolving ideas on "madness" as a kind of healing process that needed to be allowed to take its own course with minimal intervention. In tune with the counterculture's search for personal authenticity, the Kingsley Hall project encouraged, with mind-expanding substances, the discovery of the "true self." It also became an "in" place where left-wing radicals, poets, painters, and performers might be found mixing with the schizophrenic patients along with an "American invasion" of clinicians and academics from New York and California, a mecca for, especially, American visitors who "took a taxi straight from the airport . . . a hallowed shrine of the counter-culture movement." In October of 1966 Laing went back to the States again to attend a conference in Philadelphia that may have served as a catalyst for the Dialectics of Liberation conference in London the following year. By 1967 he was prepared to believe that the radical youth counterculture was engaged in "one of the most hopeful things . . . *a total dissolution of the old egoic consciousness*" through "Acid Tests, Be-Ins, Happenings." Usually reluctant to let himself be drawn into political action, the next year Laing nevertheless addressed the students at Hornsey.[39]

While the Roundhouse event celebrated Laing's radical critique of the psychiatric diagnosis and treatment of schizophrenia, the "antipsychiatry" theme was congenial to and indeed itself floated in the larger contexts of the anti–Vietnam War movement (the dehumanizing of the Vietnamese enemy) and of the counterculture generally (with its promised liberation, at least in the prosperous "First World," of the creative self). If participants saw themselves as an Underground vanguard of an inner change—Marcuse's new consciousness—that sprang from the interiority of the counterculture as personal liberation and transformation, there was recognition of the "dissociation of liberation on the mass social level . . . and liberation on the level of the individual" and the need to "effect some union between the macro-social and micro-social, and between 'inner reality' and 'outer reality.'" This, however, was easier said than done, and there was an uncomfortable clash, as Sheila Rowbotham has observed, between countercultural celebration—Ginsberg chanting the Hare Krishna, the nomadic youth who camped out on the floor of the Roundhouse to enjoy music and pot—and "a politics of anger [that] was already sweeping through the North American New Left." If there were calls for cultural guerrilla warfare, others meant something more tangible.[40]

Though the conference hardly dealt directly with issues of sexual oppression (of women and homosexuals), some of the issues raised, especially those dealing with domination and the family and internalization, were of deep interest to both emerging radical feminism and Gay Liberation. Rowbotham found it "a peculiar collection of the incompatible and reluctant forces of liberation" and "experienced a severe sense of dislocation throughout." What helped bring things into focus for her and perhaps many others were not the seminars and academic lectures but the remarkably powerful address by the American Black Power leader Stokely Carmichael—invited onto the program "to bridge the gap between theory and practice." Indeed, Carmichael's call for self-liberation, by violence if necessary, had a considerable impact. It informed with an American racial perspective the Black, Women's, and Gay Liberation movements that emerged in Britain too at the end of the sixties.[41]

PART III

Freedom

———•◆•◆•———

Freedom . . . freedom . . . freedom . . . freedom . . . freedom . . .
freedom . . . freedom . . . freedom.
    Sometimes I feel like a motherless child . . . . Sometimes I feel
like a motherless child . . . .
              —Richie Havens's opening performance, Woodstock, 1969

In the summer of 1967 Angela Davis, who had been reading philosophy with Theodor W. Adorno at Frankfurt, returned to the United States via London in order to attend the Dialectics of Liberation conference where her mentor, Herbert Marcuse, was to speak. She stayed with Robin Blackburn "in the immigrant slum of Notting Hill" and visited black neighborhoods with Stokely Carmichael and Michael De Freitas (Michael X). Far from finding Black Power inappropriate and inauthentic in this "local context,"

> I was struck by the degree to which West Indian communities in London were mirror images of Black communities at home . . . . I learned more about the new movement [in the United States] there in London than from all the reading I had done.[1]

The transatlantic counterculture, with its urban zones of anarchic liberation and its project of a radical reclamation of community and self, was as much a matter of festive performance as Marcusian-scripted ideology. "Identity through performance" strongly characterized the radical "politics of the personal" that evolved out of the sixties counterculture—from Black Power to Radical Feminism and Gay Liberation. If the Anglo-American Pop and counterculture, however, had exhibited a degree of circularity, of back-and-forth mutual influence, the angry liberationisms that followed have usually been seen as explicitly *American* phenomena that traveled uneasily across the ocean. Their common project to engage self-hatred and so to reclaim and affirm the "real" self was a politics of identity that, it has been argued, drew powerfully from an especially American model of hyphenated ethnicities. Moreover, there was little reflux from East to West; there was no "British invasion" of black, feminist, or gay rebellion.

As with revisionist accounts of the sixties counterculture, liberationism has been positioned firmly in the history of those times, both marginalized as the story of a small minority and localized in certain spatial communities (San Francisco, the Village, Notting Hill). The search for an account that is objectively distanced from that of participants has led a successor generation of scholars to contain it within a closely circumscribable era—a narrative closed with tropes of failure and fragmentation. This diminished and diminishing perspective, what Kobena Mercer has called a "selective erasure" of the recent past, draws largely from a focus on the artifacts, inflated rhetoric, unrealistic objectives, and fragile institutions of the liberationist movements qua political phenomena. In the United States, Doug Rossinow's much acclaimed study of the New Left in Austin, Texas, following the nineties' fashion for localizing the global, ends by confirming the conventional view that radical utopianism "nurtured only a small subculture . . . . [By] the early 1970s the young radicals passed over the horizon of authenticity into marginality." Such distancing has been even more insistent in Britain, where, however, late-sixties and early-seventies radicalism did have a more tangible political legacy than in the States. If Trevor Pateman's 1972 hopeful contention that militancy was "spreading into new areas" was overdrawn, his claim that "off the campus, our disaffection increasingly takes the positive form of serious political work in the communities" was accurate enough. The most enduring legacy of liberationism can be best found in the new subjectivity of racial and sexual minorities and women, aggressively counterpointed in the seventies to the neoconservative project of the "remythification" of Britishness. As an anonymous black British woman later put it, "That's when we began to come into our own . . . . I went to my first Black meeting," or as the lesbian feminist Elizabeth Wilson later observed, "It was not until I became involved in radical political movements that I ever felt I lived fully in the present or was fully myself."[2]

The following three chapters will offer as full an account as possible here of the three major examples of the radical politics of identity in this period in an attempt to challenge the dismissal of liberationism in Britain as an inauthentic import, alien in local contexts and doomed to have only a marginal and temporary influence. British blacks, women, and homosexuals were challenged by American radicalism at a critical cultural-political moment, and it is important to explore the ways in which external inspiration met local context—how deeply American ideology and practice penetrated, among whom, and how elements of the project of reclamation persisted thereafter. The vocal minority of British liberationists left a wider and more enduring legacy than their unstable politics and institutions would suggest. What William Van Deburg has said of the American Black Power movement's legacy might apply to transatlantic liberationism as a whole: it "was not exclusively cultural, but it was essentially cultural" and served as "a therapy of collective identity" for many far beyond the relatively few activists who embraced its separatist political solutions.[3] The early seventies, it now seems clear, saw a significant, and in many subtle ways irreversible, shift in "attitude" that endures in the unself-conscious mentality of successor generations of British blacks, women, and gays.

CHAPTER 7

Anglo-American Black Liberation

American race relations have long played a prominent role in the special relationship, and in the complicated ways British people, white and black, have sought to use knowledge and interpretation of American experience in their own domestic contexts. In early and mid-nineteenth century Britain, as the Royal Navy took on the task of policing the abolition of the slave trade and after Parliament had (at least nominally) abolished slavery throughout the empire, the persistence of the "peculiar institution" in the United States often served to affirm a superior sense of cultural distance from their American cousins. British visitors to the American South, indulging in what had become a commonplace form of voyeuristic tourism by the 1850s, brought back their own narratives of difference, while American abolitionists in Britain, like, famously, the former slave Frederick Douglass or Harriet Beecher Stowe, raised their voices in evangelical chapels and town halls across the country.

Subsequently, however, the narrative of American race relations came to play differently. Rather than confirming distance, it compelled a reading of Anglo-American similarity, as the optimistic theorizing about racial equality of the earlier abolitionists yielded to the on-the-ground problematic of sustaining white hegemony in a post–Civil War, post–Sepoy Mutiny, post–Jamaican rebellion world. By the turn of the century, Jim Crow America, though still containing a subtext of American populist crudeness that was flattering to British sensibility, harmonized with the intellectual and institutional entrenchment of racism in the empire. At the level of popular culture, this closeness was entrenched by transatlantic entertainments like the minstrel show and popular fiction. If American blacks like W. E. B. Dubois before the First World War or Paul Robeson in the thirties and after occasionally, as visiting agents for a more liberal reading of "race," found an audience, their influence was restricted chiefly to an intellectual left, while cultural imports that reached a larger market—jazz or Hollywood films—by and large served to perpetuate in Britain a caricature of American black culture.

The Second World War and its aftermath, however, had a significant impact on

British, as on American, race relations. For the British, the war both greatly accelerated an irreversible erosion of white supremacy out in the empire and brought to domestic Britain a significant black presence: not only thousands of nonwhites from the West Indies but also a dramatic U.S. "occupation" that included by D-Day more than 130,000 black U.S. servicemen (it also saw the importation of the racist, segregationist belligerency of white Southern American GIs).[1] If some in government were concerned "brown babies" and G.I. racism would inform and animate domestic British racism, the general public apparently regarded the presence of the American blacks as more of a curiosity than cause for apprehension.

The postwar era, however, saw both a significant permanent nonwhite immigration to the United Kingdom from the New Commonwealth and, in the United States, the galvanizing of a newly energized movement for civil rights and self-empowerment among largely segregated black communities. This simultaneous emergence of a numerous nonwhite British population, concentrated in deprived urban areas though not quite ghettoized in the American sense, and American black activism created by the late 1950s a fertile ground for transatlantic exchange, albeit a mostly one-sided one in which American race relations, black culture, and policy were drawn upon by British policy-makers, media, bigots, and the nonwhite new British themselves. When racial violence came in 1958, in the Notting Hill area of London and in the midlands city of Nottingham, the anti-immigration right was quick to draw comparisons with the unfolding confrontation in the United States, and the press was still drawing such cautionary parallels five years later during the bus boycott in Bristol.[2]

In the sixties, America's convulsion over civil rights and Black Power and its televised urban disorder offered an even more compelling text for a newly multicultural urban Britain. Those most receptive to the idea of a special American-British parallelism were academics who dominated the race relations industry that came to flourish among the sociology faculty of the new universities and the official bodies and nongovernmental boards and institutes they and the liberal great and good populated in the sixties. Concerned whether Britain would develop a "colour problem" similar to that in the States, their policy-oriented work often tracked and replicated that of American scholars similarly engaged in advancing integration and social harmony. Though some of these drew, like John Rex, on personal Commonwealth experience, the theory and methodology often derived directly from American work. Many also had significant American connections. For instance, the wealthy, well-connected Liberal, the Hon. Mark Raymond Bonham-Carter, chairman of the Race Relations Board from 1966 to 1970, had spent a postgraduate year at the University of Chicago (on a Commonwealth Fund Fellowship) before marrying a daughter of the American magazine publisher Condé Nast. In November 1966 he set out on a fact-finding tour of the United States and Canada "to discover what lessons we could learn from North American experience in preventing discrimination against minority groups." He was especially interested in the relevance of the recently instituted Equal Employment and Civil Rights Commissions for the British Race Relations Board. On the academic side, Hugh Russell Tinker, politics professor at the School of Oriental and Asian Studies before becoming director of the Institute of Race Relations in 1969, had taught at Columbia University. On taking up his post at the institute he too set off for the States to make useful contacts and recruited an academic with considerable experience in the United States, Robert Mast, to his full-time staff.[3]

By the late sixties, partly in response to Black Power criticism, race relations academics on both sides of the Atlantic were driven to re-examine an "objective" social science that was outside the phenomenon it studied and that viewed non-white communities as passive "victims" of prejudices their problematic growth inspired. In February 1971, the Institute on Race Relations, a target for militants demanding an end to the dominance of white scholars and liberal philanthropists, held a conference to compare U.S. and British responses to "minority demands"—that is, implicitly to shift focus away from racial prejudice toward a better understanding of those discriminated against as actors rather than silent victims. Convened by Mast, who had studied "urban conflict" in Pittsburgh, and funded by grants from the Ford Foundation and the cultural attaché at the U.S. embassy in Grosvenor Square, the conference included an equal number of British and American participants. There was a general acceptance that in both countries "the respective race industries" were dominated by liberals who "have a vested interest in racism." Within months the director and white board members would depart as the institute was redefined directly to represent the black community and redirected toward a more aggressive, grass roots black activism. The report, when published in *Race Today*, was prefaced with a photo of Malcolm X and his call for *self*-liberation: "By any means necessary to free our people."[4]

The originating assumption for Mast's conference, as for liberal scholarship generally in the sixties, was that British and American societies were significantly analogous. These assumptions were, ironically, shared by some of the sharpest British critics of black immigration and liberation who, like the popular press generally, drew on American sources in attacking the left's racial equality agenda. Beyond the higher journalism, populist anti-immigration politicians, from Peter Griffiths in the 1964 Smethwick by-election to Enoch Powell in 1968 and beyond, deployed a more apocalyptic rhetoric that drew on a dystopian reading of American society in the sixties in their attempts to foster an urban and suburban white backlash in Britain. Though constituency race-baiting may have been deplored by the national press, their own sensational focus on the "crisis in American society" and often-repeated assertions that America today was Britain's future ("[T]he prevailing cultural winds are carrying the same challenges and threats across the Atlantic to Europe")[5] served to create a climate that encouraged both right-wing attacks on further immigration *and* integrationist solutions that might prevent the development of ghettoes of the aggrieved (through an assimilation that was itself viewed as the death of black communities by late-sixties militants). Enoch Powell's notorious speech in Birmingham playing the race card exploited precisely the media-amplified threat of American urban violence, just as the Labour government modeled their ameliorative legislation on American Civil Rights acts to block Britain's spiral into American-style race war.

Beyond the academic race-relations experts, the anti-immigrationist politicians, and the often sensationalist press, the United States also provided a complicated race-paradigm for many black British themselves. While some black intellectuals were no doubt influenced by francophone African affirmations of *négritude* in the fifties, Fanon's texts on the mentality of the colonized, or a specifically West Indian understanding of colonialism, they were also closely attuned to events in the States because these were easily accessible to them via personal contact and the transatlantic mass media. In the sixties and seventies a new generation found in American "black pride" a source of inspiration and anger, and in black American style—absorbed not only from television images of black American radicals but also from black American music, slick American publications like *Ebony*, or the "blacksploitation" *Shaft* films—ways of self-creation and self-affirmation.[6]

To what extent, then, do the sixties and early seventies generally, and the late-sixties experience of black liberationism especially, constitute a transatlantic "moment" for black Britain? The issue is not merely whether there were some in Britain who were prepared to find in the media-amplified voices of Malcolm X or Stokely Carmichael something instructive and relevant in an era marked, as Douglas Haynes has observed, by "a crisis of white supremacy in the Anglo-American world." The narrative of black activism in Britain has tended to play down the *long-term* relevance of American liberationism in the very different local contexts of Britain and to confine its impact among an unrepresentative minority of imitative militants like Michael De Freitas. We need, however, also to look beyond the activists to those many ordinary folk who, like the anonymous black woman interviewed years later, found in Angela Davis a "powerful influence" and threw out their hot combs and bleaching creams. For some years after Black Power seized the headlines, something of its style and rhetoric and a memory of its iconic leaders continued to work its way down into a younger generation. It was an identity-affirming resource that was available not only in local left-wing black political caucuses but also more generally in some complicated way as a part of popular black street culture: "It has become almost standard practice now," as Ken Pryce observed in 1979 of Bristol's black community, "for teenyboppers to wear Angela Davis and Malcolm X badges, and Black Power badges showing the clenched black fist."[7]

This is not to deny that for many black youth in the seventies it was Jamaican culture, and especially the style and sound of reggae, rather than (or more than) Harlem or Detroit that provided the best available model around which a sense of commonality, whether one was actually of Jamaican heritage or not, was constructed. One must resist, however, the temptation to see this as a matter of choice between alternative identities—one imitative, the other authentic. Beyond the fact that any attempt to separate West Indian and continental American black cultural influences runs into the problem of their own mutuality (the origins of Rastafarianism owed a debt to American pan-Africanists like Garvey, and there was a dense cross-traffic linking the Caribbean with New York), there is clear evidence that many in Britain who sought to reinvest themselves in their Caribbean origins had been prepared, as it were, for this kind of reconstruction or retrieval of self by the barrage of North American influences from the sixties militants to Alex Haley's *Roots*. As Roger Hewitt, writing in the mid-1980s, said (from his experience as a youth worker in London), "[T]he ideas and practices" of American activists from Martin Luther King to Angela Davis had "a direct and indirect impact on the racial consciousness of black British youth." Whatever the cultural differences between the varied communities of nonwhites in Britain and the more homogeneous black culture of the United States, there was, he believed, a "common understanding" of racial prejudice "due largely to the impact of black American experience on black Britain since the 1960s."[8]

The Jamaican-born journalist, broadcaster, and novelist Ferdinand Dennis, who studied sociology at the University of Leicester in the mid-seventies and subsequently spent time in the States on a research fellowship, published a widely read exploration of black Britain, *Behind the Front Lines: Journey into Afro-Britain*, in 1988. Drawing on a series of grass-roots interviews among black British and his own Caribbean-British perspective, he argued that in retrospect the American black rebellion had simply not been "exportable." It was an American phenomenon that was short-lived in Britain, in part, he claimed, because the British black was "far less secure in his Britishness" than the American black in his right to be fully American in a nation of immigrants. This underrates the density and excitement of the Black Power "moment" in Britain. It also obscures the larger, deeper issue of ways in which the American movement, as it was understood in Britain, worked at other levels to, in fact, inspire just that *second generation* reinvestment in ethnic "roots" and diasporic (West Indian or South Asian) consciousness—an indebtedness suggested perhaps in the "Afro-Britain" Americanism of Dennis's own subtitle.[9]

While Dennis was reading sociology at the University of Leicester, the subcultural theorists at the Birmingham Centre for Contemporary Cultural Studies (CCCS), under the direction of the New Left sociologist Stuart Hall (also, like Dennis, Jamaican-born) radically transformed understanding of the settled community of black British youth (no longer "immigrants"). They offered a reading, informed by Marxist semiotics, of local black youth culture that, on the left at least, significantly transcended and displaced the Anglo-American tradition of race-relations scholarship by shifting their focus away from racial exclusion per se to the cultural system within which "race" was embedded—from, that is, the politics of race crisis to the systematized oppositional relationship between the dominant and the dominated within Britain's particular version of late capitalism. Exploring issues of representation and labeling, their work—especially their well-known study of the "mugging" panic of the early seventies, *Policing the Crisis*—on the one hand emphasized the ways in which scholars, public figures, and the press borrowed heavily from American racialized discourse and selectively exaggerated the contemporary crisis in Britain; on the other, they sought a deeper understanding of black youth, as of underclass youth generally, that required a reading of "resistance," not in the political rhetoric of activists but in the "meaning systems" buried in their lives, in modes of expression and style as ways of distinguishing themselves within a system they were impotent to challenge. In this, the black American message of liberation was either relegated to the ephemeral and epiphenomenal or folded into subcultural youth style and performance, where the emerging Rastafarian/reggae phenomenon commanded much more interest. Just as the popular journalists whom the CCCS scholars accused of inciting moral panic had quite quickly in the early seventies turned away from the subversive threat of American-style riot and revolution to the social danger of a home-grown culture of ganga-crazed black muggers, the seventies subculturalists themselves refocused on Rasta ethnicity as youth-subversion via style and performance.[10]

By the eighties the subcultural resistance paradigm seemed played out, as was, more generally, the generational crisis thesis that the sixties had nurtured. The dominant culture/dominated subculture nexus had come to seem rigid and restrictive to some of its own practitioners, such as Hall, and especially to a newer generation (often their students, like Paul Gilroy or Kobena Mercer) of engaged scholars of multiculturalism who were evolving postmodern approaches to a more complex understanding of the construction of identities. Rejecting the message of essential blackness that had resonated through the Anglo-American Black Power movement, some embraced the idea of pick-and-choose hybridity. For much of this new, anthropology-informed work, the determining realm was where culture was actually performed and served specific social purposes. Black culture scholars admitted the importance of transatlantic exchange but were committed to the idea of the primacy of local (British urban) context (Kobena Mercer preserves both readings by emphasizing a temporal shift).[11] If subcultural theory was more interested in the domestic play of class than the kind of identity politics America appeared to be exporting, the postcolonial turn in the scholarship of the eighties and nineties has moved attention away from production and diffusion toward, first, the highly selective appropriation and "cultural translation" of cultural imports by local consumers, and, second, the countervailing global-ism of diasporic communities and the complicated ways postcolonial (that is, postimperial) societies like Britain can be said to have become sites of dialectical contestation and fusion in an identity-dialogue between once-colonized now do-mestic black British and mainstream British. In this, American cultural influence, though acknowledged, is much more extraneous and contingent. While this has proved a valuable way of redressing the cruder assumptions of much earlier work on cultural diffusion, the idea of local agency, if carried too far, risks seriously distorting the special, historical role of hegemonic American cultural influence in the late twentieth century.

Many black cultural studies scholars in the nineties and since have formed their approach on the work of Paul Gilroy, and especially his influential study of *The Black Atlantic*. Born in East London of mixed English and West Indian parentage, he went to the University of Sussex in the mid-seventies after-glow of the student rebellions, and subsequently worked under Stuart Hall at the CCCS as a doctoral candidate. With a particular interest in transatlantic black musicology and the "increasingly novel configurations" that characterize black vernacular culture, his work emphasizes what he famously termed the "double consciousness" involved in trying to be both European and black. Though an oversimplification of the "double consciousness" theme might lead some to narrow the field of cultural dualism to that of white British and black West Indian (with a diasporic sense of exile), Gilroy himself adopted a wider transnational and intercultural per-spective, one that especially preserves the influence of black North American culture, reflecting in part, we are told, his own experience: "When I was a child and a young man growing up in London . . . above all black America contributed to our lived sense of racial self." Black America served then, and continued to serve in the era of hip-hop and rap, as a central circulating source of "political sensibility and cultural expression" that was "reaccentuated in London." With the emergence, however, of the domestic black vernacular of a late-twentieth-century "new generation" both more self-assured in its Britishness but also fragmented and differentiated, the American influence, Gilroy believed, if still "central," was "no longer dominant."[12]

Also of that new generation (or "new ethnicity") of localized and globalized, hybridized British, Claire Alexander, Gilroy's colleague among the sociology fac-ulty at the L.S.E., has pursued a postmodern ethnographic reading of the con-struction of identities among black and South Asian youth that emphasizes a continual process of production, and identity-formation as a "discursive accom-plishment" involving, as Homi Bhabha has suggested, the art of "performance." Consequently ethnicity is neither fixed nor unitary, and subsumes within its imagined bounds a shifting "range of positions, attitudes, and images." Indebted to the work of Gilroy and other postcolonial scholars on the dialectic of diaspora peoples within Western societies, she appears to move well beyond double consciousness to embrace and celebrate a multiplicity of selves. In this world, American black cultural influences serve merely as a reservoir of media-enhanced options for performance, and of the "symbolic boundary markers" of dress and music that enabled the negotiation of a "converging black British vernacular." While such postmodern, postcolonial scholarship has unpacked a rich treasure of symbolic, subtextual meaning in the ways modern British people of mixed or non-European heritage perform, and self-construct through performance, their complex identities, it has unhistorically dismissed tangible evidence of cultural hegemony and has also tended to strip out the *politics* of race (ideology, rhetoric, and personalities). In doing so it has displaced—indeed trivialized—much serious consideration of overtly political transatlantic phenomena.[13]

This chapter will attempt to retrieve something of the density of connections between black America in a decade of dramatic change and Britain at a critical transitional stage from a society of white hosts and black immigrants to one marked by a second generational multiculturalism. Specifically, the following sections will explore the ways in which the politics of American civil rights and American Black Power may have both inspired and complicated the development of the black self in modern Britain by tracing out the density of Anglo-American connections in the sixties but also by suggesting that, in spite of the overt failure of the utopian, separatist vision promoted by Black Power, its impact was deeper and longer-lasting than much scholarship since—whether subcultural theorizing or the more recent turn to a postmodern ethnography of hybridity, "dual consciousness," and identity-through-local-performance—is prepared to acknowledge. Instead of focusing on the short-term fate of the organizational initiatives or the hardly realizable derivative agendas of a handful of Black Power activists, we need to consider how militant rhetoric directly borrowed from the United States helped propel the evolution of a sense of oppositional community, how this "consciousness raising" as it was commonly termed persisted into the early eighties (also deeply informing the parallel feminist and gay movements) and how political liberationism was only a part of an Americanization package that included slang, music, hair-style, dress, and "attitude."

THE AMERICAN CIVIL RIGHTS MOVEMENT IN LONDON

American tourists today looking up at the gothic splendor of the restored west front of Westminster Abbey may be surprised to find directly above the entrance a familiar figure leaning out of his saint's niche, admonitory finger raised, supplicant palm extended, the imposing figure of black America's twentieth-century martyr, Martin Luther King, Jr.[14] For much of the world, of course, King has floated free from his special place in time and become like Gandhi a universal symbol that came to have a potent meaning in places, like South Africa, that

6. Martin Luther King, Jr., at Westminster Abbey. Author's photograph.

he never visited. In Britain, which King did visit—indeed in 1964 he preached from the pulpit at St. Paul's Cathedral—he left a complicated legacy. His passionate nonviolence spoke to the largely white constituency of the CND, which adopted the anthem of his Southern Christian Leadership Conference, "We Shall Overcome." More narrowly, his campaign for social justice in an affluent, suburban America spoke to the New Left in Britain—where there was at least initially less enthusiasm for King's more militant black critics—as well as to those who populated the growing field of race-relations scholars (also largely white). His legacy can be found at an institutional level, in the establishment of the Campaign Against Racial Discrimination (CARD), organized in the immediate aftermath of King's London visits, and in parliamentary legislation patterned directly on U.S. models. Less concretely but more deeply his advocacy of racial equality spoke to leading elements in Britain's black communities as they struggled in the sixties and seventies to find a voice of their own as black British rather than "immigrants" caught between two worlds.

King had been preceded by other black Americans, often Marxists or fellow-travelers like Claudia Jones, who had fled McCarthyite persecution in the fifties. But it was the global reach of U.S. media that most importantly brought his passionate rhetoric and the violent images of American racial confrontation into every corner newsagent's shop and onto British television screens well before King's visit. The Montgomery bus boycott, the Selma marches, King's Nobel Peace Prize, and his Man of the Year appearance on the cover of *Time* magazine made him a familiar figure in Britain, just as the erupting anarchy in American cities and King's own death not only fed an appalled appetite for American tragedy but also entrenched a reading of King as the martyred voice of reason—not least in the following period of Black Power excess. Well into the seventies BBC commemorative programming worked to establish King as the acceptable face of black militancy.[15]

King's movement in the United States became a resource for British blacks campaigning for equal access to jobs and housing: in 1963 the exclusion of West Indians from jobs on Bristol's buses sparked a protest boycott that was, organizer Paul Stephenson claims, directly inspired by King's work in Montgomery. Stephenson, born in Britain to a black West Indian father and white British mother, was Bristol's first black youth officer; he visited America before the Bristol confrontation and left the United States believing that "we in Britain too needed a radical approach to achieve racial and social equality." Special West Indian–American relations were built on personal traffic between the islands and the States, and on an aspirational element; many Caribbean immigrants to Britain most wished to go to the United States and fell back on the "Mother Country" as a pis aller. For these, postimperial London seemed, as Mike Phillips, who followed his parents from British Guyana to London at the age of thirteen in 1956, recalls, "a temporary and inhospitable stopping place" (in 1965 his parents managed to migrate again—to New York City).[16]

Many in the dislocated world of Phillips's youth had felt isolated—besieged in the bubble of a crowded flat and "alone" outside it, and linked to the other diverse African-Caribbeans beyond family and friends by a shared sense of anomie and marginality. Out of this emerged a defensive concept of "blackness" that had "its roots in the experience of the Civil Rights struggle in the USA." In a search for more positive ways of "being black" many found in Martin Luther King and in the more militant movement that followed on his heels, ways of retrieving a sense of worth—through an oppositional engagement with white society: "The era of blackness in the USA seemed to show us a direction. Television gave us a long line of black spokesmen—Dr. King, Malcolm X, the Panthers, Muhammad Ali." Phillips's older brother Ivor followed a common route from the politics of civil rights to the anger of the separatist Black Power movement.[17]

Martin Luther King first visited London in March 1957, en route back to New York after attending the Independence Day celebrations in Ghana (previously the Gold Coast). On his stopover in London, he was introduced to leading literary and political activist members of the black West Indian community—especially the Barbadian-born novelist and Marxist George Lamming and the (less radical) doctor and political activist from Grenada and Trinidad, David Pitt. Some of this community had in fact sojourned in the United States before being ejected or fleeing the threat of expulsion, and were already known to King. The Trinidadian author, Marxist, and pan-Africanist C. L. R. James, who served as King's London host, had lived in the States for twenty-five years before moving to Britain just ahead of a threatened deportation order. King also knew Claudia Jones, another Trinidadian who had immigrated to Harlem as a child and become a prominent community activist there for black women's rights. Deported in 1955, she, too, ended up in London's Notting Hill area, reinventing her own Caribbean identity (for her thirty years in the States she had thought of herself as American) and working to encourage in the aftermath of the Notting Hill riots local black awareness through political activism and the promotion of West Indian culture. A year after King's first visit she launched the *West Indian Gazette* with the help of Marcus Garvey's widow (Garvey, deported from the United States to Jamaica in 1927, spent his last years in London), and in 1959 she helped inaugurate a series of musical programs, "Caribbean Carnivals," that were televised by the BBC, a kind of indoors precursor to the Notting Hill Carnival.[18]

Claudia Jones was also instrumental in organizing a Committee of Afro-Asian-Caribbean Oraganizations "solidarity march" to the new American embassy to coincide with King's March on Washington in August of 1963. King's mass march on Washington, the climactic event in the American civil rights struggle, in fact seized considerable attention on the left generally in Britain. In April Bayard Rustin, who was given responsibility by King for planning the Washington March, had met with the CND leadership in London to discuss a coordination of their efforts. At the Aldeburgh festival in June a Dutch scholar of black poetry, Rosie E. Poole (who had been a visiting professor at Wayne State in Detroit), organized a jazz-and-poetry happening, while others performed poems dealing with the American civil rights struggles, Rosa Parks, and Ma Rainey, "Mother of the Blues." After the triumph of the march, King himself visited at the end of a European tour in September to attend events surrounding the publication in Britain of his book *Why We Can't Wait*; October saw the announcement that King had been awarded the Nobel Peace Prize and another stay in London en route to Norway was planned.[19]

King flew to London with his family the first week of December, preached to thousands at St. Paul's Cathedral, addressed a mass peace rally, and attended a reception with members of Parliament and the cabinet. There were three separate BBC interviews, conducted by the Jamaican-born writer Andrew Salkey. Like many among the West Indian community in London, Salkey found himself "galvanized" by King. Claudia Jones, who had been in regular contact, arranged a reception at the home of Pearl Connor, a black theatrical agent from Trinidad who, with her folklorist/singer/actor husband, that year had established a Negro Theatre Workshop. They discussed "ways and means of assisting [King's] movement.... [We] talked to him about possibilities." There was also a private meeting at Jones's home in Notting Hill where King renewed his acquaintance with David Pitt.[20]

King's visit came in the wake of the passage the previous year of the Conservative Government's Immigration Act, and debate was still swirling around that first piece of restrictive legislation. When he spoke to his British audience about the struggle in the States for civil rights, he also addressed this and other causes for grievance among the West Indian community in Britain:

> As far as housing is restricted and ghettos of a minority are allowed to develop, you are promoting a festering sore of bitterness and deprivation to pollute your national health and create for yourselves a serious situation. Second, equal opportunity for education, training and employment must be made available without regard to class or colour, if the nation is to prosper in spirit and truth. Third, the presence of immigration laws based on colour are totally out of keeping with the laws of God and the trends of the Twentieth Century. It will eventually encourage the vestiges of racism and endanger all the democratic principles that this great nation holds.

As Claudia Jones pointed out in her last editorial for the *West Indian Gazette* (she died shortly after King's visit, and Paul Robeson delivered her funeral oration), much of the commentary on King's address in the British press had, ironically, been to focus on the "threat" of "growing ghettos" rather than racial discrimination. King's public speeches and his more private conversations, however, propelled a movement already under way "to bring together coloured people in the London area" into a formal organization.[21]

The idea for CARD had originated among a group of pacifists and CND supporters that included Marion Glean, a black West Indian Quaker, Michael Randle, former member of the Committee of 100, and Theodore Roszak, the American editor of *Peace News* (Roszak had recently run a series of pieces by immigrant leaders on the topic "Is Race an Issue?"). When Rustin came to town to plan the King visit, Randle and Roszak put him in touch with Glean and they agreed that King's encouragement and involvement would significantly broaden the base for a national pressure group to resist discriminatory immigration policies and to promote antidiscrimination legislation in Britain. In the event King met a group of black spokesmen and activists at the Hilton Hotel, and CARD was formally launched shortly thereafter. Though organizers were mostly black and Pitt served as chairman, white liberals came to exercise a significant voice in CARD's subsequent campaign. For three or four years it was an effective, if later controversially moderate, influence behind the Wilson government's promotion of American-style civil rights and antidiscrimination legislation.[22]

The summer before King's triumphal passage through London, LBJ's government had finally managed to get antidiscrimination legislation past the opposition of Southern senators. The Civil Rights Act of 1964 made racial discrimination in all public places illegal, and required employers to move toward equal employment opportunity under threat of removal of federal funds from projects where hiring discrimination was practiced. It also attacked Jim Crow practices in the South that denied black voters access to the polls. A few months after King's December visit, the Wilson government brought in its own antidiscrimination bill. The British Race Relations Act of 1965 was closely patterned on the American legislation, though more limited in its reach and lacking much effective means of enforcement. It outlawed discrimination in some public places like theaters and the publication of material deemed to stir up racial hatred, but did not extend protection against racial discrimination to either housing or employment. To many it seemed a half-hearted attempt that suggested as much a politique counterbalance to restrictive legislation aimed at reducing nonwhite immigration as a whole-hearted conversion to King's principles of social justice.

Revelations of the inadequacy of the 1965 legislation led to a further Race Relations Act in 1968 that addressed discrimination in housing and employment and gave the Race Relations Board set up under the previous act enhanced powers to investigate and initiate disciplinary action. This had some impact, but on balance the Wilson government's gestures toward an American-style resolution of British racial injustice raised hopes of real improvement but quickly disappointed many British blacks with mixed results at the street level. A more aggressively political and younger, successor black generation was already receptive to the kind of militancy that had begun to challenge King's nonviolent creed in the United States. Black Power, its rhetoric of separatism and its affirmation, not of a race-blind liberal society but of cultural as well as political struggle, followed quickly on the heels of King's message of Christian humility—and was if anything enhanced and confirmed by his martyrdom in 1968. How far did this new model run in Britain?

The British version of the American Black Power movement as a political project (as opposed to its cultural impact) may have been relatively narrowly inscribed within a late-sixties activist minority—though amplified by a sensation-seeking press at the time. Nevertheless, it seems clear that, whether moderate or radical, aware nonwhites in sixties Britain generally, and especially black West Indians, were at least as likely to be influenced by a transatlantic understanding of their grievances in Britain as by a sense of their condition as a postcolonial people.

TRANSATLANTIC BLACK POWER:
AMERICAN MILITANTS IN LONDON

Just two months after King's progress through London en route to Oslo, another, angrier, black American flew in to some considerable media attention. Malcolm X, who had called King "a traitor to the Negro race," had been denied entry in France on 10 February 1965 and returned to London "seething." The next day he delivered a powerful speech at the L.S.E. Malcolm had previously been in and out of the country during King's December visit, promoting his version of black liberation—a combination of left-wing pan-Africanism and the ascetic separatism of the American Black Muslims he had recently abandoned and denounced. If King had become the darling of the white liberal left, Malcolm X spoke to the black street—or attempted to—in terms that had made him notorious, not only in the sensation-seeking press but also among the CND nonviolent respectables who were willing to listen to apocalyptic warnings from (essentially middle-class) black literary exiles like James Baldwin or a preacher's son like King, but who were distinctly uncomfortable with Malcolm's violent background as a thief and drug-addict, his erstwhile Black Muslim fanaticism, and his autodidact's embrace of militant negritude ("black racism") and Franz Fanon's anticolonialist Marxism. Closer to Garvey's "race-first" message than King's humanism, Malcolm's rhetoric had an electrifying effect among at least some of the West Indian intelligentsia (like Jan Carew) and more widely among younger West Indians and Africans in Britain who had come to regard Garvey as "an icon of black consciousness."[23]

Malcolm had quit the Nation of Islam in March of 1964 in order to join, focus, and establish his own leadership of the militant criticism of King's Southern Christian Leadership Conference that some radical American blacks had begun openly to express. Positioning himself to the left of King with a rhetoric that reached widely for the international dimensions of racism and neocolonialism (his mother was from Grenada), his increasingly vitriolic and personal attacks were disdainful of the tactics of King's leadership but also challenged the ame-liorationist, limited objectives of the whole "civil rights" movement as little more than a plea for white acceptance. The centerpiece of his first visit—he also spoke in Sheffield and Manchester on the inadequacy of legislative remedies to en-grained racial discrimination—was a televised debate arranged at the Oxford Union with a moderate Tory MP, Humphrey Berkeley. He delivered to a standing ovation a vigorous call for black people to discard "this wishy-washy love thine enemy approach." Afterward he "talked for hours" in his hotel with "spellbound" young black West Indian and Asian activists who found his sincere, direct, and fixing manner (an "electric personality") infectious; the Guyanese-British nov-elist, poet, and playwright Jan Carew was captivated by the magnetism of his personality in conversation. Malcolm was not feted like King, but his articulate forcefulness guaranteed some exposure in the British media—radio interviews and short pieces in the press—where often his sarcastic barbs were counterposed to the much broader coverage afforded to King. He left London for New York the Sunday King delivered his sermon in St. Paul's Cathedral.[24]

Malcolm X returned in February for a three-day stopover en route to France (there was time for an address to the Council of African Organizations); his expul-sion from France the next day brought him angrily back to London, where, invited by the school's African Society, he delivered a "furious" lecture to an overflow student audience at the L.S.E. He denounced U.S. military support for reaction-ary forces in Africa, the apartheid regime in South Africa, Ian Smith's Rhodesia, and the growing war in Vietnam before bringing his audience back to domestic America and Britain, where black people were conditioned to hate themselves because of the "conqueror's image" of whites in Africa.

> In America, they have taught us to hate ourselves. To hate our skin, hate our hair, hate our features, hate our blood, hate what we are . . . When you make a man hate himself, why you've *really* got it going.

But salvation would come with the realization that "the same pulse beats" in the hearts of black people all over the world. Blacks in Britain and the United States were part of a "global rebellion . . . of the exploited against the exploiter." He was frequently applauded and approvingly told a reporter from *The Times* that "most students are political revolutionaries."[25]

As in December, Malcolm followed his London address with a tour of provin-cial cities where there were significant nonwhite populations. Scheduled to speak in Manchester and Sheffield again, he also delivered an address at Birmingham, following which a BBC camera crew for the "Tonight" program attempted to maneuver him into a media event at nearby Smethwick. This was where the local Tory candidate, Peter Griffiths, had notoriously (and successfully) engaged in a racist campaign in the recent general election of October (his campaign supporters were accused of using the slogan "If you want a nigger for a neighbour, vote Liberal or Labour"). When Griffiths failed to appear, the BBC reporter (subsequently himself charged with "fanning racism") walked Malcolm around town for three hours of in-the-street interviews, commentary, and filming. The footage was not shown, but Malcolm's characteristically blunt and unguarded comments, widely reported, broke through a politeness of discourse common in Britain and energized many younger blacks who were coming to regard race relations liberals as "wishy-washy" and black spokesmen like Pitt (later Lord Pitt) somewhat—to use the American black liberation epithet—"Uncle-Tom."[26]

Malcolm X departed Britain the next day having stirred up a significant brouha-ha, and authorities were both annoyed and concerned about the probable impact of what they regarded as his egregious "race hatred" on race relations in Britain. They had reason to be. Though marginalized in the media as an "extremist" he left a strong personal impression on blacks he met, and his message of pride and resistance would speak powerfully to the coming generation of 1968 and beyond. It is doubtful whether the government would have allowed him a visa had he sought to return; he was in any event assassinated in New York eight days later. But his memory persisted among both the black community and the radical left. The transatlantic traffic in black awareness and militant liberationism was subsequently carried forward not only by the global media as American cities burned, by black style, and black music, but also by other militant spokesmen who traveled to London, especially one who was as powerful an orator as Malcolm X.

Stokely Carmichael (subsequently Kwame Touré), who could speak as a West Indian as well as an American, brought considerable personal charisma to London at a critical generational juncture. The emotive concept of "Black Power," a slogan coined by Carmichael in 1966 that invoked "race pride" and direct action, had already traveled to Britain by the spring of 1967. Its coming not only signaled the rise of new organizations, like the Universal Coloured People's Association, founded in June, and emerging self-appointed black "leaders" who in the late sixties would stridently challenge the custodial patronage of white liberals, but also a generation change from the West Indian literary spokesmen of the Caribbean migration to somewhat younger, less intellectual blacks with roots in the neighborhoods. In this transition, American style and rhetoric were to play a key role, and Carmichael's visit—preceded by media reports of his challenge to King's leadership in the United States—was catalytic.[27]

Carmichael was born in Port of Spain, Trinidad, where he attended school before following his parents to New York at age eleven. Growing up in New York and Washington, DC, he went to Howard University in 1961, was a "freedom rider" that year, and became active in the Student Non-Violent Co-ordinating Committee (SNCC). Arrested repeatedly for antisegregation demonstrating, he grew increasingly scornful of insufficiently militant blacks—calling them "niggers" and "Uncle Toms." By 1966 he was chairman of SNCC and openly began to challenge King's reliance on white support for black liberation. Things came to a head in Mississippi on a "March for Freedom" after the wounding of James Meredith. On 16 June, at Greenwood, Carmichael called for "Black Power" and armed self-defense. The next day King was confronted with antiphonic chants of "Black Power" in response to his own SCLC's chants of "Freedom Now." By the next year Carmichael's fiery challenge to King's nonviolent, color-blind integrationism was being widely commented on in the media, and King himself was moved to lay out his grounds for rejecting Black Power and Black Nationalism in a book titled *Where Do We Go from Here, Chaos or Community?* To which Carmichael (with Charles Hamilton) offered his own response in *Black Power: The Politics of Liberation in America.* Both books were available in British editions the following year (1968).[28]

Carmichael was invited by New Yorker Joseph Berke and the other antipsychiatry organizers of the July 1967 Dialectics of Liberation Conference at the Roundhouse to offer a perspective from the revolution in the street, as it were, on "the demystification of violence," and as a voice not well represented in an event where participants were overwhelmingly white and academic. In fact, Laing, concerned to establish his dominance, and Carmichael "did not hit it off." Though Laing may have been willfully provocative, it is hardly surprising that, in Theodore Roszak's words, "it proved impossible for the congress to maintain more than a stormy rapport" between Ginsberg's chanting the Hare Krishna and Carmichael's call for brothers to use violence (mystified or not) to smash the system. For his part, Carmichael, though dressed in countercultural mode—a silky golden shirt with Chinese collar—and "using his body like James Brown," was characteristically sarcastic about hippies throwing flowers at the police "while they gun you down." He did not, in any event, have high hopes for a venue where white liberals predominated ("We concluded the conference was not going to be worth much"), but agreed to attend in order "to correct disinformation about Black Power"—and no doubt to twit the white academics a little about how the real problem was not about alienation and personal adjustment but real oppression. He also intended to use the trip to reach out to as many of the local black leadership and community as he could pack into a week or two in London ("a perfect opportunity to establish contact and exchange ideas with these emerging forces").[29]

The day Carmichael delivered his main address the audience was, inevitably, mostly young and white. We can take with a grain of salt the report in *The Times* that it was also "substantially American." Carmichael later claimed to recall that there were "but few black or brown faces," though it is unclear if he is referring to the participants ("white liberals interested in theory") or the audience—where, along with some Americans like Angela Davis, there were certainly British blacks present from the recently organized Caribbean Artists Movement as well as more generally the community. A cyclostyled notice had been circulated beforehand in neighborhoods with significant black populations announcing: "Black Eyes. Black Voices. Black Power. Hear Stokely Carmichael at the Round House."[30]

By most reports the twenty-five-year-old Carmichael's address, among those by more mature luminaries like Marcuse, C. L. R. James (the only other black to speak), and R. D. Laing, was a high point of the three-day conference: "exhilarating rhetoric" (Tariq Ali), "historic" (Obi Egbuna), "an awakening" (eighteen-year-old Janet Hadley), "electrifying" and morale-boosting (Dilop Hiro), "fiery" and "genuine"—"for all its suspect morality" (the *Tribune*), and (equally grudgingly) "cool as they come, totally 'hip'" and delivered with "great charisma" (*The Times*). Angela Davis, who had come to hear Marcuse, was transfixed by Carmichael's words, "cutting like a switch-blade, accusing the enemy as I had never heard him accused before . . . . I felt the cathartic power of his speech." He laid out what he called a "system of international white supremacy coupled with international capitalism." Blacks were kept poor by "institutionalized racism" (a concept Carmichael was first to name), not only in the States: "I think you can apply a little of it to London." There were intimations of pan-Africanism as well as a special shared black West Indian–American relationship: "You can keep your Rhodes Scholars, we don't want the money that came from the sweat of our people." There were references to "our martyred brother Malcolm X" and to the work of Franz Fanon (his "patron saint"). Criticized for rejecting the support of sympathetic whites and black moderates alike in the struggle, he turned and, with a sense of dramatic audience engagement would shake his finger at the questioners, asking repeatedly: "What have you *done*? . . . What *have* you done? . . . What have *you* done?" And, while the mostly white audience stomped and chanted "Stokely" and "Black Power": "*You are the descendants of the violent society. Have you stopped it? With all of your flowers, with all of your marches, with all of your love, have you altered it?*"[31]

Carmichael's theatrical rhetoric was not confined to the Roundhouse conference, nor to the sitting rooms of black intelligentsia (he met C. L. R. James, the Barbadian poet, and dramatist Edward Kamau Braithwaite, and, among others, the Trinidadian poet John La Rose, who organized a workshop discussion in Hackney). For a week he spoke publicly to largely black audiences in Notting Hill, Brixton, the Africa Centre in Covent Garden, and elsewhere in the more multicultural parts of the capital—Dilop Hiro claimed in 1971 that he had been "instantly able to establish a rapport with his Afro-Asian-Caribbean audiences"—and often afterward more intimately with local militants like Michael De Freitas. He was also, more than Malcolm X, courted by the British media and interviewed at length for the BBC by Andrew Salkey. His strident rhetoric—about the need for blacks to arm themselves and fight violence with violence, or, quoting Che Guevara, about the efficacy of hatred—drew predictable responses from both the broadsheets and the popular press. In the event, Special Branch also took an interest and may have leaned on Carmichael to leave the country with the threat of formal prosecution for "incitement to racial hatred." In any event, he cut his visit short and departed for North Vietnam (De Freitas, now known as Michael X and an eager acolyte, took Carmichael's place at a planned event in Reading and subsequently was, ironically, the first person to be charged under the incitement to racial hatred provision of the Race Relations Act of 1965). Carmichael was banned from re-entering the country.[32]

The militant version of black self-liberation in the United States retained high visibility in Britain in the following years as a result of the media images of ever more severe social and political dislocation there: the assassinations of King and Bobby Kennedy, the anarchy in the universities, the disruptions and violence at the Democratic Convention in Chicago, and the Black Power salute of American athletes at the Mexico City Olympics were for many in Britain part of a dystopian tableau and cautionary tale. This was the middle-class audience for Jonathan Power's pessimistic prognosis on BBC Radio's Third Programme of what "Black Power" aimed to produce on the streets of America's riot-torn cities.[33] For others, especially among activists in the black communities, there was another reading—one of possibilities.

The faces and voices of black anger and militancy in the media and in print were readily available. By 1968 Carmichael's views could be found in British bookshops in an American edition—indeed Berke (though threatened with prosecution under the Race Relations Act) apparently made tapes of Carmichael's address at the Dialectics of Liberation conference available for sale shortly after the event—and in 1969, as Carmichael became more deeply involved in the Black Panther Party, Penguin brought out a cheap British paperback edition of his *Black Power* text. During the BBC-televised chaos of the Chicago convention, the black comedian Dick Gregory had been in London for appearances on the David Frost show and at other venues, sarcastically lampooning not only "the white folks" but also the nonviolent tactics of moderate integrationist blacks. Meanwhile the revolutionaries of the Black Panther Party also began to receive "dramatic and provocative visibility in the public sphere." H. Rap Brown, SNCC activist and now Black Panther spokesman who often appeared with Carmichael in the States, spoke to British Black Power activists in London in March of 1968, and there were interviews in the British media with Bobby Seale and David Hillyeard. Eldridge Cleaver's prison essays, *Soul on Ice*, appeared in Britain in both abridged and unabridged versions. After Seale's arrest in the United States in March 1970, there was a Black Panther sympathy protest at the American embassy in Grosvenor Square; and when in May fire bombs were thrown at the embassy, the caller claiming responsibility mentioned Seale (and Kent State).[34]

If the American Black Panther revolutionaries did not receive much sympathy from the Marxist left—Tariq Ali, though he published pieces by Stokely Carmichael and Eldridge Cleaver in his collection *New Revolutionaries* in 1969, was deeply suspicious of black nationalism, and the *New Left Review* was not much interested[35]—the press of course found them sensational material. Beginning in March of 1968 *The Times* commenced a six-part series of prominent articles on "Black Man in Search of Power," exploring the theme in Africa and the United States researched by a special "News Team." The third part, "The Fire This Time," dealt with King's "Negro movement in the U.S." and the long summer in the cities to come. The final three sections focused on the threat of "black violence" in London: "Attempts are being made to export features of the urban violence [in American cities] to this country." In these pieces, published on 14, 15, and 16 March, straightforward reportage yielded to a heightened sensationalism.

The central message of the (one assumes white) researchers was that the "tub-thumping visits of two Americans preaching black violence" (Malcolm X and Stokely Carmichael) had "set militant thought alight in Britain." Some "coloured people" in Britain had already armed themselves, and Malcolm X's call for black self-respect had been particularly attractive to "some of the more disillusioned West Indians here"—as was indicated subsequently in the violent "speeches by coloured men at Speakers' Corner." *The Times* guessed there were only about 150 core militants, but the "appeal of what these black politicians preach is astonishingly wide." Threats of armed violence, and especially of assaults on police, were common, and there were rumors that "shadowy Snick [SNCC] supporters" were advocating acts of provocation against both blacks and whites to spark a backlash that would inspire racial violence in the streets: "The News Team has seen no arms, but other evidence tells its own story." The final message, somewhat calmer and with some sympathy for a black British population that was discriminated against and harassed by the police, was that, while there were marked differences between the ghettos in the United States and Britain, where the black population was more diffuse, nevertheless "foreign activists" had increasingly found fertile ground: "The danger is . . . that the pattern forming in America will, like so much else in the way of fashion exported here, encourage imitation," especially among embittered West Indians, "Britain's deep south," who "look towards America for example."[36]

The underground press, as one might expect, presented a rather more enthusiastic message, one that endorsed Black Pride, worked Black Power symbols and slogans into its graphics, and reprinted its rallying manifestos. The first issue of *OZ* (in January 1967) featured a piece by Colin MacInnes on the probable rise of Black Power in Britain following the American model. The black social worker and local activist Courtney Tulloch (whose own Ladbroke Grove-based *Hustler* offered, according to Richard Neville, "an angry, bitchy voice of British black power") guest-edited *IT* in 1967 and contributed to *IT* and *OZ*. And it was an interview with American black militant and comedian Dick Gregory ("I say fuck white folks") that got *IT* busted by the police.[37]

There was, as Stuart Hall observed at the time, some affinity between the hippies and their dropout culture of disillusionment on the one hand and the alienated black militants' turn away from the politics of liberal integrationism on the other. But if, as with the "White Negro" beats in the fifties, the white counterculture of the sixties loved Hendrix and his Afro, appropriated black argot, and reveled in a pot/ganga recreational culture borrowed from the black ghetto, there was not much reciprocal interest. Hendrix himself, the one black superstar closely caught up in countercultural style, was uninterested in radical politics or Black Power—indeed, seemed, surrounded by his groupie blondes, to offer a bundle of clichés drawn from white fear and longing: he was, *Rolling Stone's* John Morthland pronounced, "the flower generation's electric nigger dandy, its king stud and golden calf, its maker of mighty dope music." Another critic called him "a psychedelic Uncle Tom." Dick Gregory may have performed at Jim Haynes's Arts Lab while Michael X hovered marginally around all the major countercultural institutions, but relatively few blacks on the street in Britain had, it would appear, much interest in the California dreamin' counterculture of white hippies. As Courtney Tulloch put it, citing a local Rasta referring to LSD trips, "That's for *them* . . . you've got to discover your African-ness."[38]

Many British blacks did, however, respond to American black liberationism. Short-lived but vocal Black Power organizations sprouted, and the editorial collective behind the Race Relations Institute's *Race Today* (more militant than the parent body) gave the movement on both sides of the Atlantic significant coverage. The journal and its editorial board in fact lay at the heart of the struggle in the institute between moderates and black activists, who finally emerged victorious in 1972 when moderate white board members quit over a controversial piece in *Race Today*. Two years later editorial control was given to a nephew of C. L. R. James and one of the Mangrove Nine, the Black Power–inspired militant Darcus Howe, who was determined to emphasize "grass-roots self-activity." Tariq Ali dismissed these British Black Power militants as mere "mimics" of their American counterparts, irrelevant to a situation that was "totally different from that of the United States," and praised C. L. R. James for having completely "demolished" the black nationalist case that Carmichael had advanced at the Dialectics of Liberation Conference (of course as one of South Asian heritage, Ali's own lived experience had not been within a community that was especially sensitive to the legacies of slavery and black self-hatred).[39]

Without our taking either the self-justification of the contemporary Black Power militants themselves or the cautionary sensationalism of *The Times* at face value, it remains, pace Ali, very much an issue, not sufficiently examined, just how deeply the American Black Power "import" bit into the West Indian community, how its rhetoric may have especially resonated there, and among whom, and for how long and in what ways thereafter. The first step is to remind ourselves of the density of its presence in at least a part of the younger and more activist black leadership of the time. This is not to suggest that the political goals of Black Power separatism could have had any more success among British blacks than they had ultimately in the United States, but rather to look uncondescendingly at that moment with an eye not for its obvious limitations but for its more subtle legacies.

BRITISH BLACK POWER, AMERICAN STYLE

[We] aim to define and encourage a new consciousness among black people . . . pride rather than shame. . . . Black people must redefine themselves, and only *they* can do that.
                                        —Stokely Carmichael, 1967[40]

"Black Power" in Britain, as in the United States, was as much a matter of culture as politics. Its power to command attention among especially younger African-Americans and African-Caribbean British can only be appreciated in the context of a postwar world of advertising and commodities aimed at exploiting black self-hatred—the bleaching creams and hair-straighteners—and in Britain especially a first generation immigrant culture of just getting along through passivity and low profile. King's movement had of course manipulated and built upon a rhetoric of Negro "self-respect," but seemed to many by the mid-sixties—unfairly no doubt—to have defined that respect as respectability, a church-going, upwardly mobile mainstream blackness that mimicked the values, style, and aspirations of the white middle class. In addition to attempting to mobilize a mass following beyond its racial constituency, it also pursued a politics of strategic alliances with white liberals in the social and political Establishment and in the academy both as a practical necessity in securing antidiscrimination legislation but also as an advertisement of the kind of inter-racial cooperation that itself signified victory over racial animosity and prejudice. For those who saw the struggle as one for integration into an inclusive color-blind society for "*all* of God's children," those alliances, then, were illustrative of hands reaching across the racial divide; for others, there was more than a suggestion of the kind of relationship visually available in those nineteenth-century images of kneeling former slave and benevolent philanthropist. It was this ambiguity that the Black Power radicals exploited to significant effect.

Founded after King's December 1964 visit to London, the Campaign Against Racial Discrimination was emblematic of such progressive white-black alliances, a pressure group headed by the moderate West Indian doctor David Pitt that aimed to get American-style legislation onto the statute books as quickly as possible. CARD was to be the first victim of a growing militancy inspired to a large degree, not by the Marxist left represented by C. L. R. James and other West Indian and

South Asian intellectuals, but by the more aggressively race-conscious movement in the United States—its visiting spokesmen and its media-sensationalized messages. Malcolm X's brief but dramatic appearance in Britain in February of 1965 sowed seeds of a more strident form of activism that complicated from the outset the course of CARD and led directly to the emergence of militant, all-black organizations like Michael De Freitas's Racial Action Adjustment Society (RAAS). His message, however, also had significance for a cultural politics of black West Indian awareness that was attractive to some of the younger diaspora Caribbean blacks in London, often postgraduate students connected with the arts and literature of Jamaica.

The Caribbean Artists Movement (CAM) was organized in December of 1966 by the poet E. K. Braithwaite and his wife, Doris, John La Rose, Andrew Salkey, and others upon whom, as with Jan Carew, Malcolm X's visit and subsequent assassination "had a profound effect." There would be symposia, conferences, and annual memorial meetings (in 1969 there was one with the West Indian Students Union that included a filmed documentary of Malcolm's life) celebrating, in La Rose's words, a coming together on the basis of "Our Blackness." Active from 1966 to 1972, CAM paralleled the similar Black Arts Movement in the States and its cultural nationalist playwrights, artists, and poets like Leroi Jones (Amiri Baraka), who emphasized a special black aesthetic, black pride, and black unity. Like the Black Arts Movement and its workshops, conferences, and publications, CAM sought to institutionalize the Black Power message, if with an especially West Indian resonance. In the event, however, it was a somewhat uneasy coalition of those who saw themselves primarily as artists and writers laboring to advance black self-worth and awareness and others who saw their role much more as that of a countercultural agit-prop body enlisted under the quite specific program that transatlantic Black Power seemed to be advancing (at a CAM conference in 1968, La Rose, endorsed by Stuart Hall, claimed Carmichael's visit to have been a "catalyst" for "fantastic development" toward black mobilization in Britain).[41]

Like Jan Carew and some members of CAM, Michael De Freitas had met Malcolm X and also found him personally captivating—they listened, he claimed, to Aretha Franklin records together in Michael's flat and drove around London.

> He wanted to see the areas where black people lived . . . . I took him to Notting Hill and the other ghettos . . . . [He] suddenly asked me: "What are you guys doing in England? And what do you aim to do in the future?" And then he looked me in the eye and added: "What are *you* going to do?"

Malcolm X's speeches, according to Carew, were "sophisticated, brilliant and conciliatory" (and were available in London on Transatlantic records for those who had not heard them in person). But unlike Carew or La Rose and the poets and artists of CAM, De Freitas was a marginal figure, close to the street, with—like

Malcolm X—a rough past as a pimp and hustler who had served time for theft. He also, unlike the West Indian Marxist and literary intelligentsia in London, had been intimately involved with the sixties transatlantic radical counterculture.[42]

After the still-cloudy circumstances of De Freitas's conviction for murder and execution in Trinidad in 1975, his role in the history of black radicalism has been, as it were, rather remarginalized. The sensational press coverage of the crimes and the trial, and exposure—perhaps exaggeration—of his past life subsequently proved an embarrassment to many militant activists, like Darcus Howe, who scrambled in the seventies to distance themselves from him. For moderates like Mike Phillips or the Trinidadian-British novelist Sam Selvon (of the somewhat older generation of West Indian intellectuals in London), De Freitas's fate confirmed a larger sense that there had all along been something inauthentic, foreign, and suspect in the British Black Power idea: the extravagant posturing, the outlandish gladrags and hairstyles, the "kill the pigs" rhetoric, and RAAS itself (the acronym is a Jamaican vulgarism) had been a regrettable joke—designed it seemed largely to funnel donations from, alternatively, white liberals or the American Black Muslims into the pockets of opportunists like De Freitas. Selvon published a savage caricature of De Freitas in the year of his execution in *Moses Ascending*—in "Galahad," a Mercedes-cruising "rabid disciple" of a visiting American militant with a sharp interest in the party's funds. Such readings were elaborated and entrenched in what passed for serious biographical treatment in the years following his death. It also rapidly encouraged a dismissive tone in some quasi-sympathetic (white) academic treatments of black leadership.[43]

But De Freitas was a much more complex phenomenon than his detractors suggest. Admittedly from a rough background and, when he came to London, almost entirely uneducated, he managed in a few years to achieve a largely self-created presence in the fluid environment of the sixties London counterculture: this can't have been entirely a matter of connections, pretence, self-promotion, liberal guilt, and newspapers' need for copy from an "instant black." Living for a while with "Hoppy" Hopkins and later with a Canadian journalist, Nancy, who turned him on to American authors like Mailer ("whose 'White Negro' knocked me out") and Baldwin, he continued to read widely under the guidance of mentors like Trocchi, MacInnes, and Carew, and aspired as an adult learner to get into Ruskin College at Oxford. He was involved in the "Sigma" movement, wrote poetry, contributed a piece to Wholly Communion, and was invited to read his poems at the Commonwealth Arts Festival at Cardiff in September of 1965; he wrote articles for *IT*, provided (black-clad, shaved-head Black Nationalist) security for UFO at the Roundhouse, and helped start the Free School with Hoppy Hopkins and Joe Berke. In 1967 and 1968 he was often found at Jim Haynes's Arts Lab, where he introduced Haynes to Leonard Cohen and organized a "Black Power Week" with Carmichael on film as a centerpiece. And it was De Freitas who suggested reviving Claudia Jones's Carnival and moving it outdoors into the streets of Notting Hill on August Bank Holiday. The Notting Hill Carnival in the mid-sixties was as much hippy counterculture as West Indian heritage, reflecting De Freitas's own location at the juncture of these phenomena.[44]

If Ambalavaner Sivanandan's protest in the early eighties at the "fashionable" dismissal of De Freitas did not succeed in restoring De Freitas's character, his insistence on the centrality of RAAS in the evolution of black British self-awareness bears serious consideration. Just how much the wider black community knew about and responded to "Michael X" and RAAS may be questioned, but his notoriety—which his militant pronouncements and his indictment in 1967 and six-month imprisonment ensured—made him better known than many less provocative activists. His rhetoric, modeled on that of the American Black Power radicals he admired—and which the press and the authorities took at face value—was an often humorous inversion of white racism: as when he called for the killing of whites who "lay hands on a black woman." The laughing, mostly black, audience understood the parody, if the press and authorities did not. While some found (then as now) De Freitas to be either unbalanced or a morally dubious opportunist, Stokely Carmichael, who saw much of him when he visited in 1967, took him seriously and formed a more positive opinion: "He was a black-consciousness militant, quick-witted with a real mastery of that sharp, in-your-face, verbal comeback that in Trinidad they call *picong*."[45]

The American Black Power movement did not resonate only among London's African-Caribbean activists. De Freitas set up RAAS with the help of Abdul Patel, an Indian, and Roy Sawh, a Marxist Guyanese Indian accountant who, after the decline of RAAS, founded his own small group, the Universal Coloured People and Arab Association, as well as a "Free University for Black Studies." Now an academic sociologist but with personal recollections of the militant groups of the period, Harry Goulbourne has lately reaffirmed that American black militancy exerted a strong influence on a broad spectrum of nonwhite activists in Britain from the sixties on: "[The] vocabulary, symbols, icons of struggles of black America became those of people from Africa, Asia and the Caribbean in Britain."[46] Sivanandan's own path to black activism owed much to American example.

Born in colonial Ceylon in 1929, the son of a Tamil postmaster, Ambalavaner Sivanandan came to London after the war to learn banking. As his insight into the nature of colonialism matured he abandoned his career for activism, eventually taking a position as librarian at the Institute of Race Relations. What turned him into a *black* activist, however, was more a matter of transatlantic than South Asian connection. In 1970 the institute sent him to the States, where he spoke to black leaders in California, New York, and Washington (including Black Panthers Bobby Seale and Huey Newton) and toured American black ghettos (a likely future for Britain that, he thought, spelled social death without the kind of political sense of self and resistance the Black Power leaders were offering). He also met and was un-impressed by white race relations scholars in Denver, Buffalo, and Berkeley. This American journey precipitated, as Mullard has observed, "Sivanandan's personal journey . . . to being a *black* radical activist."[47]

If Black Power had a message for South Asians, especially those with a Caribbean background,[48] the resonances may have been less powerful for black British with an African rather than West Indian heritage. In part that is because the leadership of most of the black activist groups formed in the late sixties and early seventies was dominated by West Indians, the fact that west Africans, espe-cially Nigerians, in London notoriously held themselves aloof from what many regarded as the lower class, less African-authentic, mixed character of Caribbean migrants, and the fact that Africans in Britain may have been less prone to the kind of "double consciousness" that marks the transatlantic culture of the islands/New York/London world. The striking exception, however, was the Biafran Nigerian militant the media most closely identified, next to De Freitas, with Black Power, Obi Egbuna.

A young African novelist and playwright, Egbuna was one of those singled out by *The Times* reporters in their "Black Man in Search of Power" series in 1968. With RAAS in decline, Egbuna's Universal Coloured People's Association was the flag-carrier, as it were, for American-style Black Power in the capital. Founded in the Ladbroke Grove area of west London a month or so prior to Carmichael's appearance at the Dialectics of Liberation Conference, the UCPA was recast more completely in the image of the American movement by Egbuna, who used the buzz surrounding Carmichael's appearance ("Stokely's arrival was like manna from heaven") to convert it into a Black Power vehicle.[49]

A scholarship student in Britain and already a published author, the twenty-five-year-old Egbuna had toured America's black metropolitan centers in August of 1966 (New York's Harlem, Philadelphia, Cleveland, Chicago where he met Elijah Muhammed, Atlanta's Vine City, and Watts in Los Angeles). Armed with the writings of W. E. B. DuBois, he sought out black nationalists like Carmichael who, as Egbuna later put it, signaled the end of the mentality of the "house-nigger." At SNCC's head office in Atlanta, "I saw them in their police-scaring revolutionary outfits, jeans, threadbare old clothes . . . . Their spirit of dedication, hard work and organisation was incredible." These he found to be more genuine and "aware" than (perhaps there is a note of Nigerian hauteur here) black West Indians he had encountered in Britain: "Tom-intellectuated and cowardly, I-am-alright-Old-Boy and Oxford-accented-hustler-type Black 'Englishmen.'"[50]

Back in Britain, Egbuna (who had also signed on to lecture for Berke's Anti-University) and a small following in UCPA worked to raise consciousness by deploying Black Power symbols (he brought badges back from the States) and rhetoric ("whitey establishment") in an assault on black and white moderates in the antidiscrimination movement. Under assault by UCPA and other such dissident groups, CARD began to fragment, and by the end of 1967 it had substantially lost influence. In October Egbuna led calls for Black Power at the Anti-Vietnam rally in Trafalgar Square. By early 1968 his strident attacks not only on the white British Establishment but on insufficiently radical blacks and on Marxists who were reluctant to endorse a movement that they regarded a diversion was undermining his position as president of UCPA. In April he left to help found a British version of the Black Panthers.[51]

The British Black Panthers were politically a marginal force, divided over tactics, and as a revolutionary institution narrowly located in time and place—but they had a loud voice that was amplified by the mass media, their community-distributed publications, and word of mouth. Egbuna edited their monthly organ, *Black Power Speaks*, and consistently drew analogies with the American scene and lessons from consciousness-raising and race-affirming black American style ("Black is Beautiful," the "natural look") as well as the politics of Carmichael, Rap Brown, and others. Eventually the authorities began to take serious notice, and Egbuna went to jail for six months for language that threatened the lives of policemen. Whether the Black Power movement in Britain actually posed the kind of threat that the authorities feared—that is, whether it in fact achieved much traction at the street level—is open to debate. Never a mass movement of course, it nevertheless was able to attract a core of earnest supporters, some of whom, like Darcus Howe, were prominent in militant confrontation in the early seventies and would go on to become influential leaders of the black British community thereafter. Did it also have some influence in undermining CARD and the radical transformation of the Race Relations Institute by shifting the central issue from that of white prejudice and discrimination to the construction of black self-regard and self-assertion?

In 1972 one of the best known of the white practitioners of race relations scholarship and progressive influence, Michael Banton, then director of the Social Science Research Council Unit on Ethnic Relations and a professor at the University of Bristol, looked back at the collapse of CARD from a sociologist's perspective, and complained that the role of Black Power in its demise had been exaggerated and "over-simplified": "Whatever the merits of the Black Power philosophy, any claim that CARD abandoned its pressure group role simply and solely because of the strength of this outlook cannot be sustained." And yet Banton protests rather too much—of course he had himself been a prime target of black militant rhetoric—and no one would argue that Black Power was the only cause of the weaknesses that undermined CARD. The same year another postmortem appeared, written by a Rhodes Scholar from Harvard, Benjamin W. Heineman. Heineman had come to Britain typically expecting a "journey back into the past" and found himself instead in the midst of heated debate about a new "coloured"

Britain in the inner cities. With less of an ax to grind than Banton, he argued that an over-reliance on American experience by British race-relations activists, the dramatic changes in the United States at the time, and the prominence of Black Power in the media inflamed self-fulfilling expectations of a breakup of CARD.[52]

By 1972 the Black Power moment in Britain, as in the States, and its overt adoption of American style, rhetoric, and program, had begun to recede. This was not necessarily clear to participants and sympathetic observers at the time. Chris Mullard, in his book *Black Britain* (published in 1973), believed that the British Black Panther Party was still "growing fast" and that "Assimilation is a utopian dream." Black Power's high water mark however, to use Sivanandan's retrospective expression, had been the 1970 confrontation with police at the Mangrove Restaurant in All Saints Road involving some 200 demonstrators, and the trial of the "Mangrove Nine" that followed the next year. This had been preceded in the spring of 1970 by police confrontations with black demonstrators outside the U.S. embassy and elsewhere (in March, sixteen British Black Panthers were arrested protesting the arrest of Bobby Seale in the United States; twenty were arrested in April in a thirty-minute battle with police at Speakers' Corner, where Black Power militants attempted to take over an anti–Vietnam War rally). Sivanandan's own campaign to turn the Institute of Race Relations into a more activist, politicized center led by blacks rather than white liberals, similarly marks an apogee: this was a power struggle that lasted from 1969 to 1972, when he and his supporters triumphed and John La Rose became its first black chairman.[53]

But Black Power also left in its wake a proliferation of organizations and publications that maintained a grassroots presence (the British Black Panthers with its *Freedom News* carried on well into the seventies), even as their own "utopian dreams" (of a separatist and inclusively "black" nationalism) subsided. The Black People's Alliance, the Black Eagles, the Black Liberation Front, the Black Unity and Freedom Party with its newspaper *Black Voice*, or the Black Liberation Collective and its publication *Grassroots*[54] were often more specifically attuned to the Caribbean and African heritage of their constituents than the originating African-American movement had been. In the seventies *American* Black Power, itself in steep decline, had less direct influence in Britain, though American black style continued to be influential. British black liberation groups developed more anchorage in local contexts (the Black Panthers were largely based in Brixton), often recruiting a coming generation of those who were either brought to Britain as young children or were born in the U.K.—the Hackney Black People's Defence Organisation, the Croyden Collective, the South East London Black People's Organisation, and many other groups in the London area and, like the Bradford Black Youth League, in the provinces. The *Black Liberator*, self-described as a "theoretical and discussion journal for black revolution," began in September of

1971 under the editorship of Ricky Cambridge promising a largely cultural focus that would mark a transition from the "formative period of black consciousness." Its alternative press look and language ("pigs" for police, and so forth) were, however, still closely indebted to transatlantic liberationism (and the first issue was dedicated to George Jackson who had just been killed; the next featured articles on Angela Davis, the Black Workers' League Manifesto, and "Black Liberation in Britain"). By mid-decade, however, it had evolved into a more expensive journal with a concentration on domestic Britain, the arts, and left-sociology—and less comradely attention to the American scene. Nevertheless, some of the earlier transatlantic rhetoric and symbolism survived well into the seventies and beyond: into the eighties the *Black Voice* banner portrayed a black man with an Afro raising a clenched fist with broken chains.[55]

The transatlantic politics of antidiscrimination, "Black Liberation," and "Black Power" existed within a wider field of American black cultural influences that worked among the nonwhite British communities to heighten a sense of identity and pride-through-association and the general British public to facilitate acceptance of a multiracial society in which there were, by the seventies, prominent role models (often Americans) in the media, entertainment, and professions. An early example of this was the enormous appeal Muhammad Ali had in Britain and the enthusiasm surrounding his fights (at Wembley in 1963 and Arsenal in 1966) and his subsequent visits among both black and white working-class communities. Though briefly associated with Malcolm X, Ali had remained outside the Black Power movement. His reputation however—not only his successes in the ring, but his famously articulate "attitude," projected in television interviews—meant that his popularity was available for appropriation. Local gyms attracting, especially, black youth sprang up in the wake of these visits—like the one set up by Jan Carew in Finsbury.[56]

In the arts there had been other prominent American blacks—from Robeson who played Othello for a Tony Richardson production at Stratford in 1958, to Sidney Poitier in the British-made films *Cry the Beloved Country* and *To Sir with Love*—who performed in Britain, were interviewed in the British media and, later, lionized on television talk shows, at a time when there was hardly a black *British* presence on stage or in film. By the end of the sixties the British mainstream media itself began—in direct response to the high visibility of the Black Power movement—to pay more attention to black cultural issues both for general interest and with some hope perhaps of a black market. In the seventies American television's use of blacks as newsreaders or in prime time sitcoms was emulated in Britain (Michael Grade at London Weekend Television bought Norman Lear's scripts for *Good Times*, a black working-class comedy, and adapted them for *The Fosters* with Lenny Henry). In 1973 Alex Haley's *Roots* commanded attention from the British viewing public generally and had a special interest for blacks (the 1970s British answer to *Ebony* was called *Roots*). Radio, however, was by and large uninterested in offering music of special interest to the African and West Indian communities, nor was there any hurry to enlist black D.J.s. From 1970 soul music was available to London listeners, but from the pirate station Radio Invicta.[57]

Any assessment of the American-inspired Black Power movement in Britain is a complicated affair. On the one hand, as the violence of the late sixties receded, media coverage of American race relations tended to present its British audience with a more benign view of American black leadership—the rise of a new generation of local political rather than revolutionary activists, an increase in the number of black professionals, the integrationist successes of blacks in the American media. On the other, if black revolution had been safely contained, indeed often relegated to the realm of humor, the American media, responding in part to the rhetoric of Nixon's "law and order" campaign in the 1968 election and after, smoothly segued into stories about urban crime. By the early seventies the British press and television followed the American lead and largely abandoned its concern with the threat posed by the direct subversion of black Britain by American-style militants. In its place, as has been well detailed in *Policing the Crisis*, was a panic over "mugging," strongly coded, as in the United States, as *black* crime that grew, like drug abuse, out of a general urban social crisis, especially pronounced in areas of black concentration. Here again, the American paradigm—with all its referential contexts—was important ("[S]lowly mugging is coming to Britain"): "We might as well begin to learn the lessons of America now, for our own traditional standards are under the same kind of attack."[58] In this, British Black Power became one of many symptomatic signs of a general social malaise within alienated communities rather than an active agent of change.

Within the nonwhite communities, American-inspired black liberationism had all along, of course, had a divisive as well as cohesive influence. There was the generational divide that it deepened between the earlier West Indian intelligentsia of the fifties and the young militants of the late sixties—expressed most sarcastically in Sam Selvon's 1975 *Moses Ascending*. Andrew Salkey, as one might expect, was more sympathetic in his 1976 novel *Come Home, Malcolm Heartland*:

> You all gathered in London in the early fifties, mainly for metropolitan approval and recognition. The approval "thing" is finished now, and so is the recognition "bit." Malcolm, Stokely, Rap, the Panthers and the others broke the back of that. The young Brothers, here, stepped good and hard on the pieces. That's left the intellectuals without aim and purpose.[59]

And its legacy—its memory within the "black" community—remained an issue that separated not only moderates and assimilationists from militant separatists, but, with the growth of the politics of ethnicity through the seventies and early eighties, the African-Caribbean from others—especially as the balance of population shifted from Caribbean to South Asian, whose neighborhoods (in

Southall in London or Bradford in Yorkshire) became more tightly knit around ethnicity, extended family, and religion than was the case generally in the African-Caribbean areas of Brixton or Notting Hill.

Some, like Tariq Modood, have taken the view that by splintering the coherence and unity of the sixties civic coalition, by alienating many South Asian British who did not consider themselves "black," Black Power seriously undermined the struggle against political and social discrimination, and encouraged racial animosity between African British and South Asian British. Some might argue further that the assertion of a common "blackness" among nonwhite, once-colonized people in Britain ironically sustains the ideology of the colonizer—that is, the privileged white perspective that seeks to define all those of a non-Western heritage as the "Other." Of course the answer to this charge, that which Sivanandan continues to insist upon, is, first, that nonwhite immigrant peoples in Britain did often face a quite similar prejudice and exclusion whatever their ethnic background, and, second, that Black Power's subsuming nonwhite oppressed peoples into a common blackness had a powerful pragmatic advantage in organizing a politics of resistance and amplifying its message in that time and place. One can only observe that Modood's view is shaped by and located in the evolved social circumstances of the eighties and nineties. On the ground in the seventies, at Grunwick (where the South Asian woman at the center of the strike, Mrs. Jayaben Desai, said, "The treatment we got was worse than the slaves in *Roots*") and elsewhere, it was not unreasonable to believe that the Black Power and black awareness movement offered some tangible advantage to non-Africans—while admitting that the course of ongoing assimilation in Britain in the following decades has greatly eroded the inherent unity of "immigrant" peoples from the Commonwealth.[60]

On another level, it is commonly asserted—now as then, and both in the United States and Britain—that the rhetorical excesses of the Black Power movement were dramatically counterproductive. By inciting racial hatred and white backlash, the argument goes, they encouraged a reactionary opposition in the seventies and eighties to the kinds of ameliorative measures for *social* justice envisioned by Martin Luther King at the end of his life as the necessary next step beyond civil rights. Here too, though, there are grounds for dissent. It may be, as Mullard disapprovingly suggested in 1973,[61] that the violent militancy of the Black Power movement actually made ameliorationism and assimilationism more acceptable in white society as a way of undermining militancy—black middle-class integration into white society was the price white society had to pay to keep more revolutionary change at bay.

Whether the Black Power movement was divisive or unifying, whether its tactics and rhetoric enhanced or retarded social progress for nonwhites in Britain, it was a transatlantic phenomenon that left its mark in the popular culture of the time. This is not to say that Black Power, as closely indebted as it was in Britain to its American originators, did not play out in contexts that were strikingly different than in the States—something Michael Banton in his denial of the relevance and influence of Black Power in Britain asserted with some exaggeration in 1972: "The black experience in America is unique. So is the West Indian or the Pakistani experience in Britain."[62] This difference in Anglo-American contexts will be a common issue as well when we examine the other forms of British liberationism that were inspired by Black Power—the radical feminist and gay rights movements. But the most significant legacy of Black Power was not in the realm of practical politics at all, or in the internecine wrangling within the various race relations institutions, or in any tangible achievement of social justice, but in *mentality*.

Black Power was a struggle, first of all, for a sense of self-worth, for, as Carmichael insisted, a positive, *self*-constructed identity in the face of a long history of internalized negative stereotypes. It is here that Banton and others mislead. The cultural life, the lived experience, of any community is always in some sense "unique." But transatlantic Black Power "spoke" with forcefulness in Britain because its message answered a psychological need in the lives of many nonwhites in London just as it did in Detroit, and consequently some of its cultural influence persisted well beyond its political moment. When he traveled around Britain interviewing black people in 1985, Ferdinand Dennis was surprised to find black people in Bristol "who have abandoned their European names. Their new names are drawn from all over Africa, with little respect for ethnic consistency."[63] This was a fashion begun in the United States when militant blacks abandoned their "slave names."

In fact, it might be argued that British blacks had a special need for the reinforcement of self-confidence that Black Power/Black Pride offered in the face of the special, historical force of British class prejudice and social exclusivity. In the United States the struggle for civil rights—for equality before the law and against legalized, indeed mandated discrimination—played out in the context of a society where the dominant national myth was that of the self-made man. In Britain the struggle was not against legal exclusion but against social discrimination in the context of a society famously knit together at the top by coteries of insiders, where even intellectual and artistic success had a dynastic side, and where race prejudice was vastly amplified by polite caste-snobbery. Imperfect grammar, unusual cadence and accent unmarked by Received Pronunciation, and unrepressed manners conspired with dark skin not only to inhibit economic and social self-advancement but also to erode self-confidence—arguably to a much greater degree than in the States. Black Power's legacy should be sought, not in its failed political agenda but in the consciousness-raising "attitude" it encouraged, in the hardly measurable unapologetic self-regard and self-confidence it incubated. In 1972 Peter Stevens noted in a book on *British and American English* that "Black English has quite suddenly become a major cultural possession of the entire black population." It was not only a matter of the recently borrowed American slang he instanced, but of a deep attitudinal shift whereby such dialect was no longer regarded by many as an embarrassment.[64] Whether the dialect in question was current American slang or lilting Jamaican patois, it seems reasonable to suppose that its validation had something to do with American Black Power's affirmation of black identity and with the unapologetic portrayal of black jargon and culture on imported American television.

These messages crossed the Atlantic not only with King, Malcolm X, or Carmichael, but with Muhammad Ali or the images of the black American Olympians, with distinctive hair styles and black American music and with the in-your-face sassiness of a Dick Gregory or a Richard Pryor. Though the messengers and their messages were often trivialized, willfully misrepresented, and manipulated by the mainstream media,[65] by the seventies and eighties a new, less defensive and more assertive Black British identity was commonplace; to a very significant degree, it was invented in the United States.

Recently Ministry of Defence documents have become available for 1975. In them we find that among the concerns the officer class had about their black recruits was an anxiety about the spread of Black Power ideas among them— there had been clenched fist salutes at an athletic meeting in Britain, Black Power literature was found among the soldiers' effects, and "coloured British and US drivers" were exchanging clenched fist salutes "when passing on the autobahns in Germany."[66]

CHAPTER 8

Riding the Second Wave: The American Face of Women's Liberation in Britain

In 1967 Piri Halasz cautioned American tourists in search of Swinging London that the status of women in England was "still not on a par with that of women in the United States." Visitors in search of male companionship might profitably emulate "quieter and more submissive" British women by "being demure, helpless and slightly more cooperative than usual." This was already somewhat dated, if tongue in cheek, advice. When radical feminism crossed the Atlantic in 1969, with its consciousness-raising tactics of disruption and confrontation, it found already fertile ground. Many young women, no doubt a mostly metropolitan middle-class minority, had been encouraged by the creative individualism of Pop modernity, the libertarian hedonism of the counterculture, and the radical politics of universities—which significantly larger numbers of women attended in the sixties than ever before—to think beyond the gendered norms of conventional behavior.[1]

In the United States, the free speech, free love, and antiwar movements had helped shift the character of reemerging feminism by elevating the personal nonconformism of the happening into a politics of radicalism as self-liberation-through-performance and spectacle. By the late sixties there was a similar trajectory of experience and activism for many university-age British women, from the disruption of the Miss World Contest at the Albert Hall in 1970, to the gigantic red, white, and blue penis paraded around Trafalgar Square on International Women's Day in 1971 and the Flashing Nipple Street Theatre.[2] At the same time, women attracted to the counterculture often experienced a deep frustration with its masculinist bias, not only in the groupie world of hippy chicks and cock-rock, but often in the radical politics of the new New Left as well. Much as militant blacks had felt that they were subordinated—with their concerns shelved until after the revolution—by the white romantic-Marxist left, radical feminists came to see sixties militancy, with its rhetoric of guerrilla warfare, as inherently sexist in both its macho posturing and its domestic character, where women made the sandwiches and tea and were rarely called on to speak at meetings.

The coming of radical feminism to London was prepared not only by the physical presence of militant American feminists in the city, the transatlantic reach of radical feminist publications, or the model offered by radical feminist organization in Chicago, New York, and Boston—though each of these is a crucial factor—but also by the way *Black* Liberation, its evangelizing experience and confirmation of self-through-unity, spoke directly to young women. As Juliet Mitchell observed in 1971, "The Black Movement was probably the greatest single inspiration to the growth of Women's Liberation." When Janet Hadley threw herself, at age nineteen, into the work of the Women's Liberation Workshop and its militant alternative-press publication *Shrew*, she had already been given "the courage to see that women *should* organise on their own" by her experience of black separatism in Notting Hill, where she lived. Involved with "an older West Indian man," she had heard Stokely Carmichael talk about Black Power, and from his eloquence she "learned about internalised oppression, issues of identity and colonialism": "It was definitely an awakening."[3]

As in the United States, Black Power rhetoric about a need for *self*-liberation and rejection of self-hatred resonated with many women who had previously been involved in the male-biased, Anglo-American counterculture: Marsha Rowe, who had been recruited for Neville's *OZ* in both Sydney and London and worked on *INK*, and Rosie Boycott, who coordinated the first women's issue at *Friendz*, went on to found the feminist magazine *Spare Rib* in 1972; Lynne Segal, who fell in with David Cooper and the Laing antipsychiatry crowd in London, threw herself into the Women's Liberation movement in north London; Anne Coote and Alison Pell wrote for *INK*; Michelene Wandor wrote for *OZ* and had been married to *INK*'s American editor Ed Victor; and Germaine Greer wrote extensively for several Underground papers.[4]

Histories of second-wave feminism in Britain, while acknowledging transatlantic influence, have tended to emphasize difference rather than similarity, to stress the distinctiveness of British attitudes and class locations. Some defenders of British feminism, like Juliet Mitchell, acknowledged a debt to the American movement, had been to the States, and had American friends, but found it difficult to understand the American movement in all its complexity and strangeness. Antifeminists, and not only British men, were of course prone to dismiss "bra-burners" in the States as typically Amazon-American middle-class women of the kind long caricatured in Europe. When Kate Millett spoke about the women's movement and her own work on Radio 4 in March 1971, a woman from Dorking in Kent wrote in to *The Listener*:

> I haven't been to America, but it is very likely that the crux of the trouble there is not that men have too much power, but too little . . . . [It] could be that these men are what they are because American women are as they are. Now this disruptive attitude in the US is spreading over here.

This was, in fact, a quite common reading of Anglo-American difference in the era of Women's Liberation, one that played, for instance, a role in Gordon Williams's violent 1969 potboiler *The Siege of Trencher's Farm*, in which the English wife of an American academic (with a somewhat diminished libido) has been caught up in "the classic American syndrome" where women are encouraged to relieve men of their masculine responsibilities: "*She* had organized the move from America, *she* had done most of the house-hunting, *she* had taken care of all the details." It is only in the surprisingly brutal English countryside where George must play the real man that she rediscovers her feminine self. They have passionate sex and she "felt the way she'd always wanted to feel, like a woman. Protected. Given a man to lean on."[5]

Not only did popular constructions of American difference complicate the transference of feminism across the Atlantic, but some of the "economistic" feminists on the political left held American liberationism to be lacking a proper ideological grounding. American feminists affirmed the self, the personal, in their assault on male privilege while their British sisters, especially those with some experience of academic Marxism, often claimed to be more in tune with issues of class oppression. Some British feminists, such as Sheila Rowbotham, were early on in the struggle at pains to contrast the movement in the United States as "very inward-turning because of exhaustive consciousness-raising," whereas in Britain the "real political initiative has come from the labour movement." If the American movement achieved an "independent strength" that British women could not manage to find, the domestic British variety, she implied, had a deeper sympathy for the reality of poor women's lives. It has also been suggested that the women's movement was stronger in the United States because, as with the youth culture generally, expectations had risen faster there. While rising expectations were hardly an exclusively American phenomenon, it may be that the buoyant American economy was uniquely able to nurture a radical middle-class feminism as an aspect of an especially American modernity. When Joyce Gelb set out to assess the doubtful state of feminism in Britain in the mid-eighties she began with the belief that British culture and political institutions emphasized "social integration rather than individual representation," while the backwardness of the British economy worked to limit women's aspirations and foment pessimism about the role of women on their side of the Atlantic.[6]

This emphasis on difference has come to characterize histories of British feminism—as less successful in terms of the reconstruction of the self and perhaps qualitatively different.[7] First, this risks losing sight of the importance of the transatlantic moment in setting the British movement going, and, second, by a simplistic polarization of typically moderate, British social-agenda feminism against a consciousness-building radical separatist American feminism, one does not do justice to the complexity of the movement on either side of the Atlantic. Moreover, whatever the real differences in substance and context, any analysis of the failure, stagnation, and fragmentation of radical feminism in Britain as somehow drawing from the inherently alien and shallow nature of an American export plays to the same preoccupation with "authenticity" that limits so much of the current understanding of the British versions of Pop, counterculture, student rebellion, or Black Power.

Recently, a reflective Sheila Rowbotham posed the question, just "where did all those ideas about reinventing ourselves come from?" Specific ideas often came from the United States, like the slogan "the personal is political," which she ironizes by noting that "the personal" meant "big money" to those cashing in on feminism as lifestyle. The deeper question she raises, however, is not that of origins, but why and how were young women like herself responsive to them? This is a much more complex matter, and, as she says, calls for a search for the sources of the "heightened awareness of subjective identity" that marked British as well as American popular culture since the fifties. Answers, she suggests, may be found in the same influences that shaped New Left politics generally in Britain in the sixties: "oral life stories on the radio, realistic TV drama, a dynamic view of class in social history, a sociological interest in the marginal, the stigmatized and disregarded."[8] Though Rowbotham more than most historians of the feminist movement has recognized its Anglo-American character, she reflexively searches here, like Raymond Williams more widely, for difference grounded in a reading of the special cultural landscapes of Britain. This chapter will, while acknowledging, certainly, the need to be sensitive to local contexts, re-emphasize the transatlantic nature of both the ideology and the practice of feminism in a period, the late sixties and early seventies, that needs to be re-evaluated as a special moment rather than a prelude to failure.

FROM BLACK POWER TO WOMEN'S LIB

Our oppression is more internalized [than that of American blacks] . . . .
My own realization of the depth and extent of my colonization came with
the force of an electric shock.

—Sheila Rowbotham

Second wave feminism in Britain has a complicated provenance, one that draws not only on important Continental and American sources but also on the traditions of a particular domestic history—on local memory and the lived experience of women of very different classes, communities, and sexual and ethnic identities. That said, the "electric shock" of self-awareness that galvanized renascent feminism into a Women's Liberation Movement owed much of its rhetoric and something of its practice to American Black Power. Rowbotham's tropes of internalized oppression and cultural colonization signpost this. Her own encounter with the writings of Fanon, Cleaver, and Carmichael dovetailed with her evolving feminism, her growing discontent with the rigidities of much Marxist analysis, and her discovery in Gramsci of the concept of cultural hegemony: "Black Power provided a crucial language of cultural domination, because it gave voice to a subjectivity obliterated in Marxist versions of socialism." Some took the messages directly from hearing Carmichael in London or his black British followers; others, through an American Women's Liberation Movement that was itself inspired by the attitude, language, and tactics of American black ghetto militancy.[9]

The easy analogy in this era of liberation of the oppression of (male) blacks and that of (white) women was later subjected to a sharper scrutiny and critique. By the early eighties bell hooks could observe that such constructions, ripe for deconstruction, seemed to imply that all women were white and all blacks were men—that is, they ignored the "intersectional" category of black women—for whom much of the (white, middle-class) woman's liberation agenda (countering self-hatred, facilitating abortion, securing pay for housework) was a bad fit. As instructive as this critique has proved, it is important not to lose sight of the force of the analogy between Black and Women's Liberation in the special context of the time and its mobilizing power as a basis of militant praxis. As with the radical counterculture and the antiwar movement, Black Power in both the United States and Britain inspired feminist militancy through its example. It also encouraged black women to participate, though rarely as self-conscious "feminists," in caucuses within the Black Power organizations in London and gave them a voice (the Black Union and Freedom Party's organ, *Black Voice*, carried articles on and by black women from its first issue in 1970).[10]

Unintentionally, however, Black Power also encouraged feminist self-consciousness and separation through its own provocative relegation of women as objects of desire and convenient service. Stokely Carmichael's dismissal, "endlessly repeated" in the press ("The only position of women [in the civil rights movement] is prone"), may have, as Anne Coote and Beatrix Campbell have claimed, done "as much to fuel the fire for a new women's movement as the publication of *The Feminine Mystique*." It may be that the media exaggerated off-hand comments by Carmichael, twisted out of context Cleaver's analysis of black rape, and sensationally and prejudicially focused on the subordination of women in the Nation of Islam. It has been also argued that "gender and gender roles were far from static" within the Black Panthers and that by mid-1969 they were turning away from "masculinist flourish" to an emphasis on the kinds of community-based programs that made use of black women at the grass-roots level who "had a significant impact on the development of gender consciousness." Nevertheless militant (white) feminism both absorbed much from Black Power's ideology and recoiled from what nearly everyone read as its sexist practice.[11]

What of black women themselves? For some activists in Britain, as in the United States, the problem of sexism within the Black Power movement raised issues of conflicting identities and the intersection of forms of subjugation. As Stephen Ward has observed of the movement in America, their engagement with black patriarchy should not, however, be taken to mean that "black feminism" was inherently antagonistic to Black Power; its critique was itself in some sense an extended form of black consciousness. As John McLeod has reminded us, black women's "insurgency" in Britain, though focused by the emergence in the early and mid-seventies of such activist bodies as the Brixton Black Women's Group, the Liverpool Black Sisters, the Manchester Black Women's Co-operative, or, later, the Organisation of Women of Asian and African Descent, was present before and beyond such activities in the "spatial practices and subaltern resistance of women in London." This receptivity among black women in Britain to the need for self-empowerment—whether or not they regarded themselves as feminist and signed on to the agendas of the Women's Liberation Movement—parallels similar evidence in the United States where polls taken during the 1970s indicated that black women were *more* likely than white women to agree with "feminist values." Both African-Caribbean and South Asian women were often ready to listen to the, albeit foreign, messages of American activists (and especially to Angela Davis, who, as one activist recalls, "seemed to have liberated herself mentally and fought in her own right, showing us all a lead"):

> Thanks to our sisters in the United States, this silence is at last beginning to be broken, and for the first time ever Black women have a voice. But that voice comes from America, and although it speaks directly *to* our experience in Britain, it does not speak directly of it.[12]

Women's Lib in Britain, as in the States, is sometimes derided as an anomaly whereby angry white mostly middle-class young women employed a rhetoric of exploitation somewhat at odds with their privileged social condition. This, however, is to elide the presence in the movement of black (and white) feminists who came from unprivileged, working- or lower-middle-class urban milieus, had not attended university, and whose perspectives on oppression no doubt differed from those of Betty Friedan or Germaine Greer. Ironically, as Yasmin Alibhai Brown has suggested, white British feminists were often more likely to know and credit *American* black women—writers like Alice Walker, Nikki Giovanni, or Maya Angelou—than their Asian and Caribbean sisters in Britain. Black feminists in the seventies who felt that the movement was ignorant of black women's lives were more inclined to "listen" to black women's voices within the American movement than to those of white feminists at home.[13]

Though uncommon, personal transatlantic experience for some independent black British women could itself play a role in developing an independent sense of self. The black drummer Terri Quaye, for instance, born in London of an African (Ghanaian) father and a West Indian–English mother, sang and played for her father's jazz band in the fifties. When "[n]ews filtered into our communities about Blacks in America and their insistence on claiming their identity," she recalls, "how proud I felt and how instinctively they seemed to rekindle that sense of extended family, so that I too felt part of that struggle." In the sixties, "inspired" by visiting American black performers, she managed to get gigs in New York. Back in London in 1970 she played her drums in Jack Goode's Black Othello musical "Catch My Soul" at the Roundhouse and the same year toured Ghana in a "back-to-roots" trip. Quaye found Britain sexist—club managers would ask her to "show a bit of tit"—as well as color-prejudiced. By the seventies her material was often political. American jazz, like her West African drum routines, "helped to reflect yourself."[14]

AMERICAN FEMINISM COMES TO LONDON

On 14 September 1969 the *Sunday Times* discovered radical feminism, New York style. In a lengthy section of its magazine supplement, with photos by Diane Arbus, Irma Kurtz explained to the paper's mostly middle-class readership just what American bra-burners were about and warned that, presumably even in Britain, "Thousands of women are preparing for the coming fight." There were pictures of Betty Friedan, but also Roxanne Dunbar, "a karate expert" and member of the Boston Women's Liberation Movement, Rose May Byrd, "a Black Panther leader," and Anne Koedt, who had revealed the myth of the vaginal orgasm. "Hard-core" militants like Valerie Solanas—self-published author of the *SCUM Manifesto* then in prison for shooting Andy Warhol—and the leftwing Redstocking radical feminists were angry and violent: "Make war not love." By early the next year, there was simultaneously in the United States and Britain an "avalanche of publicity" surrounding "Women's Liberation"—in Sunday supplements, weekly news magazines, daily papers, and television programs.[15]

In the Anglo-American world, "second wave" feminism, in its liberal "equal rights" form, was kick-started by Betty Friedan's 1963 American best-seller *The Feminine Mystique*, brought out in a London edition the same year by Victor Gollancz (and by Penguin in paperback in 1965). Influenced by King's civil rights movement, Friedan's campaign gained a national momentum that culminated in Washington in 1966 in the creation of the National Organization for Women. The second NOW conference a year later demanded a bill of rights for women that included civil rights but also maternity leave, child-care tax deductions, child-care centers, and reproductive freedom (abortion, legal and available). Though dismissed by some radical feminists subsequently as a political lobby of middle-class housewives and professionals, Freidan and NOW were in fact instrumental in initiating a larger exploration and expansion of the "woman's question" as one as much of culture and mentality as of law, opening issues of consciousness-building and self-empowerment that became the stock-in-trade of the more radical and often younger women of the liberation era.

If British women were slow to imitate NOW's politics in the sixties, nevertheless Friedan's work was influential among those who would at the end of the decade eagerly respond to a more militant call for Women's Liberation. Eva Figes, though a Continental by birth, recalled in 1978 that she had been more moved by Friedan than by Simone de Beauvoir. Sheila Rowbotham, who had lived in France as a student, knew de Beauvoir's *The Second Sex* ("an extraordinary achievement") and was suspicious of Friedan's liberal remedies, nevertheless claimed in 1971 that it was *The Feminine Mystique* that had been "a revelation" for many women in Britain "because it was so determinedly about everyday matters." Similarly, Juliet Mitchell, who rated De Beauvoir's "massive work" the "greatest single contribution to the subject," also admitted that Friedan's book had been the single most important "inspiration" for the movement, while Audrey Battersby, a seventies liberationist and member of the Belsize Lane Women's Group, told an interviewer that reading Friedan and the more radical American feminist Shulamith Firestone had indeed been revelatory: "Then the bells rang and the connections were made."[16]

Organized radical feminism in the States emerged in 1967 out of the sense that women's concerns were being marginalized within the New Left. Though in Britain Juliet Mitchell had drawn attention a year earlier, in a subsequently often-cited essay in the *New Left Review*,[17] to the blindness of much Marxist theory and practice to women's issues, it was in New York and Chicago that women's caucuses first consolidated into separatist organizations using the language and symbols of militant liberation. Jo Freeman and the Chicago Westside Group and Shulamith Firestone and the New York Radical Women became the models for similar groups in London a year or so later, just as the New York Radical Women's street-theater demonstration against the Miss America Contest in Atlantic City in September 1968, which signaled a general challenge to beauty contests across America, also inspired picketing at the Miss World ceremony in London the next year and a more theatrical confrontation at the Albert Hall in 1970.

Militant feminism in the States often conferred a kind of celebrity status. Indeed, in Jane Fonda liberationism found an actual celebrity, a feminist icon already made notorious by her antiwar career, while Diana Rigg, somewhat to her surprise, found that her exported television role as Emma Peel became a great hit among women in the States to a large degree because of what was taken to be its feminist subversion of Bond-era machismo.[18] More intentionally, Germaine Greer also crossed the Atlantic to become something of a celebrity feminist in the States, thanks as much to her televised confrontations with Norman Mailer and talk show hosts in the early seventies as to the ready availability of a paperback edition of her one big book. The traffic in feminist imagery, however, flowed more often from West to East.

Women in Britain had long sought images of the feminine in American fashion magazines and American cinema, and for young women especially this "Star-gaz-ing" was a "female spectatorship" that provided in the fifties and sixties a relief from the dowdy respectability and conventional restraints of local lives. Whether this was mere escapism that inhibited the construction of a more activist self or served to unsettle and undermine British norms may depend on context, class, and generational expectation. Certainly feminism in Britain as in the States had a complex relationship with the celebrity icons Hollywood offered, finding in trousered Dietrich or Hepburn models of a kind, and even in Marilyn Monroe at least a martyr. By 1968, the fiftieth anniversary of Women's Suffrage in Britain, with the increased participation of young women in Vietnam demos, the lifestyle liberation of Pop fashion and the pill, and, as Elizabeth Wilson recalls, a growing "awareness of their own situation," some young British women were especially receptive to American images of *feminist* celebrity. Indeed, in the context of the counterculture the definition of celebrity itself shifted, and Janis Joplin offered a raunchy style simply unavailable in a Britain where Julie Christie was still the chief avatar of a cool modernity. With the new American feminist images came also American agents of feminist challenge, visitors "constantly expressing their amazement at the backwardness of their sisters on this continent"—antiwar students and academics like Kate Millett, who came to live in London after the appearance of *Sexual Politics*.[19]

From the abortion campaign in 1967 to the "Clit Statement" declaration of a radical lesbian feminism in 1974 in the London Women's Liberation Workshop newsletter, transatlantic traffic—of feminist writings that "quickly found their way across the Atlantic" and of American women who traveled to Britain and British feminists who visited the States—played a significant role in the women's movement in Britain. Anita Bennett, who came to London in the mid-sixties already disenchanted with the American New Left, was involved in the campaign for David Steele's 1967 Abortion Act. Advocating a specifically woman's voice on issues affecting them, in the seventies she wrote for *Spare Rib* (itself a British answer to Gloria Steinem's *MS* magazine) on international feminism and became an articulate figure on the radical-lesbian wing of the movement. Though it is often asserted that the more radical forms of Woman's Lib in Britain drew especially from American example and by implication were less solidly grounded than moderate feminism in British culture and experience, mainstream feminism was also deeply responsive to transatlantic influence and resident American voices. These need to be further interrogated. What exactly did the American movement and its agents in London bring that spoke, in that time and place, especially forcefully to those British women who responded? American feminism may have brought a focus on the personal and, in its radical manifestation, a sometimes fanatical separatism that was off-putting to many activist women in Britain, but it also often impressed those like Rowbotham with its organizational drive.[20]

The American women who met in Tufnell Park, already involved in antiwar politics, were a vanguard of Women's Liberation in London. Among them Sue Crowley and Shelley Wortis brought a refreshing "anti-authoritarianism and belief in participatory democracy," and an understanding that the organization of the liberation groups itself "prefigured a desired future." Another was Sue O'Sullivan, from an American Quaker family, who had been in and out of Britain from the late fifties. A summer in the States in 1968 introduced her to Women's Liberation, and she returned to the Tufnell Park women's group where she committed herself to radical feminist journalism. American feminists in London like O'Sullivan or the American Jewish New Left mother Cora Kaplan provided, according to Lynne Segal, a "critical catalyst." Rowbotham found that they often "possessed an openness to new realities and perceptions and a respect for knowledge rooted in experience." Others were not always as impressed, especially women who had begun their radicalism on the Marxist left. Val Charlton, a post-grad communist arrested in 1968, found the American feminists at her first Women's Liberation meeting middle class, overly confident, and not "terribly warm" or inviting.[21]

The experiences of Lois Graessle, an American feminist active in London, suggest, however, a presence that was more interactive than domineering, both contributing and evolving along with the British movement. She had been involved in the civil rights struggle while a student at Northwestern University in Chicago before hitching around Britain in the mid-sixties. Returning to London in 1967 to be a part-time student at the L.S.E., she took a secretarial job at University College. In 1968 friends introduced her to a woman's group from the Essex "Festival of Revolution" and to the Tufnell Park women, where she felt "at home, familiar." She participated in the Miss World disruption, zapped sexist ads in the underground and department stores with feminist stickers, joined the London Women's Liberation Workshop, attended the Ruskin conference, and marched on International Women's Day in 1971. Having met a West Indian man, a south Asian from Trinidad, she moved to Notting Hill where she belonged to a local women's group, participating but not attempting to dominate: "I felt it wasn't appropriate to have an American with an accent stage centre in the woman's movement in this country." Graessle's feminism, which matured in London, contrasts with the caricature of the shrill American radical separatist. Uncomfortable in "consciousness-raising" sessions, she "took the chance to go and work with girls at Clapham Junction which is what we'd all been talking about, 'getting to working-class women.'"[22]

A snapshot of how some American women in Britain interacted with radicalism on the ground is also provided in some of Wandor's interviews with English women. Anna Davin was then a student at Warwick and a socialist who had spent a year in the States and read de Beauvoir and Juliet Mitchell. She knew American exchange students at Warwick who had been in the SDS and who "brought feminist pamphlets and ideas" with them. In 1969 Davin and friends from the Socialist Society started a woman's liberation group at the university and ran a bookstall stocked, in part, with pamphlets from the New England Press. With perhaps a British rather than American reticence, she found the more open sexual discussions inspired by Koedt's "Myth of the Vaginal Orgasm" and radical lesbianism "difficult"—though ultimately she was led to explore her own bisexuality. Audrey Battersby remembers being challenged in London in 1967 by an American woman who came to give a talk on the women's movement in the States. The English women had heard Juliet Mitchell speak on women's issues, but it was the American who demanded why they hadn't actually organized: "We just gaped at her." Another "extraordinary" American woman in an Islington commune, an antiwar activist with a Vietnamese flag along one wall who smashed windows at Selfridge's, "changed," Battersby said, "my ideas about my own femininity." Similarly, Amanda Sebastyen was impressed in 1969 by an American discussing abortion ("very obviously not wearing a bra, which only a few people over here did then"), and by the *Sunday Times* spread on radical feminists in America: "[T]his is it, this is for me, where are the English ones?"[23]

A number of late-sixties, early-seventies American feminist texts, often quickly published in British editions, exerted a particular transatlantic influence. Kate Millett's doctoral thesis, *Sexual Politics*, not a quick or easy read, appeared in a British hardback edition a year after its 1970 publication in New York, and was followed by a paperback edition in 1972. Millett herself, surprised at her sudden celebrity status—*Time* magazine called her "the Mao Tse-tung of Women's Liberation"—fled to London and became a somewhat reluctant resident American resource for the woman's movement for some years. The 1977 Virago Press edition of *Sexual Politics* presented it as "one of the most important documents ever written on the relationship between the sexes" and, downplaying Millett's American origins (she "read literature at St. Hilda's College, Oxford"), offered the work as a revolutionary analysis of "*our* history and *our* culture."[24]

But the text that arguably caused the most excitement among the nascent liberation movement in Britain was the New York Redstocking activist Shulamith Firestone's call for "feminist revolution," *The Dialectic of Sex*. Born in Ottawa, Firestone grew up in St. Louis, moved to New York, and was a founder of the radical feminist movement there in the late sixties. The book set out a radical agenda to free women, "a slave class," from "the tyranny of reproduction" through economic independence. Shifting the burden of child-care to society as a whole would spell an end to family-centered repression: "[In] our new society, humanity would finally revert to its natural polymorphous sexuality—all forms of sexuality would be allowed and indulged." She both acknowledged and contested feminism's debt to other liberationisms, preferring the term "radical feminism" to the derivative-sounding "Women's Liberation," and provocatively arguing that sexism "presents problems far worse than the black militants' new awareness of racism: feminists have to question, not just all *Western* culture, but the organization of culture itself." Moreover, she asserted that racism itself was "a sexual phenomenon": "[We] can fully understand racism only in terms of the power hierarchies of the family . . . . *[R]acism is sexism extended.*"[25]

Juliet Mitchell may have seized upon the blindness of Marxist theory and the New Left to the oppression of women in her article of 1966, "The Longest Revolution," but that work hardly initiated a movement (Mitchell herself flew to the United States the month it was published, where she discovered in New York and Chicago "lots of women who were beginning to think about feminism," and, though she had gone "to lecture on literature and Marxism," she "ended up attending women's groups"). Firestone's tract amplified this grievance more forcefully for an activist audience, arguing that Marx and Engels "knew nothing" about women as an oppressed class and that the New Left "seemed ashamed to acknowledge any relation to feminism." She arrogated to radical feminism a primary position as "the most important revolution in history" aiming to overthrow "the oldest, most rigid class/caste system in existence."[26]

If Mitchell's protest was grounded in the cultural work of Raymond Williams and the old New Left she challenged, she also paid her own somewhat guarded respects to the counterculture. American work, however, often drank more deeply at this well. The same year Elizabeth Gould Davis, though hardly herself generationally a member of the Age of Aquarius (she was a sixty-one-year-old librarian), concluded her widely read *The First Sex* (perhaps as fantastic in its historical imaginings of a vanished matriarchal world as Tolkien's myth-making) with an apocalyptic paean to "the overthrow of the three-thousand-year-old beast of masculinist materialism":

> The ages of masculinism are now drawing to a close. Their dying days are lit up by a final flare of universal violence and despair such as the world has seldom before seen . . . . Only the complete and total demolition of the social body will cure the fatal sickness.

Firestone's rhetoric and agenda are also situated within this realm of countercultural utopianism. The disappearance of traditional motherhood would usher in a "cybernetic communism," drudgery would yield to "play," "love" would "flow unimpeded."[27]

Though Mitchell would later engage what she took to be the casual, erroneous dismissal of Freud and the sloppiness of "Reich—Laing—Firestone" psychology as misguided and "deleterious," the women she brought to feminism in the consciousness-raising classes she offered at the Anti-University devoured these tracts with enthusiasm. For her part, Germaine Greer, who did not care for Kate Millett's "'Bible' of Women's Liberation," proclaimed that *The Dialectic of Sex* was "a beginning," and "more unanswerable than *Sexual Politics.*" For Gillian Hannah,

"[It] was like finding the pot of gold at the end of the rainbow, finding something that suddenly made sense of my life, everything I had felt was wrong with my life and the world." The same year there appeared another American publication that was quickly seized upon and endorsed (like its eponymous slogan) by the British movement, *Sisterhood Is Powerful*.[28]

If Firestone employed the rhetoric of the counterculture and the radical feminist press reproduced symbols and slogans that drew on those of the antiwar and Black Power movements, the Miss America/Miss World protestors deployed the *practice* of the counterculture and constructed an identity of sisterhood through performance. What began as liberal protest ended as radical spectacle—both alternative Happening and Situationist challenge.

However much the televised beauty contest could be represented as simple popular entertainment (much the same was defensively said about the *Black and White Minstrel Show*), they were a god-send to the radical feminists, perfectly enshrining the idea of the commodification of the woman's body in commercial culture. Mecca's Miss World compere Eric Morley read out not only the national origin of his "girls" but also the "vital statistics" of their breast, waist, and hip sizes. He also banned married women from competing in the major feeder contests in Britain (though not in Miss World itself) because of the risk of domestic "trouble": "I could not easily envisage a wife returning to scrub the kitchen floor who might, in the previous six months, have dined regularly at the Dorchester or Savoy." And in the early years the young women were indeed commodities: "[We] used to try and offset some of the girls' expenses by allowing firms and wealthy companies to dine them out with their executives for an evening." Or as the organizers of the 1970 protest rather more crudely put it, Mecca were "superpimps selling women's bodies." Reigning "Queens" would also expect to earn significant income from commercial sponsorship deals—using their glamor to sell often the kind of products that feminists decried. Though perhaps never achieving the status of the Miss America pageant, the Miss World event was not far behind, at least in TV ratings by the mid- and late sixties. Both offered radical feminists irresistible sites for consciousness-raising confrontation and spectacle that would seize a wider public attention than manifesto screeds or thin street demos. In 1968, the feminist disruption of the Atlantic City Miss America contest—bras and girdles were thrown into buckets—pointed the way.[29]

The coming of color broadcasts encouraged Mecca to lift the British event into something more like the lavish American showbiz productions, and Morley had long wanted a grander venue. In 1970, Miss World moved to the Royal Albert Hall, to be televised by the BBC in color and hosted by British-born comedian and American star of radio, film, and, latterly, troop entertainments in Vietnam,

Bob Hope. Hope had served on the Miss World panel of judges in the sixties and often employed the Miss World winner in his own shows (in 1966 Miss India, Reita Faria, won and was recruited for his Vietnam tour—against the advice of the Indian High Commissioner in London). He was still a celebrity, though his routines involving statuesque buxomly young women and scripted, mildly risqué, jokes were like himself aging. Often in London for charity performances, he would stay at the Savoy, play a little golf and hobnob with the great and the good. Not as politically partisan as John Wayne, Hope's support for the war, however, and for conventional, mainstream values made him an unexpectedly polarizing figure, a red flag to feminists and those generally on the other side of the countercultural generation gap. As the activist author of *Why Miss World?* put it, he "made more connections than we ever hoped to put across."[30]

These "connections" extended beyond feminism. Though the bathing beauty contest may have had prewar roots in British popular seaside culture, the event as lavish television-promoted national ritual seemed somehow "American," as a showbiz species of commercialized popular culture. Moreover, as in the United States, there were racist overtones from the beginning. In the late forties Mecca had organized beauty contests in central London at the Paramount dance hall in Tottenham Court Road. But they "had to put an end" to these events in the fifties when they became popular with "a large number of coloured men" who would ask white girls to dance: "[We] had," Morley said, "to close the Paramount to protect our good name." In spite of the "international" character of Mecca's Miss World competition, "beauty" was judged, as often in America also, to be that of a European ideal: straight hair, often "put up" (on Morley's advice) in a statuesque Grecian mode, and light skin. The first two winners were blonde Swedes, and none of the others while Morley hosted the event were "black"—including, of course, Miss South Africa (1958) but also Miss Jamaica (1963) and Miss India (1966), who was of Portuguese Goan heritage. In the States, the Miss America competition actually barred women of color until the 1970s.[31]

The move from peaceful protest outside the doors of the Lyceum in 1969 to disruptive spectacle inside the Albert Hall in 1970 was more than a tactical escalation. It represented the arrival in London of an American-style radical Women's Liberation Movement. Cadre-building and headline-grabbing, direct action, like the symbol it borrowed from the radical left (a raised fist inscribed within the international female sign), had less to do with a political agenda of amelioration of grievances than, as with Black Power, establishing attitude and identity. It also significantly raised the visibility of a minority radical fringe, one that was especially influenced by American sisters studying at British universities or living in London. Inevitably parallels and connections were drawn with the Angry Brigade, a violent, Situationist-style underground blamed for the January bombing of the house of the Home Secretary, Robert Carr, though it is not clear that the women who planned the Albert Hall disruption had anything to do with the bombing of the BBC van the night before the Miss World pageant.

On the night of the contest, 20 November, Hope began badly. Responding to recent feminist criticism that beauty contests were cattle-markets, he opened with "I'm very happy to be here at this cattle market tonight . . . . But I wanna assure you . . . nothing is going to get blown up here tonight—they've checked every costume in the place." As the event developed, before live TV cameras relaying the program to an American as well as British audience, radical feminists began to shout from the stalls—perhaps as many as a hundred—and caught Hope off guard. His nervous jokey attempts to deflect their anger only drew jeers, the noise of rattles and whistles and a rush for the stage; he beat a retreat amid lobbed sacks of flour, bags of ink, and smoke and stink bombs before Mecca bouncers removed the most aggressive of the women and Morley hurried on stage to appeal for calm. After the interruption, Hope ("Is it safe yet?") returned to crown Miss Grenada but then lashed out against the protesters: "You'll notice about the women in the Liberation Movement—none of them are pretty, because pretty women don't have those problems . . . . They're exhibitionists, these people."[32]

The spectacle inside the hall spilled outside, where demonstrators paraded a pantomime cow—leading the *Daily Express* to title its front-page story "With a moo moo here and a protest there." Two of the feminist disrupters, as no doubt they intended, were arrested outside the hall for assaulting police and carrying offensive weapons. Others made their way to the Cafe de Paris, where the contestants were having dinner, and two more women were arrested for throwing flour and rotten tomatoes and using abusive language ("fuck off pigs"). The arrests ensured that the event would be replayed for the media at Bow Street two months later.[33]

More dramatic, and angrier, than Jerry Rubin's Frost Freak-Out, the Miss World disruption brought a "politics of theatre," borrowed from the counterculture and alternative left, to the women's movement. Indeed it drew reinforcement directly from the flourishing underground street theater: the following year's protest outside the Albert Hall was led by the Gay Street Theatre and the Women's Street Theatre Groups, who parodied the contest in their own "Flashing Nipple Show." Its importance lay less in any tangible result—Miss World and other media-supported beauty contests continued into the eighties—than in its announcement that radical feminism had arrived, a defining moment that remains in the memory of the era. A media coup, it provided a narrative of action that could produce in some, like Lynne Segal, "moments of sudden awakening" as she read the militants' pamphlet *Why Miss World?* in her bath. It encroached on the masculine terrain of physical force and "We're not gonna *take* it anymore" direct action and as such drew on deeper roots than the American counterculture, especially on memory of the British Suffragettes (a movement that "also had been coloured by a heightened sense of spectacle"), though the earnest seventies project of recovering the

Suffragettes itself profited from the notoriety and increased visibility that the infusion of American countercultural flair gave to radical feminism in Britain.[34]

In the early seventies street spectacle and radical theater provided "symbolic acts against symbolic targets," and played a role in the Feminist and Gay Liberation movements out of proportion to the number of militants involved. As Marwick has well described, radical theater offered new forms of expression for women suffering from a heightened sense of social constraint, communal spirit, and creative collectivity, roles as writers, directors, and actors unavailable in conventional theater, and a means of proselytizing that could seize attention in a world conditioned not to listen to women's voices. Most large demonstrations, like the International Woman's Day demo in Trafalgar Square in March 1971, had an orchestrated theatrical element engineered by small cadres of activists, as did the carnivalesque, parodic disruptions of the counterdemonstrations of middle England: men from the Gay Street Theatre Group dressed as nuns and wandered through a Festival of Light rally while feminists from the Women's Street Theatre Group pushed in with a pram and placard saying "Fuck the Family." Alison Pell, a member of the Women's Street Theatre Group who took part in the Festival of Light affair, had just returned from the States, carrying "some of the seeds of the American sexual liberation movements with her." Her enthusiasm for women's-revolution-as-theater at the Women's Liberation conference at Ruskin College in January had already captivated Michele Roberts, who "experienced a conversion moment," gave up wearing a bra, and signed on for the Woman's Day demo, as well as the theatrics of the Miss World affair and "Situationist drama" in the lavatories at Selfridges.[35]

As with Yippie antics, the element of subversive "play" in radical feminism was meant to expose through ridicule the pretense, hypocrisy, and pomposity that cloaked the real machinery of social oppression. As a tactic it depended on provoking anger for its effect, but lost much of its public impact when, as quickly happened, the commercial media turned the "Wimmin's" revolt itself into humorous text. But radical feminism was also concerned, perhaps more concerned, with creating through performance a new mutuality and self-awareness. For many of the increasingly separatist radical groups that proliferated in London and elsewhere in the early seventies, such consciousness-raising, though decried by some, was more important than the event itself, the undermining of Establishment values, or the furthering of a legislative agenda.

If the sober conferences at Ruskin College and Sheffield promoted a less confrontational political agenda and sought to enlarge women's role in socialist organizations, the trade unions, and the Labour Party, by 1969–70 small local groups of radical feminists had also already begun to coalesce out of the fragmenting counterculture. Berke's Anti-University promoted woman's consciousness through courses like that offered by Juliet Mitchell on "The Role of Women in Society." Some women touched by that experience went on to organize loose local collectives to explore feminist literature. These discussion groups were often formed around American women living in London and British women who had been to the States, or those who had been active, as at Essex and Nottingham, in the university rebellions. The American-dominated Tufnell Park group was one of the first and inspired by example other local collectives—as many as 300 perhaps by the end of the seventies. Many of these joined together under the common umbrella of the London Women's Liberation Workshop.[36]

The radicalism-shading-into-lesbianism of these small local organizations, the influence of an especially radical American element within them, their focus on consciousness-raising practice, and their ephemeral smallness has conspired to marginalize their importance in histories of the women's movement in Britain. Eve Setch, then an LWLW activist, has recently argued, however, for a grass-roots perspective that restores some importance to these local radical feminist organizations and to consciousness-raising as "the bedrock of the women's movement," more enduring than Millett's weighty tome, Greer's entrenched media presence, or any legislative agenda. She emphasizes the "progression" of grass-roots groups from sites for planning confrontation to women's centers and information service providers: "[T]he Women's Liberation Movement was centred in lived politics, not abstract thought, producing feminist ideas and structure through experience."[37]

At the same time there was emerging an alternative press of radical and mainstream feminist publications, as well as a spate of "style" magazines aimed at the "new woman." The LWLW's newsletter *Shrew* was founded in 1969 and "aimed at women outside the [radical] movement." Its *Newsletter* was meant for insiders and was a more provocative and contested site, containing American separatist articles (notably the lesbian "Clit Statement") that sparked controversy within the group and led to complaints that material by British women had been turned away to privilege American extremism. These were followed by others with different constituencies: the less separatist *Socialist Woman* (founded by the Revolutionary Socialist Students' Federation) in 1970 or *Woman's Voice* in 1972. *Spare Rib*, which achieved a larger circulation, was launched the same year by a collective of women journalists headed by Marsha Rowe, who had been urged to "start a magazine" by an American woman, Bonny Barton. As we have seen, the women behind the emergent feminist press often had experience in the Underground press and brought something of its subversive mockery. In May 1969 the first issue of *Women's Newsletter* appeared; its second issue was called *Harpies Bizarre*.[38]

Like the Underground out of which much of it sprang, the women's press closely followed formulas and material from the United States. The first six issues of *Shrew* "took up themes already widely discussed in the American movement: female separatism; developing feminist theory; the politics of housework; sex, contraception, and childbirth; Freudian psychology; make-up and deodorants."

More mainstream style magazines like *Cosmopolitan* also followed an American (commercial) formula aimed at the "New Kind of Woman." These bore roughly the same relation to feminism as *Ebony* or *Roots* did to black consciousness. *Cosmopolitan*, a Hearst Corporation magazine revived by Helen Gurley Brown (author of *Sex and the Single Girl*), crossed the Atlantic in 1971 and was given an English editor from the women's section of the *Sun*; Brown came over for talk shows on BBC television. Though liberal-minded and occasionally featuring mainstream feminist writers, *Cosmo* was hardly radical. When the American version ran Burt Reynolds as its first male nude in 1972, the closely parallel London edition featured Germaine Greer's unknown working-class (and temporary) husband Paul De Feu—"as a sort of anti-feminist in-joke." Its readership of half-a-million of course vastly outnumbered that of the most popular of the radical feminist productions; indeed, one assumes, the readership of all the feminist movement press combined.[39]

As in New York, feminism proliferated also in the arts—closely allied in any event to ideas of expanding identity through performance and spectacle. A Women's Liberation Art Group, organized in 1971, promoted women artists and feminist themes, often involving graphic representation of women's bodies (countering what Greer called the "mystery" that served to deny active female sexuality) and a feminist (rather than rape-inducing masculinist) eroticism. This was very much in inspiration an American project (Suzanne Santori's plaster casts of her own genitalia displayed in Rome in 1970, and censored by the Arts Council in 1976, or Betty Dodson's genitalia slide presentation at a NOW conference in New York in 1973), as was a Women's Film Group formed in London, with provincial spin-offs. An outgrowth of the radical, antiwar Angry Arts/Liberation Films group, they produced agit-prop footage from both the Ruskin Conference in 1970 and the International Women's Day march in 1971. As with alternative film generally, American influence was prominent, and critics, especially those with an already jaudiced eye for American "silliness," were prone at the time to damn British feminist arts by association. Irma Kurtz visited the subject in the second of her articles on Women's Liberation for the *Sunday Times*, "Boadicea Rides Again." She, however, found some virtue in the English scene: "[O]ver-statement and violence rarely happen here in the wild, deadly way they happen in America." If the London Women's Liberation Workshop's guerrilla theater "in the style of the *Witch* girls in America" had resulted in artistic "fiascos," they nevertheless possessed, she thought, a sense of humor, "a grace which will save them and one which their American counterparts totally lack."[40]

A THEORY OF THEIR OWN? ARTICULATING DIFFERENCE

The closeness of the American relationship in the British women's movement, both at the level of personal relationships and in the transatlantic traffic in key texts, rhetoric, organization, and practice, itself encouraged a degree of denial and a search for difference. This ultimately focused on what were taken to be the contrasting agendas, class location, and, especially, sexual separatism of the extremist fringe in the States. Mainstream feminist strategists and their sympathizers in the press searched for an authenticity that located the movement in British cultural contexts. This need by moderates to flatter British norms and special virtues was driven in part by the Conservative media's dismissive characterization of feminism of any kind as mere Americanism. Irma Kurtz's bemused pieces in the *Sunday Times* magazine were not dismissive of feminism-as-American-nonsense in the manner of, say, a *Daily Telegraph* editorial. Arguing that American radical feminists were grounded in symbols and precedent to which their British sisters did not have ready access and that validated an extremism that was rare in Britain—the struggle for colonial independence, a pioneer tradition, and the fight for the abolition of domestic slavery—British feminists by their pragmatic cultural conditioning were, she claimed "more articulate, intelligent," "cooler and more logical."[41]

Looking back from 1980, Elizabeth Wilson reflected on those feminist writers who had, she thought, been most influential in driving forward the movement in Britain. It is a relatively short list that begins, predictably, with Betty Friedan and does not include Simone de Beauvoir. There are four Americans (Friedan, Mary Ellmann, Millett, and Firestone) and three British theorizers of the feminist cause. Of these (Mitchell, Figes, Greer) it was Juliet Mitchell who many in the mainstream of the movement in Britain came to think most clearly served to differentiate American and British feminisms. Mitchell's 1966 article "Women, the Longest Revolution" was indebted to what she called de Beauvoir's "theoretical innovation" of fusing the "'economic' and the 'reproductive' explanation of women's subordination by a psychological interpretation of both." Informed less by American example than by the British context of sixties sexual permissiveness, and the ambiguities it posed for the liberation of women, her central concern—as indicated by her choice of publishing journal, the *New Left Review*—was to locate the exploitation and subordination of women more centrally within contemporary socialist theory and to interrogate its "silence" on the issue. By focusing on ways in which women's condition was "overdetermined" through women's *multiple* roles in production (especially), reproduction, and family (the socialization of children), as well as sexual relations, she implicitly cast doubt on the promise of liberation through "sexual freedom" alone: "[T]he main thrust of any emancipation movement must still concentrate on the economic element—the entry of women fully into public industry." Moreover, reformist demands (an allusion, perhaps to Friedan and NOW) for equal pay for work were of less elementary importance than "*the right to equal work itself.*"[42]

This largely (though not exclusively) economistic approach was grounded in a European tradition of Marxist analysis, though seeking to expand beyond its narrow preoccupation with the commodification of women as property in the bourgeois family. Much of the article speaks to an academic left in Britain in a language largely absent from the reformist movement around Friedan and drew attention to a subject—working-class women in the industrial workplace—unaddressed by its concerns for middle-class equality. Nevertheless, it would be wrong to see Mitchell's piece as establishing a clear and early line between distinctly American and British approaches to feminist meaning. In the first place, the article's importance was somewhat retrospectively constructed. It was the infectiously spreading transatlantic radicalisms after 1968 that seem to have refocused attention on her 1966 version of the women's revolution (Rowbotham *re-read* Mitchell amid the rage of radical engagement in 1969 and apparently found in it ground to reject, not American personalism, but the simplicities of economistic Trotskyists who claimed the women's struggle was a diversion from the fight against capitalism).[43]

By that time radical elements of the women's movement in the States as well were invested in at least rhetorical elements of a post-countercultural version of romantic Marxist liberationism, and in Marcusian "Freudian Left" concepts that linked sexual and social repression. The language of class, economic exploitation, and revolution was quite commonplace in the student, black, *and* women's movements on both sides of the Atlantic after 1968. If the separatist radicals focusing on sexuality and gender relations were often seen to be at odds with an economistic feminism, there was in fact more commonality in analysis and agendas on both sides of the ocean than has perhaps been suggested. Nor can Mitchell's work itself be categorized as narrowly economistic. She invokes psychological issues of alienation and mentality, of women *choosing* not to seek a role in production, nor does she reject the idea that the psychological impact of sexual permissiveness *might* be a force for liberation rather than simply presaging new forms of oppression. A liberated sexuality was becoming "the weakest link in the chain" in regulating bourgeois social behavior.[44]

Ultimately, Mitchell's chief criticism of the American element in the woman's rebellion lay not so much in its refusal to engage issues of economic analysis or an agenda that ignored the condition of working-class women, but rather in what seemed to her its misreading and misuse of Freudian psychology, the subject of her major, if somewhat querulous, text *Psychoanalysis and Feminism*. Here she let fly at the "personalism" of the "Anglo-Saxon" sixties counterculture and its (posthumous) guru Wilhelm Reich and mentor R. D. Laing and at the radical feminist writers, mostly American, who, from Friedan to Millett, historicized Freud as culture-bound and dismissed, along with his masculinist assumptions about penis-envy, analysis that had, she believed, much to offer feminists that was constructive.[45]

Mitchell suggests that in Britain Figes and, especially, Greer, drew their opinions uncritically from mostly American feminist writers who had seized upon the early work of Karen Horney to promote their own inadequate, reductionist or erroneous criticism, who twisted Freud into false contexts (Friedan, Millett, Figes, and Greer), and who either misused specifically psychoanalytical concepts in order to appropriate elements for their own purposes (Reich, Laing, Firestone), or, like Figes, used those works of Freud that are technically outside psychoanalysis in order to develop an ad hominem critique. Though she focuses her argument on those feminist writers who engage Freud most fully and directly, she implies that their mistakes and illegitimate elisions informed a wider field of, largely American, "underground literature."[46] Greer, in this regard, comes in for special criticism: "an Australian," though writing in Britain, who in her erroneous "misreading" of Freud was more attuned to "the diversity of the American movement" and its counterculture-inspired "deleterious" "vocabulary of protest" than to the "relatively homogeneous and [more sensibly?] organised British movement." Mitchell dismissed *The Female Eunuch* as "probably as deeply influenced by [Greer's] experience of American culture as she was by living and working in England."[47]

The two writers on the British side of the Atlantic who had most annoyed Mitchell, Germaine Greer and Eva Figes, published the works for which they are best known in 1970, within months of each other. Figes's *Patriarchal Attitudes* was more self-consciously of the feminist movement in that she aspired (as she later said) to "stir women out of their apparent passivity" and found in the surge of American feminist writing that was flooding into Britain (feminist books were "selling like hotcakes") the promise of an end to her own sense of "intellectual isolation."[48] Though *Patriarchal Attitudes* remained a key text in the British feminist canon (it was republished by Virago in 1978), it did not achieve anything like the high visibility in popular culture that Greer's rambling, colorful, bawdy, and intentionally provocative work did. *The Female Eunuch*, though subsequently often a set text at university, broke free of what was becoming an academic feminist lit genre and became a best-seller on both sides of the Atlantic (and has never been out of print). It is the most successful example of a work of "British" feminism that crossed the Atlantic against the flow, as it were, of most feminist theory and practice. Indeed, it probably found a more receptive audience in the States than among either mainstream or radical feminists in Britain, who have never exactly seen Greer, with good reason, as a dependable Sister.

It is misleading to surrender the seventies to ideas of backlash and extremist fragmentation. A feminist perspective of sorts crept into television programming, overtly in Midge Mackenzie's popular "Shoulder to Shoulder" documentary about the Suffragettes, or obliquely in *Upstairs Downstairs*'s Rose, and even in *Coronation Street* (where there had never, in any event, been a shortage of

strong-willed women). Ironically what began as Americanization was for complicated reasons also more politically productive and enduring in Britain than in
the States, where the religious right found more traction than the Festival of Light
and Mary Whitehouse could. This is of course partly the result of the way central-
ized parties and leadership are privileged in the British political system, which is
significantly more resistant to provincial backlash than that of the United States.
The work of the centrist left feminists in the seventies entrenched feminist issues
within the Labour Party, however much one may doubt that "Blaire's babes" were
the lineal inheritors of Women's Liberation. NOW's Equal Rights Amendment
failed in the United States; in 1975 British feminists rejoiced in the implementa-
tion of both Equal Pay and Sex Discrimination acts. The year 1975, "Women's
International Year," also saw the inauguration in London of the alternative theater
groups Monstrous Regiment and Gay Sweatshop, the publication of the British
edition of Kate Millet's *Flying*, and the foundation of Virago Press.

Rather than viewing the struggle in the early seventies between mainstream
and radical feminism as symptomatic of fragmentation and failure, the one
achieving some success because it rejected a neurotic American-style "separatist
extremism," the other self-exiled to the far margins of impracticable politics, one
might rather see the radical feminists as exemplars of what Eva Figes called the
"real victory" of feminism generally—a fundamental change in self-awareness.[49]
Lesbian feminism, though at the time often dismissed as the logical conclusion of
American man-hating, was not, of course, simply a minority fringe of the Anglo-
American woman's movement. It is doubly located—within the awakening and
recovery of self that marks sixties and early seventies feminism generally, but also
specifically within another phenomenon significantly inspired by a transatlantic
special relationship, Gay Liberation.

CHAPTER 9

Coming Out and Coming Together:
Anglo-American Gay Liberation

———◦◆◦———

"There is a sense in which the homosexual is our current 'nigger' of love."
"Chick equals nigger equals queer. Think it over."[1]

Gay Liberation, the third of the triad of militant late-sixties movements grounded in the retrieval and affirmation of the self, has yet to receive quite the same attention in the general literature on the sixties, often—outside of specifically gay scholarship—being relegated to the margins of a territory defined by hippies, student revolutionaries, blacks, and women.[2] Nevertheless, like the Black Power and Women's Liberation movements it followed, Gay Lib is centrally and importantly located in the militant subjectivity that defines the era, and it too has a complicated transatlantic character.

When Gay Liberation arrived in London in 1970 it drew directly on American gay organization, rhetoric, and symbolism (the word "gay" itself was apparently a postwar American import that, like the San Franciscan artist Gilbert Baker's rainbow flag or the New York Gay Liberation Front's "gay day" marches, traveled eastward from the United States). Indirectly, the British militant gay movement was also indebted to American sources through its self-conscious appropriation of elements of both the Black Power and Women's Liberation campaigns, and more generally to the personal liberationism of the radical transatlantic counterculture. Like both the black liberation and the radical feminist liberation movements, Gay Liberation was also viewed with uneasiness and annoyance by the left, as both ideologically suspect and problematic for any project to radicalize a socially conservative working class. The *New Left Review* group stayed largely silent during the national debate over the Wolfenden Report, and a decade later the more radical liberation movement still had difficulty getting comradely support. As Dennis Altman observed in 1971 and David Fernbach recalled later, in neither America nor Britain was it possible for the organized gay movement comfortably to caucus within the New Left. As late as 1972 Trevor Pateman's radical student movement handbook *Counter Course* could offer advice on Marxist critiques of capitalism, student rebellion in the United States and Britain, the Underground and the arts, Black Power and Women's Liberation, but nothing on Gay Liberation. Many gay activists had been, like hippy-bearded Arthur Evans at Columbia University in 1968 or Nigel Young at the L.S.E., politicized and radicalized through their experience of the sixties antiwar movement and continued to employ Marxist phraseology and militant symbols of revolution, but inevitably a strong sense emerged that separatist organization was necessary. Some, especially perhaps in Britain, struggled to maintain personal connections in both camps, like Bob Cant who was a member of the Gay Liberation Front *and* the International Socialists until 1973, when he too abandoned the "economistic" left "as most other members of the Gay Group had already done."[3]

GAY LIBERATION AND THE COUNTERCULTURE

The counterculture emphasis that dominated the early movement stressed personal change as the key to social change and the elimination of sexism . . . . But the power structures of society were left completely untouched, and the lives of the majority of gay people were left completely unchanged by the sweet smells of incense, inspiration and home-baked bread.
—"Collective Statement," *Gay Left* 1 (1975)

After the utopian phase of the GLF had run its course, those on the left in the gay movement in Britain attempted to recover a socialist reading of the homosexual rights struggle in the face of a rapidly evolving consumerist, lifestyle gay scene in London. Dismissal of the excesses and presumed limited social reach of the countercultural liberationist moment in fact came to characterize a rather eager postmortem on both the right and the left after 1973, and yet there is something deeply misleading in that assertion that most gay people's lives and values were "completely unchanged" by the sixties generational revolt. A thesis that is easily made but hard to confirm, it also begs much larger questions about how change operates in history, how paradigms shift, and how subjectivities are subtly reshaped. In 1975 the Gay Left Collective had of course its own ax to grind, but one might as reasonably ask from this distance whether "the lives of the majority of gay people" were in fact somehow more tangibly and enduringly affected, shifted out of their settled orbits if not directly impacted, by the liberationist moment than by anything the GLC was able to achieve.

The *hippy* counterculture had nurtured and encouraged the freer exploration and expression of the self. Those freaks streaming through Portobello Road market celebrated the liberation of desire, and an androgynous style that put women into jeans and long-haired men into caftans and beads—"gay-looking young men who were not gay" as Elizabeth Wilson, who found the "hippy life" both attractive and boring, would later remember. It may be, as Altman observed, that in the pop and rock scene androgyny and sexual ambiguity drew especially on British style, but Ginsberg's flower power children on both sides of the Atlantic were tolerant of homosexuality as a cool part of the spectrum of free love in an Age of Aquarius that celebrated the ideal at least of a universalized bisexuality, while Richard Neville proclaimed the Underground's goal of "turning sex back into play." When Carl Whittman penned a brief clarion call for gay liberation in San Francisco—a mecca for both hippies and gay people ("refugees from Amerika")—he drew the obvious:

> A major dynamic of rising gay sentiment is the hip revolution . . . . Emphasis on love, dropping out, being honest, expressing yourself through hair and clothes, and smoking dope . . . . The gays who are least vulnerable to attack by the establishment have been the freest to express themselves on gay liberation.[4]

At the same time, the libertarian counterculture proved an inadequate resource for young homosexuals searching for an end of isolation and communities that openly validated same-sex desire, just as it had for militant blacks and feminists. Though adult male homosexual relations had been largely decriminalized in Britain in 1967, the commercial alternative press, *Time Out* or Nicholas Saunders's *Alternative London* guides, was relatively slow and hesitant to advertise the newly open gay scene until after Gay Liberation had achieved a tangible presence. There were of course gay hippies, though Lisa Power believed they were "suppressed" by the sexism of the counterculture. According to Aubrey Walter the hippy scene in Britain was less inviting for gay men and women than that in New York or San Francisco. Nor was there yet a specifically gay alternative press like San Francisco's *Gay Sunshine* or *The Advocate* in L.A.[5]

Though Ray Gosling announced in *New Society* in August 1968 that there had been an explosion of gay-themed magazines in Britain, some with contact ads, these were mostly behind-the-counter "adult" publications rather than countercultural (one of the ads he reprinted specified "no hippies"): there was a risk, he primly observed, of leaving developing gay culture to the pornographers. The counterculture press, like *IT,* where the openly homosexual American Jack Henry Moore served on the editorial board, was certainly gay-friendly. Before Stonewall, Neville's *OZ* had occasionally devoted space to gay items as part of its general effort to be outré and hedonistic; its first post-Stonewall issue, *OZ* 23 (August/ September 1969), was entirely devoted to gay-themed articles (and featured a cover photo of two nude men, one black and one white, embracing). Though inside, *OZ* 23 had been more interested in sex and its "shock content" than sexual politics, the magazine later, thanks in part to the role there of Jim Anderson, also a GLF militant, provided space for GLF articles proclaiming that "gay is good," not just permissible.[6]

The urban spaces of London that the counterculture laid claim to had become, by the late sixties, pockets of anarchic diversity and relative tolerance that encouraged an existential search for self, display, and, ultimately, out-behavior and gay performance—Chalk Farm and Camden Town, Fitzrovia and Soho, the King's Road, Earls Court, and, especially, Notting Hill. In 1966 the first street procession of what would become the annual Notting Hill Carnival was led by "Queen Victoria," a white gay man in drag. It was perhaps inevitable that the radical fags of Gay Liberation should gravitate to such zones of liberation, though Notting Hill never quite managed the bohemian character of New York's Greenwich Village or San Francisco's North Beach, nor did it evolve a sustained and focused gay village area like San Francisco's Castro Street.[7]

In 1971 the Gay Liberation Front, founded at the L.S.E. the previous October, moved its meetings to the counterculture venue at Covent Garden, Middle Earth, and then in July to All Saints Church in Powis Square, Notting Hill, where radical liberationism entrenched itself in the surrounding racially mixed streets and squares just south of All Saints' Road—gay communes, militant street theater, and pub protest in a permissive and narcissistic era where both pop rock and hippy play had prepared the way for the "gender fuck" tactics of radical gay militants. There was, perhaps, more scope for gender-bending radicalism as performance in at least London (if not the rest of Britain) than in an America where conventional morality was less tolerant of art-school happenings and boundary-teasing display. Nevertheless, when Toby Marotta looked back in 1981 to the early seventies in the United States he was convinced that "the proliferation of gay subcultures is perhaps the most dramatic evidence today that the counterculture survives."[8]

Beyond flamboyant style and gender-bending costume, the Anglo-American counterculture's most explicit legacy to the gay movement was R. D. Laing's challenge to conventional psychological diagnosis and therapy. By the end of the decade, the assault on a mental health establishment that characterized homosexuality as a sickness was a primary objective for militant gays seeking to distance themselves from liberal homophile organizations. Laing's Dialectics of Liberation conference had foregrounded ideas that inspired both the American Gay Liberation movement and its English counterpart: "[T]he analogy with racial oppression, a generalized rejection of bourgeois models of mental health, and the alienation which is inescapable from capitalist modes of production."[9]

The GLF organized its own Counter-Psychiatry Group in the summer of 1971, following those already established on the West coast and in Chicago: in May, 1970, the national convention of the American Psychiatric Association in San Francisco was invaded by both gay and women's lib activists protesting aversion therapy; a few weeks later Chicago gays staged a similar invasion of the American Medical Association's national convention shouting "Gay is Beautiful," and in October a talk by a British psychologist at a Behavioral Modification conference in L.A. was disrupted. By the summer of 1971 the British movement, led by lesbian activists Elizabeth Wilson and Mary McIntosh, followed suit with similar "zaps" in Harley Street, at London psychiatric clinics and hospitals, and at conference venues.[10]

If Gay Liberation was, like the Black Power and Women's Lib movements, closely imbricated with the radical nonconformist Anglo-American counterculture, it was also symptomatic of a rapidly spiraling fragmentation of that phenomenon. The seeds of a radical "minority" separatism sprouted and flourished in the soil of the counterculture, but they also took direction, strength, and confirmation from each other. Most obviously, both radical feminism and the gay movement drew deeply on the rhetoric and tactics of the American Black Power phenomenon, but this was a spiritual affinity that was, to say the least, problematic. Women, as we have seen, found black identity politics both powerfully suggestive and analogous and also frustratingly sexist on both sides of the Atlantic, and black women felt especially caught up in the ambiguities of their intersectional condition. Such contradictions were even more sharply present in the debt gay militants openly avowed to a black liberationism that was more overtly hostile to gays than it was to liberated women.

Gay liberationism, as a politics inspired by the oppression of a minority, was especially attuned to the reports of black self-empowerment that saturated the transatlantic media from about 1966, when SNCC in the States, and shortly thereafter black militants in Britain, renounced white sympathy and patronage. The new gay militancy, turning from the lobbying for civil rights that had characterized the Mattachine Society in the States or the Homosexual Law Reform Society in Britain toward "unashamed assertiveness" and "pride," drew directly from Carmichael, Cleaver, and Rap Brown a rhetoric of self-affirmation and an agenda of confrontation. And yet, it would be hard to find a more offensive homophobic text than Cleaver's widely read manifesto *Soul on Ice*, with his contemptuous dismissal of James Baldwin's "sickness" that had conspired, he argued, to perpetuate the feminization of the "castrated" black man (nor did Cleaver have much good to say about "frigid" lesbians). Though some Black Power leaders came by 1970 to acknowledge solidarity with other minority movements, rank and file black power culture was clearly unfriendly to a Gay Liberation that threatened to undermine the pride that was the chief construct of their own liberation. In August 1970, Huey Newton famously called for black brothers and sisters to welcome revolutionary feminists and gay liberationists in spite of "your personal opinions and your insecurities about homosexuality." But at the Panthers' Revolutionary People's Constitutional Convention in Philadelphia in September, to which the American GLF had been invited, members of the audience were unfriendly, leading to a walk-out by radical lesbians.[11]

In Britain as well, militant black organizations, including black feminist organizations, were at best cool to overt expressions of homosexual identity and at worst aggressively dismissive, leading some to look to attempts in the States to organize groups like the Combahee River Collective in Boston (from 1974) which focused on issues of sexuality and race not dealt comfortably with in either the

Black Power or the white feminist organizations, and to American writing: "I actually found it very useful to read Black lesbian literature from the USA"; it provided "inspiration and energy," even if "you also feel frustrated that it is always coming from the USA and you want to hear what British Black women are saying." If it was also true that black British lesbians drew on global voices beyond the United States, these too were often brought to their notice by American sisters, like Diane from New York, who shared with the Black Lesbian Group in London her research on West African female bonding.[12]

Contexts were of course different. In the United States the Black Power movement drew almost entirely from African-American and Caribbean sources; in Britain, if it drew from those sources as well, its message was deployed among a more ethnically diverse community, and the issue of homosexuality no doubt played differently among West Indians, Africans, and South Asians, and differently as well when the issue was male or female homosexuality—though untangling these threads of relative accommodation and prejudice is difficult. What is clear is that the Gay Liberation movement in the States and, latterly, in Britain, drew heavily on Black Power rhetoric while exploring a separatism that was both propelled by the logic of identity politics and a defensive reaction to the prejudice it encountered in both the black and feminist camps.

It is also true that in both countries Gay Liberation was, in its leadership and much of its militant rank and file, largely a matter of white males—in part no doubt an artifact of both the historic legal situations (where it had been male homosexuality that was criminalized) and the fact that white male homosexual subcultures were more tangibly inscribed in their urban milieus. This itself heightened the contradictions involved in Gay Liberation's borrowings, not only from Black Liberation but also from radical feminism and its same-sex—if not necessarily same-sexual—consciousness-raising. If both radical feminism and Gay Liberation were avowed offspring of the Black Power movement, like many siblings their own relationship was conflicted—both close and distant, marked by mutuality but also by suspicion and schism. Juliet Mitchell had as early as 1966 been prepared to find a close commonality between feminists and homosexuals in their mutual need to dissociate reproduction from sexuality, and this was reaffirmed in *Woman's Estate*, her feminist call to arms published in 1971 just as the British version of Gay Liberation emerged in London ("[O]ur solidarity with Gay Liberation—gay sisters and brothers—is of paramount importance, as is their solidarity with us"). It was, however, a somewhat qualified solidarity that warned of the dangers "coy flirtation" and sexual hedonism posed to the larger objectives of liberation.[13]

Simon Watney later observed, in his essay on "The Ideology of GLF," that by 1971 the radical call for consciousness-raising, "to free the brothers and sisters . . . it is necessary to free ourselves," represented "perhaps the high-water mark of the popular assimilation [by the gay movement] of Kate Millett's *Sexual Politics*." On both sides of the Atlantic, however, Women's Lib rapidly developed its own internal tension between those who saw self-empowerment as a means of achieving equality with men and those who turned to the community of women as an alternative to a masculine world of power games, aggression, and sexual domination. For the latter, radical feminism was often a bridge to a radical lesbianism that others viewed with deep misgiving, suspicions that were amplified in Britain where the ideological left was more important in the movement and often, as Power says, "regarded homosexuality as a bourgeois perversion."[14]

ANGLO-AMERICAN CONTEXTS

The cultures of same sex intimacy were roughly comparable on the two sides of the Atlantic in the postwar era—its somewhat subterranean lived experience, the at times derisive, at times brutal tenor of popular (and populist) prejudice, the legal disciplines imposed upon it, the liberal sympathy that sought to shield it, and the modernist psychiatric therapy that theorized and treated it. Shared Anglo-Saxon legal and cultural systems meant that male homosexuality, if not lesbianism, was situated in a public discourse of immorality and criminality, while the professionalization of what were increasingly transatlantic social science and scientific communities since the late nineteenth century had lent authority to views of homosexuality as illness or maladjustment, views that came to underpin much liberal opinion in Britain and the United States by the 1950s. There was, by the fifties, what Frank Mort has called a "dialogue of ideas" across the Atlantic: "[T]he history of modern sexuality can rarely be understood as a purely domestic scenario, comfortably bounded by national formations." And yet beneath the similarities of official and professional discourses and the parallel trajectories of liberal reform and metropolitan homosexual self-consciousness before the late sixties, there were complicated differences. As Mort has also observed, "While national routes do not securely de-limit homosexuality, they do continue to shape its appearance and positioning."[15] There are of course boundaries other than the presumed differences of "national character"—the contrasting contexts of the metropolitan and the provincial (significant in both countries) or the urban and the rural. Varieties of prejudice, and of homosexual accommodation to them, may also be traced into differences of ethnicity, no longer by the sixties an especially American phenomenon, or class, a more self-conscious factor perhaps in Britain, or gender—or complicated permutations of all of these factors.

If in Britain working-class culture was in dialect and traditions tenaciously local, the social and political elites were historically more unitary than in the United States. This is a significant difference in national context as we consider the ways in which transatlantic homosexual reformism, and latterly Gay Liberation, played out. It certainly made decriminalization, and the debate surrounding it, a more straightforward affair in a country where elite opinion commanded greater leverage than in America and where a unitary system of parliamentary sovereignty promised a resolution (even if ambiguously and partially delivered) not possible in a federal system where states and even municipalities pursued their own course. Moreover, the British elite was arguably somewhat more insulated from populist pressure. America's Cold War fifties were marked by a Red scare that surpassed the British version in its virility. There was a homophobic subtext in both countries in the press-driven anxieties about moral standards, and a sharp postwar increase in police surveillance and prosecutions of homosexual activities, but McCarthyite witch-hunting in the United States was altogether nastier. There was also arguably a closer linkage in the popular culture of prejudice in America between homophobia and anti-Semitism, a familiar connection but one that was sharpened by the prominence of Jews in the homophile and liberation movements in New York City. If homosexuality was a "stigma symbol" in both countries, America, with its religiosity and its cruder policing, was, Ken Plummer claimed in 1973, "probably more hostile to homosexuals"—a hostility that was in some sense amplified by the small-town character of an America that historically idealized the public and private moral virtues appropriate to a republic in constant need of self-construction and re-affirmation.[16]

However, it is also true that the rhetoric of liberal homosexual reform in the United States was able to draw on a civic ideology of the desirability—indeed necessity—to integrate "minorities," and concomitantly on the powerful sense of the plurality of a nation of immigrants. Dennis Altman, an Australian scholar who researched his path-breaking book on homosexual oppression and liberation in both New York and London, noted the way the homosexual, as a *minority outsider*, was a central theme in American literature and believed that this was a major difference between American and British writing about homosexual relationships: it was "as impossible to talk of current American culture without talking of homosexuality as to talk of it without discussing Jews or blacks: the self-affirmation of minorities . . . is a central part of present American literature."[17] Andrew Lumsden later reflected similarly that there was a sharp "difference" in cultural and political contexts between the American and British liberation scenes—that the American GLF "came out of the ethnic melting-pot . . . where people identify themselves as Italian Americans, Chinese Americans, Jewish Americans and so on . . . . [In] Britain we didn't and we don't think like that."[18] Difference in national cultural attitudes toward "minorities," however, was eroding by the seventies, as Britain came to grips with the permanence of its rapidly acquired nonwhite immigrant population, the emergence of a born-in(or at least acculturated-in)-Britain second generation, and especially a developing politics of *racial* identity within the British black communities.

Another area of some difference, it seems clear, surrounds the libertarian Cold

War ethos, the "ideals of individual liberty" that Toby Marotta later invoked and that, arguably, exerted greater force among Americans in the movement than among their British counterparts. Indeed, the American version of *both* liberal reformism *and* Gay Liberation was especially marked by a kind of possessive individualism, a right to do as one wished with one's *own* body anytime anywhere. In New York City the Gay Liberation Front treasurer, Jim Owles, held libertarian views that would have been very unusual in the movement in Britain (he "had read several books by Ayn Rand and dug her objectivism philosophy"). The Gay Activists Alliance that he helped found late in 1969, and that rapidly became the dominant successor group to the GLF at least on the East Coast, quickly abandoned much of the rhetoric of countercultural utopian radicalism and instead hoped to ground the struggle more narrowly in the defense of a political "right" to subcultural "self-expression," on the right of gays to cruise and cottage as "the right to express our own individuality."[19]

Toby Marotta, the early historian of this phase of the struggle, and others who have followed his analysis, probably exaggerate the degree to which the American movement at any point could be simply divided into reformists, radicals, and revolutionaries, not merely because this may overprivilege the tactical debate among some of the East Coast leadership, but because it tries too hard to tidy up what was in fact a swirling confusion, especially among the rank and file, of mentality, motive, and objective. Ultimately the unstable utopianism of Gay Liberation, quite specific to the late sixties and early seventies, precipitated out into hardened alternative positions between the left and those defending personal choice. The radical left never had much traction among American middle-class homosexuals, but in Britain it was, at least for much of the seventies, somewhat otherwise. Though there was considerable tension between a socialism that distrusted the politics of the personal and the gay and feminist sexual liberationists, the London GLF had for its part consistently avowed its revolutionary, anticapitalist credentials. Don Milligan, writing in 1973 on the eve of the disintegration of the group, affirmed that "Homosexual equality is not possible under capitalism"—while injecting some distance and realism in his observation that their experimentation with communes, though good at showing what might be possible beyond capitalism, was inadequate itself to challenge and break the system.[20]

After 1974 the Gay Left Collective in Britain turned a yet more jaundiced eye toward the fissiparous and utopian GLF while attempting to sustain a socialist reading of the gay struggle in Marxist and Fanonian terms. They continued into the eighties to condemn and contest the lifestyle liberationism (the "libertarianism and spontaneism" in Frank Mort's words) that came to characterize London gay life. The late-seventies disco-driven third-wave scene celebrated an American-style hedonism and consumerism that threatened even in Britain to wash lingering left ideology out of the idea of being gay.[21]

In the United States a left reading of the struggle had all along been a harder sell, and there was little room for the discourse of class oppression in the politics of the personal and the consciousness-raising of the feel-comfortable-in-your-sexuality therapies of encounter groups (Altman thought that in America there was a preoccupation with homosexual *sex*, in Britain with "the extent to which the gay world is stratified by class").[22] In Britain, generally, class was certainly a more familiar category—in the rhetoric of the political left and in the social sciences taught at the newly expanded universities and polytechnics of the sixties; class *self*-identification was also more common in Britain than the United States. Issues of class were prominent not only in the general historical discussion and literary presentation of homosexuality—as a perversion of the effete upper (or pretended upper) classes or the criminality of a rough-trade underclass—but also in the elaborate homosexual culture of camp behavior.

In both countries the stereotype of the affected "queen" had been available well before the postwar era—notably portrayed in Hollywood by a few camp film stars like Frank Pangborne, but in Britain the role was more culturally entrenched and rather more precisely situated as an upper-class affectation that had a specially tolerated, if always precarious, place. This place was in fact threatened by the discourse around legal reform that undermined the special mystique of being thought queer, and finally by liberationism itself, which exploded the codes of innuendo and secrecy that had characterized a world of insider outsiders. Carl Whittman's agitprop "gay manifesto," copied from the San Francisco original and distributed by the London GLF, called the "closeted queen" an "Uncle Tom . . . the most harmful pattern of behavior in the ghetto." Similarly, class affectation was pronounced in the long British music hall tradition of cross-dressing, and in the comic drag of both amateur panto and commercial popular entertainments—which might or might not convey even a superficial reading of "homosexuality" but which suggests at the popular level at least an especially British area of gender ambiguity largely absent in U.S. culture. Drag reviews like Danny La Rue's show at the Palace Theatre (1970–72)—an entertainment "fit for families"—could draw heterosexual audiences of thousands. On 30 September 1972, the "annual" Miss U.K. Drag Queen dinner/dance was held at the Hilton Hotel in Park Lane.[23]

From the standpoint of 1969, the chief difference on the ground between the American and British contexts for Gay Liberation, however, was the fact that the legal situation in Britain, after a decade of reformist lobbying, parliamentary discussion, sexology paperbacks, and even BBC documentaries,[24] dramatically changed in 1967 with the decriminalization of private, consensual adult homosexual behavior—a change that heralded a significant shift in gay consciousness if not in police harassment. In the States, with a longer history of liberal homophile lobbying organizations, only a few states had made gestures toward changing antihomosexuality laws by the late sixties—though there were wide variations in the aggressiveness of police enforcement. On the other hand, though reformism in Britain in its organizational and rhetorical character in the late fifties had sometime taken its cue from across the ocean, it was slower to respond to the rising militancy there. Nor did British homosexuals, in spite of, or perhaps because of, the legal change in 1967, anticipate the militant liberationism exported by the American movement in the summer of 1969.

The American campaign to reform public opinion and the law, the so-called homophile movement, had its origins, shortly after the war, in California, inspired by the Negro civil rights movement. In 1951 Donald Webster Cory's *The Homosexual in America* presented homosexuals as a persecuted minority who were the innocent victims of discrimination and negative stereotyping. "Cory" (a pen-name) advanced the essentially liberal integrationist view that, their sexuality apart, homosexual men and women, stigmatized by pejorative labels, were largely indistinguishable from other moral, respectable citizens. This strategy of representation involved the creation of as much distance as possible from the subcultural underworld of the criminal and secret homosexual community that was stock-in-trade of the exposé press in both the United States and Britain in the early 1950s. Something of the same insistence on the respectability of the individual, (otherwise) law-abiding homosexual can be seen in Peter Wildeblood's testimony at his trial in 1953 and subsequent self-presentation in *Against the Law* (1955) and as the Wolfenden Committee's first homosexual witness.[25]

In the United States, a more robust agenda was presented by the Mattachine Society, founded in 1951 in Los Angeles by left activists, some with ties to the CPUSA. Securing minority rights would require education and organization of homosexuals themselves as a deprived minority like "the Negro, Mexican and Jewish Peoples" who could demand their rights, though the tenor of the organization was toned down a couple of years later at the height of the McCarthy panic. By the time a New York chapter was organized in Greenwich Village in 1955, the Mattachine Society, and after 1956 its sister homophile organization, the Daughters of Bilitis, presented a front that was largely professional and liberal, determined through its own respectability and the suppression of homosexual stereotypes to disarm prejudice and further legal reform.[26]

Analogous organizations like the Homosexual Law Reform Society and the closely associated Albany Trust emerged in Britain in the late fifties, in respectable character and liberal tone much like the Mattachine Society in New York. Though these may have been propelled into activity specifically by the opportunity that the recommendations of the Wolfenden Report in 1957 seemed to offer for reform of the criminal law, there had been from the late forties some "signs of a new self confidence" in metropolitan homosexual circles. By the sixties there was also an emerging lesbian activism in Britain to some extent modeled on the American scene: in 1963 the first publicly lesbian social organization, the

Minorities Research Group, was founded to promote discussion and research on sexuality. As Rebecca Jennings has described, the MRG was closely connected with their American counterparts (their publication, *Arena Three,* mirrored the American lesbian monthly, *The Ladder*) and sought collaboration with American sexologist researchers. In 1965 an MRG project on "theories of lesbianism" was supervised by an American psychologist at Cambridge, June Hopkins.[27]

In the United States the Wolfenden investigation and its report were "closely monitored" in the emerging gay press, and "offered hope for a future" of sympathetic allies and enlightened experts. There was a certain circularity of influence. Post-Wolfenden British homophile lobbying organizations, themselves in part inspired by American developments, now offered moderates in the United States a model for a liberal program of influence. Curtis Dewees of the New York Mattachine looked to the Homosexual Law Reform Society, a body that "consisted of some of that country's most respected citizens," to confirm his view that the best hope for progress in the United States lay with moderation and influence rather than militants and a mass movement. The complete Wolfenden Report was available in an American edition by 1963, and by the mid-sixties mainstream media—*The New York Times, Newsweek,* and *Time* magazine—as well as the gay press commonly referenced the British findings when discussing the course of the American reform effort. By this time, however, things were changing in the American homosexual reform movement, very much following the shift in character of the civil rights movement toward a more assertive black militancy.[28]

If British homophile organizations had closely paralleled the American example in the fifties, they were much slower to embrace this new activism, evident among the more militant younger leaders like Franklin Kameny in Washington, DC, or Charlie Hayden and Craig Rockwell in New York. By 1965, with Carmichael's call for Black Power setting the tone and with the rapidly evolving antiwar movement generating a new politics of in-the-streets demonstration, the respectable American homophile organizations began to develop serious fissures between those still intent on mollifying and lobbying straight politicians and those who looked to force the pace by militantly contesting discriminatory practice. But militant tactics required a radical change in the self-protective quietism of middle-class homosexual culture. For the new activists, Black Power offered the precisely appropriate paradigm of self-awareness, self-empowerment, and "pride." Out of this Gay Power and Gay Liberation were born.

In Britain, there was, in the beginning, very little resonance with the new activism. In part this was due doubtless to the expectations that had been raised by the election of a Labour government in 1964 and the possibility that the Wolfenden Report would finally, and in the near future, bear fruit. Perhaps it is also the case that the special resonance of homosexual and black grievance and the ways in which the gay campaign could draw on the rhetoric and tactics of the civil rights movement did not obtain in Britain with anything like the same force, at least until black militancy manifested itself there late in the 1960s. In Britain, 1967 was the culmination of a post-Wolfenden decade of the politics of liberal sympathy. In the United States it was the beginning of a new politics of activist confrontation, visible already in the universities: a Student Homophile League was organized at Columbia in 1966, but rapidly, in the radicalizing spirit of the time, evolved beyond the liberal implication of its name; in 1967 Greenwich Village saw the beginning of Craig Rodwell's campaign "to bring Gay Power to New York." By 1968 there were new-style gay activists on the fringes at least of the campus antiwar revolt as it spread across the United States, while Columbia's militant gay student organization itself became the model for gay student chapters on campuses across the country.[29]

Securing legal reform in Britain had seemed neither to require nor inspire homosexual militancy (though once achieved, its limitations provided fuel for what was to come in 1969 and 1970). If anything there was, in the realm of liberal opinion, a certain smug satisfaction that Britain in matters of sexuality, as in its abolition of the death penalty, was considerably in advance of what Diana Trilling called the "puritanical and prurient" United States.[30] Medicalized definitions of homosexuality, however, had been prevalent in the public debate leading up to the change in the laws, and this aspect of "liberal pity," along with the kinds of aversion therapy advanced and practiced on both sides of the Atlantic, helped prepare many for radicalization at the end of the decade.

After taking an Oxford BA in sociology, Mary McIntosh spent a year at Berkeley in 1960–61 and was drawn into student civil rights activism and protests in San Francisco—which turned violent—against the excesses of the Un-American Affairs Committee. Back in Britain as a junior lecturer at the University of Leicester, she was involved in a pub sit-in with a black friend (a tactic that re-emerged when, as a GLF activist in 1972, she helped organize pub protests). By the mid-sixties she was committed to the view that the "homosexual role" was largely social rather than an aberrant medical or psychological construction, thanks to "cross-cultural" (that is, Anglo-American) research: she was deeply influenced by Kinsey's studies of American sexual practices, Ford's and Beach's *Patterns of Sexual Behaviour*, and her reading "a lot of the American homophile movement's literature." In the event, she published her work, not in a British journal ("I would not have known what journal to publish it in in this country"), but in the main American forum for labeling theory, *Social Problems*.[31]

Subsequently, radical sociologists in Britain generally, and in particular Kenneth Plummer writing on homosexual identity and homophobic stigmatization, drew heavily, like Carol Warren in Los Angeles, on American social theory that contested traditional approaches to deviancy with ideas of labeling and social interactionism. Plummer, writing in 1973, found in this body of work an especially useful approach to his exploration of sexual stigma "in this culture" (by which he meant preliberation United States *and* Britain). But he also found in the GLF a corrective that "served as an important—if transitory—stimulant for me to remember ideas that could easily have got lost in the welter of interactionist subjectivism." Anglo-American Gay Liberation not only offered some scholars a personal "stimulant" to explore the uses and limitations of American deviancy theory, but itself became an object of study in the (re)construction of identities. At the Ninth Symposium of the National Deviancy Conference, held in Sheffield in January 1972, Mary McIntosh, now an active member of both Women's Liberation and the London GLF, delivered a paper on "Gay Liberation and Gay Ghetto."[32]

TRANSATLANTIC GAY LIBERATION

In June 1970, when I read about the Christopher Street Gay Pride march in New York, I remember feeling that *that* could never happen in London—and a good thing too. But by November of that year I was enthusiastically attending meetings of the London GLF and feeling that my whole outlook and life were being transformed.

—Jeffrey Weeks

Within a year after the Stonewall riots in New York City in the summer of 1969 a Gay Liberation movement exploded onto a London scene that had not, unlike the American East and West coasts, seen the local evolution of a militant cadre. This quite sudden takeoff can best be explained by the quickening of transatlantic traffic of both people and media in the last years of the decade. There had long been a traffic of sorts in those who sought sexual adventure and discovery, either as a chief motive for traveling or as an additional attraction. When police surveillance was increased in London in the early fifties, American tourists and servicemen were sometimes caught up in its nets—like the U.S. naval chaplain who was found to have visited urinals in Piccadilly some nine times in a twenty-four-hour period. London may have been especially attractive to American men looking for an anonymous urban world where homosexuality was thought to be more common than back in middle America; in the context of significant growth in tourism and professional and commercial cross-traffic, "homosexual men traded their own apocryphal versions of the city." The supposedly relaxed moral regime of Swinging London further heightened the attractions of the city for American visitors: both Hunter Davies (1966) and Piri Halasz (1967) included information in their guides to London aimed at, presumably, both flaneurs (homosexual dives being part of the "London experience") and those with a more active interest. Both were precluded, in these last years before the law changed, from offering "any precise directions as to where a queer may find a companion," though Davies could direct his readers to Piccadilly for "rough rent" and generally to "West End lavatories . . . thronged with queers obviously importuning—many of them visitors and tourists." Harasz was less candid, but noted, "Homosexuality is discussed much more openly and matter-of-factly in London than in the United States," and the law was "largely unenforced."[33]

The legal change in 1967 and the rapid elaboration of openly gay clubs and pubs enhanced such tourist attractions. There was also some traffic in the other direction as well. There had long been well-heeled frequent travelers like Gielgud or Coward who expected to move in certain circles in New York or Los Angeles, but there were in the sixties and seventies an increasing number—often students and young professionals, women as well as men—who flew to the States and discovered the developing gay movement and social scenes there—like the BBC presenter Jackie Forster, who from the late fifties had traveled back and forth to the States for lecture tours and appearances on U.S. television. Her first lesbian affair was with an American woman in London, and on her next trip to the States they toured Miami and the Keys, the start of a three-year relationship ("I never even knew there was a gay scene"). When this ended she met a Canadian woman with whom she explored, and found disturbing, "diesel dyke" venues in New York City. Subsequently, Forster became involved in the Campaign for Homosexual Equality. This is not to say that every homosexual who traveled sought sexual adventure. Philip Derbyshire was a Mancunian who discovered Gay Liberation in the early seventies while an undergraduate at Cambridge. In the States to study for a Ph.D., he "went back into the closet" because of his foreigner's sense of "extreme disorientation," "a sort of inner suicide." Nevertheless, his American experience ended in an American solution of sorts: he sought "the ministrations of a very sympathetic therapist" who convinced him that it was "the repression of my homosexuality and not my being gay that was at the root of my 'breakdown.'" When he returned to London in 1976 he became a committed left liberationist.[34]

The American Gay Lib *movement*, its consciousness fostered by the counterculture and its "attitude" by Black Power, famously exploded in the aftermath of the Stonewall Inn riots in Greenwich Village in late June of 1969, a series of events that quickly assumed the status of key foundation moment and myth for "Gay Liberation" as self-liberation. The continuing demonstrations that summer, the organization of an "action committee" of a "Gay Liberation Front," the spread of militant gay activity to other American cities, and the rapid emergence of a radical gay presence in the media—first in countercultural organs like the *Village Voice* and the *East Village Other* and then in the national press (*Time* magazine ran a cover story on gay militants in October)—amplified the meaning of the confrontation in Christopher Street and shifted it from its local context to the global as a kind of universal signifier of resistance to homophobic oppression.[35]

If British mainstream media was slower to pick up on this message than it had been on militant feminism in the United States (the *Times* took no notice of either the riots or the "gay power" demonstrations that followed), transatlantic word of mouth in the gay community and the Underground press in London ensured that the Stonewall moment would "travel" and seed a new militancy there. The ground was prepared by growing concern over the apparent inadequacies of the reform of 1967 and the more aggressive policing that seemed to have followed this liberalization, as well as the gathering international movement to challenge the understanding of alternative sexualities in the medical profession and the academy. In Manchester Alan Horsfall's Northwest Homosexual Law Reform Society rechristened itself the Committee for Homosexual Equality (later the Campaign for Homosexual Equality), dedicated to a more activist, if still liberal and reformist, national program. In the spring and summer of 1970 the gay and feminist disruptions of psychiatric conferences and further developments in both New York, where there was a mass rally in Central Park on the first anniversary of Stonewall, and on the West Coast did finally receive some attention in the British press. The news persuaded some, like Aubrey Walter and a radical L.S.E. student, Bob Mellors, to go to the States themselves.[36]

Walter and Mellors, who was "hanging out with New York GLF," met at the Black Panther convention in Philadelphia and "decided that when we got back to London we would call a meeting to organize a GLF there." They first attempted to raise interest at the L.S.E.: "I think we were still rather full of American rhetoric and gay liberation slogans such as 'We gotta get out of the ghetto' and 'Out of the closets and into the streets.'" There was already some ferment among gay radical students in Britain, and following their rapid proliferation on the East and West coasts university gay organizations began to appear in Britain. By the early seventies "GaySoc" groups had been organized at most British universities and at many polytechnics and colleges, often with some support from their student unions.[37]

Inaugural meetings at the L.S.E. for a *British* Gay Liberation Front took the New York name along with much of its countercultural style, though Elizabeth Wilson later argued that it quickly "transcended the 'head' and left scenes from which it sprang." While some may have been further removed from the counterculture than others, the movement as a whole in fact remained close to its origins—in its street theater, performance art, happenings and zaps, in the widespread use of marijuana and LSD "to break down," as Walter said, "their internalisation of repressed social norms," and in awareness groups and communes. In the open, indeed exhibitionist, declaration of nonconformist sexual identity there was a significant debt to "beat" self-expressiveness and hippy sexual freedom. As John D'Emilio has said of the gay-friendly milieu in bohemian San Francisco, "Through the beats' example, gays could perceive themselves as nonconformists rather than as deviates, as rebels against stultifying norms rather than immature, unstable personalities." John Phillips, who joined the GLF in London in his early twenties in 1970, has argued that the movement derived much more from the bohemian street counterculture than from a swish "swinging London" style—long hair, jeans and sneakers, street theater up and down Portobello Road market, and the American Black Power movement (which "had been particularly influential with me"). Gay Liberation's social makeup unsurprisingly confirms a continuity with the radical counterculture: "[A]rtists, drop-outs, social-security claimants and the young"—as well as the kind of "new professional people . . . students, teachers and sociologists" who had characterized the university rebellion and were often—like Jeffrey Weeks in Britain or Toby Marotta in the States—among Gay Lib's first chroniclers.[38]

The inevitable "manifesto," published in October 1971 (Carl Whittman's *A Gay Manifesto* had been published in San Francisco earlier that year), was closely formed on the familiar model of the American black, feminist, and gay declarations, ending with "Gay is Good!" and "All power to oppressed people!" Don Milligan, active in the GLF in London after graduating from the University of Lancaster in 1972 and an early propagandist for its work, saturated his presentation with closely drawn rhetorical associations with Black Power, with "self-oppression" and "self-revulsion," and the need for "a sense of pride." Gay liberation promised, not integration or assimilation (which for minorities "always means cultural submission" and "the destruction of their culture"), but taking "control of who they are": "In the same way that 'niggers' are Beautiful and Black, 'queers' are Glad to be Gay."[39]

If the chants of "Right On!" the raised fists, the Afros, the use of "brother" and "sister," were borrowed from the militant Black Power movement, there was also, as with the black rebellion, a determination to break free from dependence on liberal supporters: "Having straight people around was a very big issue at the start, over the elections to the Steering Committee [of the London GLF]." This issue had already come to a head in the United States in November 1969, when militant activists challenged the right of a "straight" representative from the Mattachine Society, Madolin Cervantes, to attend the 6th biannual convention of the Eastern Regional Coalition of Homophile Organizations. Also as with the Black Power and radical feminist movements, the object early on was not only to challenge straights but also to disrupt the protective strategies of nonradical homosexuals, to disturb and radicalize passive and closeted gays via confrontation and consciousness-raising groups and, generally, to bring the revolution into the open, into people's faces.[40]

In Britain, radical homosexual liberationism—its organization, rhetoric, and tactics, and the subjectivity it advanced—was for the three or four years it flourished in London more directly and self-consciously emulative of its American counterpart than had been true of the reformism that preceded it or the rapid localization of gay culture that followed, though this too was strongly indebted at least to American style. While the Westward-looking enthusiasm of gay men and women caught up in the excitement of the liberationist moment may have involved some forgetting of the ways in which the opening-out of gay culture in

London was indebted to local urban experience and past connectivities, as Neil Bartlett has argued, even he admits that his search for the local was a kind of reaction against his own previous transatlantic enthusiasm: "[L]ike a lot of other men, I'd seen America and 1970 as the start of everything."[41]

Gay Lib in London closely tracked and replicated tactics and modes of the New York, L.A., and San Francisco movement. Gay "sit-ins" in the United States (borrowed from the civil rights campaign) became British "pub occupations" in 1972; GAA "zaps" of political figures and media in New York from October 1970 were followed by the London GLF's zapping of the Festival of Light in September of 1971; "Gay-ins" and "Gay-Days" crossed the ocean like the rainbow flag. Communes, already inscribed within the radical left and the hippy counterculture, followed the same pattern, with the 95th Street Collective in New York preceding the Colville Street commune in Notting Hill. The performance art and "gender fuck" tactics of the radical fem "Flaming Faggots" in New York were mirrored a few months later in the antics of the Notting Hill Radical Drag Queens.[42]

Annual Gay Pride marches, "those hugely symbolic rallying events" that became a global institution by the eighties, also first emerged in New York in the summers of 1970 and 1971. The first *British* "Pride march," from Trafalgar Square to Hyde Park, and the first "Gay Day" at Primrose Hill, followed in 1972 (though these were anticipated a few days earlier by the Notting Hill drag queens who joined an anti-Vietnam protest by the Boilermakers Union at the American embassy and then marched on to Piccadilly). Through the seventies Pride marches retained much of their "fight-back" political protest character in London, with participation varying from a few hundred to a thousand or so and confrontation not only with the authorities and right-wing moral campaigners but with the "ghettoized" recreational gay scene itself.[43]

In August 1971, Victoria Brittain finally brought Gay Lib somewhat belatedly to *The Times* with a relatively sympathetic leader, "An Alternative to Sexual Shame": "Recently under the banner of the Gay Liberation Front young homosexuals in England have developed a campaign begun in America." She cited a young Canadian and a "serious articulate American girl in dungarees" with whom she had spoken. The other broadsheets and Sunday papers had begun to pay attention somewhat earlier as London GLF agitation-performance began to provide sensational copy. If the national press was slow to bring Gay Lib to a mass readership, the *countercultural* press in London had, as we have seen, been eager to appropriate gay themes and hoped to generate much-needed income from serving as a notice-board for gay events and organizations as well as from "contact ads." When Keith Birch, age eighteen, came down to London from the Midlands in 1971, it was an advertisement for a GLF dance in *IT* that attracted him to an event that became his personal "catalyst." Within weeks he had joined a "consciousness-raising group" and a gay commune, and had his first homosexual affair.[44]

The nascent gay press itself was very much formed out of the Underground style, ethos, bawdy humor, and distribution tactics of publications like *IT, OZ, INK,* or *FRIENDZ*—both the liberationist agit-prop publications and, in the beginning at least, the commercial press pioneered by *Gay News.* As with radical feminism, their relationship with the counterculture was fraught with contradiction, being both derivative and oppositional. On the one hand, the subversive libertarianism of the Underground encouraged openly gay expression; on the other, the content of much of the radical and countercultural press was ostentatiously hetero-sexist. The first public action of the London GLF in October was to invade the office of the L.S.E. student paper, *Sennet,* to protest against homophobia and send a message to the Underground press that "the same would happen to them if they persisted in operating on . . . a 'tits and arse' basis."[45]

The London GLF's own press publication, its haphazardly produced, hand-distributed agit-prop organ, *Come Together,* was clearly modeled on the style and format of Anglo-American Underground papers like *INK*—from which it sometimes reprinted material. Its specifically *gay* models, though, were American ("We used to pour over all the American publications"), and especially the New York GLF's own short-lived paper, *Come Out!,* which had first appeared in November of 1969. This, like *Come Together* subsequently, was produced by a radical "collective" that emphasized a left-reading of the movement and collaboration with radical feminism—though it collapsed after only eight issues when the women walked out. A "media workshop" at the London GLF produced the first issue of its *Come Together* in November 1970. There were sixteen issues in all, appearing at odd intervals under a variously collective editorship, before closing down in the spring of 1973. As with most of the London Underground press, news from the States received much attention and pieces were reprinted directly from the American gay papers—like the Radicalesbian Martha Shelley's "Stepin Fetchit Woman" in issue 3. Police were invariably "pigs"; comrades, "Brothers and Sisters."[46]

In North America there was also by 1970 a significant expansion of a commercial gay press. Pre-Stonewall titles like the L.A. *Advocate* (from 1967) were quickly joined after Stonewall by a host of more specifically "out and proud" community newspapers like *Gay Sunshine* (San Francisco, 1970), *Gay Liberator* (Detroit, 1970), or *Body Politic* (Toronto, 1971). There was no parallel in Britain until *Gay News* began in the summer of 1972—propelled, perhaps, by the recent addition of a "Gay News" section in *INK.* Like *Come Together,* it was initially published by a collective (with staff taking shares), dependent on volunteer workers and donations, and distributed by hand. But whereas the *Come Together* collective refused to accept personal contact ads on the grounds that "it is sexist to advertise for a partner," *Gay News* did and quickly moved to emulate the more commercial Underground papers. It adopted a large format like *Friendz,* with spot color, and aspired to appear regularly with a national distribution, generate operating income from sales, advertising, and contact ads rather than donations, and be open to "any possible viewpoint" within the broader gay world. Densely American connections were suggested in these early issues in the reportage of events in the United States, the movie reviews, the reprinting of content from the American gay press, interviews with, for instance, David Hockney or Allen Ginsberg, the advertisements for North American gay papers—and even in the personal ads: "Gay student visiting States July–September wishes to contact other people planning same."[47]

Under the editorship of Denis Lemon—the collective idea was dropped within months—*Gay News* rapidly put its GLF origins behind; indeed it became hostile to militant Gay Lib in its communes-and-radical-drag form and developed a closer relationship with the reformist Campaign for Homosexual Equality (CHE). It managed to survive the rapid collapse of the countercultural press in 1973 through a financial reorganization that further distanced the enterprise from its liberationist quasi-leftist origins. At the same time that the front page lost its countercultural lettering, genitalia in illustrations (including cartoons) disappeared as well—a move away from Underground obscenity that was also, presumably, an effort to secure over-the-counter distribution and avoid police suppression in a climate of moral backlash. The key figure in this rapid shift from radical liberationism to entrepreneurial libertarianism ("as in America") was Lemon, later described by disgruntled colleagues as "a hard-faced man who has done well out of the Gay Liberation Wars, and [who] proposes, it is suspected, to do even better." From a working-class background, he was less committed to a liberationist utopianism than to servicing the unfolding gay male recreational culture; he was personally "entranced by the American gay lifestyle and this fascination was increasingly reflected in the contents of the paper."[48]

Transatlantic Radical Lesbians

From the start, Anglo-American Gay Lib drew heavily from the rhetoric and practice of radical feminism, and in its manifestos, militant press, and public performance echoed the feminist assault on "sexism" and traditionally gendered role-playing. But the feminist movement in the United States itself was in some crisis by 1968 and 1969, its goals bitterly contested and its organizational form fragmenting. At the center of this ferment was the problematic of cross-gender collaboration and the militant call for exclusively female institutions and communities, and by extension the possibly constructive and revolutionary role of "political lesbianism."[49]

In the spring of 1973 *Gay News* reprinted (from a San Francisco paper) the angry feminism-as-lesbianism essay "Woman-Identified Woman." This collective statement had first appeared in May 1970 in New York at the Second Congress to Unite Women and had subsequently been widely circulated and reprinted. By 1973 it was already known in Britain in militant circles as the defining statement of radical separatism and of the lesbian as "the rage of all women condensed to the point of explosion." It suggested that, on the one hand, women who did not abandon relations with men were collaborating with the enemy, while on the other homosexuals who simply inverted traditional role-playing (as masculine women and feminine men) remained "inauthentic" constructs of a sexist society characterized by male-centered definitions of self. Lesbianism was therefore "different" from male homosexuality in its ability not just to subvert, but to step outside the male-dominated "system" through an act of rejection that was part of a general shift of "primal commitment" to a woman-defined culture.[50]

Following the May Day conference, "lavender menace" militants organized themselves into the *Radicalesbians*. Drawing support away from both the radical wing of the feminist movement—the Redstockings and the New York Radical Women—*and* from the homophile and new Gay Lib organizations, lesbian separatists threatened to "leave [both] the straight women and gay men behind."[51] For those who adhered to their reading of the radical feminist struggle, collaboration with gay men interfered with the construction of a sisterhood defined by lesbian self-sufficiency. In both New York and London, this message attracted the active support of only a small minority of women, and many lesbians remained active in both the GLF and CHE. Nevertheless "Woman-Identified Woman" was part of a storm of ideas about sexuality that crossed the Atlantic from 1968 to 1974 and served further to unsettle already uneasy cross-gender alliances that had formed within both the Feminist and the Gay Liberation movements.

Lesbian separatism was in Britain often identified as especially American-inspired, by both those who deplored it and those who embraced it; it had been gathering force since the publication of Anne Koedt's widely read article on "The Myth of the Vaginal Orgasm" the same year, 1968, that Valerie Solanas's *SCUM Manifesto* appeared. The pivotal year, however, was 1970 when, following Koedt, Susan Lydon, then involved in feminist consciousness-raising groups at Berkeley, published "The Politics of Orgasm" in the West Coast radical journal *Ramparts*, developing further the idea that clitoral-stimulation made male penetration unnecessary for female pleasure. This essay, like "Woman-Identified Woman" the same year, was known and discussed in Britain, where the feminist film-maker Alison Garthwaite, for instance, found Lydon to be "an inspiration." Also traveling across the Atlantic in 1970 was the "outing" of Kate Millet in December by *Time* magazine. The period of greatest American influence closes in 1974 with the publication of Millet's own tortured engagement with self-hatred and bisexuality, *Flying*, as well as that radical summation of lesbian feminist separatism, "The Clit Statement," a collection of American articles made available by the London Women's Liberation Workshop newsletter that managed to offend not only nonlesbian feminist sisters but also gay male liberationist collaborators as well: "Straight women . . . come on like male transvestite femme drag queens."[52]

Divisions, instability, and rapid disintegration characterized Gay Lib organizations in both the United States and Britain. If from the start there was great difficulty in sustaining a common front that included both the Marxist left and the lifestyle libertarians, even more difficult was the alliance of radical (lesbian) feminists and the mostly male organizers of the Gay Liberation movement. Cross-gender alliances were widely advertised as at the heart of Gay Liberation, but were problematic from the start. The fact that the movement for militant homosexual separatism was dominated—in London as in New York—by men quickly raised suspicions among some feminists. This was true of both those who were committed to what they saw as the larger issues of Women's Liberation generally and, within the gay movement, lesbians who regarded their male allies as, in their relationship with women, men first and homosexuals second. Many feminists—both straight and lesbian—in any event found the gender-parody of militant gay male performance—bearded men parading in make-up, dresses, and high heels—to have disturbing, perhaps misogynist subtexts. In London the launch party for the new feminist journal *Spare Rib* in June of 1972 was awkwardly and uncomfortably gate-crashed by "Radical Feminists" from the GLF—men in "gender-fuck" drag and clown costumes.[53] The rapid drift into mutual suspicion and separate organization that characterized the New York scene was, if to a lesser degree, replicated in London.

In Britain the GLF proclaimed itself to be a movement of gay men and women, "sisters and brothers," united in revolutionary purpose to overthrow sexism—whether in society at large or within the gay scene itself (and some marched together to liberate men-only and women-only gay social venues like the lesbian Gateways Club, zapped on 20 February 1972). Two issues of *Come Together* (whose editorial collective included men and women) were devoted entirely to women's issues, but in fact the women's group within GLF was riven with dissention well before the separatist "walk-out" in February of 1972. Some disillusion (as expressed by Carla Toney in *Come Together* 10) among the women of GLF drew from the sense of "tokenism" within a movement that was preponderantly gay male, while the debate then raging among American feminists over the necessity for lesbian consciousness took concrete form in the radical feminist Faraday Road commune in W10 north of Notting Hill, the subject of an article in the second women's issue of *Come Together*. But significantly the "power struggle" in the women's group of the London GLF was not just about the cultivation of feminist self-sufficiency and pride but also the role of *socialism*.[54]

An undated (probably late 1971 or early 1972) cyclostyled memo among Mary McIntosh's papers, "What Happens Next?" complained, from the socialist point of view, "that something has gone wrong with the Gay Liberation movement" and blamed the (American Radicalesbian) focus on separatism and consciousness-raising: "We cannot solve anything by trying to bring about a revolution in our heads." This issue of ideological grounding proved divisive as well at the second national feminist conference at Skegness in October 1971, where the lesbian radical minority split with the dominant socialists—ultimately establishing their own national conference in 1974.[55]

If Gay Liberation had a tendency to pull apart at the seams of gender and ideology—with socialist women reinvesting themselves in Women's Lib, the radical lesbians emulating their American sisters by withdrawing to consciousness-raising communal cells, and spin-off collaborationist institutions like the alternative theater group Gay Sweatshop almost immediately falling into separate organizations for women and men—it is nevertheless easy to exaggerate fragmentation as somehow indicative of the collapse of collaboration in the movement as a whole. Jeffrey Weeks claims that the women's walk-out at the GLF was "largely symbolic" and many "centrally involved" gay men and women continued to work together. Certainly Gay Pride marches developed into a major demonstration of movement unity by the end of the decade in both the States and in Britain and consistently drew men and women together in celebration, just as some local gay pubs drew a comfortably "mixed" clientele and icons of gay culture enjoyed a popularity with both gay men and lesbians. Dusty Springfield, London-born but since the early sixties a recording star who lived much of the time in the United States, who greatly admired Aretha Franklin and patterned her own musical style on Nashville and Motown, who sang with Jimi Hendrix on BBC TV in 1969 and who declared her own bisexuality in 1970, may have seen her popularity decline with the general public in the seventies, but it remained solid among London's gay community, who turned out for her live performances; "You Don't Have to Say You Love Me" was a pre-disco constant in gay male and lesbian locals.[56]

If there were lesbians within the London GLF who were *not* committed to radicalesbianism, nevertheless, those who were were a vocal and significant minority of activists very closely attuned to American radical feminism. They often had American activist friends in London and avidly read and promulgated American radical tracts. For many of these the discovery of a new personal *and collective* subjectivity as out lesbian sisters was as transforming an experience as coming out had been for many closeted gay men ("realizing what it's all about . . . feeling my own self-oppression for the first time. Realizing my isolation"; "I left my husband"; "I felt very much in the middle of things"). Often their radicalism was evolved not in large movement organizations but in the kind of local discussion groups that coalesced under the umbrella of the London Women's Liberation Workshop. Janet Dixon, for example, found her separatist "extremism" and decision to leave the London GLF confirmed by reading the American "Clit papers" in 1973 and the next year Elizabeth Gould Davis's *The First Sex* ("[An] American friend brought me over from the States a copy"). An active member of the LWLW, she was one of those who caused a storm by deciding provocatively to make the Clit Statement—controversial even among radical feminists in the States—widely available, an action that apparently drove many moderate women out of the LWLW.[57]

Transatlantic Gay Liberation in its utopian countercultural mode was relatively short-lived. By the end of 1973 the American GLF, as well as the Daughters of Bilitis *and* the Radicalesbians, had disintegrated, and the rival Gay Activists Alliance was near collapse. In London, the British GLF was rapidly fragmenting by the end of 1972 and its organ *Come Together* ceased publication in the following spring—following the general trend of the Underground press. Characterized by instability and division, Gay Lib's organizational form if not the positive sense of self it promoted rapidly expired. In both the United States and Britain there was, on the one hand, a return (for some) to a more practicable reformism, and, on the other, the elaboration (for many more) of an open "lifestyle."[58]

When Denis Lemon interviewed David Hockney, who had become a celebrity icon in the transatlantic gay world, the subject arose of how gay life differed in America where the Yorkshire-born artist had been living and working (in southern California) since 1963. Hockney noted the larger number of gay papers available in the States, which he thought a good thing, but also what he called "the American tendency to ghettoize," which he hoped would not happen in Britain.[59] Of course it did, at least in some degree, and very much took its cue from American style. By the mid-seventies militant consciousness-raising group discussions, zaps, dances in church and community halls, and commune experiments in squats—though some of these lived on in an increasingly attenuated form—had largely disappeared as sign-posts of modern gay life. They never managed to replace the "ghettoized" gay social scenes they contested; indeed these flourished in the seventies—an increasingly differentiated, largely commercial leisure world of pubs, clubs, and discos. A gay-themed commercial press, fueled by advertising and contact ads, promoted (actual or virtual) gay villages and services for gays by gays ranging from house-cleaning to financial advice and travel agents.

In a sense this marks a return to the local after the exhaustion of a global liberationism—a less discreet, hidden-away localization than that of the preliberation scene. But, though local in its organization, seventies gay "hedonism" was also often openly derivative—as American styles of dress, music, and venue permeated (even if via Amsterdam or Berlin) the increasingly variegated gay social scenes. John Phillips, an early GLF activist in London, left the liberation movement to spend seven years in New York City. When he returned to London in the late seventies he found a transformed postliberation world: "[L]ike gay politics, much of American gay male lifestyles and fashions had crossed the Atlantic." For most homosexual men, preliberation social life in London as in American cities had revolved less around specifically gay pubs and clubs than would be the case in the out-and-proud scene of the seventies. Lesbian culture was even more domestic than that of gay males—though "domestic" developed a new meaning in the sixties with the growing fashion for lesbian house parties. A distinct lesbian pub-and-club subculture had emerged after the war, but there were relatively few venues, like the well-known Gateways in Chelsea, where women could meet, dance, and enjoy (often American) music and a drink. Like the Gateways, they were also perhaps distinctively British in their low-key respectability; there was hardly anything like the well-developed and specialized bar scene in New York where Jackie Forster found the extrovert "diesel dykes" so unsettling.[60]

Male Gay Liberation in the United States, in its early somewhat Puritanical manifestation, aggressively denounced the world of backstreet bars and clubs, as it did the anonymous netherworld of "cruising" in public parks, toilets, baths, and—perhaps unique to the New York scene—parked trucks. The object was to drag homosexuality out of a ghetto that was both imposed and self-constructed, reflecting also a radical countercultural commitment to "love" and authenticity rather than "mere" sexual gratification and objectification. A vigorous, confrontational, and divisive campaign against distinctively homosexual social routines and practices was ultimately unsustainable in New York as it was in London and led, as we have seen, to a countermovement that affirmed "gay difference" and, rejecting not only the heterosexual family but also the ersatz family ideology of utopian communes, rationalized and justified a uniquely gay approach to (demystified, casual, and libertarian) sex.[61]

In London, the Puritan idealism of the New York GLF had been enthusiastically adopted as a central part of liberation ideology and practice. As Don Milligan explained in 1973, "One of the results of gay oppression is the 'gay scene' . . . composed simply of bars and clubs." If many of the bars were "meat-racks," expensive gay clubs also encouraged class exclusivity with their "piss-elegance." According to Aubrey Walter, "Very early on we recognized that . . . we had to create an alternative social scene." Partly this was tactical ("[T]he vast majority of gay men and lesbians hardly ever went to gay pubs, clubs or discos"), but the London GLF's aggressive assault on the gay scene—the protest marches into gay and lesbian pubs or outside well-known "cottages"—also drew from a radical commitment to reconstruct mentality and gendered role-playing in order to "break down their internalisation of repressed social norms": out of the pubs and toilets and into consciousness-raising groups, communes, and "collective acid trips." Liberationist "alternatives" faded however with the counterculture from which they sprang, while the "ghettos" of gay social life throve in the seventies as in no other era, in unabashed celebration of virtual neighborhoods of gay taste and style.[62]

Gay Lib began by admonishing homosexuals not only to get out of gay bars and clubs but to demand their right to be served in "straight" establishments—to assert that any space was gay space. Beginning in 1966 militants in the New York Mattachine Society inaugurated a campaign of "sip-ins" to challenge restrictions on serving homosexuals in bars—a direct borrowing from the civil rights movement's antisegregation sit-ins—only to find to their disappointment that after they declared themselves to be homosexuals most bartenders served them anyway. In London the GLF conducted their own campaign of "gay-ins" at Notting Hill pubs in the autumn of 1971 in response to being barred (refused service), overcharged, and harassed at pubs in the area. In the beginning they were refused at a number of locals, but many quickly caved in. Much depended on the prejudices of pub management and staff, but also on the attitude of the breweries that owned most pubs.[63]

The British "tied-house" system (in the United States most pubs were locally owned, apart from the queer bars in New York controlled by the Mafia) meant that the national breweries might lean on local pub managers to resist serving gays out of fear that their straight clientele would withdraw their custom—initially an issue at the Chepstow in West London, where the police were called in. But most of the older pubs already serving a largely gay clientele were also tied to major breweries (like the Champion in Bayswater or the Coleherne in Earl's Court—both owned by Bass-Charrington), which, by the mid-seventies, were eager to cash in on the "pink pound" by extending their list of gay venues. Some locals (often in areas where neighborhood straight custom was in decline) were simply recast as gay—recruiting staff who were gay or gay-friendly and introducing gay entertainments. Not long after the confrontation with Gay Libbers, the Chepstow was itself reinvented as a gay pub. In both the United States and Britain the rapid emergence of a scene of openly gay bars aiming to service various special tastes was commercially driven. In Britain, however, the national organization of the drink trade made this trend both easier and more "local," pubs converted to serve gays being part of a larger licensed network that ran throughout the inner London neighborhoods. In America, where drinking was less a matter of neighborhood socializing than of singles cruising, gay bars were more likely to be in derelict and "red-light" districts.

In 1973, a young C of E curate in London who worked with youth observed that there had been since about 1969 a marked shift of the gay scene away from the seamier sex-trade areas of Soho, and establishments where the clientele appeared largely to be middle-aged men and young hustlers, to the brighter parts of West and South-West London where new pubs and clubs were springing up to cater to a younger, more "out" crowd. This was the beginning of a migration to "new centres of a burgeoning gay community," especially in Kensington and Bayswater, a phenomenon quite distinct socially from the Bohemian, countercultural gay colonization of Notting Hill. The new scene was much more diversified, anticipating the "proliferation of urban sites of homosexuality" that came to characterize the post-seventies era. A relatively open subculture (defined as a recreational culture) was rapidly emerging—though still harassed by police, toughs, and moral campaigners—to celebrate "their own" urban space. In the States there was a "huge migration" of gay men to New York, San Francisco, and Los Angeles; the British focus was almost entirely a London one, with its parallel "migration" one-directional—from provincial cities to the capital. The elaboration of gay culture in London reflected the exuberant commercial scene then exploding in American cities, with its "proliferation of identifiably gay bars, discos, restaurants, bath-houses, bookstores, sex shops, artistic enterprises, publishing ventures, hotels, community centers." But the British experience, as Jeffrey Weeks has suggested, never attained quite the same degree of frenetic hedonism.[64]

The seventies London scene was marked, in the vast expanse of the capital, by an apparent increase in the number and specialization of pubs and clubs, with different atmospheres catering to different tastes. There had of course long been some specialization in homosexual venues, and some of the apparent increase was no doubt an artifact of their now being listed and advertised in commercial guides and the gay press rather than depending as in the past solely on word of mouth. Successive editions of Nicholas Saunders's *Alternative London* included ever larger sections on "gay London" (its 1977 edition rather unnecessarily informed its readers that its gay section was "written entirely by a homosexual"). By mid-decade there were upwards of sixty pubs and clubs of various kinds listed for gay males (many fewer for the lesbian scene) in such publications and in the gay press. If London proved inhospitable for British versions of New York's exuberantly erotic gay sauna scene (police came down hard on two West London saunas in February and March of 1977), the masculine American "clone" was a successful import, already entrenched as a subcultural style before the late-seventies American disco group Village People popularized "an extreme macho, Western American look" that was "self-assertive, highly consumerist and not at all revolutionary."[65]

In London the clone look and ethos (in which casual sex was "desacralised and uncoupled from the context of romantic love") never defined the London scene as a whole. David Bowie's feline androgyny, and Glamrock ("faggot-rock") generally, achieved a special niche that drew on British traditions of camp and drag and was a native counter to American machismo. Rather more ambiguously, mid- and late-1970s British Punk (arguably an American import, at least in inspiration) both rejected hippy counterculture and was closely associated with (Americanized) gay subculture—in its early venues, the prominence of gay people in its audiences, and its appropriation of gay-hustler-derived leathered, sadomasochistic style. Punk (and Clone), in Frank Mort's view, projected but also subverted traditional ideas of masculinity through a "language of pastiche and bricolage."[66]

Charles Silverstein was an American psychologist dedicated to providing a psychotherapy for gays that worked to counter sexual guilt about their identity. In 1977 he copublished with the not-yet-well-known Edmund White a gay version of Alex Comfort's 1972 best-selling guide *The Joy of Sex*. Though both authors were American, *The Joy of Gay Sex* as a publishing project in fact originated in Britain, where the prospective publisher had been frightened off by their solicitor's advice that the book risked prosecution for obscenity. In the event, the U.S. editions proved hard (though not impossible) to get commercially in the U.K., where Customs and Excise would often confiscate imported copies or police would raid and seize what they deemed to be "pornographic" stock at the newly established gay bookshops like "American Boys" in Earl's Court. The book nevertheless became well known in the male gay community (a companion volume, Emily Sisley's and Bertha Harris's *The Joy of Lesbian Sex*, followed within the year)—as an American import by American authors with a message that sex was uncomplicated fun. This harmonized with the proliferating recreational scene promoted in the commercial gay press. *The Joy of Gay Sex* not only provided advice on gay sexual techniques; it also offered helpful hints on cruising.[67]

In a sense, cruising became global by the end of the decade as cheaper and faster air travel allowed many to expand their horizons. Tourism in general encouraged in many cities a "commodification of space" that from the seventies included rapidly developing "queer space" and a marketing that aimed, in the beginning, to attract the pink dollar or pound (but that ironically would subsequently attract straights to gay areas as "a geography of cool"). There emerged in the United States and in Britain a tourism industry that was especially aimed at the gay male market. The near Continent provided British gays—their copies of *The Spartacus Guide* in hand—with relatively cheap access to a wider and often much more liberal gay sex scene. And, if things were less liberal in Roman Catholic and Eastern European countries, international guides might at least direct interested visitors to "cruising spots and places where gays congregate (always Hilton hotels . . .)." What *America* had to offer was not just a liberalized scene in many of the major cities, especially San Francisco, where out gay life was, if not majoritarian, at least commonplace, empowered, and localized in neighborhoods, but also getaway resort sites specializing in an affluent gay holiday trade—Fire Island, Provincetown, South Beach, the Keys.[68]

Transatlantic gay tourism was in both directions, and in the seventies Americans might be found in the Coleherne in Earls Court as well as the National Gallery. Others, like the gay artist Philip Core, came looking to stay. Born in Dallas and graduating from Harvard in 1973, Core dabbled in pop and experimental art and film in New York before moving on to Britain where he attended the Ruskin School of Drawing at Oxford. He moved permanently to London, age twenty-four, in 1975 where he developed an artistic style of painting and sculpture that drew on his own hedonism for images of the erotic and dark evocations of gay cruising. By 1976–77 he had established, at least among the cognoscenti of the Anglo-American gay art world, a presence through a number of exhibitions in public and commercial galleries in London. The avant-garde in London, it has been argued, was especially marked in the seventies by "the emergence and widespread influence of the homosexual subculture," often available as an American export—influential not only among gay male artists but also in radical feminist "body art."[69]

Two things appeared to be determining the future of gay life in Britain a decade after the drama of gay liberationism jumped from New York to London. Both were disparaged by the socialist gay left as characteristically American: the "invention of the ethnic homosexual," that is, the reification of gays and their "alternative" sexuality into an essentialized community comparable to (American ideas of) minority ethnicity; and the dominance of lifestyle commercialism over a politics of anticapitalist liberation and the primacy of "enjoyment" and "self-awareness" as a "new ideology . . . so current in the United States." Especially focusing this latter complaint that the United States, as the hegemon of capitalist culture, was exporting to Britain a consumerist form of gay identity, was the disco boom in the second half of the decade. Though disco may have lost some of its American (gay and black) overtones as it was transplanted from New York into British heterosexual youth culture generally, it shifted the recreational London gay scene away from the local pubs and clubs. "Bang" was the first gay megadisco, opening with great success in the Charing Cross Road in 1976 and signaling a fashion for large commercial venues, youthful clientele, loud American disco music, light shows, and a sexually charged environment—"a new hedonism, where sexual pleasure was placed at the heart of a new gay identity." It was followed in 1979 by "Heaven Under the Arches" off Villiers Street, a vast venue of four floors advertised as "Europe's biggest gay disco."[70]

Whether or not one accepts the left critique—and since the nineties there has been a useful revisionist scholarship on the "enchantment" and life-affirming aspects of "commodity culture"—the highly commercialized scene that emerged in the eighties and nineties and the gay leisure zones that followed in Soho, Brighton, or Manchester seemingly confirm a definitive, generational turn away from the residual idealism of the liberation movement (it also meant that many "gay villages" were by the nineties in danger of being swamped by voyeuristic heterosexuals— what one critic has called the "straightening of gay space"). But this oppositional binary—and ironically *both* the earnest utopians and the celebratory hedonists were "born in the USA"—may be more apparent than real. As with the misleading opposition of the global and the local, it may be that, as some postcolonial critics of modernism aver, it is more a case of "both/and" than "either/or."[71]

As with the other liberationisms we have studied, the reconstruction of the gay self in the late twentieth century was as much a matter of "performance discourse" as manifesto argument and political lobbying. The reclaimed, unapologetic subjectivity of the liberation moment importantly "survived"—this would certainly also be true of the women's and the black liberation movements—not in fringe communes and generational nostalgia, but in the mentality of a perhaps unreflective successor generation. One can find such "attitude" as much wired into the "hedonist" performance culture of the disco as in celebratory Gay Pride marches. For gays, as for many feminists, the most powerfully popular disco song of the era was not the BeeGees' "Night Fever" but the black American Gloria Gaynor's soulfully defiant "*I Will Survive*," released in 1978. Played endlessly in pubs, clubs, and discos, it already achieved the status of gay anthem well before AIDS gave it an added poignancy.

PART IV

Postmodern, Antimodern

If the United States shaped ways in which modernity was read in Britain, it also helped generate its seventies antithesis, the several forms of both empire and village-England nostalgia. With the fragmenting of the radical counterculture and the rapid marginalization of at least political liberationism, and in the context of Britain's apparent slide into urban decay, economic decline, and social chaos, America provided both an available "fall guy" for the failure of British modernity but also a market for the restorative myths of Heritage Britain.

The export to the United States of heritage Britain and Britishness was hardly new—reaching back at least to empire epics of the thirties and to wartime cinema, which, however much it may have denigrated blimpish mentality, also continued to celebrate clichés of British character for both the British and American popular markets: the nobility of "the few," the stoicism of the many, and the enduring decency and representativeness of an idealized England of the shires. If in Britain these myths were challenged by the New Wave filmmakers of the late fifties and early sixties, such films did not, with perhaps the exception of the arguably late–New Wave but also "swinging London" film *Alfie*, export well to the States, where provincial accents could not be understood and the themes contradicted the stereotypes that were being marketed by the tourism industry. Tony Richardson made his American name, not with *Look Back in Anger*, but with the period romp *Tom Jones*.

In the sixties the Bond films marketed, not history but clichés of Britishness in modern dress. As an entertainment industry, they were a transatlantic enterprise presided over by Harry Saltzman, a Canadian-born Jewish American "wheeler dealer showman on the grand scale" who went West to Hollywood and then to London, where he formed Woodfall Productions with Osborne and Richardson and produced many of the "new wave" films. If these didn't sell well in the United States, his next venture, with the U.S. millionaire Albert R. Broccoli, did when he gambled and got the option to produce the first of the Bond films. Their transatlantic success encouraged commercial television producers like Lew Grade successfully to export to the United States spin-offs like *The Saint* or *The Avengers* that marketed, as did many of the British invasion bands, British style and accent. If Emma Peel was a leather-booted feminist, her unflappable insouciance was as "British" as Steed's brolly, jag, and bowler hat.

The great export success of the seventies, however, was that of nostalgia television, first by the BBC, as it came to specialize in historically costumed literary dramatizations, and quickly followed by the commercial companies. There is perhaps a more complex interaction between British self-presentation and American market than meets the eye. In Britain the turn away from kitchen-sink realism or swinging London farce toward the Edwardians of *The Forsyte Saga* and *Upstairs, Downstairs* is conventionally located domestically (both were very popular at home before being exported to the States) as responses to the failure of the promise of modernism and the collapse of national self-confidence in an era that sought comfort in the imagined social cohesiveness of a past deferential society. And yet, also at play was a kind of circularity of transatlantic cultural relations. In the seventies it becomes especially difficult to distinguish the domestic from the transatlantic in the nostalgia business, especially in a "heritage television" that was increasingly intended for the American market, cofinanced and coproduced transatlantically, but also consumed at home, or in the expanded antiques markets in seventies London that throve on rising domestic but also tourist and export demand.

Analysis of the nostalgia phenomenon in both countries has often remarked its essentially middle-class ideology and social geography. In the United States those who responded most enthusiastically to PBS and its offering of cherry-picked high culture and literary costume drama programming from Britain (by and large British low comedy did not cross the ocean until the nineties) often seem to affirm what some have seen as a characteristically upwardly mobile, status-conscious desire to embrace British programming as "real quality." Speculation about social class and viewers' motives draws attention to the way a fixation with the idealized past may entrench class prejudice and justify antidemocratic, perhaps even antimeritocratic social values. Others,[1] however, have argued that the culture of nostalgia, including a hunger for heritage and historical preservation, escapes a simple identification with the defensive strategies of status and status quo. There had long been a deep nostalgic vein in much of the socialist left's lament for lost communities, or in the counterculture's longing for innocence in a simpler prelapsarian world, just as black communities searched for their own "roots" in a past unsullied by slavery. Nostalgia was never entirely a monopoly of the right.

CHAPTER 10

Dystopias

———◆———

For much of the twentieth century the American built environment, especially that of New York City and Chicago, provided both inspiration and cautionary in envisioning the modern British metropolis. By the late sixties it was, however, the rather different sprawling shopping-mall-and-expressway aesthetic of the American West, and of Los Angeles in particular, that came to exercise an especial influence. In four talks on the southern California city on the Third Programme in August and September of 1968, Reyner Banham explored L.A.'s sprawling formlessness, enchanted with the "freedom of movement" symbolized by what he called one of its four ecologies, autopia. But if Banham refused to acknowledge L.A. as "an indifferent dystopia," just that reading became a commonplace in the British press, where the earlier wonderment over its excesses was displaced by darker images of dysfunction. Searching for the "real" L.A. beneath the clutter, Banham's 1971 book on the city was a not entirely convincing answer to journalist critics like James Cameron:

> It is as though London stretched unbroken from St Albans to Southend in a tangle of ten-lane four deck super parkways, hamburger stands, banks, topless drug-stores, hippie hide-outs, Hiltons, drive-in mortuaries, temples of obscure and extraordinary religions, sinless joy and joyless sin . . . all shrouded below the famous blanket of acid and corroding smog.[1]

By the time that the Brutalism-inspired South Bank exhibition venue, the Hayward Gallery (which had opened in the summer of 1968), mounted a show on Los Angeles in October of 1971, British foreign correspondents like Charles Wheeler, who crisscrossed the United States for BBC television from 1965 to 1973, had constructed a picture of the chaos and violence of U.S. politics framed by a relentlessly dystopian view of the modern American urban environment, in both its social and physical character: race riots, the decay of social housing and public services, the graffitied mess of Mayor Lindsay's subway system in New York, the police-riot chaos of the Democratic Convention in Chicago, the mean streets of the hard-drug-saturated Haight in San Francisco, and Richard Nixon's massaging of crime statistics to promote a law-and-order regime. The United States by the early seventies had become emblematic of the failure rather than promise of urban modernity, mirroring and amplifying Britain's own sense of the failure of their version of the modern.[2]

British apprehension of "decline" in its many postimperial manifestations was hardly a new phenomenon, while dystopian fantasies like William Golding's *Lord of the Flies* (1954) or Peter Watkins's suppressed BBC TV film, *The War Game* (1965), had characterized a particular Cold War apocalyptic bomb culture in the fifties and early sixties. But the dystopian vision of the early and mid-seventies was a much more generalized motif of economic, social, and political commentary and of literary and cinematic representation in the wake of the failed modernist promise of the Wilson era, the collapse of countercultural idealism, and the political and ideological divisions and apparent social chaos of the Heath years. This sense of not just decline but also the failure of hope, a deep and persistent sickness, and dysfunctionality seized the collective (or at least literate, suburban, middle-class and elite) imagination. Moralists from Mary Whitehouse to Christian-convert Malcolm Muggeridge, the similarly newly evangelized Christopher Booker, Paul Johnson, a Catholic who recanted his left-wing past, or the young Tory hopeful and Church of England loyalist John Selwyn Gummer, charged "permissiveness" with threatening the utter decay of British social and ethical disciplines. As we have seen with Booker, such indictments were, however, often accompanied by a powerful undercurrent of transatlantic animus. Calls to reclaim British moral certainty and character not only were directed against the permissive and socialist left but also targeted explicitly or implicitly a cultural corruption that had its origins in and agents from America.[3]

The surge of revulsion against the sixties centered not only on the counterculture, but on modernism itself and assumed an instructive parallelism between American modernity and its British derivative. Gummer's 1971 tract on *The Permissive Society,* though by no means the most acerbic of this genre in its targeting of the American contagion, repeatedly draws parallels with American society in its assault on sex, pornography, drugs, and second-rate television programming. It was, he argues, *American* student radicalism and the *American* Gay and Women's Liberation movements that had moved blame from the individual to "the immorality outside themselves." Americans were leaders in narcotic abuse and "the main promoters of 'blue' films." American television companies bore "the greatest blame" for the "set formulas—mindless quiz shows; poorly-made cartoons; and purposeless talk programmes" that had come to characterize British programming, while American left-wing militants could be heard on British TV using American vulgarisms like "motherfucking" that were shocking, he thought, to the majority of British viewers.[4]

Ironically, much of the early seventies moral assault on sixties modernism in

Britain not only was derived from a negative reading of media images of American social chaos but also was explicitly instructed by the "moral majority" rhetoric of the Nixon-Agnew campaign against American liberalism. This was especially true of the law and order society promoted by the Tories in the general election of 1970 and the mugging/black-crime panic of the early seventies. When John Mansfield interviewed the American urban planner Oscar Newman on BBC2's *Horizon* program in March of 1974, transatlantic parallelisms of violence and social dysfunction were assumed. Newman, who had recently written about crime in high-rise urban housing estates, and who instanced the infamous 1964 case of Kitty Genovese in Queens, New York (murdered while neighbors refused to get involved), feared that on housing estates in Britain as well there was a danger of crime becoming a "normal hazard of everyday life" and people unwilling "to go out at night for fear of being mugged."[5]

IMAGINARY DYSTOPIAS

Crime and violence, environmental decay, and social alienation are central to the literature, theater, and cinema of dystopia—and of its belated analogue in popular music, Punk—that flourished in Britain from the late sixties to the late seventies. In some ways it was a reworking and updating of the urban jungle themes of the fifties and early sixties moral panic, just as the iconic seventies film of urban dystopia, Kubrick's *Clockwork Orange* (1971), took Anthony Burgess's early-sixties teens-on-a-rampage novel and gave it his own slick postmodern lyricism (echoing the "lyricism of violence" in American films like Arthur Penn's *Bonnie and Clyde* [1967] and Sam Peckinpah's *The Wild Bunch* [1969]).[6]

Deracinated, violent, working-class teens were directly transposed from the fifties to the seventies in the popular cult novels of Richard Allen. *Skinhead* (1970) may seem uniquely Cockney in inspiration, but like much of the more literary dystopia novels of the era often uses the United States as referent, portraying in Levi-wearing, American-hating Joe Hawkins an alienated youth who kicks out at a world he both aspires to and hates—like despised hippy Cherry who "had taken part in practically every demonstration in Grosvenor Square" and her friend, draft-dodger Joel, whose "American accent bit into the wind" and who evoked "California and the communes . . . orgies where the girls were all naked and the pot was freshly imported from Mexico." In the 1971 sequel, *Suedehead*, Joe, who listens to *Voice of America* on a stolen transistor radio, makes "the leap from poverty street into the affluent society" and affects a posh English accent while "devouring anything with a sex-violent theme coming from the States." His cultural and sexual confusion—he takes to hustling and queer-bashing—is a mark of his alienation in a multicultural world where the targets of his anger are queers, women, and blacks in a Soho of drug rings, bent antiques dealers, and tourists looking for pornography.[7]

Allen's somewhat egregious gloss on his stories, that they represent an "instantaneous explosion" of youth in a "climate of anarchy," locates them in a post-sixties world of permissiveness and countercultural detritus—the major theme of much of the dystopia genre that flourished both on the left after the failure of 1968 and on the right. Howard Brenton led the way with his play *Revenge* (first staged at the Royal Court in September 1969) about a comic duel between the Old Lag Hepple ("I have been a life-long admirer of the works of Al Capone") and MacLeish of the Yard that ends in a near future where there are "Rapes every night. No citizen abroad after dark. The coppers armed. Gangs roaming at will . . . brothel villages, the cities red with blood and pleasure." If Brenton's lament seems to be for the failed socialist community in a successor-world of Selsdon Man, the (American-style) New Tory individualism that anticipated Thatcherism's "no society" ethos, the more conventional dystopian reading of the crisis (present and to come) belonged to the right's assault on the double disaster of liberal permissiveness and radical American-imported counterculture.[8]

It is this package of media-sensationalized assumptions that the young Martin Amis opportunistically exploited in a satirical second novel, *Dead Babies*, set in the near future (though its subject "is not tomorrow . . . it is today"). Here the legacy of the counterculture has been made flesh in its grown-up children, transposed from Notting Hill to a country-house commune, Appleseed Rectory (a warped version of *Howards End*, symbolic of England itself). This "place of shifting outlines and imploded vacuums . . . of lagging time and false memory" is dominated by an American sexual triad—a drug-pushing postgraduate from Columbia University, a young runaway halfwit matricide, and a proto-punk girl. The innocence of hippy free love has been replaced by a manic search for a "good time." The future, in the person of Andy Adorno, child of the sixties counterculture, raised in a commune, educated at Holland Park Comprehensive, "where he studied nothing but the modern American novel," is bleak, abusive, and ultimately mortally exhausting. As Diana, whose clitoral orgasms were practiced, frequent, and casual, observed to Andy: "[We] must have made a mistake a long time ago to end up like this . . . . [T]hat's now why we're all so dead."[9]

Robert Hewison has observed that by 1975 "the liberal world view, both inside and outside the novel, was at breaking point."[10] The mid-seventies can serve as literary focal point for the anti-sixties/anti-permissiveness dystopian genre— running from Amis to J. G. Ballard's dark techno-apocalypse, *High-rise* (1975), Ian McEwan's collection of short stories *First Love, Last Rites* (1975), or Anthony Powell's *Hearing Secret Harmonies* (1975)—most notably in his self-delusional character Lord Widmerpool, who crossed the Atlantic to take up an academic appointment at an Ivy League university, moved on to California, and converted to the counterculture before returning to become chancellor of a "newish" university and an acolyte of a dangerous New Age Svengali: "I take pride in ridiculing what is—or rather was—absurdly called honour, respectability, law, order, obedience, custom, rule, hierarchy, precept, regulation."[11]

Margaret Drabble's novel of national decline, *The Ice Age*, presented a portrait of corrupt property dealers like Len Wincobank with his passion for big buildings and cement, making millions "raping the city centres of Britain," and whose "monument" was "a gleaming office tower"—but also tower-block estates with broken lifts, graffiti-covered walls, and "dog shit on the stairs (was it dog shit?)." Britain had "a new egalitarian culture" (with its "parasitic teenagers") in an "illiterate television age," but was bankrupt, living beyond its means "on the ruins of their own past excesses": "Where was the new bright classless enterprising future of Great Britain? In jail with Len Wincobank," or, she might have added, offshore in a tax haven of the sort (now Sir) Charles Clore left Britain for the same year *The Ice Age* appeared. Like Muriel Spark's "parable of the pagan seventies," *The Takeover* (1976), Drabble's postmortem and many other novels and plays of that collective gasp of apprehension offer angles of vision about the failure of communities and the passing (or warping) of Englishness itself, in the context of both an American-fostered modernism and its countercultural enemies—many include Americans themselves as agents provocateurs of decline. Most deal in urban social and moral chaos, fantasies of violence, and the claustrophobia of decayed or ersatz family relations. John Osborne's gratuitously violent play *Watch It Come Down* (1974) is set in a converted country railway station in a "last of England" countryside where Texans slaughter the pheasant, grouse, and deer in a "Wildlife Vietnam of their own."[12]

The New England expat and Anglophile Paul Theroux lived in London. His *The Family Arsenal* (1976) with its floating American drug-pushing escapee from Vietnam, one of a "family" of misfits thrown together with a Trotskyite actress, Irish provos, feckless Cockneys, and other post-countercultural misfits in a neighborhood of "decay pushing towards ruin" ("[T]here was nothing worth preserving"), cashed in on the genre as well, with an American publisher's dust jacket that says it all: "*London Today*, dangerous and antique—where once elegant districts decay into slums jammed with former colonials, where terrorists' bombs rip holes in historic stone, and football graffiti read like a veiled threat." Similarly, at the end of the era though anticipated in some of his earlier short stories, Ian McEwan's *The Cement Garden* (1978) offered another deformed "family"—of incestuous orphans isolated in a condemned house in a postmodern desert of a neighborhood without neighbors where deserted houses await demolition for the next motorway and high-rise.[13]

Most characteristic of the dystopia genre were stories of *high-rise* modernism gone wrong, like Caryl Churchill's radio play *Not Not Not Not Not Enough Oxygen*, broadcast on Radio 3 in March of 1971 and set in 2010 in a window-sealed, waterless flat in a London tower block, both a last refuge from the rampant violence and deadly pollution outside and symbolic of fatal social isolation. Eve Figes found it "all too possible," a "grave new world." Churchill had immigrated at age ten to North America (Montreal) in 1948, returning to England and Oxford in 1957. J. G. Ballard, eight years older, was also exposed to American culture at an early age, being raised in the International Settlement in Shanghai, a place "dominated by Americans, by American cars, by American styles and consumer goods." In the fifties he worked briefly for a London advertising agency, did RAF training in Canada, and, back in London, was impressed by the 1956 Whitechapel Art Gallery Pop exhibition "This is Tomorrow." Flirting with his own Pop art collages (Warhol was "a tremendous influence on me") he discovered his writing inspiration from American film noir ("[T]hey conjured up a hard and unsentimental image of the primeval city") and American science fiction ("[T]hey described an American imperium colonising the entire universe").[14]

Following Ballard's "inflammatory" 1969 mélange of violence, sexuality, Vietnam, and American Pop celebrity, *The Atrocity Exhibition* (withdrawn by his American publisher Doubleday), his interest in avant-garde art and dystopian late-modernity coalesced in an exhibition of crashed automobiles in 1970 at a "New Arts Laboratory." A trilogy of urban novels commenced with *Crash* in 1973 (inspired by the combination of sex, violence, and twisted technology of the London exhibition), followed by *Concrete Island* the next year—the story of an architect trapped in the wasteland of a motorway intersection. In 1975 he published *High-Rise*, a novel of social stratification made concrete, of isolation and gradual psychological decline, of "no social organization at all." The affluent tenants of Ballard's glass tower revert to an atavism of violence as the electricity fails, walls are covered with graffiti, corridors are choked with garbage, and lifts cease to operate. Though *High-Rise* may be set in London, Ballard's "real spiritual home" was Los Angeles, and, he says, his literary "stuff" is "about the fall of the *American* empire," about the end of technology, the end of America . . . what America is going to be like in 50 years time." His own American Dream, nourished by the ice cream and comics and gregarious American servicemen of his childhood, was darkened and warped by the Kennedy assassinations, the Vietnam War, "the casualties of the hard drug scene, the determined effort of the entertainment culture to infantilise us—all these had begun to get between us and the new dawn."[15]

The perceived failures of the public modernism of fifties and sixties architecture became by the mid-seventies a conventional symbol for a larger failure of optimism and confidence. Journalists, novelists, and film-makers mined the drab waste of a collapsing urban ecology in mutually reinforcing visions of a dystopian present. Such a vision was available at either end of ideological spectrum, from Christopher Booker writing in 1976 of "Dreams That Crack Like Concrete," of the stench of urine, of tenants who "shuffle past to wait for the only lift that is still working" to Derek Jarman's vision of London as wasteland in his Punk-era film *Jubilee* in 1977.[16]

TELEVISION AND THE AMERICAN ASSAULT
ON (BRITISH) CHILDHOOD

As a signifier of modernity, television—television viewing and television pro-gramming—had a special importance in the antimodern warnings of cultural crisis and visions of future dystopia that characterize the era. Thanks to hire-pur-chase credit arrangements, by the end of the sixties the large majority of British homes had a set and viewing had become—it was, after all, part of the eager promise of a modernized Britain—a mass activity, displacing to a large degree cinema as common weekend social entertainment and shifting radio toward its special divergent roles of provider of Pop and rock to youth, easy listening for many others, and, for a small minority, the more intellectual stimulus of the Third Programme.

From the start of the television era there had been predictions of cultural dam-age from the left as well as the right in both the United States and Britain. In Britain these had often taken an anti-American turn in deploring the unhealthy narcotic effect of the ever-extending daily rituals of watching and the supposed erosion by American imports of "British culture" (whether of the authentic working-class communities eulogized by Hoggart and Williams or of an elite historically defined by its valorization of quality). Such fears, carried over and magnified from earlier concerns about Hollywood cinema, extended beyond content to the contamina-tion of language itself. By the end of the sixties these anxieties, heightened by the growing density of satellite-delivered media, constitute a special area of dystopian rhetoric.

Concerns about the moral danger (as opposed to cultural vulgarization) of mass television programming moved from journalism and academic discussion[17] to populist political organization in 1965 with the founding of the National Viewers and Listeners Association by fifty-five-year-old middle-England housewife and teacher Mary Whitehouse. The target of her "Clean Up TV" campaign, begun the previous year, was the portrayal of sexual themes and violence in program-ming readily available to, especially, children and young persons. Though fiercely directed at metropolitan permissiveness generally and the kitchen-sink realism of early and mid-sixties British docu-drama, the campaign's indictment often carried a subtext about the United States. Charges that Hollywood sensationalized sex and violence were of long standing and, with the importation of American movies into daily television programming, especially by ITV companies searching for low-cost filler, were easily transferred to the new medium. In the fifties and sixties popular American Western and police-and-gangster genre television series fed the same apprehension, while it was an episode from, one would have thought an ordinarily innocuous American medical drama, *Dr. Kildare*, that started Mary Whitehouse on her career of television protest. The episode dealt graphically with a woman in labor and was watched by her schoolgirls. It left, Whitehouse claimed, such an impression on them ("There were close-up shots of her screams and agony") that "in one fell swoop all that I had been telling them about how wonderful and challenging an experience it was to give birth to a child was wiped out." And so to immorality: "Most of the girls were quite sure there would be no babies for them if they could help it."[18]

As what might be called a minor moral panic over sex and, especially, violence developed, not only as viewer protest but as a subgenre of media sociology, imported children's programming was scrutinized for gratuitous mayhem. Hanna and Barbera's *Tom and Jerry* cartoons, a popular American import at the afternoon children's slot on BBC1, came in for sharp criticism. And yet, the critique of sex and violence on television, while often searching for American pollution, was also significantly dependent on American media studies and public enquiry for shaping its own investigations. The media-promoted and politician-massaged concern about rising crime rates was a transatlantic phenomenon, and fed in both Britain and the United States into quite similar policy-driven, sociological exploration of some kind of crime and television nexus. In the States commercial television itself, supposedly "self-policed" rather than state-regulated, responded to viewers' concerns—with an eye to public relations.

In 1969 the network giant CBS assembled a conference of social scientists to discuss "ways and means of securing realistic estimates of the different effects of exposure to television violence." The next year a *British* media researcher, William A. Belson, received a very substantial grant from CBS (£157,000 to be administered by the L.S.E.) to investigate the "real life" effects of television on adolescent London boys. Belson was an Australian who had come to England in 1950 to join the BBC's Audience Research Department (the statistical analysis of listeners and viewers and the social-psychological effects of media programming was a postwar American preoccupation). His study (1972–73) exposed several thousand London boys age twelve to seventeen to "25 types of violence" in, for the most part, American programming (cartoons, Westerns, and gangster films). By the time he published his findings (1978) the issue had perhaps lost some of its immediacy, though he purported to have confirmed a definitive link between some of what the boys viewed and the degree to which they later engaged in violent activity. He recommended "immediate steps" to reduce violence on television. *Tom and Jerry* was, however, acquitted.[19]

By 1970 there was a rapidly rising concern in Britain about urban violence, fears that clearly were derived in part at least from concern about violence in imported American media. In the last months of the Wilson government, the Home Secretary, James Callaghan, called the heads of both the BBC and the Independent Broadcasting Authority in to discuss televised violence, and the BBC subsequently set up a special advisory committee, headed by David Attenborough. This continued to sit for several years, and was subsequently (1972) influenced, Alasdair Milne later recalled, by the published report from a scientific advisory committee set up by the U.S. Surgeon General suggesting a causal connection between screen violence and social behavior. British critics of television programming also took note of the findings (1970) of a U.S. National Commission on the Causes and Prevention of Violence, which had questioned representatives from the major networks. When the British mass communications scholar James Halloran published on "the effects of television" in 1970 he extensively cited American research, though remaining somewhat skeptical about the "tendency to use TV as a scapegoat for social ills."[20]

The issue persisted throughout the seventies, though by 1972, when the BBC presented its own commissioned report on "Violence on Television," Clive James, Australian-born television critic for the *Observer*, treated the subject with some sarcasm—suggesting that the whole issue, at least as a scholarly field, not only was being made too much of but was somewhat risibly American: "The two researchers [Irene S. Shaw and David S. Newell] have each grown an American-style middle initial, but thankfully fall short of the commensurate sociological self-confidence." He also found scholarly investigation of the threat of American cartoons to be especially "boring" (Peckinpah's extended rape scene in *Straw Dogs*, cut by the British censor, was one thing, but animated violence in *Tom and Jerry*?).[21] Nevertheless, the issue of the probable impact in Britain of American television programming for children shortly came to a head in an extended debate over what would be one of the two iconic children's programs of the seventies—*Sesame Street*.

Programming for preschool children was a somewhat underdeveloped field in sixties Britain. Freda Lingstrom, head of Children's Television at BBC, had pioneered with *Watch with Mother* in 1951—a combination of education and entertainment that, with its Andy-Pandy and Flower-Pot-Men puppets, was popular with mums—and her successor oversaw the launching of what would be BBC's longest running children's program, *Blue Peter*, in 1958. Lingstrom "despised American fare," however, and refused to import or imitate American children's series. ITV was not so reluctant in fashioning directly derivative American-style children's programming; the most successful of these, presented by Rosalyn Thompson from 1964, was Anglia's franchised version of the American-created *Romper Room*, designed to inculcate "Do-Bee" politeness and respect, with (in the States) a dose of "I Pledge Allegiance" patriotism. For ITV companies at least, American commercial and, by the end of the decade, public-financed programming became ever more attractive—either as direct imports or as models for imitation.[22]

Some animus against children's programming imported from the United States persisted at the BBC long after Lingstrom left in 1956. As with informed opinion generally, the obvious issue was the "foreign" acculturation of British children—the inappropriateness of American urban, multicultural contexts, and the presumed danger to British codes of behavior and British pronunciation. It was a debate that drew force from the more general turn against American-styled modernism in the aftermath of the era of youth revolt and urban violence there and targeted especially American liberal approaches to child-rearing and education. These fears came to a head in 1971 over whether the BBC ought to import the most liberally informed, innovative, and popular of new American children's programming, *Sesame Street.*

In 1966 a New York–based noncommercial organization, Children's Television Workshop, proposed to develop a "cognitively based" program for children three to five years of age. Its goal was not only to provide noncommericalized educational content, but to do so in a way that would bridge the cultural chasm between ghetto and suburb and draw both "street kids" and their more privileged counterparts into a positive, multicultural experience. Securing public and private charitable sponsorship, the project came to fruition in 1969 with the pilot broadcast on public educational television in New York and other large metropolitan areas. Catching the rising tide of public broadcasting in the States, *Sesame Street* quickly proved popular in both poorer households and the wealthier suburbs. In the transatlantic media world it also became a hot property. When, in the autumn of 1971, the BBC concluded it was "too American" for British audiences and declined to pick it up, the IBA stepped in and authorized London Weekend Television to screen a limited run. LWT received "an extraordinary volume" of positive response from viewers to the *Sesame* formula (puppets, bright color, cartoons, rock music, and a fast pace to keep children's attention), and this success led to a wave of imitative preschool series on other ITV sites as well as to an outburst of concerned public discussion—mostly negative—over the reliance generally on television imports from the States. The IBA held (in January 1973) an anxious "Consultation on Children's Television," though it was poorly attended by ITV leaders, who were already moving forward to meet the apparent demand for U.S.-style programming.[23]

The case against *Sesame Street* was vigorously deployed on both the left and the right, if for different reasons—though Raymond Williams came down on the side of cautious approval (because of its "identification with a poor, minority-group community . . . a vital and particular job, for the educationally deprived"). Complaints ranged from the inappropriateness of its Americanisms of speech and habit (peanut-butter and jelly sandwiches being unknown in Britain) to its "frantic pace"—"the children's *Laugh-In*"—and, especially from those on the left who distrusted the hidden messages of any American programming, its use of techniques drawn, it was argued, from commercial advertising. An American writer resident (and married) in England, Brenda Maddox, echoed these charges to BBC listeners and in a book on American mass media. Those who attacked the polluting influence of American television in Britain focused on its violence, commercialism, multiculturalism, vulgarization, and inappropriate, un-British Spock-inspired modernist psychological approaches to child rearing. Ironically, perhaps, once the minor storm over *Sesame Street* subsided, a teapot tempest that played to larger fears of the collapse of British identity into the black hole of American anticulture, Lew Grade's ATV scored its biggest transatlantic export success with its own *Sesame Street*–derivative feature, American puppeteer Jim Henson's *The Muppet Show*, launched from London's Elstree Studios in 1976.[24]

ECOLOGICAL DYSTOPIAS

In the Persian Gulf, turtles, dolphins, even the sea cow . . . die in a huge oil slick. Throughout Europe acid rain—more acidic than lemon juice—is feared to be killing millions of fish . . . . In Britain the otter is disappearing, beautiful butterflies are extinct. Lovely orchids barely cling on. Radioactive waste from Windscale is found in polar currents off Greenland. Great natural forests are torn down in South America, valleys are flooded.

—David Bellamy, 1984[25]

The crisis rhetoric of early-seventies environmental activism was, and continued to be through the eighties and beyond, infused with the imagery of the Apocalypse. The threats it posits in fact closely parallel those of dystopian science fiction. Motivated by an Edenic nostalgia, it often shared something of J. G. Ballard's vision of a probable future-shock world, as Des Wilson, chairman of the U.K. Friends of the Earth, made clear when he spoke of the need to "project ourselves forward into the middle of the twenty-first century, or even the beginning of the twenty-second," when it was an open question whether "the human race will have survived at all." The ecology movement in Britain, if it had its own native sources in the long English idealization of the countryside, was powerfully indebted to an especially American "back to nature" ideology, U.S. conservation and recreational management regimes, American mainstream lobbying from Rachel Carson's *Silent Spring* (1962; British edition, 1963) to Barry Commoner's *The Closing Circle* (1971; British edition, 1972), and, especially, the recent American-inspired style of countercultural protest.[26]

Among architectural avant-gardists in Britain like the Archigram Group, the New England architect and inventor Richard Buckminster Fuller exerted a profound influence, while the alternative architecture of the "Drop City" movement in the States also found notice in *Architectural Design*. If limitations of space and climate made Drop City experimentation improbable in Britain, Buckminster Fuller's designs for sustainable, environmentally friendly living and his populist promotion of these ideas had some appeal well beyond the counterculture. He became a kind of touring evangelist for an environmentally friendly lifestyle that had radical, egalitarian overtones. He turned up at the Hornsey School (where he was "especially influential") during the occupation of 1968.[27]

If Anglo-American environmental activism embraced the countercultural aesthetic of Buckminster Fuller's holistic forms, it also drew from the antiwar critique of the chemical devastation of the Vietnam countryside and from the counterculture's rejection generally of the supertechnological society of the military-industrial complex. Late-sixties ecoradicalism in Britain was saturated with American influence, as were others closer to the more moderate liberal-left mainstream of the ecology movement. When Barbara Ward published *Spaceship Earth* in London in 1966, she was using a metaphor already deployed by Adlai Stevenson in the United Nations and by Buckminster Fuller, whose 1963 *Operating Manual for Spaceship Earth* was republished in paperback form in 1969 after the unprecedented blue and green photos of the planet taken by the *Apollo VIII* astronauts in December 1968 had given an American-sponsored reality to the trope. The next year Sir Frank Fraser Darling, an animal ecologist who the *New Statesman* thought "exemplifies an unusual combination of British and American environmental attitudes," sounded an alarm in the annual Reith lectures, and early in 1970 the Wilson government set up the first Royal Commission on Environmental Pollution.[28]

In Britain the new environmentalism drew on long-standing domestic aesthetic and political traditions of antiurbanism, especially John Ruskin and William Morris (both of whom enjoyed—like the Pre-Raphaelite art with which they were associated—a small renaissance of appreciation among sixties university students). Organizationally, environmentalism, at least the moderate, respectable, and ameliorationist version of, say, the Conservation Society (founded 1966), looked to the National Trust (1895), the Council for the Protection of Rural England (1926), or the Nature Conservancy (1949). *Eco-activism,* however, more immediately had its green origins in the United States with the West Coast lobby, the Sierra Club, and the more militant Friends of the Earth—the creation of David Brower, whose call for direct action rather than pressure tactics drove him from the Sierra Club. In 1970 Brower met with the vice president of the National Union of Students in Britain, Graham Searle, to discuss the founding of an autonomous British version that would appeal directly to the younger, counterculturally informed. The U.K. Friends were established in Covent Garden in October and were commissioned by Ballantine to write a British version of the American *Environmental Handbook.*[29]

Friends of the Earth, U.K., were also indebted in the early years to an American research fellow at Merton College, Amory Lovins (Brower's "representative" in Britain) in marshaling the case against the British mining company Rio Tinto-Zinc's plans to strip-mine Snowdonia for copper and, especially, in mounting a powerful indictment in the media against the British nuclear power industry.

Their first "publicity coup" was a countercultural happening in May 1971 when a hundred young activists dumped 1,500 disposable bottles on the steps of the headquarters of Cadbury Schweppes, a theatrical protest that was repeated in October at eight Schweppes depots. By 1973 FoE, UK, had proliferated into seventy-three local groups and radical environmentalism in Britain achieved its own momentum: it developed a domestic base, an articulate leadership, and also soon had its own British guru in E. F. Schumacher, whose *Small Is Beautiful: Economics as If People Mattered*, published in London in 1973, was a major influence on the nascent greens in the United States as in Britain. Nevertheless, British ecoradicalism, if achieving a global presence in the decade that followed, remained significantly indebted to its transatlantic origins and connections. Such connections characterized, for instance, the transatlantic campaigns against Boeing's plans for a supersonic passenger aircraft (the SST) and the British-French development of *Concorde*. The anti-*Concorde* effort, a riposte to the promises of technological modernism in Wilson's Britain, made use of the American protest's anti-SST sonic boom "evidence"; Richard Wiggs, a CND activist, worked closely with William Shurcliff, an American physicist who organized a Citizens' League Against the Sonic Boom in Boston in 1967 (Wiggs went to the States to help Shurcliff bring the case to local neighborhoods near airports and to lobby Congress, where he gave testimony at the hearings that would ultimately kill the SST project). In 1970 the anti-*Concorde* movement was joined by the FoE UK's G. W. Searle and Thomas Blair and others on the radical environmentalist left.[30]

In 1976 a group of British political scientists asserted that the British environmental movement, though inspired by the United States, was a distinct phenomenon less driven by "hysteria." This echoes other attempts to assert difference in the face of cultural-political transatlanticisms. What is not debatable is that radical environmentalism drew heavily on American sources like Jane Jacobs's *The Death and Life of Great American Cities* (1961, reissued in Britain in 1972), Paul Ehrlich's controversial *The Population Bomb* (1968), Wesley Marx's *The Frail Ocean* (1967), or Alvin Toffler's *Future Shock* (1970). Its literature commonly employed a high level of Apocalyptic rhetoric, as in Wigg's "case" against *Concorde*—represented as dangerous not only to passengers because of cosmic radiation, ozone leakage, catastrophic risk of explosion, metal fatigue, depressurization, hail, lightning, air turbulence, and pilot strain but also as a substantial addition to "the man-made environmental crisis . . . constituting the ultimate threat to man's survival . . . the final catastrophe."[31]

Tony Aldous was "environmental correspondent" to *The Times* who, like Larkin or Betjeman, turned a sense of looming cultural loss into an angry indictment of modernist architecture and urban design ("'develop' was beginning to mean 'destroy'")—something he associated explicitly with Americanization and "the soft lies of public relations officers." The danger extended to preservationism itself, where tourist heritage sites threatened to become mere stage sets and England "a few acres of preserved countryside between concrete fly-overs." For preservationists like Aldous the goal was "natural towns" that were, somehow, "tourist-free." As Larkin put it in a dystopian poem commissioned by the Heath government for a white paper on the environment, "[T]he whole/Boiling will be bricked in/Except for the tourist parts . . . And that will be England gone . . . it will linger on/In galleries; but all that remains/For us will be concrete and tyres." Aldous's 1975 preservationist polemic, *Goodbye, Britain?*, like his articles for the *Illustrated London News*, advanced the idea of small-is-beautiful "village London" and "cohesive communities" in the face of bureaucracy and modernizing city planners. But the vision of a sustainable, historical, local-villagey Britain closely mirrored that of tourist-brochure Britain, an uncomfortable paradox to those preservationists who struggled against confusing theme-park artifice with the historically authentic. That the profits from American tourism necessarily underpinned and helped shape heritage preservation in Britain was an awkward reality.[32]

CHAPTER 11

British "Heritage" and
the Transatlantic Marketplace

The cultural turn away from an optimistic modernist ethos in the mid-sixties to one of defensive nostalgia after the end of that decade has been the subject of much journalism then and scholarship since. That this phenomenon—though no doubt partial, contested, and shaped by specific local cultures of class and history—was transatlantic, raises issues, however, not only of context but also of a circularity of causation and amplification. It happened in an era of rapidly thickening Anglo-American contact, both virtual in the form of denser media traffic and actual in the great increase in transatlantic travel. A competitive and well-differentiated tourist industry was positioning itself to accommodate this increase. In 1971 the Duke of Bedford claimed to "have just seen the catalogue of a Texas department store which offers the ultimate in tours of elegance and distinction": twenty-two days of "sheer luxury as guests of the aristocracy," chauffeured from castle to stately home. "They will feel they are living in a novel or movie."[1] However much there may have been a domestic appetite for heritage consumption, all of the markers of the nostalgia turn in Britain—the growth of the antiques trade, the rapid expansion of country house visiting, the development of "heritage" museums, and the costume-drama fashion in television and film production—can be related to a growing American market, real and potential.

In 1970 Christopher Dunn reported that the sale of rare books to American collectors was growing dramatically, leading to not only an increase at the auction houses (Sotheby's reported selling some 100,000 rare books a year; its chairman was honored for "services to export") but also a specialization in the U.S. market among local dealers like Richard Booth of Hay-on-Wye, who estimated that 70 percent of his business was with North America and Australia. By the early seventies the development of public broadcasting in the States advertised British style to just that part of the population—more or less educated, middle-class, tourism prone, relatively affluent white suburban Americans—likely to buy into British heritage. While many Britons may have been prepared to seek refuge during a time of malaise and emerging multicultural reality in a heightened sense of Britishness-as-historical-whiteness, it is remarkable how closely aligned their nostalgia is with the simplistic expectations of the American market—a market that the British media (television, film, and publishing) increasingly needed in a world of transatlantic corporate mergers.[2]

It may be that, as Shaun Sutton, head of the BBC's Drama Group, claimed in the late seventies, the turn to heritage programming would have happened irrespective of American demand—though according to Eric Paice (a playwright who worked on BBC television series), "[He] appears to be the only one in the building under this illusion." Costume drama was more expensive to make than kitchen-sink TV. Not only were British programs increasingly made with the hope of American sales (and, as Paice said, "Who in the States is going to get excited about series set amongst Sheffield steelworkers?"), but increasingly British producers trolled the U.S. networks for "front money" financing. By the early and mid-seventies, a series like *Upstairs, Downstairs* cannot be understood as merely reflecting a domestic turn away from the identity-challenging crises of the times. As the decade wore on, it and many other nostalgia-drenched programs were crafted to appeal, like Alistair Cooke's avuncular, Edwardian voice on PBS's *Masterpiece Theatre*, to an American audience that, as Antoinette Burton has observed, "has been and remains the audience perhaps ripest for performances of Britain's eternal Britishness." In the process, there was what one might call back-flow. Programming designed to advance a stereotypical version of historic national identity and class relations that would sell in the United States was also consumed at home. Paradoxically, the British search for a challenged national identity was in some degree reinforced and encouraged by products crafted for the transatlantic market. As Dominic Strinati has perceptively if tentatively suggested: "Americanization may also take the form of Britain selling to Americans 'Americanized' representations of itself, and bringing back American produced and validated versions of constructions of 'Britishness.'"[3]

It is also likely that middle-class America's appetite for British historical costume drama, like the student-cult status of the Pythons, had some effect on the volume of transatlantic tourism—as had been the case in the sixties when the American tours of the Beatles and the media's hyping of Swinging London conspired with cheapening air travel to generate mass tourism. By and large, tourists did not come to Britain, however, to "swing" or to hear British rock bands in their domestic venues. They came to find what they romantically imagined England or London to be—Dickensian, small-scale, quaint, class-defined; different, that is, in aspect and character from the modern familiar back home. They came to see storied sites, wander through village London street markets, shop (at least the affluent) at Harrods, and have tea at Fortnum and Masons. "Heritage" perfectly resonated with their expectations. While the preservationists seized upon the American redesign of San Francisco's Ghirardelli Square and Boston's Haymarket as models for the saving of Covent Garden through tourism, churches throve as tourist sites while their congregations declined and obsolescent warehouses and docks became, as Booker crossly observed, "twee" museums and restaurants: "[O]ne is no longer in a grim survival of nineteenth century commerce, but a sub-Williamsburg fantasy world."[4]

As a literature of dystopia Gothicized the failures of (an essentially American) modernism, Americans themselves not only played a part in the recovery of a struggling British economy but had a significant and unappreciated role in the redefining and retrenching of Britishness itself. American tourists expected to experience a Britain that was historically familiar and perhaps bring some of it back home, and the "industry" accommodated their expectations. At the same time, the British media were more vigorously exporting to the States (or hoped to) and needed to present themselves in a language the American market expected and would understand. In an increasingly internationalized media world, with a growing trend toward cofinancing and coproduction, there was circularity of production and consumption as distinctions between home and export markets, especially in the area of high-end "quality" television and film, significantly eroded.

GOING FOR A SONG IN PORTOBELLO ROAD[5]

> In his tastes and character [Steed] embodies tradition and the qualities that people overseas have come to associate with the British way of life—gracious living, a London house full of family heirlooms and handsome antiques . . . .
>
> —American publicity notes for *The Avengers*[6]

From the late sixties to the early eighties there was a keen and widespread interest among both the British and their American visitors in artifacts of the past. In the antique shops, fairs, arcades, and street markets of London Victorian mementoes of no great inherent value—horse brasses, chamber pots, blue-glass medicine bottles—became talismanic objects of desire. This phenomenon was one aspect of a flood of nostalgia, a longing for "heritage," that was much commented upon at the time. Among the British at some level it was a compensatory reaction to a sense of national entropy and more specifically the rapid erosion after 1968 of the optimistic, progressive modernism of the early Wilson years. Subsequently, the morass of "stagflation," IMF humiliation, and "ungovernability" further served to encourage the cult for the past already evident in the "retrochic" of the late sixties. But commercializable nostalgia was also intimately related to forces extraneous to British domestic anxieties—specifically the expanding U.S. market for British cultural commodities at a time when the white American urban-abandoning middle class was coming to grips with its own status anxieties. At the same time the "loss" of British culture to money from abroad served further to encourage a dystopian reading of the present crisis and spurred a defensive mentality that, spurning

American modernism, absorbed some version of the simplistic (American) reading of British culture as hierarchical-elitist, traditionalist, nonurban, and fixed.[7]

Throughout the seventies, National Trust visiting—both foreign and domestic—surged dramatically, as did the tourist-driven profits of some stately homes
still in private hands. The Duke of Bedford ("interviewed quite frequently on
American television") reported in 1970 that well over a million paying visitors a
year came to Woburn Park and house, among them groups of up to three hundred Americans at a time who "would come down for tea and a look round the
antiques market": "I find this reverent interest in Englishness rather comforting
nowadays, when mourning our decline has become such a fashionable pastime."
At the same time nostalgia-driven preservationism became "a widely popular
cause" and, for Roy Strong, ultimately "an addiction." The very pervasiveness of
nostalgia suggests that it enfolds very different "values." On the radical left, the
seventies environmental crusade, which had its own ethos of nostalgia, inherited
a long tradition of popular protest filtered through the late-sixties counterculture
that was far removed from the kind of longing for traditional social hierarchies
and fear of derogation of taste that marks the campaign to save the Country House
and its gardens as somehow symbolic of "the real" England or from the different
kind of nostalgia evoked by the New Right's espousal of the values of Victorian
enterprise.[8]

The past as commodity had long been available to collectors and antiquar-
ians in the west-end shops of the London antiques trade. Following an earlier
American trend, this market (both demand and supply) expanded explosively
after 1968. It promoted a snob-aesthetic that was attractive on both sides of the
ocean to the socially mobile salaried class with suburban homes to decorate. On
the other hand, the largely unregulated trade in antiques was marked by an extreme entrepreneurial individualism, and, responding to opportunity provided
by not only expanding domestic demand but also that of tourists and American
commercial importers, became a model of the sort of enterprise that the New
Right praised. The trade increasingly appeared to be in the hands of a new breed
of dealer eager to ship off "heritage" en masse to American buyers: in the seventies
a number of firms began to specialize in bulk shipment to the United States—like
Stephen Morris, "Shipping, Specialist Packers & Shippers of Antiques and Bric-
A-Brac," who advertised "a special 'All-in' rate for full containers [up to 40 cubic
feet]."[9]

If the counterculture of the sixties appropriated Victorian military jackets and
street-market paraphernalia either ironically or as mere bricolage, by the seventies the exploding mainstream market suggests that heritage commodities evoked
comforting associational meanings. But what meanings and whose heritage? The
market had long depended upon a degree of nostalgic sentimentality, entwined
with whatever satisfaction the collecting of status objects, especially if they were

"bargains," might hold for the modestly well-off—the audience from the late sixties for Arthur Negus, the avuncular antiques expert of BBC1's "Going for a Song," an audience that grew to more than 13 million viewers for its successor "The Antiques Roadshow."[10]

It can be argued that the anxious and entropic climate of the mid-seventies, the "Ice Age" of Margaret Drabble's novel, encouraged a reading of artifacts of the past that was coded as a *Tory* form of nostalgia, a flight from modernism-read-as-socialism—the "heritage" of one-nation Toryism, royalist and embracing the country house aesthetic, and promoted in publications like *Country Life,* which also had some transatlantic appeal (in the United States it enjoyed a significant increase in sales with, in Stephen Haseler's words, its "'how-to-do-it' kind of Englishness"). Nostalgia is a deeply subjective force suggesting, not an objective historical reality, but a wished-for mirror opposite—as when in the eighties the Prime Minister, offering her own gloss on the dystopian seventies, counterpoised an image of a traditional Britain of self-discipline and personal morality to one of socialism, strikes, hooliganism, and urban chaos. Some have seen such rhetoric as a kind of "double-coding" that allowed the New Right to sound traditionalist while concealing the deep disjunction with the past that their American-style enterprise ideology entailed, of disguising the future as a narrative of the past. But there is also a sense of the past that can be said to have grown very widely in popular culture through the seventies. It is a kind of history that relates directly to the commodities found in the seventies antiques markets or in BBC TV prop rooms—that is, it is a history fixed as *things* ready to be picked over to illustrate heritage myths and heritage morality. This is history seen from the antiques marketplace, where the past *is* its physical detritus—commodities stripped of social-historical meaning, of social relations in their production or use, and intended above all for a transatlantic consumer ready to invest them with his or her own myths about the Britain of their imagining.[11]

The commercial world of antiques was torn between a sense that going too down-market would tarnish the reputation for quality and snobbery upon which the trade depended and embracing wholesale the North American and tourist markets that drove on the rising sales figures and infused what had been a relatively quiet and modest sector with an element of American-style enterprise ethos. When David Coombs, the editor of the oldest established trade journal, *The Antique Collector,* lent his support to the heritage preservation, anti–Wealth Tax lobby in the mid and late seventies, he was at pains to justify *private* (domestic) collecting of fine art and antiques: "[E]very antique we buy and cherish . . . makes a contribution to the maintenance and improvement of the nation's total heritage."[12] In fact, however, antiques dealers (as opposed to tax-paying domestic antique collectors) were likely to be of two minds about Labour's proposed Wealth Tax—on the one hand they didn't want potential buyers deterred from collecting (that was not, of course, an issue when consumers were American tourists), or the market swamped and prices suppressed with goods put up for sale to pay tax; on the other they naturally looked forward to a market made lively by the increased circulation of goods otherwise locked up in private collections. Not many were much concerned about the "threat" posed by the "loss" of Britain's heritage to the United States—a trade in which they looked to do quite well.

Though some, like the art and antiques columnist in the *Sunday Telegraph,* Deborah Stratton, might complain that "[g]reed affects every aspect of the art and antiques market," the fact was that, combined with nostalgia-driven buying, such motives—avoiding high inflation and uncertain stock and real property markets—played an important role in the U.S. and Britain in driving the antiques trade to ever-higher levels of volume and profit. In the depth of the recession in 1974–75 Christie's total sales for "antiques" rose sevenfold (to £1,780,000), and in the following years, just when it seemed that the collecting mania had peaked, that "the euphoria was over," trade activity would climb to new heights. In 1979, on the verge of the "winter of discontent," Coombs himself could write that "the antiques and art market has seldom if ever been so prosperous." Much of the money came from abroad.[13]

Speculation about the growth of the antiques market has usually emphasized demand factors, the growth of American buying as well as that of domestic buyers inspired by television and radio shows that demystified the process of bargain hunting. But there were also changes in the structure of the trade that pushed along demand, notably the rapid development in London, from the mid-sixties, of selling beyond the traditional shops. At the top end, there was the increased role of the great auction houses like Christie's and Sotheby's and the importance of the annual antiques "fairs" in prestigious locations like Burlington House or the Grosvenor House Hotel—with increasingly a wealthy clientele (or their agents) from abroad. At the other end, and perhaps most important for the downwardly democratic growth of the trade, was the explosion of arcades like Antiquarius and street markets like those at Camden Passage, Bermondsey, and, most dramatically, Portobello Road (popularized as a tourist site for Americans in the 1971 Disney film *Bedknobs and Broomsticks*). Here tourist demand was critically important.

The fashionable, expensively organized, and slickly advertised fairs, often with royal or aristocratic patronage, catered to the wealthy buyer and those who responded to their "snob element."[14] By the late seventies the London season for these extravaganzas extended from early spring to autumn. Of the major fairs, that at the Grosvenor House Hotel, one of the oldest (from 1934), was arguably the most prestigious and often commanded the largest turnover. Major dealers, and those aspiring to become major, had to participate; some operated only at the fairs. The apparent success of the fairs as a minor if expanding export industry that boomed while others faltered helped fuel growing claims that this aspect of the heritage industry was important to the future economic health of a trading nation—a way of neatly turning a liability ("the museum society") into an asset. But if the art and antiques fairs were the trade at its most elegantly posed, at that juncture of high aestheticism, heritage, and conspicuous consumption, the down-market end of arcades and street stalls represented the business at its most democratic, and it was here where the real revolution occurred from the late sixties.

The New Caledonian second-hand goods fair at Bermondsey was not new, but it evolved in the sixties into an important market for specialist dealers, as did Camden Passage; Portobello Road was transformed in the late sixties by the influx of "hippy crafts," vegetarian food stalls, and a general carnivalesque atmosphere of street entertainers and voyeurs—to the dismay of the "legitimate" shop owners in the Westbourne Grove area. At the same time indoor arcades like Antiquarius in Chelsea offered places for traders that were a step up from the street markets but much less expensive than a high street shop. By the mid-seventies Portobello Road was twice the size it had been a decade earlier, with an indoor "Antiques Supermarket" at its central junction, and more than 2,000 stall-holders and shop-owners. This rapid increase in small dealers was a response to rising demand, but it also may reflect the economic difficulties facing those in the more traditional shops, with their high overhead of rising rents and rates. A stall in a multitrading unit was relatively inexpensive and provided access to a larger, less discriminating market (casual shoppers, including tourists, rather than knowledgeable collectors).[15]

The structural change in the London antiques trade was not the only supply-side reason the market expanded. Importantly, a new kind of antique dealer became common, a younger trader on the make with little capital and only a small range of stock, eager for a quick turnover, with a lighter regard for "professional" ethics. The trade also experienced a kind of Americanization of entrepreneurial ambition suggested by the successful dealer and picture gallery owner Gavin Graham when he told Deborah Stratton simply, "I'd like to be rich." Some new traders could employ family money and connections to start at the top—like the ill-starred fine art dealer Robert Fraser, who had been inspired by the gallery scene in New York City when he opened his shop in the West End in the sixties. But most served a period of apprenticeship, and even among the grand West End shops there could be found a wide spectrum of social origins. At the lower end, where little start-up capital was needed for stock (often borrowed and sold on commission), selling antiques had particular attraction for young men with few resources or useful connections.[16]

The seventies saw a significant change in the social world of antiques dealing, reflecting the rising volume of the tourist-driven market but also an Americanized ethos. The market was much more volatile, and success (or perhaps failure) seemed to come earlier in life. *The Antique Collector*'s interview pages are full of success stories about very young dealers. There is, for example, the case of Jack Ogden, who left school at sixteen in the mid-sixties to go into the modest family jewelry trade, discovered the market for ancient jewelry, and, by his early thirties, had his own fashionable West End shop selling Egyptian pieces to "the intelligent rich." Or there was Francis Raeymaekers, who began in 1979 with a stall in Antiquarius dealing, at age twenty-three, in silver. He found that Americans were less diffident than the British about buying Sheffield plate, prospered, expanded a "telephone trade" with American clientele, and was able (still in his mid-twenties) to go "up market," moving to the Knightsbridge Pavilion as "A.D.C. Heritage."[17]

Beyond the youth (and often flamboyant lifestyle) of the dealers by the late seventies, there is the question of a change in the culture of dealing at the lower end of the trade where the expansion had been greatest. There was a general perception of an increasingly speculative element, widely commented upon by (usually older) traders themselves and those who have studied the industry. Ronald Pearsall commented in 1974 that in the market stalls, "A type of entrepreneur has joined in, a person who is not really interested in antiques but knows the prices down to the last five pence." E. R. Chamberlin, in 1979, observed that there seemed to be a high entry and mortality rate among contemporary dealers, and in 1981 Frank Taylor, in the *Sunday Times*, echoed the complaint that "a new type of antique dealer had appeared in the last decade," one who was motivated, he suggested, by quick profit rather than a love of the objects themselves: "[He] knows what he likes when he's sold it." Such impressions are inevitably difficult to substantiate. There had always been a speculative, opportunistic side to the trade in antiques, though it is reasonable to assume that this did grow more pronounced as foreign demand mushroomed.[18]

In June, 1979, Esther Rantzen's BBC TV program *That's Life* did an exposé of antique dealers who greatly undervalued items brought to them by naive sellers. The trade, of course, loudly complained, but even *Art and Antiques* admitted that "*some* dealers do *sometimes* make a quick buck." There was also a resonance between charges of shady practices (misrepresentation of goods, over-restoration, and so forth) and a sense that, like many of the things they sold, the young dealers themselves were often not what they seemed. Though many were self-taught school-leavers from relatively poor East London, Essex, or very modest provincial backgrounds, affectation and a camp snobbery were common among them (it helped to sell)—most favored among the stalls was a kind of "sub-county" accent, especially effective, one imagines, with Americans. Many dealers were gay, an important subculture in the trade (a theme that Anthony Powell made use of in *Hearing Secret Harmonies* and Martin Amis in his 1978 novel *Success*): the older were often camply preliberation in their character ("resting" actors and overage dancers had long been drawn to the profession); the younger embraced the liberated hedonism of the seventies and saw in the trade itself an entertaining theatricality, enjoying perhaps the art of a little deception in selling over-the-top goods of doubtful provenance. In 1974 Jeremy Cooper, in a guide to antique street markets in London, went so far as to ascribe some part of the phenomenal growth in the Portobello market, not only to the revulsion against the "horror of industrial progress" fomented by the radical ecology movement but also to "the 'Gay is Good' campaign," which had played, he thought, its own recent role in the "liberation of taste and ideas."[19]

Finally, loss of respect for the customer—in an era when the faceless tourist or suburban shopper may be thought to be a nouveau-riche with more money than sense—clearly played some part in defining the morality of the "cowboy" end of the antiques trade. The distinction was between dealing with a canny collector who came early to the markets and knew the dealers, and selling to the arts-illiterate who only wanted something to decorate a mantel, would passport in hand never walk into the shop again, and would dumbly overpay for shoddy goods if they were cheap but balked at a fair price for an expensive item. Fair game, many thought, and a temptation, especially among those who were young and new to the trade (and remarkably non-nostalgic about the goods they shoveled in bulk to America), who came to it as a speculative venture, and who were themselves dealing on credit and caught in the volatile trade or fashion cycles of the period.

UPSTAIRS WITH ALISTAIR COOKE: BRINGING BRITISHNESS
TO AMERICA . . . AND TO THE BRITISH

The opening shots of WGBH's extraordinarily successful series of imported British television drama, *Masterpiece Theatre*, take the viewer into a gentleman's library, camera lovingly caressing the Edwardian leather and desk-top *objets*, the elegantly bound books and silver picture frames that invoke the "quality" of British culture on offer—rather like the fine things to be had in the transatlantic antiques market—before settling on the comfortable figure of Alistair Cooke, folded into his leather armchair. Cooke was himself an avid collector of Georgian furniture and on trips to London had a shrewd eye for undervalued bargains he could ship back to the States.[20]

Without the somewhat intimidating character of a Sir Kenneth Clark (though many Americans had responded enthusiastically to the de haut en bas cultural elitism of the *Civilisation* lectures), Cooke was a reassuring, avuncular presence, well-read and well-spoken but no know-it-all snob as he gently drew the less-well-read, less-informed American viewer into the world of British literature and history. The affecting hesitation in speech and diffident, self-deprecating manner evoked a kind of Britishness that played well in the States and was familiar as a Hollywood cliché of the kind long exploited by actors like Wilfrid Hyde-White, Leo G. Carroll, or Roland Young. Cooke's own version of the role, as a naturalized

British journalist resident in the United States since the thirties, had been long maturing.

In America, Cooke was central to the remarkable success the seventies witnessed in the transatlantic media-marketing of Heritage Britain in an era of dystopian malaise. In Britain, though he played a significant role as explicator of the American scene to a curious public, his transatlantic identity was necessarily a rather more complicated affair, just as the voice Americans heard as "British" could seem to English ears to have acquired a flattened American tone. Nor were his origins as upper-class as his media-presence in the United States might imply. His Lancashire accent, like his name (Alfred), had been adjusted when as a scholarship boy he made his way to Cambridge from provincial Blackpool. As his biographer says, to a significant degree, "Alistair Cooke is his own invention."[21]

Alfie Cooke at an early age was exposed to American influences—American troops in Blackpool during the First World War (he was nine in 1917) had been billeted with his family, and he had an early taste for American jazz. After Cambridge, a Commonwealth Fund fellowship (provided by American philanthropist Edward S. Harkness) enabled him to spend two years in the United States, first at Yale and then traveling across the country, and to take courses at Harvard, where he was especially fascinated with idiomatic American language (he would later heartily advocate importing American expressions into British English). Back in Britain in 1935 he took a job with the BBC, proposed a radio series on American life, and was allowed to broadcast a program on "English on Both Sides of the Atlantic" both in Britain and, thanks to an early contact with NBC, in the States.[22]

Cooke spent the war years in the States as a journalist and took American citizenship in 1941. Immediately following the war he signed on to be, first, United Nations and then in 1948 chief American correspondent for the *Manchester Guardian*, inaugurating a popular column that, along with a fifteen-minute weekly BBC radio piece, "Letter from America," made him familiar in Britain. By the fifties he had become a kind of transatlantic chameleon, with an accent, as Basil Willey remarked, that was "adopted with such characteristic finesse so as to offend neither American nor British ears" (a 1951 profile in an English magazine claimed that the English assumed he was American, Americans that he was English). His reportage on the United States was usually generous (though he had no use for the student rebellion, Black Power militants, or the counterculture)—and he was sometimes criticized in Britain (there were in any event lingering suspicions about his abandoning them in the war) for being too pro-American. If indeed he became a kind of "public relations officer" for the States, this can be explained in part as a measure of self-justification.[23]

By the fifties, though Cooke's journalism, family, and friends drew him regularly back to Britain, he was firmly planted in the States—his first and second wives were both American, and he had begun a successful career on American television as a presenter of the popular CBS arts and culture series *Omnibus*. For *Omnibus*, though he had been living in the States for some thirteen years when the series began in 1952, Cooke's carefully presented image was, as later for *Masterpiece Theatre*, that of a well-spoken Englishman—a persona that sold well on a culture program that Cooke himself admitted was "perhaps a little pretentious." Originally funded by the Ford Foundation, *Omnibus* won an Emmy in 1958 and made his U.S. reputation—as well as an income that, with his American freelancing, significantly surpassed that of his continuing work through the fraught sixties for either the *Guardian* or the BBC. It was in large part the prospect of significant profit that persuaded Cooke at the end of the decade, after the success of Sir Kenneth (subsequently Lord) Clark's *Civilisation*, to accept an offer by the BBC to put his long familiarity with reporting the American scene to use in a television series and book on "American civilization" ("if one can call it that," Alastair Hetherington at the *Guardian* gratuitously commented).[24]

The *America* project brought an end to Cooke's *Guardian* column, which he gave up to free himself for work on what was to be, after Clark's *Civilisation*, one of the first transatlantic series at the BBC produced in collaboration with American commercial partners—something that would characterize an especially seventies approach at the BBC to transatlantic financing, production, and marketing. This was a phenomenon of growing media internationalization, the deep pockets of American backers, and the potential size of the American market for products that could exploit middle-American hunger for "culture" as, like the new American taste for wine, croissants, and cappuccino, something that was best learned from Europe.

Cofinancing and coproduction were somewhat controversial. Criticism focused on issues beyond injury to national pride. Foremost was the likelihood that content would be (was already being) affected if British television production had to be accessible by Americans who were only interested in (or capable of understanding) stereotypes of a historical, literary Britain. The need for marketability abroad might act, that is, to discourage good contemporary domestic production. The veteran journalist and radio broadcaster William Hardcastle, writing in 1969, observed that "the worry must be over what happens to national programmes when they are tailored," by either the BBC or ITV companies, "for an international market." It might represent "splendid business acumen, but is it British television?" It was, in fact "mid-Atlantic television ... slanted to an American audience." For the BBC, financed by the license fee, there was the further issue that production for profit (abroad) and collaboration with commercial interests raised concerns about to whom they were answerable. Fears were heightened when the Time-Life Company, a book and music marketing division of the media empire established by the right-wing anticommunist Henry Luce and family, "fell on" Clark's BBC series *Civilisation* and then moved to initiate future prefinanced coproductions.[25]

Hardcastle rightly predicted that coproduction and overseas sales would significantly expand. According to one source, in the seventies perhaps 10 percent of the BBC's television program budget came from foreign financing and sales; BBC2 alone netted some £2 million in cofinancing from 1971 to 1974. Whether that was a good or bad thing or inevitable continued to be debated, especially when significant production effort went into projects, like *The British Empire*, that proved not to be as successful in either the domestic or American market as anticipated. The debate, played out in the BBC's widely read house journal, *The Listener*, continued into 1972 and 1973, but criticism did not significantly slow the trend toward transatlanticism. In fact only a relatively modest percentage of BBC television was coproduced and cofinanced in the seventies, and profits from exports to the United States—including "spin-offs" like books, commercial videos, and recordings—at least allowed the BBC to survive without the political risks of repeated appeals for increases in license fee.[26]

Foreign sales of BBC programs, if not cofinancing and coproduction, had in fact been pursued, albeit not very aggressively, for some time in the Commonwealth and U.S. markets. What happened post–*Forsyte Saga* was a largely unanticipated opening—the unprecedented growth of American appetite for British programming—that American management, itself increasingly transatlantic in its contacts and experience, moved to exploit in a developing competition between the commercial networks and PBS for the high end of the market. As late as 1970, Dennis Scuse, who had been the BBC's representative in the United States in the early sixties and general manager since 1968 of their television export division, BBC Television Enterprises, was pessimistic about American sales, claiming that the "high quality" of BBC programming inhibited their sale in the United States and predicting, wrongly, that the *Civilisation* series would not be able to find an American network. But Scuse was living in the past and a quickening pace was already apparent: BBC television sales worldwide rose by nearly 17 percent in 1968/69 and a further 15 percent in 1970/71.[27]

The BBC's television series *America—A Personal History*, cofinanced by Time-Life with support from the Xerox Corporation, and the accompanying book (Cooke made his own very profitable separate arrangement with the New York publisher Knopf) made "serious money" for Cooke in both the U.S. and British markets. There were sniping complaints from some (similar complaints sometimes appeared over the conservatism of his *Guardian* column) about his representation, say, of Native Americans or his lack of interest in negative, alternative voices in contemporary America; as the film scholar James Leahy, just returned from Daley's Chicago, put it, "In his desire for us to love him and love America, he has ceased to relate to and describe the America that is." But it was just this calm, generous, cheerful, and nondystopian presentation that apparently appealed to those searching for a conventional and familiar reading of America that made its screening on BBC2 a great success (with twice the viewing audience achieved by Clark's *Civilisation*).[28]

Distribution in the States followed—with some editing (no nudity)—but at first proved problematic. Placed with NBC (which had previously taken the BBC's historical docu-drama *In Search of the Nile*), in competition with mass entertainment programming the series began with disappointing ratings. This led to its transfer to PBS and success with public television's more precisely targeted demographic—the educated, relatively affluent. The same shift happened in 1971 when CBS had trouble finding sponsors for two BBC historical dramas, *The Six Wives of Henry VIII* and *Elizabeth R* and sold them on to WGBH's *Masterpiece Theatre*—where they had considerable success. The accompanying large, color-illustrated book, *America*, was also a "publishing phenomenon" in the States and displaced *The Joy of Sex* from the top of the hardback bestseller list. It made Cooke a rich man. In Britain, sales were brisk as well, and continued through the seventies. The U.S. Information Service bought the *America* series for embassies and consulates worldwide, while a philanthropic foundation put a copy of the book in every public library. On 25 September 1974, as part of the celebration of the bicentennial of the first Continental Congress, Cooke was, remarkably, invited, like LaFayette and Churchill, to speak before a joint session of Congress—an event that was broadcast both in the United States and on BBC2. [29]

With *America* largely finished toward the end of 1971, Cooke was pressed by public television's WGBH in Boston to sign on as presenter of a series of high-culture British drama imports they intended to produce with the help of Mobil Oil. *Masterpiece Theatre* (the British spelling was intentional) was designed to build on the remarkable success of WGBH's imported *Forsyte Saga*, which had finished that January. Public television in the United States was rapidly evolving from its roots in local educational TV to position itself as the provider of high-quality programming as an alternative to the mass market networks. Initially subsidized by the Ford Foundation in the wake of the mid-sixties race riots in urban America with the hope that local public networks might be able to provide cross-racial dialogue and programming more relevant to minorities, public television's mission shifted significantly by the turn of the decade. Deprived by the Nixon administration of hopes of BBC-like public funding, its recourse, ironically, was to relocate its niche among relatively affluent white audiences, supported by a combination of corporate philanthropy and viewer donation. Screening *The Forsyte Saga* and *Civilisation* signified this shift toward the "discriminating viewer."[30]

The attractiveness of British productions lay in their off-the-shelf relative cheapness as well as marketability to that part of the American public that associated British with high culture. For its part, the BBC had been attempting to break into the American media market since the fifties but with indifferent success as Lew Grade's commercial productions effectively targeted American entertainment opportunities in ways the BBC by and large could not. This changed dramatically with a growing viewer appetite for costume drama, a market that both the BBC and the ITV companies rushed to encourage and fill, and the waning of the Anglophobia that had long been familiar in at least some sectors of the American market.

The Pilkington report in 1962 had criticized what the committee regarded as the low cultural quality of much ITV programming. The turn toward historical and literary drama and documentary at ATV and Granada in the early and mid-seventies would help improve the "respectability" of commercial television. This motive dovetailed with the prospect of increased sales to the A and B demographic in the American market, once the success of the *Forsyte Saga* and Clarke's *Civilisation* revealed the possibilities for profit there. Moreover, the apparent oversaturation of a diminishing American market for Bond spin-off, secret agent series further propelled Lew Grade's ATV network toward quality programming as a way of saving his transatlantic business by convincing not just PBS stations but also the commercial channels with which he had connections of long standing that British independent producers could do high-end production as well. In 1972 he persuaded ABC to take his film of the National Theatre's production of *Long Day's Journey into Night*: "You may not get ratings, but think of the prestige." He also sold them *Anthony and Cleopatra*, *The Merchant of Venice*, and *Twelfth Night*—with "stars" already familiar to suburban America like Olivier, Gielgud, and Guinness. By the early and mid-seventies Grade's Elstree Studios was busy producing historical docu-drama of the kind the BBC was marketing to PBS: a mini-series, *Edward the Seventh*, was made for the domestic British market but also hawked around the U.S. commercial channels before being sold to Mobil, which was financing *Masterpiece Theatre*. This connection led to Mobil's taking a number of historical series on Disraeli, Nelson, and William Shakespeare.[31]

Though it has been estimated that ATV's production of "prestige programmes" made expressly for the international market was a small part of their total output (perhaps less than 3 percent), there were many more productions made for domestic consumption with an eye for selling on to the States. By the seventies it is not possible easily to distinguish those productions, whether BBC or ITV, that were intended for the domestic market from those meant for export. For Grade, of course, quality programming was only a piece of the picture, and he continued successfully to promote profitable mass audience productions he could place in the American market, like the sixty one-hour television programs of *The Tom Jones Show* he sold to ABC.[32]

At PBS generally, and especially at what was possibly the most Anglo-oriented of the public stations, WGBH, British television already had some influence and connection. Christopher Sarson had been a producer at Granada before coming to the United States in the mid-sixties ultimately to take a position as a leading producer at WGBH; Frank Gillard, after he retired as Director of Sound Broadcasting at the BBC in 1969, joined the Corporation for Public Broadcasting in Washington as a distinguished fellow. Both would be influential in pressing American public broadcasting toward the kind of historical and literary drama that could capitalize on the nostalgia and high-culture market. It was Gillard who recommended that WGBH ask Alistair Cooke, regarded at the station as "a kind of quintessential Englishman," to present a series of programs imported from Britain. *Masterpiece Theatre* with, especially, *Upstairs, Downstairs* in 1974, would bring something like a mass audience to PBS. This was made possible by funding from Mobil Oil, in a significant shift at PBS to corporate support (Mobil had previously provided early funding for *Sesame Street*).[33]

The oil industry was especially interested in public relations at a time when its lobbying effort to deregulate gas and oil prices and expand offshore drilling was encountering a more aggressive environmentalism. At Mobil the goal of the chairman and chief executive officer, Rawleigh Warner, and of his vice president for public affairs, Herbert Schmerz, was to counter what they perceived to be the "anti-business" environment of the late sixties and advance free market ideology generally: "In our minds," Warner later commented, "Mobil's support of public broadcasting (and other cultural activities to which we contribute) is all of a piece with our outspoken support of the American system of democratic capitalism." Moreover, the contributions to PBS were tax-deductible. In 1960 Humble Oil had sponsored National Educational Television's broadcast of *An Age of Kings*—fifteen episodes from Shakespeare's history plays produced by the BBC.[34]

Schmerz, who flew to London to talk to the BBC and view programs on offer (for "an absurdly low figure"), was no right-wing Republican but a progressive if Establishment Democrat—a labor lawyer with connections to Robert Kennedy and his 1968 campaign—and Cooke found him very agreeable to work with, not least because of his deference: "[T]he best sort of patron: loyal and unobtrusive, never once questioning our choice of play or author." Pressed to accept the job of presenter, Cooke accepted when Mobil's underwriting allowed WGBH to meet what he had, so he said, intended to be a prohibitively large fee. The press release announcing the coming series called it "intelligent television for people who don't ordinarily watch television." In fact, the first *Masterpiece Theatre* installment of BBC-produced historical drama, *The First Churchills*, was bawdier by American television standards, more soap opera with a sexy co-star, Susan Hampshire, than "intelligent television" might have implied. Cooke himself was unimpressed ("The script was not a masterpiece, either original or adapted"), and it had not been especially successful in Britain. But, introduced by the "quintessential Englishman," it found viewers ready to respond, not only to "powerful signifiers for an American audience" (it was advertised with a picture of Susan Hampshire as the Duchess of Marlborough, described as "Winston Churchill's Great Great Great Great Grandmother") but also to a sense that even entertainments like this meant superior British viewing.[35]

Masterpiece Theatre, with the Union flag prominently displayed in its title sequence, was launched with popular success—considerably expanding the demographic of public broadcasting. Other BBC productions followed in steady succession on Mobil's Sunday hour. Most were nineteenth-century literary dramatizations. The twentieth century was served by productions of Dorothy Sayers's "novels of manners," the mystery stories that starred another "quintessentially [that is, upper-class] English" actor, Ian Carmichael, now made familiar to a large American audience. The taste for dramatized history was served by the transfer to PBS of *The Six Wives of Henry VIII* and *Elizabeth R*, a mini-series that made Glenda Jackson a household name in the United States. It was, however, the American broadcast from January to March 1974 of the first series of *Upstairs, Downstairs* (shown in Britain from 1971) that established public television, at least on Sunday evenings, as a competitor with the commercial networks for general audience: Edwardian soap opera like *The Forsyte Saga*, but without the *Saga*'s literary derivation and with more sympathetic characterizations. It was produced by London Weekend Television, and had been successful on British television—Rawleigh Warner heard about *Upstairs, Downstairs* from the dowager Duchess of Bedford at a dinner party in London.[36]

WGBH, comfortable with its association with what was generally regarded as the superior cultural programming of the BBC and its, by 1974, long succession of televised versions of great literature, took some convincing that, as mere "entertainment," LWT's Edwardian soap would not damage their reputation for "intelligent television." Staff interviewed director, writers, and actors and in the end were persuaded by the promise of its "split sociology" (what Cooke called "a foolproof formula for ensnaring a mass audience")—Upstairs for "the snobbish kick" of elegantly costumed aristocratic elitism, Downstairs for the cozy realm of humanized ordinary folk. The three months it was shown confirmed that there was a large soap-and-nostalgia market—it managed at least the viewing audience (around 7 percent, or 10 to 12 million) that the *Saga* had achieved, and quickly built a following. There was a second series in November through to the next year, a third in January to March of 1976, and a fourth finally finished in May of Jubilee Year, 1977. The success with a loyal, eager part of the viewing public was such that WGBH and LWT were able to profit from spin-off commodities—novelizations, Mrs. Bridges cookbooks, jams and marmalade, and tea towels, while the cast was used (as also was the case with the Python team) for WGBH fund-raisers. Among at least the relatively affluent, white, educated PBS audience, the historical and social detail of the long-running series wove an attractive representation of

Britain-as-Edwardian-London. And as with those fantasists who sought out the Baker Street residence of a historical Sherlock Holmes, "American tourists were seen wandering up and down Eaton Place, just off Belgravia Square [*sic*] looking in vain for number 165."[37]

In the films and television series that signaled the transnational production and consumption of heritage, Andrew Higson has observed, there was a tension between the "Englishness" consumed in either Britain or the United States and the reality of what he calls (writing of eighties films like *Chariots of Fire*) "a much more hybrid and transgressive sense of cross-cultural identity." Stitched together pastiches of English historical locations and interiors "masquerade as the real thing," when in reality it is America's modernity that is "a constant and often ironic reference point." A central issue arises, then, of just whose heritage is being circulated in a production like Thames Television's 1974 historical drama *Jennie, Lady Randolph Churchill*, with the American actress Lee Remick as Winston Churchill's mother. Its Welsh director, James Cellan Jones, had done *The Forsyte Saga* and other literary dramatizations for BBC2; the writer, Julian Mitchell, had worked on *Elizabeth R. Jennie*'s theme, cast, and transatlantic export intentions (it quickly transferred to PBS's Great Performances series) certainly embodied ambiguities of transgressive cross-cultural identity as well as encouraging quite distinct "readings" in Britain and in the United States (where, as Jeffrey Miller has pointed out, such heritage programming involved an additional problem of "a negotiation of 'otherness' and 'our-own-ness'"). Another scholar has argued that *Masterpiece Theatre* revealed a subtextual strategy of defensively fusing together the apparently incompatible national myths of England and the United States (good breeding and rugged success) in an era of Western decline, and offered lessons in the "manners" necessary for running a (perhaps declining) American empire. Without completely accepting that such popularizations of high culture offered exactly an "ideological commodity" of this nature, we can appreciate that *Jennie*'s fusion and its forward-looking premise (that American savvy and British class would combine to produce a twentieth-century hero for both "Anglo-Saxon peoples") represents a transatlantic conationalism flattering to many.[38]

Finally, a parallel example of transatlanticism can be drawn from the print media. The *Times Literary Supplement* aimed to achieve a degree of export success in seventies America in much the same market as the BBC and ITV (whose costume drama often had the effect of increasing the sales of British literature). In 1974 a cartoon by Everett Opie in the *New Yorker* suggested that the *TLS* might massage a nostalgic fantasy of British Heritage and social éclat. A man reclined in his library chair with a book while his wife observes, "It all started with that trial subscription to the T.L.S. Then came that Nigel Nicolson book, the smoking jacket and pipe, the pint of bitter, and, bingo, little West Tenth Street has become Bloomsbury." The *TLS* had been concerned to expand its American presence since

*"It all started with that trial subscription to the <u>T.L.S.</u> Then came that
Nigel Nicolson book, the smoking jacket and pipe, the pint of bitter, and
bingo, little West Tenth Street has become Bloomsbury."*

7. "It all started with that trial subscription." Everett Opie cartoon, the *New Yorker*, 20
May 1974 (Everett Opie/The New Yorker Collection/www.cartoonbank.com).

its editor, Arthur Crook, went to the United States for four months in 1961 (and
again in 1965) to meet editors, writers, academics, and publishers to drum up sales
and advertising and to negotiate reprint rights.[39] As with the television media, the
effort to attract American sales had a circular impact on what was consumed in
Britain: not only was there subsequently more American content, but arguably the
end of anonymous reviewing in 1974 was in part dictated by the need to increase
sales in an American market that did not much care for the time-honored insider
game of guess the reviewer.

Whether the transatlantic antiques trade, the transatlantic circulation of television nostalgia for an imperial past, or the American marketing of the *TLS* necessarily much furthered an "Arnoldian project of civilizing an American international ruling class" with lessons from reified British history and the emulation of
imagined upper-class English manners and taste, as one critic of British media
exports has proposed,[40] the successful transatlantic marketing of nostalgia and

heritage did achieve a kind of success, and can be found in yet other, sometimes surprising, realms. In international sport America was historically isolationist—calling the annual denouement of their national pastime a "World Series" when no one else but Canadians was allowed to compete, and whose "football" was not the world's football. Baseball, poised for terminal decline, profited immensely from the turn toward a culture of nostalgia in the seventies. Britain, on the other hand, had extended from its home base to its empire and beyond truly internationalized sporting traditions—whether the populist professionalization of football or the more elitist traditions of cricket. Britain's cricket, "soccer," or rugby never found much of a media market across the Atlantic, but its tennis did.

HERITAGE TENNIS: THE MARKETING OF WIMBLEDON

Like the Henley Regatta, Royal Ascot, or the Glorious Twelfth, the lawn tennis championship at Wimbledon, with its royal patronage and quasi-military organization and trappings, its champagne and strawberries, the discouragement of overt commercial sponsorship and the tasteful insistence on white outfits for players, can be seen as one of those traditional rituals of the upper classes that have somehow survived—even flourished—in the democratic, modern postwar age.[41]

Like some other class-defining traditions, however, lawn tennis as an organized "national" sport is neither especially ancient nor, despite its origins among the late-Victorian country-house set, an especially upper-class phenomenon. By the twenties a passion for tennis in suburbia was encouraged by cheaper private clubs and public courts as well as the huge international reputation of a "star" player, the American Bill Tilden. The popularity of the game—both as leisure activity and spectator sport—was a largely middle-class phenomenon, though one that, as at Wimbledon, retained a cachet of class and tradition suggested by its amateur character, or the Kipling stanza from *If* above the players' entrance to center court. In the postwar world of democratized national pastimes, however, the Wimbledon tradition was under increasing threat from domestic and international commercial pressures for professionalization and popularization. It was also vulnerable, as were other class rituals, to a modernist and ironic attack on the fusty traditions of an obsolescent Britain. Ray-Jones's devastating black-and-white photo of "Wimbledon, 1968" captures this sense of a washed-out, defiant, unsmiling class clinging to its privileges. And yet, as the sixties progressed the sport throve as never before both in attendance at the championship matches and in television spectator audiences.[42]

The survival of Wimbledon as both a distinctive "English" ritual and the primary grand-slam international championship provides an interesting and instructive example of a curious conjunction of modernity and the marketing of "heritage" in the late sixties and seventies, a remarkable example of how

8. "Wimbledon, 1968." From the Tony Ray-Jones Collection at the National Media Museum/SSPL.

Britishness itself was first challenged and threatened by Americanization only to emerge, if dependent upon, also enabled and sustained by, American money and, as with *Masterpiece Theatre*, an American appetite for transatlantic tone and style. Ironically, in the late twentieth century traditional form was, so to speak, emptied of British content. There has not been a British men's singles championship winner at Wimbledon since Fred Perry's in 1936, and he retired to California.[43]

The year before Ray-Jones snapped his black-and-white photo, the BBC used the Wimbledon final for its first color broadcast (the other program broadcast in color on the first of July 1967 was the *Andy Williams Show*). The matches had been televised since before the war, but in the sixties the game became an especially important piece of BBC's sport programming, it having successfully seen off the threat of commercial competition by offering two channels to ITV's one. But the tenacious traditionalism of the sport, a fear of down-market Americanization, and a lack of sufficient resources to sustain the reputation of a modernized Wimbledon worked to delay professionalization. When in 1968 tennis finally yielded to the threat that the best players themselves were abandoning amateur status, the "open" era brought immediate challenges. The first was how Britain might retain its status in a field where, as Rod Laver pointed out in 1970, there were five American tournaments to Britain's one, many of which provided a larger purse—not to mention invitationals with much more substantial prizes—than Wimbledon. Money, especially American money, came to seem the most prominent threat to Wimbledon's continued position. [44]

In the late sixties feminist pressures were also mounting to address the purse-money inequality of the women's game. In the United States, Billie Jean King, who eagerly embraced pro status, was increasingly vocal in her dissatisfaction with the unequal prizes available to women at Wimbledon and elsewhere. After women players boycotted the Pacific Southwest tournament, the American tobacco company Phillip Morris offered to sponsor a women's "Virginia Slims" tour in 1971 that saw prize money of nearly $200,000—rising to almost $1 million three years later. The pressure to raise the purse for women's championships in the grand slam tournaments increased, and in 1974 King helped launch a union of women players, the Women's Tennis Association, that successfully lobbied for prize money equality at the U.S. Open at Forest Hills that summer, while "sponsors other than Virginia Slims seemed to line up to give money away."[45]

As the seventies dawned, Britain's only grand slam event had to scramble for resources. What Wimbledon had to market was its historical reputation. The largest potential source for increased revenue, vital if the club was going to be able to meet professionalization's demand for prize money, was the United States: from ticket sales to well-heeled American tennis tourists, merchandizing spin-offs, and, by far most important, the sale of television rights to American networks—a source that would come to generate more than half of Wimbledon's income. Previously, though the BBC paid fees for facilities, it did not pay for the right to broadcast, having after the withdrawal of ITV a monopoly on domestic broadcasting of the championships. The American networks came in with substantial offers from the late sixties, however: the championship that Laver won in 1969 was transmitted via satellite to the United States, and, by 1977, the All England Club could get upward of a million dollars for the right to broadcast in the States. There is a double story here—of the successful marketing by the British of Wimbledon to the American networks, but also the emergence of a substantially enlarged market for a televised sport that had not previously had much mass appeal.[46]

By the early seventies, according to one scholar, it was "clear that the power base of tennis had shifted to America because of the money players could make [there]." The game was "ripe for TV exploitation of all kinds" in a satellite-fed medium that presided over a vast expansion of tennis spectatorship. But if Wimbledon retained a special appeal and was now viewable live in North America, it also had to compete with ever-growing prize money available through televised "challenge" promotions, like the $100,000 winner-take-all match between Jimmy Connors and Rod Laver or the $250,000 match between Connors and Newcombe shortly after—both in Caesar's Palace, Las Vegas. Or the antics of even more gimmicky mass entertainment promotions, like the heavily advertised Bobby Riggs/Billie

Jean King farce, promoted by CBS as "the battle of the sexes," in the Houston Astrodome in 1973. The more immediate challenge to traditional world tennis, however, came from a Texas millionaire.[47]

Lamar Hunt, heir to a vast oil fortune and an avid sports entrepreneur and promoter, cofounded World Championship Tennis in 1967 and immediately began signing amateur and professional players. That year a WCT tournament, just weeks after Wimbledon, negotiated BBC coverage to provide a purse several times as large as that for the finals' champion at Wimbledon. By 1970 Hunt had signed thirty-two top world players, directly challenging the International Lawn Tennis Federation with his intention to run international tennis as a flamboyant, spectator-pleasing business. A key issue arose over the WCT's demands for "expense money" in exchange for allowing its signed stars to compete at Wimbledon. When in 1972 the ILTF refused to pay, Hunt's players stayed away (the next year there was another, larger boycott organized by the Association of Tennis Professionals). WCT's alternative circuit ultimately failed, but its innovations showed where tennis might go in the business of increasing the spectatorship that kept the all-important cash flowing from media sponsors: bright clothing, changes to rules that increased the pace of the game, and encouragement of noisy spectator participation—in 1973 a short-lived World Team Tennis experiment initiated by Billie Jean King's husband, Larry King, urged spectators to "behave as if [matches were] a football game" (Evonne Goolagong, the Women's Singles champion at Wimbledon in 1971, joined the WTT Pittsburgh Triangles for a $1 million five-year contract). Attempts to reorganize championship tennis along the lines of other glamorized American sport entertainments like the Super Bowls, however, offended many within just that demographic that television executives found most attractive—the "affluent, well-educated, upwardly mobile, and trendy"—and the WTT suspended play in 1978.[48]

The threat of innovation and modernization that commercial, spectator-oriented entrepreneurship represented nevertheless pushed the grand slam tournaments along in self-defense. In 1970 the ILTF experimented with tie-breaks, which both added tension to the game and met (American) television network objections to interminable matches. The introduction of more visible colored balls was also prompted by media concerns. Media-fueled, spectator-driven "American influences" threatened to proliferate in lawn tennis, as they did in the hard surface, indoor court game—from the shift toward a more exciting style of power and speed, the raised visibility and style of women's tennis in a postradical feminist world, or what was regarded by many British observers as the "breakdown" in "gentlemanly" player behavior toward officials. As the elderly classics scholar Harold Arthur Harris complained in 1975, the problem was an especially American habit of playing to the crowd: "If spectators want to see players throwing their rackets at umpires, then rackets will be thrown at umpires. And if the trend now being set by the promoters of World Team Tennis in America follows the logical course, the game will soon be on a level with all-in wrestling." Many traditionalists also feared the threat of a change in the style of British sports commentary toward incessant American patter (this phenomenon, much resented by Alistair Cooke, was in fact slow in coming), the introduction of the American obsession with "statistics" (counting unforced errors, service aces, speed of serve), and, especially, the noisier participation of crowds. When, in July of 1972, there was a "crescendo" of "fan" noise during the women's final (King vs. Goolagong), one British television reviewer complained with Swiftian humor that "a committee of inquiry ought to be set up without delay, with a view to transferring the Wimbledon Open Lawn Championships to another country: nothing is easier than to call another place Wimbledon—say, Wimbledon, Massachusetts."[49]

While professional tennis enjoyed a general increase in spectator popularity and televised visibility in the United States in the seventies, due to expanded media coverage and vigorous promotion, Wimbledon's special appeal lay in its own added value for much of the American viewing public—the heritage and quality that the grass courts of the All England Club and its royal sponsorship seemed to offer. In the gloves-off struggle for share in transatlantic and world tennis spectatorship in the seventies, this was a critical element in keeping Wimbledon *the* prestige venue as the only grand slam that was chiefly identifiable by its presumed uniquely "national" character. Its success lay in retaining its traditional appearance while in fact yielding to the commercial pressures that lay behind a growing entertainment industry. When in 1971 Evonne Goolagong took her transistor radio into the Wimbledon changing rooms, playing the black American soul singer Otis Redding's posthumous hit "Sittin' on the Dock of the Bay," Billie Jean King had voiced her approval at the challenge to the fusty routines of the Lawn Tennis Association's prestige venue—"About time we had some music in here to liven the place up." But "livening the place up" was not to be, at least overtly, where Wimbledon's survival strengths would lie.[50]

Unlike cricket or (world) football or, in the other direction, baseball and (American) football, British tennis successfully crossed the Atlantic divide as a televised spectator sport that commanded for NBC impressive ratings and audience share throughout the seventies (staying high from 1973 to 1982, paralleling almost exactly the popularity of heritage television). Arthur Ashe put his finger on the unique attraction of Wimbledon to many Americans in the seventies: "Part of the reason that Wimbledon attracts such great attention is that it is a bone fide, certified British tradition, and British traditions are just a bit more traditional than anyone else's." It was certainly sold to the Anglo-American market, as in Ronald Atkin's 1981 coffee-table-size, glossily illustrated *Book of Wimbledon*, as an artifact of British heritage, with its "tradition" and "exclusivity," an "efficiency more normally associated with Trooping the Colour," the military discipline of its ball-boys or the uniforms of its umpires: "Even the Americans, who possess the monopoly of most that is biggest and best, refer to Wimbledon with a touch of awe as The Big W . . . a national celebration that is internationally renowned."[51]

The Britishness of Wimbledon, and its marketing as a self-consciously crafted national-historical institution was a green-purple-white image that effectively masked modernization and the degree to which it was increasingly dependent on American commercial media sponsorship. Its centenary year, 1977, was also Jubilee year, and American viewers were treated to images of the Queen herself, recently returned from North America, in attendance, and Virginia Wade making at least the Women's final again a cause for national celebration. The same year H.R.H. the Duke of Kent opened a Wimbledon Lawn Tennis Museum that promised to draw a substantial proportion of its paying visitors from across the Atlantic. Shortly after, the marketing of Wimbledon as heritage tennis was made explicit in the States by its most prominent American sponsor, NBC, which aired its own Wimbledon documentary, narrated by Peter Ustinov. The Wimbledon museum, Ustinov happily informed his viewers, was open and ready for business.

Wimbledon was, of course, a "bone fide, certified British tradition," but one whose managers and sponsors came to realize risked losing much of its unique appeal for the ever-larger attendances and the vastly expanding television sales in the United States if it appeared to be yet another commercialized entertainment. Heritage sold in the seventies and beyond, and the "traditional" aspects of Wimbledon became its brand. As Paul Kelso reporting for the *Guardian* in 2005 said, "Wimbledon crowds are no fans of modernity."[52] Or as James Meikle and Esther Addley reported in 2008, "[T]he world's oldest tennis tournament wins game, set and match when it comes to global marketing."[53]

CHAPTER 12

Mecklenburgh Square

For many of the growing number of American postgraduate students who found themselves living in the late-imperial, once-elite establishments London House and William Goodenough House in Mecklenburgh Square, Bloomsbury, the game of tennis—whether on BBC in the basement television rooms or on the courts in the gated Square and those at the Hurlingham Club in Southwest London to which London House residents had access—was a part of their British experience. For those Americans who played as well as watched, tennis was more familiar and accessible than cricket, rugby, or squash-rackets. There were House teams for each of these sports, though few U.S. students played on them, because of lack of interest, ability—or encouragement. The teams, for the men a significant means of integration into the life of the House, were recruited by staff who were often former colonial officers not very keen on the changing character of the institution generally and especially its slide toward American colonization in the sixties and seventies.

Television room tussles at London House may reveal a little about fault lines between those domestic British and Commonwealth students who were happy with common entertainment (appropriate only for a "mindless audience," as one aggrieved Canadian put it in 1972)—reruns, say, of the *Phil Silvers Show*, popular in the seventies—and North Americans expecting refined difference as part of their British experience. London House was in fact a kind of cultural oasis: chamber music and lieder performed by residents, poetry readings, and the House phonograph collection well stocked with opera. There were frequent guest lecturers—prominent historians or Establishment figures from politics (including, usually, the sitting Lord Chancellor) and the professions, royals like Mountbatten, former ambassadors like Lord Harlech (Sir David Ormsby-Gore), and for balance a few newsworthy political gadflies. It offered North Americans and some of the white South Africans, Rhodesians, or Australians recruited from privileged backgrounds a rather self-conscious, somewhat anachronistic Britishness—if just a little worn at the heels—in a chaotic, democratic, multiracial postcolonial world.

If dinner was no longer five-course affairs attended by white-coated former servicemen stewards, as had been the custom in the thirties and forties, London House still represented "class" to many—especially when compared, say, to the University of London's nearby modernist knockabout casual and very multicultural International Hall (built in 1963).[1]

HISTORY

The Dominion Students' Hall Trust was founded in 1930 to provide a genteel residential setting for postgraduates from the Dominions and colonies who were expected to carry something of the high culture and British heritage of the late-imperial metropolis back out to the governance of empire and commonwealth. There was significant Establishment patronage from royals, the City, Dominion statesmen, and Tory empire-enthusiasts like Leo Amery. It was, of course, a whites-only, all-male establishment, and the only North American residents were Canadian.

The resolutely unmodern buildings, not completed until the sixties, reflect this founding ideology (a gilded flaming torch was carved into the plaster of the Great Hall with the motto of the late-nineteenth-century Conservative Primrose League—*Imperium et Libertas*). The original designs, closely followed over the decades of construction, were by the late-imperial architect Sir Herbert Baker, who lived some years in South Africa and helped Lutyens plan New Delhi. Much of Baker's work—he designed South Africa House in Trafalgar Square and India House at the Aldwych—was deeply disliked by Pevsner for its insufficient modernity, decorative "foibles," and the "timidity" of its "weak" efforts at combining domestic idiom with heavy grandeur. London House, built around a quadrangle on the south side of the square, is typical of Baker's approach, a historicist combination of 17th-century-style flint and stone base with brick upper stories and a pitched tiled roof of cottagey dormers.[2]

The Dominion Students' Hall Trust chose neither to mirror the cosmopolitan elegance of the stuccoed and columned Georgian terrace that originally defined Mecklenburgh Square nor to accommodate internationalist fashion. Located in a historic and leafy enclave in the modern capital, London House represented a domestic refuge protected from the intrusion of the modern world by its additional defense of a closed, cloistered quadrangle—an island of calm in a square of calm—while its rituals, tone, and aspirations required rather formal interiors. Baker had bequeathed "characteristically pompous"[3] public spaces, a high-ceilinged "common room" with bronze statuettes of Nelson and Wellington in niches by the mantelpiece, and especially the "Great [Dining] Hall" with gilded imperial emblems high on its walls, heavy red velvet drapes, a grand polychromed "Empire Clock" that indicated time of day in the Dominions and India, and paintings of larger-than-life imperial statesmen like Smuts looking down. As late as 1963 the

9. London House: Inner Quadrangle and the Great Hall. Author's photograph.

Establishment character was underscored by the opening of a Church of England chapel—with resident chaplain—in the southeast corner. Other postwar additions included a formal "Churchill Room," while more functional projects like a basement swimming pool faltered as the late-imperial idea encountered a falling off of interest and resources.

Originally intended as part of the infrastructure of a forward-looking *modern* Empire-Commonwealth, the Trust in a postimperial world ultimately, if reluctantly, abandoned one raison d'être for another, more generalized one, that of facilitating ties of understanding in the English-speaking world. But it also remained a somewhat self-conscious vestigial relic, a living artifact of heritage, like its country house in Scotland, The Burn, where residents could escape for walks, fishing, tennis, croquet, and bowls—as "really British" as the much-thumbed copies of Trollope in the House library. In the early seventies a mural painted in the lower refectory/bar, caught the mode of the times—a pastiche of wraithlike historical figures in the leafy square that included Dickens, Disraeli, and Virginia Woolf.

London House, by the seventies, was in fact as much an American enclave as South Kensington and Hampstead had become, a presence—like that of women or nonwhites—not envisioned in the original plans. As late as 1957 it could still be confidently proclaimed that residents were "heirs to great traditions and great names . . . a Smuts or a Menzies . . . [who] will find themselves somewhat better equipped than most to serve as leaders."[4] But hopes for substantial financial support from beyond Britain proved illusory: the Dominions, busy expanding their own institutions of higher learning, proved less interested in incubating their future leaders in Britain.

The first students were admitted in October 1931; the first stage of Baker's London House was opened for residents six years later by Queen Mary. There were more than 650 white, male residents, mostly Australians and Canadians, drawn from the fields of medicine, accounting, economics, and the arts. When the war came the premises were turned into a club for officers from overseas services, there was bomb damage, and a new appeal was launched in 1944 with a ceremonial visit from the King and Queen. But though construction continued, finances proved even more parlous in the postwar period of austerity. Probably under pressure from Attlee's government, the race bar was ended (though there was a quota system thereafter) by 1949, when the Trust concluded the purchase of most of Coram's Foundling Estate (some 25 acres and 800 houses in Bloomsbury). The next year it was announced that a goal of the Lord Mayor's National Thanksgiving Fund would be the admission of women and Americans—ostensibly in thankful recognition of gifts of food from the States during the war, but also no doubt in hopes of extending the catchment area for future donations. These continued, however, to fall below expectations.[5]

AMERICANS

The quota of Americans slowly expanded. In 1952 Fulbright Scholars and their families were admitted to the new residence built for women, William Goodenough House, and in 1955 Rhodes Scholars at Oxford were offered honorary membership. As long as the late-imperial ideal survived, however, their presence remained something of the anomaly suggested in the original plan, soon abandoned, to house all Americans separately in "a building of their own" as an alternative to "a more intimate participation" in the corporate life of London House. Americans were tolerated by administrative staff, mostly former military men like the long-serving Warden Brigadier Peter Pepper (1946–69), who appears to have quickly developed a distinct, if obliquely expressed, animus, shared by at least some of the older staff well into the seventies, about what he regarded as a class of complaining residents who lacked the stoicism of British students. Though pleasant enough "*on the whole*," the Americans, he claimed in 1970, regarded their accommodation as "archaic" and "were fiends for hot water, and would lie in their baths with the hot tap turned on till every overflow pipe in the building was cascading down into the small yard outside." Things came to a head first in 1954 when he faced down demands by North American students, led by "two vociferous, 'power without responsibility'" representatives, for a place on the Dominion Students' Hall Trust Council and "various committees" as well as lower fees and better food. With some satisfaction he reported that they "retired discomfited." The sixties would bring much deeper misgivings and a nostalgia for days when "no one had ever heard of hippies or the generation gap." Pepper implicated both "the steady and ever-increasing demand" for places in Mecklenburgh Square from the States and that from "the new independent countries of the Commonwealth" in what he regarded as the vulgarization of the institution. It was "the End of an Era."[6]

Though the new warden, Sir Francis Loyd, H.C.M.G., was a long-serving colonial official, the new controller (from 1966), Lt.-Col. E. C. Wilson, V.C., a former military man and colonial administrator, and patrons continued to be drawn from royalty and the Establishment, the seventies saw the final collapse of the Empire-Commonwealth idea (except as a kind of heritage concept) and a more liberal regime that was prepared to embrace not only the multicultural character of the institution but its increasingly transatlantic nature as well. Loyd, a Commonwealth Fund Fellow in 1953, traveled extensively in the States studying conservation practices, while the chaplain appointed in 1970, the Rev. Dick Thornley, had been assistant minister at an Episcopal church in Pennsylvania. Down at the daily operational level, though, there remained some frisson between Americans and their British hosts—a deputy-controller who would turn on his heel and "cut" students with long hair, a struggle for a Coca-Cola machine, complaints at the absence of the *New York Times* or the *Herald Tribune* at breakfast, or a campaign for barbecues in the square on the Fourth of July.

As Christopher Hitchens has observed, the special relationship in the postwar world "rests in many respects on mutually sustaining elites in the two countries." Though the culture of the special relationship is wider and deeper than the cross-traffic enabled by scholarships and fellowships or the economic and foreign policy institutions in which Hitchens was primarily interested, London House does provide insight into the ways in which some young Americans from more or less privileged educational backgrounds encountered the Britain of their imaginations—not a world of Pop, rock, or counterculture but of Establishment, class, and nostalgic framing.[7]

The steady increase in American residents at a time when the American presence in London was generally becoming denser was symptomatic, in a minor way, of what John Updike called "the outcroppings of American power" in a city whose virtues seemed to the visitor to be "combined for his pleasure." For a decade after they were allowed to apply to the Dominion Students' Hall Trust, the numbers remained modest (no more than a score or so in 1956). Thereafter they began to climb. By and large from elite universities and colleges, they differed often from other residents in their fields of study, pursuing history (including art history), economics and political science, or English literature, whereas the Commonwealth and British residents were much more likely to be training in medicine, law, or accountancy. London (and London House) was especially attractive for Americans engaged in dissertation research in the arts and humanities (the number of historians expanded significantly into the seventies) rather than professional certification programs. This meant that many of the Americans were especially vulnerable to heritage nostalgia, where clichés of Britishness melded with their explorations of history and literature. American long-stay residential numbers continued to climb—from 49 in 1963 to 70 the next year and 86 in 1966—by which time they may have surpassed the number of South Africans (still admitted, though South Africa had left the Commonwealth) and were gaining on the dominant contingents from Australia, New Zealand, and Canada. By the seventies the Americans were established as a more or less coequal presence with those from what had been called the White Dominions. Numbers did not mean, of course, that they had a coequal part in the life of the House. At all-male London House the dominant tone remained that of the hearty rugger-and-cricket crowd from Australia and South Africa.[8]

Amateur house sport was where the late-imperial ethos of the place was most tangible. Dominion residents dominated, though a growing number of nonwhite new Commonwealth students were recruited in the sixties and seventies. Indeed an ability to play cricket or squash may have figured in their admittance in an era when the staff felt increasingly challenged to preserve at least this part of the House culture as "British." In 1963–65 there were no Americans playing on any of the London House teams, due to their inexperience and lack of interest no doubt, but also perhaps to exclusion (or at least lack of encouragement). Americans, though a rapidly growing proportion of residents, kept apart, except for an occasional eccentric, from what was, if the "fond" recollections of sport friendships in the House magazine are any guide, an important socializing experience. For the deputy controller (former colonial service, Rhodesia), who had a keen interest in the House games (his own son was on the House squash team), sport was a means of preserving the character of an institution, as probably he and certainly Brigadier Pepper felt, under assault from Americans, new Commonwealth blacks, and modernization generally.[9]

LIBERATION?

Americans living in Mecklenburgh Square in the late sixties and early seventies were not agents of countercultural liberation. Some may have signed on to London House or Willy G simply for the convenience of the place, of course, and others were soberly pursuing their postgraduate work without much regard for their surroundings. But many, perhaps most, also subscribed at some level to the view that the Dominion Students' Hall Trust provided a singularly British refuge—by the seventies, even a unique survival—in a metropolitan world that was changing in ways Mecklenburgh Square appeared to resist. The leafy elegant physical location, the sport, and the slightly anachronistic rituals of the House encouraged a misleading sense of its timelessness, though in reality its contextual location in the city, the times, and the larger culture were continuously and considerably shifting.

A decade earlier many Americans at the institution, still relatively few in number, would have regarded life there—like the afternoon teas or tennis in the garden—as uncomplicatedly representative of quietly respectable British society itself, and if some complained about the food and the exclusion of students from governance, that was simply to rail against British difference. One resident, a historian's daughter from New England pursuing a doctorate at the L.S.E., found life in the women's house 1961–63 socially comfortable (compared with the loneliness of bed-sit land). Though she did not participate in rituals like the annual ball in the Great Hall, the Queen's visit in 1963 was a matter of some excitement—she made a dress for the occasion and practiced curtseying. There were casual excursions for theater and music, day-trips to historic towns, and a bicycle tour of Holland with friends. The only political activism she can recall was that of *English* friends in CND.[10]

By 1970, however, it seemed to some Americans that the institution no longer represented modern British society, that the Trust had become unmoored from its founders' aspirations and was drifting in search of a "role," and that the older generation of management saw themselves as a rear-guard serving out increasingly uncomfortable times. For the (ever larger numbers of) Americans who had some sense of what London life was like beyond the Square, the London House experience was now viewed as an anomaly, a curiosity. Some put themselves on the side of *libertas* rather than *imperium* and complained a little, some merely found London House life alternately amusing and annoying, and many in the heritage-minded seventies relished its anachronistic character in a postcolonial, multicultural metropolitan world—like the South Carolinian who, acting out some fantasy of his own about Southern social exclusivity, would loudly comment that some other member of the House was "not the sort of person one knows."

Mecklenburgh Square was not in fact entirely immune to American-inspired countercultural liberationism. Some of the student residents themselves were, like one young woman who came from Berkeley in 1969 (to work on a thesis about Chairman Mao), conduits back to the radicalism running through American universities. If the challenge of student governance was kept largely at bay—House "clubs," run by resident representatives, pushed on a number of issues but were, as the then-bursar recalls, kept "under the watchful eyes of the Wardens"—resident pressure did secure at least the inclusion of radical voices and issues among the common run of Establishment, often Tory, speakers at invitational House lectures. These included Germaine Greer, Bernadette Devlin, and the then left-wing president of the Cambridge Union, Arianna Stassinopoulos (now Huffington)—though also the judge at the *OZ* trial. In contrast to the student rebellions elsewhere in Britain and the late-sixties, early-seventies shouting-down culture of angry undergraduate confrontation, the debates at London House were relatively sedate affairs, "without any hooliganism, minor terrorism or even just plain bad manners," as one Australian resident somewhat ingratiatingly commented in 1970. They engaged, however, most of the touchpaper issues of the time—racism, feminism, and "permissiveness"—and could draw scores, on occasion hundreds, of residents. If, unsurprisingly, few of these postgraduate preprofessionals seem to have committed themselves to the street politics of the anti-Vietnam and student protests of the time, many nevertheless were sympathetic fellow-travelers—in October 1969 the house defeated a motion (39 to 13) that "Student riots are unjustified." Black, feminist, and gay identity politics and consciousness-raising also had an interesting, if muted, resonance in the Square. Most obviously there was the problem of the Trust's heritage of racial exclusion.[11]

The original terms of the Dominion Students' Hall Trust were intended to keep the residences white, specifying that only applications from "Dominion students of European origin" might be considered—a color bar that mirrored common practice in the Dominions themselves. In the last days of the war, after Labour's great election victory in 1945, however, there was movement within the Trust to remove what had become an embarrassment—and perhaps a political liability. Though there was no overt dissent, it appears that many of the fund's subscribers chose to remain silent on the issue. Amendment of the exclusion clause proved a complicated affair, however, requiring a decision in the House of Lords. The ideal of a multiracial Commonwealth brotherhood was, with Indian independence looming, in line with liberal thinking generally, and Attlee lent his public support once it was clear that the Trust would play along. In November 1946 he attended a dinner at London House—in the presence of the Archbishop of Canterbury and the Lord Mayor—and spoke of its drawing "closer the ties of unity." The *Times* approved of the Trust's decision to "bring the foundation in line with modern conceptions of the Commonwealth," though of course only a few "carefully-selected" nonwhites were to be admitted—a quota of "about twenty"—and, the paper assured its readers, about half of these "coloured students" would be "by arrangement with the Colonial Office" intended for Colonial service—probably they would be chosen from those who were already serving in that service. The chairman of the Trust, Sir William Goodenough (who that year followed his father as the new chairman of Barclay's Bank), might be regarded as "a modern imperialist in the good sense of that word."[12]

In practice, of course, the change fell well short of a full commitment to a color-blind, well-integrated house. Ironically, the liberalizing of the terms of the

Trust to include Americans after 1951 probably helped to rationalize the increase of places (via a new charitable bursary) for white Afrikaner "stock"[13] and the continued selection of white South Africans ("English-speaking peoples" rather than "Dominion students") after that country ceased to be a member of the Commonwealth in 1961 (and Rhodesians after their Unilateral Declaration of Independence). The numbers of nonwhite students in any event were relatively small, considering the vast field of potential "coloured" applicants. The culture of the institution, influenced as it was not only by the former colonial officials in its administration but also by white students from South Africa, Rhodesia, and Australia, remained for years somewhat intimidating for nonwhites who made it through the selection process. Later, when the world had changed significantly, one could still find blacks at London House who spoke the language their selectors no doubt wished to hear (one South African resident could claim in 1976: "My people will need years of education before they are ready to govern themselves"). Moreover, for years there was some de facto segregation at London House, with nonwhites, especially Pakistanis and Indians, often taking less accessible, crowded, but less expensive quarters high up in the older block—an area commonly referred to as "the Khyber Pass."

The idea that the Empire-Commonwealth was "family" (given the post-war surge in emigration from Britain to Rhodesia or Australia, this was rather more than a metaphor) died hard, especially one imagines among many of the Conservative sponsors of the Trust, the Trust's administrators, and indeed many of the white students themselves. The argument taken to the House of Lords set out the intention of establishing not a single integrated charity, but two "complementary" charities side by side, one for whites and one for coloreds. In 1957, anticipating a formal visit from Queen Elizabeth, the House magazine republished an article by the popular historian Arthur Bryant that dwelt on the concept of the Dominions as kith and kin. While in the fifties and sixties Lord Mountbatten, a long-time supporter of the Trust, might, like some of the more progressive one-nation Conservative members of the Round Table, endorse the idea of multiracialism, for many other prominent supporters there was great reluctance to turn away from the racial coding of "family." The Marquis of Salisbury—then Lord President of the Council and a last-ditch imperialist who vigorously resisted black majority rule in Africa and attacked nonwhite immigration to Britain—attended the opening of London House's Churchill Room in 1955, while another prominent right-wing opponent of the "winds of change," Julian Amery, followed his father, Leo, on the Trust's board of governors.[14]

When the winds of change came to London in the form of civil rights agitation and black liberationism, London House was somewhat insulated from criticism because of its avowed multiracial character; indeed, Philip Mason, long-time (if soon-to-resign white) director of the then-beleaguered Institute of Race

Relations, was invited to London House to give a talk on "race in a homogenous society" (subsequently, however, none of his more radical [black] successors at the Institute were asked).[15] As the number of nonwhite residents increased steadily, if modestly, over the years, an increasing number of nonwhite males appeared on the rosters of the House sport teams—some indication of a widening integration of the institution, though most of these were South Asians, rather than Africans or West Indians, recruited to the cricket and squash teams (in 1969 a Pakistani, Zubair Shaikh, captained the cricket team). Rugby and hockey remained all white, or nearly so, into the seventies.

The most divisive race issue at the end of the sixties in fact involved sport. As one might imagine, there was intense interest in the debate over whether the South African cricket and rugby tours ought to go ahead in the face of calls for a sports boycott over the Apartheid policies there (Julian Amery was a prominent and loud opponent of the ban). Peter Hain, a pro-boycott student leader, was invited to Mecklenburgh Square to debate the issue with the pro-tour Conservative MP Edward Taylor and others. The turnout was the largest of any debate at London House. Surprisingly, perhaps, the motion to oppose the boycott failed by a large margin, an indication that the sentiments of, certainly, many of the numerous white South African and Rhodesian residents were buried in the largely liberal opinion of many of the rest (Americans included).[16]

Women's liberation was, one suspects, actively endorsed by only a small and eccentric minority of house residents, though, as with racial issues, there was (outside the rugger crowd) a largely sympathetic audience for feminism generally—especially among the preprofessional women in "Willy G." In January 1969 a somewhat ambiguous motion that "The Western attitude to women is decadent" was defeated. The next year Germaine Greer was invited to a debate on Women's Liberation and the motion, put to a larger audience of more than a hundred, that "This House believes that marriage can survive women's liberation," failed. There were, in fact, local issues. There had long been a sense that the Dominion Students' Hall Trust was as an institution more interested in the men. The exclusively male residence London House was grander and better resourced than that for women. Only in 1969, under sharp pressure, did the London House Club committee rescind its long-time ban on women in the House's Large Common Room and bar.[17]

If there was a core of feminist sentiment in Mecklenburgh Square, it is reasonable to imagine that careerist American women were at its heart. They made up a significantly larger proportion of the residents at Willy G than the American males did at London House. Through the sixties women getting the kind of professional qualifications many were pursuing while resident in Mecklenburgh Square still had to face significant struggles to secure jobs on anything like equal terms with men. One American resident in the early sixties, for example, came to London to do a doctorate at the L.S.E., having previously, with a master's degree from a prominent school of international relations in hand, applied for a government job and was told to learn shorthand—which she refused to do. With her doctorate completed, she applied again and was told that she was now "overqualified."[18]

While the measured respectability of the women's residence hall was hardly conducive to radical consciousness-raising, there were those whose academic work reflected the radicalized times generally and in some instances the heightened interest in the culture and history of women. Sociologist Cynthia White was at William Goodenough House at the beginning of the second wave of the feminist movement (1963–66). Subsequently at the University of Michigan she researched the transatlantic history of women's publications, and in 1969 chided readers of the House magazine that British women's magazines had yet to follow "America's lead" in contributing to the "full emergence of women as socially responsible citizens."[19]

Whether there was much sympathy for feminism-as-lesbianism at Willy G is a more complicated issue not easily discovered—in part because of the reticence about issues of sexuality that the social respectability of the institution encouraged, and the defensiveness that single-sex living arrangements inspire. While, in the postliberation environment of the seventies and eighties, it may be that attachments were neither uncommon nor especially secret at Willy G, there does not seem to have been an especially gay culture there. Things were somewhat different at London House, as may be suggested by the well-used copies of Christopher Isherwood's *A Solitary Life* in the house library. It is hardly surprising that an institution more or less dominated by the rugger ethic should also have cultivated a somewhat closeted but active culture of homosexuality—not that these were by any means entirely oppositional parts of the House. Unlike feminism, which was quite likely strongest among the American women at Willy G, the male gay subculture at London House before and after Gay Liberation was not an especially American phenomenon. But the American students who were interested either found access easy enough or already knew the reputation of the House as a free-wheeling site of sexual opportunity.

Gay organizations may have proliferated at British universities after 1970, but overt liberation activism was unusual at London House—though at least one resident from this era, an Australian, became a campaigner for lesbian and gay equality back in Victoria. Homosexual liaisons offered one kind of "Commonwealth brotherhood" that crossed racial and national lines. Its very prevalence in Mecklenburg Square, as a system that operated more or less freely, perhaps worked against a liberationism that threatened to damage what many clearly regarded as its intriguing semisecrecy. For some Americans the (barely) closeted gay side of London House seemed a part of its Britishness, and its somewhat bitchy society of intimate circles within circles a kind of gossipy analogue of what many imagined with some accuracy to be the characteristically enclosed and incestuous nature of upper-middle-class British social and intellectual life generally.

If some British gays were eager to import the language and flamboyant practice of a liberated identity, Americans at a place like London House found a well-established same-sex subculture that appeared to need no liberation, that, indeed, might be regarded almost as an historical artifact of British difference. As Mark Turner, the historian of Anglo-American urban "cruising," has observed, "I wouldn't be the first American to be seduced by the presentation of old, fastidious London, to romanticize a past that wasn't mine." In 1971 an American resident of London House commented more generally on the gendered nature of British culture: "American television will inform one that all people who make pretence to intellectual tastes are either phoney or effeminate; here, fortunately, men can get away with it."[20]

BRITISH HERITAGE AND AMERICAN FANTASY

London House arranged coach tours in and around historic London or to country houses in the Home Counties and the ancient universities of Oxford and Cambridge. Major R. Battcock's "visits" (he was awarded an MBE "for services to British tourism") were popular with Americans in large part because of his own distinctive style, which was as much an anticipated cliché of Britishness as that of the cheeky Cockney night porter Stan. As an American resident claimed in 1969, if "few in London House circulate in the crowds described in *Newsweek*'s [*sic*] swinging London," the historical London of Dickens and tradition was a "dream." For many of these, presumably, the charm of the institution lay precisely in the fact that it was not "Mayfair Modern." Those who signed up for Major Battcock's visits, or "enjoyed beagling with the Mid-Essex Beagles," or wandered along the "heritage walks round the City of London" laid out in 1975, or who ate their kippers, kedgeree, cold toast, and porridge at the Burn before a game of croquet were tourist-consumers participating in a fantasy of heritage. Their search for an imagined Britain endorsed and encouraged the British drift toward nostalgic self-representation that so marks the era—and beyond. When the Trust finally if somewhat reluctantly came to grips with its need to "sell" itself to transatlantic alumni-donors, it was its heritage brand that came foremost. In 2003 the summer events for visiting alumni included a day-trip to the opulent Rothschild country house Waddesdon Manor, and in the summer of 2005 alumni were "cordially invited to a Clay Pigeon Shooting Day at Sandhurst."[21]

This National Trust view of modern Britain harmonized with the snobbery of some American residents who were also especially impressed by ritual and royals: "For most of us, [the visit of the Duchess of Gloucester] was the first opportunity . . . to feel first hand the warmth of that unique and royal talent of being interested in us." Such sentiments were not, of course, universal, especially among those engaged in a form of low-level combat against rules and the casual arrogance of some officials, but they do represent an important mode of American sensibility within and beyond the House. One American resident from California who had been an undergraduate at a red-brick British university before moving to London House for postgraduate studies—where he affected a bowler hat—may have been more candid than most when he wrote about the unpleasant "whine of the Brummie accent" or the fact that he fortunately moved in a circle of upper-middle-class friends with career military fathers. For him, culture in Britain was simply a matter of class.[22]

Cultural tourists were certainly not new. Numbers were increasing, but Americans had long lived in London; blue plaque memorials give them a modest amount of recognition—and suggest that they lived mostly in the posher parts of town, as one might expect (many of the nineteenth-century American ex-pats were anglophiles from a relatively well-heeled Brahmin tradition). This tendency for Americans in London to colonize the better parts of the city, South Kensington and Mayfair, and in the sixties and seventies increasingly Hampstead, left many visitors with a particular class-bound sense of Britishness and the tendency to equate it with a high culture that was, like the theater and concerts, so much more accessible and affordable than in the States (it also meant that in the postwar world Americans were often viewed by the British as much wealthier than they in fact were).

What was changing was not the disappearance of this phenomenon—wealth of course still headed for wealthy parts of the city and entrenched itself there—but the expanded contact between those who were not genteel in the more everyday parts of town. By the mid- and late sixties the new American presence was especially marked by students, postgraduates, and junior academics who, though usually middle class, nevertheless lived in bed-sits, very modest flats in less fashionable parts of town like Islington or Camden, or in residence halls like London House. It was especially from among these visitors, often seeing in even postwar socialist Britain a refuge from democratic materialism and vulgarity, that some Americans pursued their own sometimes quite elaborate fantasies of self-constructed Britishness. There was Stanley Olson, a Jewish American from Akron, Ohio, who arrived age twenty-two in 1969 with the intention of becoming "Stanley Olson, Esq.," an English gentleman. Financed by his American family made wealthy through their electronics retail and mail order business, he led a largely solitary and fastidious "stylish, literary life," and published a biography of another American expatriate, the painter John Singer Sargent. But, as Stephen Haseler has observed, Olson's story was "not so odd."[23]

American poseurs were not new, nor was tourist fraud—like that perpetrated in 1963 by an American writer, Douglas Stuart Crawford, a frequent visitor to Britain who was arrested at the recently opened Hilton Hotel, where he was found to be living, on credit, the life of a gentleman of leisure in a suite of rooms, having for months apparently defrauded a number of hotels in Mayfair and South Kensington.[24] Sometimes there were those on the run who sought to lose their identity in the anonymity of the metropolis, like James Earl Ray in the summer of 1968. For many others, posing became an internalized fantasy of nostalgia, made possible in a London of literary and historical imagination. By far the most memorable of these transplants was Dennis Severs.

Born to an affluent family, Severs, as a child in California in the fifties and early sixties, developed a fascination with Dickensian London through film and television adaptations. After a first trip to England in 1965, as he says in his memoir, he lived a teenager's life of imagination where he dreamed of traveling "past picture frames" into "a warmer, mellower and a more romantic light." After his mother's death and just five days after graduating from high school in 1967, he came to London to escape what he called "the ramshackle ordinariness from which I came." London became his permanent home, where, inspired by the furniture department of the Albert and Victoria Museum, he devoted the rest of his life to collecting antiques: "Soon I was combing all the early morning street markets in London . . . . I was collecting *auras*: signposts to the thinking of other times." A frequenter of country houses, from 1969 he became himself a kind of heritage tour guide, taking visitors in a horse-drawn carriage "into the back streets of west London . . . a time machine, and I was soon beginning to speak in the 'dramatic present,' as if things were happening right now." What might have seemed to some as signs of a rapidly decaying mental condition, Severs's eccentricity found a creative outlet in the world of seventies transatlantic heritage tourism and preservation nostalgia. He bought a run-down house, 18 Folgate Street, in Spitalfields, which he turned into a living museum filled with eighteenth-century furnishings and which he inhabited with an invented Huguenot family, the Gervaises.[25]

If Severs's story is one of extreme obsession, there are elements in other less eccentric American narratives of his fascination with Britain-as-an-old-country where fantasy can have a free play. The well-known travel writer Bill Bryson came to Britain in 1973 from Des Moines, Iowa, age twenty-two, to backpack in the English countryside with hopes of being a writer. He found himself "thrilled by the prospect of a nation which could keep him in a state of almost perpetual bemusement." After twenty-some years married to an Englishwoman, in 1995 his own Defoeian tour, *Notes from a Small Island*, prospered in both the United States and Britain, and he has become a leading figure in the preservation of historical monuments and countryside. Raymond Seitz, appointed ambassador in 1992, was an avid teenage reader of English literature and as a young Yale graduate in 1965 flew to Glasgow, "bought a green Vespa motorscooter and strapped a guitar to the side," to make his way to London "looking for the New Britannia." Uncomfortable with the word "Anglophile," Seitz would distinguish himself from "a breed of

American for whom the allure of English manners, English vowels and English titles seems to cast a spell," those who often seem to "hanker after class by association, as if to say that if the United States also had an aristocratic class they would naturally be members."[26]

Britain's heritage appeal resonated strongly within the transatlantic special relationship and extended well beyond the class of the socially pretentious. In 1977 a distinguished British historian at Yale said of himself, in the introduction to his *An American's Guide to Britain,* "I am a bit book-bound, nostalgic, romantic, and certainly Anglophilic throughout." The results of a GLC survey published in 1974 suggest that the appeal of heritage Britain was strong among Americans generally. Nonbusiness visitors to London from the States were significantly more inclined to visit historic sites and museums than were the French, German, or Spanish. While of course many Americans, not least Irish-Americans, have long been relatively immune to Anglophilia, an aggressive Anglo*phobia* was clearly in decline in this period. Easier access to Britain for leisure, the addictive entertainments of heritage programming on television, and commonplace student and professional academic cross-traffic offer a significant part of the explanation.[27]

Postscript: To the Bicentennial/Jubilee

One of the more curious moments of the two hundredth anniversary of the American war of independence was, among the bunting-draped civic celebrations, historically uniformed re-enactments, *Yankee Doodle*–playing fife and drum processions, and pious television docu-dramas, the appearance of H.M. Queen Elizabeth II and H.R.H. Prince Philip on "walkabout" in the North End of Boston, the heartland of the original rebellion. They also attended a service—where lessons were read by Prince Philip and the American ambassador to Britain, Anne Armstrong—at the historic North-End church (Episcopalian) from the tower of which Paul Revere et al. received the signal to ride "through every Middlesex village and town" warning of red coats. There was an open-top limo tour of Boston and, near the Old State House where the Queen made a short public address, the royal party reviewed the "British 10th Regiment of Foot," a re-enactment group in eighteenth-century uniform founded and led by Vincent Jeffre-Roux Kehoe, a television makeup artist.[1]

The previous year had seen bicentennial re-enactments at Lexington and Concord, but also the annual *fete champetre* laid on by the English-Speaking Union to celebrate the Queen's official birthday. There were strawberries and cream while twenty "Minutemen" fired a round in honor (rather oddly) of the reigning British monarch.[2] Three weeks later Princess Anne and her husband, Mark Phillips, arrived, not to celebrate the Revolution but for horse-trials in Hamilton, Massachusetts.

The Anglo-American Bicentennial properly got under way the following June 1976, when the Lord Chancellor and the Speaker of the House of Commons traveled to Washington to present "the Magna Carta" for display under the dome of Congress while a "Bicentennial Bell" cast at the same foundry that had cast the original "Liberty Bell" also crossed the ocean as a gift from the British nation to the United States. The British role in the theater of Bicentennial was, as in many Hollywood films of a previous era, that of a well-spoken supporting actor—reserved in this instance for the Queen herself, who, like Alistair Cooke before her, addressed a joint session of Congress. There were reciprocal dinners in Bicentennial week in Washington, with music provided at the British embassy by Yehudi Menuhin (actually an American citizen) and young members of his London school. The Queen and Philip were entertained at a presidential banquet (with live television coverage) the night before her appearance before Congress. It was a long night with dancing in the East Room of the White House—where Bob Hope, who had been made an honorary CBE by the Queen at a ceremony at the British embassy a week earlier, provided amusement. As so much of Britain was being shipped to the United States, he quipped, "It's not like you lost a colony, it's like you found an attic."[3]

The royal party visited New York and joined HMY *Britannia* off Newport, Rhode Island, where a gala dinner was given for President Ford, Vice President Rockefeller, and a select list of the great and good. The next day, a Sunday, the *Britannia* made its stately way into Boston harbor at 9:20 a.m., the USS *Constitution* offering a twenty-one-gun salute. That same evening, after a hectic day of royal display followed by a reception on board for some 200 ordinary citizens (mostly in fact the local social and political elite), the *Britannia* sailed away to Canada, where the Queen was to open the Olympics at Montreal. The *Boston Globe*'s front-page headline the next morning offered a touch of irony: "200 Years Later, Queen Charms Boston."[4]

Back in London there were celebrations at the embassy, where the *British* great and good were entertained without having to worry about the loud protest pickets and mass demos of a few years earlier. The Vietnam War was over, Nixon had resigned, and Britain was again a supplicant—a familiar postwar role—for U.S. support as it struggled to secure an IMF solution to fiscal crisis. The previous year a rather sour Kenneth Tynan had found the embassy's pre-Bicentennial exhibition on the lives of Benjamin Franklin and Thomas Jefferson—mounted at the British Museum—to be "[o]ne of the emptiest occasions of my life," a "disappointing collection of reproductions" and "no alcohol on offer." More entertaining, perhaps, was a "debate" between Alistair Cooke, the voice of Anglo-America, and the heir to the throne, Prince Charles. Staged at Windsor Castle, the topic was the reputation of George III—both agreed he had been much maligned. Cooke was the televisual embodiment of a particular version of the special relationship; *America* continued to sell well in Britain, and from January to March he had introduced an enthusiastic American public television audience to yet another series (the third) of *Upstairs, Downstairs*. His abridged remarks before Congress were published in Britain and the United States in a collection of essays entitled *1976 Declaration of Interdependence.*[5]

For his part, Prince Charles was emerging as that oddity, a Windsor who read books and had views. The elaborately mounted "Investiture" at Caernarvon Castle in 1969 was, like the BBC documentary *Royal Family*, broadcast in the States, and in 1972 he had written an admiring foreword for historian John Brooke's sympathetic biography of George III. *George III*—not itself populist but resonating with television's historical bio-dramas of the time—sold well on both sides of the ocean and helped encourage an American fascination with royalty. Prince Charles's observations, naive as they may have been, represent a kind of testimony to a progressive erosion of Anglo-American "difference" that could reduce the foundation myths of national identity to simple misunderstanding: "The tragedy is that the American colonies never received a visit from [George III]—if a royal tour had been a conceivable undertaking in the eighteenth century, the leaders of the colonies might have understood him better."[6]

There was a flurry of Bicentennial events in London and on British television. The Post Office issued a commemorative 11p Bicentennial stamp (the cost of an airmail letter to the United States) with a portrait of Benjamin Franklin; Pietro Annigoni was commissioned by a commercial firm to design a special "limited edition" "Royal Bicentennial" silver plate, with silhouettes of the Queen and President Ford together, offered at £145 each. The Maritime Museum at Greenwich mounted its own Bicentennial exhibition, more successful apparently than that at the British Museum, as the hours had to be extended on Sundays. The U.S. ambassador in London, Anne Armstrong, announced there would be Bicentennial Arts Fellowships, funded by the United States and Britain, and the Royal Society and the British Academy launched a conference on "Anglo-American intellectual relations" with the American historian Bernard Bailyn giving the opening address.[7]

If for many Americans the celebrations, in an election year, carried a sense of relief at putting the trauma and disgrace of the war and Watergate behind, the fulsome celebration of a "special relationship" of law, heritage, and contemporary "interdependence" served to flatter the British, mired in their own economic and social crisis, while veiling the unequal reality of transatlantic influence. The limitations of "interdependence" were in fact made all too clear in the fate of one trumpeted Bicentennial aspiration: in February British Airlines announced that it intended to begin *Concorde* flights to the United States in May in time to inaugurate a Bicentennial summer of tourism.[8]

A few miles beyond Boston, at Concord Bridge, where British and colonial American blood was shed in 1775, a nineteenth-century memorial to the British fallen enshrines their vain attempt to "keep the past upon its throne." Two hundred years later, in the heritage-obsessed seventies, the past seemed ready to reclaim its throne. The predictable grousing of some of Boston's Irish-American community aside, the royal tour was warmly received and well televised (though Senator Edward Kennedy did not show up for Mayor Kevin White's luncheon in honor of the royal couple). The *Boston Globe* report of the Queen's address was titled "Heritage Is Shared."[9]

Elizabeth, as David Wilson, an editorial writer for the *Boston Globe*, put it, reigned over a country that had become a place not of greatness but of "inexpensive vacations." She herself, however, had "grace, dignity and civility" in an age of mere media celebrities like, he listed, Mick Jagger, Lenny Bruce, and the outspoken feminist congresswoman Bella Abzug. The Queen was "a thread of fine gold in the often shabby fabric of our unruly times." The same edition of the paper published a piece by its in-house book review editor on the death of George Jackson and the end of the era of Black Power titled "Epitaph of a Counterculture": "There was a counter culture, wasn't there?"[10] The nostalgic Anglo-American Bicentennial celebrated this end of the special relations of an overtly American form of late modernity and its replacement by another.

Concluding Remarks

⸻◆⸻

This has been an excursion through two decades of the postwar Anglo-American relationship—approached as episodes of transatlantic popular culture rather than a narrative of diplomacy or political economy. The period, from the mid-fifties to the mid-seventies, has, for both peoples, a kind of coherence, enfolding as it does what might be called the high tide of American-defined modernism. This was for western Europeans, and the British especially, a period of American Cold War leadership and hegemony. After Suez there could be no further illusions about a coequal Anglo-American "partnership." The tide, however, significantly ebbed after the early seventies with worldwide economic recession, the American embarrassments of withdrawal from Vietnam and Watergate, and British entry into the European Common Market. As we have seen, the narratives of various aspects of popular culture follow a somewhat analogous course, from the powerful Americanization of the fifties and sixties, accompanied by a degree of hybridity and circularity of essentially American forms, to a seventies marked often by a progressive localization—sometimes accompanied by a self-conscious rejection of American models.

This study begins with what we have called "Mayfair Modern," roughly running from the late 1950s to the mid-sixties and embracing both the modern architecture of key sites of post-Suez London and the "Swinging London" ethos for which Pop modernism was a stage set, read in the context of a significant increase in the cross-Atlantic traffic of architects, property developers, arts professionals, and tourists. The construction of the Hilton Hotel in Park Lane focused contemporary concern about commercial development in central London but also larger issues surrounding modernization as Americanization; the American embassy in Grosvenor Square was highly symbolic of American hegemony and arrogance and raised issues of intrusive American modernity in a historic part of the capital at a time when the British were especially sensitive about their own post-Suez, postempire identity. It quickly became a site for large, highly publicized mass demonstrations against the American war in Southeast Asia, and serves to preface an examination of the anti-Americanism of the British New Left from CND to Vietnam and the student rebellions after 1966. Both often reflect a "special relationship" of their own with America—the one drawing deeply from liberal social analysis of American capitalism, the other from the rhetoric, organization, and sometimes direct agency of radical American dissidents.

Part II focuses on the Anglo-American "counterculture" of the mid-to-late sixties, arguing that its various manifestations—from Ginsberg and the Beats to transatlantic rock and the Underground press—paradoxically constitute, though subversive of mainstream American culture and its technological modernity, another form of Americanization, drawing deeply on American style and content and often initiated and promoted by Americans in Britain. As a discourse of pleasure, youth versus age, and individual liberation, the counterculture was itself a part of what might be called late modernity, and is intimately related to the larger postwar sense in Europe that cultural Americanization offered (or threatened) an antielitist form of social democratization. The transatlantic counterculture both inspired and provoked the politics of the personal, leading to its own fragmentation and the radical reconstruction of minority subjectivities that mark the liberation movements of blacks, women, and gay people, the subject of Part III of this study.

Radical liberationism crossed the Atlantic in the late sixties and enjoyed a brief but intense period of activism and high publicity. Often condemned at the time for an alien American style and rhetoric (as were the student rebellions), the Black Power, radical feminist, and Gay Liberation movements in Britain have often been relegated to the margins of general histories of the time. This study attempts to re-establish their centrality, though inspired by American example and agency, as British phenomena and argues that they had a larger, more penetrative and lasting legacy than much scholarship left or right currently is willing to admit. While acknowledging that the American-inspired radicalization of nonwhites, women, and homosexuals played out in the distinct social and political contexts of late-twentieth-century Britain, we conclude that local difference and the fact that these movements took their own course thereafter may be less significant than the subjective "attitude" that utopian liberationism successfully instilled in many and passed on to successor generations.

Finally, the last section of this study, Part IV, examines the apparent turn against American-styled modernism in mainstream early and mid-seventies Britain—in a literature of dystopia that emphasized urban chaos and the environmental and social failures of modernity, often blaming American technology and American cultural (and countercultural) agents for a loss of authenticity in a globalized American world. This ushered in an era in which a nostalgic search for "heritage" seemed to replace the American dream, a shift in vision away from an optimistic Mayfair modern of Swinging London to a romanticized (if also commercialized) longing for past times. This nostalgic turn toward the authentic and traditional must also, however, be placed in the context of the close cultural special relationship. To the extent that heritage became commercializable, it depended on a view of "real Britain" that ironically reflected the tourists' image of an old country, an entrepreneurship that was instructed by American methods, and a market that extended to not just visitors but a consuming audience overseas. This section looks closely at the export of British heritage—antiques, costume dramas, and televised Wimbledon championships—in an era that saw American expectations endorse, not democritization, but traditional, antiurban elitism, a simplistic reading of British culture as high culture that was recirculated by the media in Britain itself. It ends with a portrait of a fading late-imperial institution, London House, and its attractiveness to some American postgraduate students who were determined to find there a version of their own imagined Britain, who were, that is, not agents of the modern but co-conspirators in a project to fix and essentialize its opposite.

A significant theme that runs through this study has been the ways in which, responding to the implication or threat of Americanization, many have insisted on an essentially native, authentic character in cultural productions that to an unbiased observer seem clearly American in form and, often, substantially American in content. Theorizing about the pre-eminence of the local over the global, of reception over production, is, on one level at least, but a late version of this defensiveness. Architects who have produced something very like the Seagram Building talk about the distinctive character of British modernism; folk purists insist that a privileged Oxbridge student singing a northern miner's song rather than Joe Hill is somehow being truer to his "own tradition."[1] A jazz musician at Ronnie Scott's or a psychedelic rock performer at UFO may have added something British, but to claim that the form is anything but American is as unconvincing as Ian Birchall grousing that Eric Burdon's the Animals playing rhythm and blues were more "authentic" (to their roots in Newcastle) than the late Beatles.[2] Or that British art-school whimsy somehow makes the extremely derivative British versions of the late-sixties Underground press very significantly less American in inspiration, organization, and content. Similarly, the insistent search by some revisionist scholars for domestic difference in the character of the British black, feminist, and gay movements, however much these phenomena may subsequently have evolved locally, displays a defensiveness that may say more about a psychological need to imagine authenticity than an accurate analysis of cultural reality.

That reality was grounded in the powerful American cultural hegemony of these two decades of ever-thickening personal cross-traffic and synchronous media saturation. There was give and take, circularity and hybridity, and local evolution subsequently as America as avatar of the modern faded (though arguably Anglo-American *elite* culture is *more* similar now than then). But the evidence in this study pretty uniformly suggests that cultural relations between the United

States and Britain were specially close and indeed changed the cultural landscape in enduring ways that are not always obvious. The best metaphor for this may not be that of a rising and falling tide, but of a kind of ecological event that shifts the course of the future.

As Britain in the decades after 1976 painfully reoriented and regrounded its economy, as its European project deepened, as social and industrial relations were transformed—not by the pragmatism of Wilson's hoped for white heat of technology but by Thatcher's rebarbative, ideologically driven, and nostalgically coded assaults—the "role" it "found" was culturally grounded to a significant degree in its postwar dance with America. However much the Blairite years of New Labour came to celebrate the new, cool, multicultural Britannia of a "stake-holder" national community "at the heart of Europe," in reality the transatlantic connection at the popular level continued to grow, thicken, and intensify. The period covered by this book witnessed the continual elaboration of ever denser networks of casual recreational, professional, and commercial Anglo-American cross-traffic and media exchange that entrenched and normalized the transatlantic nature of popular culture. While this study has not been a systematic history of that process, and the ways in which it has been hard-wired into social, economic, and cultural institutions, it has used a series of moments to restore some of the original, and accurate, reading of the modernized cityscape, sixties Pop, antiwar protest and radical student rebellion, media culture and counterculture, and the triad of racial, gender, and sexuality liberationisms as closely bound up with the American relationship and with American agency—and long-term in their effect. As one of those "agents," Charles Marowitz, correctly observed in 1990, "It is not only in the baby-boomers that much of the 1960s idealism lives on, it is also in the intellectual vestiges which continue to influence contemporary behaviour, both private and public."[3]

Whether or not one wishes to use the term "Americanization," it is hard to escape the fact that in Britain "America" was for many a strong and often determining influence in the shaping of mid- and late-twentieth-century mentality and aspiration—however much it may have melded with the postcolonial and the new European.[4] The twenty-year dance with America that this book only partly captures engaged attitudes and subjectivities which, once shifted, belie their relegation as the epiphenomena of an upper-middle-class, youthful London elite in a relatively brief period. This study attempts to restore a reading of the radicalizing later sixties and early seventies as much more than an inauthentic, short-lived flirtation with American-inspired utopianism, but rather, in Bernice Martin's phrase, a "transformation point" for "values, assumptions and ways of living."[5] Long-term legacies may be obscure, and no doubt some are embedded in debased and twisted form in commercial popular culture, as Leon Hunt has observed of what he calls "permissive populism," the "popular appropriation of elitist 'liberationist' sexual discourses, the trickle-down of permissiveness into commodity culture."[6] Hunt echoes the general disappointments of many in the seventies and the eighties who judged the stripping out of countercultural idealism from the practice of liberated lifestyles to have resulted in a "cruel parody" of the sixties. This is to undervalue, of course, the special meaning of "the personal," of lifestyle culture, among some communities—blacks, women, or gays—and may misread the importance of shifting attitudes among the young generally. At the very least, the forms of expression survive—if in attenuated and sometimes nostalgic style—as more than "cruel parody" but as, for some, practice-shaping memory. In February of 2005 the walls at University College were covered with posters demanding "Make Love Not War" and "Bring the troops home now!" calling for civil disobedience, workshops, and mass demonstrations against another war, with music provided by rock bands.

Notes

———•◆•———

PREFACE

1. See, for instance, Michael Billington's review of the television coverage in *The Times;* Peter Black for the *Daily Mail* (both on 21 July 1969); and William Hardcastle in *The Listener,* 24 July 1969.

2. Michael Palin, *Diaries 1969–1979: The Python Years* (London: Weidenfeld and Nicholson, 2006), 3–5.

3. Black in the *Daily Mail,* 21 July 1969. See also Stanley Reynolds, the *Guardian;* Billington, *The Times.*

4. *Evening Standard,* 21 July 1969.

5. *Daily Telegraph,* 13 July 1962, 24; Steven Morris in the *Guardian,* 27 December 2006.

6. *Daily Telegraph,* 13 July 1962, 24. For a scholarly study that assumed the world of satellite communications greatly enhanced American hegemony, see Herbert I. Schiller, *Mass Communications and American Empire* (New York: Augustus M. Kelly, 1969).

7. Rod Laver [with Bud Collins], *The Education of a Tennis Player* (London: Pelham Books, 1971), 248.

8. Brenda Maddox, *Beyond Babble: New Directions in Communications* (London: Deutsch, 1972), 22.

9. Palin, *Diaries,* 4–5.

10. In the British magazine *Wireless World.* See Maddox, *Beyond Babble,* 66.

11. Reginald Turnill, "Anglonauts," *The Listener,* 4 December 1969, 780–1. He had in mind John Hodge, who was in charge of NASA research and planning for a space station, and Ian Dodds at Rockwell.

12. Mary Ellman, *Thinking about Women* (London: Macmillan, 1968), 4, 6.

13. William Hardcastle, "Mid-Atlantic," *The Listener,* 13 November 1969, 679–80; *OZ* 23 (August/September, 1969).

14. Gordon Williams, *The Siege of Trencher's Farm* (London: Secker and Warburg, 1969), 5. See also Christopher Booker, *The Neophiliacs* (London: Pimlico, 1992 [1st pub. 1969]), 79; James Goddard and David Pringle (eds.), *J. G. Ballard: The First Twenty Years* (Hayes, Middlesex: Bran's Head Books, 1976), 27.

INTRODUCTION

1. For work before the mid-1980s, see David A. Lincove and Gary R. Treadway (comps.), *The Anglo-American Relationship: An Annotated Bibliography of Scholarship, 1945–1985*

(1988). More recently, there is W. R. Louis and H. Bull (eds.), *The "Special Relationship":* *Anglo-American Relations since 1945* (1986); Oliver Wright, *Anglo-American Relations:* *The Atlantic Grows Wider* (1986); Christopher Grayling and Christopher Langdon, *Just* *Another Star? Anglo-American Relations since 1945* (1988); Alan P. Dobson, *The Politics of* *the Anglo-American Economic Special Relationship, 1940–1987* (1988); Peter Hennessy and Caroline Anstey, *Moneybags and Brains: The Anglo-American "Special Relationship" since* *1945* (1990); Robert M. Hathaway, *Great Britain and the United States: Special Relations* *since World War II* (1990); C. J. Bartlett, *"The Special Relationship": A Political History of* *Anglo-American Relations since 1945* (1992); Alan P. Dobson, *Anglo-American Relations in* *the Twentieth Century: Of Friendship, Conflict and the Rise and Decline of Superpowers* (1995); John Baylis (ed.), *Anglo-American Relations since 1939: The Enduring Alliance* (1997); Ritchie Ovendale, *Anglo-American Relations in the Twentieth Century* (1998); Jonathan Hollowell, *Twentieth Century Anglo-American Relations* (2001); Christopher Hitchens, *Blood, Class and Empire* (2004); Fred M. Leventhal and Roland Quinault (eds.), *Anglo-* *American Attitudes: From Revolution to Partnership* (2000); Howard Temperley, *Britain and* *America since Independence* (2002); and Bernard Porter, *Empire and Superempire: Britain,* *America and the World* (2006).

2. John McLeod, *Postcolonial London: Rewriting the Metropolis* (London and New York: Routledge, 2004), 7.

3. Among the extensive literature on Americanization, see, esp., Dominic Strinati, "The Taste of America: Americanization and Popular Culture in Britain," in D. Strinati and S. Wagg (eds.), *Come on Down? Popular Media Culture in Post-War Britain* (London: Routledge, 1992), which differentiates between the anxiety with which elites and intellectuals regarded the United States and the "populist view" of America as promising egalitarian modernity, a perspective taken up in Alan O'Shea, "English Subjects of Modernity," in Mica Nova and Alan O'Shea (eds.), *Modern Times: Reflections on a Century of English Modernity* (London: Routledge, 1996); and George McKay (ed.), *Yankee Go Home (& Take Me With* *U): Americanization and Popular Culture* (Sheffield: Sheffield Academic Press, 1997), who wrote of Americanization as both imperialism and liberation (20).

4. The English novelist and social critic J. B. Priestley coined the term "Admas man," as one dazzled by commodities, in 1954 after a trip to the United States. "Coca-Colonization" comes from the title of Reinhold Wagnleiter's *Coca-Colonization and the Cold War: The* *Cultural Mission of the United States in Austria after the Second World War* (1994). For a recent study of the export of consumerism as a way of life, see Victoria De Grazia, *Irresistible* *Empire* (Cambridge: Harvard University Press, 2005).

5. Jean-Jacques Servan-Schreiber, *The American Challenge* (London: Hamish Hamilton, 1968 [1st pub. Paris, 1967]); see also Claude Julien, *L'Empire Americaine* (Paris: Grasset, 1968). For a scholarly study, see Richard F. Kuisel, *Seducing the French: The Dilemma of* *Americanization* (Berkeley: University of California Press, 1993).

6. According to Richard Pells (*Not Like Us: How Europeans Have Loved, Hated, and* *Transformed American Culture since World War II* [New York: Basic Books, 1997], 190), a thousand American companies set up operations in Britain between 1958 and 1963 alone. James McMillan and Bernard Harris claimed that there were at least 1,600 "U.S.-owned subsidiaries, associated companies, and branches operating in the United Kingdom" in 1967 (James McMillan and Bernard Harris, *The American Take-Over of Britain* [London: Leslie Frewin, 1968], 237–45) and listed more than 106 common American products found

in an average British home (1–3). On American Studies, see McKay, "Americanization and Popular Culture," in McKay, *Yankee Go Home*, 12.

7. C. W. E. Bigsby, *Superculture: American Popular Culture and Europe* (London: Paul Elek, 1975), 2. See also Duncan Webster, *Looka Yonder! The Imaginary America of Populist Culture* (London: Comedia, 1988), 25. As Stephen Haseler has observed, "Americanization might more properly be defined as modernization—a metaphor for the growth of cultural democracy and the spread of consumerism" (*The English Tribe: Identity, Nation and Europe* [London: Macmillan, 1996], 91).

8. See, for instance, Daniel Snowman's *Britain and America: An Interpretation of Their Culture 1945–1975* (London: Maurice Temple Smith; and New York: Harper Torchbooks, 1977), whose chapter title "The Americanization of British Culture" is punctuated with a question mark.

9. Jeremy Tunstall, *The Media Are American: Anglo-American Media in the World* (London: Constable, 1977); Richard Rose (ed.), *Lessons from America: An Exploration* (London: Macmillan, 1974), 10 (Rose, then Professor of Politics at the University of Strathclyde, was born in St. Louis); and Jonathan Zeitlin and Gary Herrigel (eds.), *Americanization and Its Limits: Reworking U.S. Technology and Management in Post-War Europe and Japan* (Oxford: Oxford University Press, 2000).

10. For the positive case, see Peter Duignan and L. H. Gann, *The Rebirth of the West: The Americanization of the Democratic World, 1945–1958* (Oxford: Blackwell, 1992). For revisionist approaches to transnational cultural contact, see, for example, R. Kroes, R. W. Rydell, and D. F. J. Bosscher (eds.), *Cultural Transmissions and Receptions: American Mass Culture in Europe* (Amsterdam: VU University Press, 1993); John Tomlinson, *Cultural Imperialism: A Critical Introduction* (Baltimore, MD: Johns Hopkins University Press, 1991) on the problem of cultural "reception"; or Mike Featherstone and Scott Lash (eds.), *Spaces of Culture: City, Nation, World* (London: Sage, 1999).

11. Richard Pells, "American Culture Abroad," or Rob Kroe, "Americanisation: What Are We Talking About," in Kroes, Rydell, and Bosscher, *Cultural Transmissions and Receptions*, 67. See also Pells's sustained examination in *Not Like Us*.

12. Philip Crang and Peter Jackson, "Geographies of Consumption," in David Morley and Kevin Robins (eds.), *British Cultural Studies: Geography, Nationality, and Identity* (Oxford: Oxford University Press, 2001), 331.

13. See Avtar Brah and Annie E. Coombes (eds.), *Hybridity and Its Discontents: Politics, Science, Culture* (London: Routledge, 2000).

14. Pells, *Not Like Us*, xiv, 279.

15. As Simon Frith pointed out in "Anglo-America and Its Discontents," *Cultural Studies* 5, 3 (October, 1991), 264.

16. Of the large literature on this topic, see Albert Marckwardt and Randolph Quirk, *A Common Language: British and American English* (1964); Brian Foster, *The Changing English Language* (Harmondsworth: Penguin, 1970); Peter Strevens, *British and American English* (London: Collier-Macmillan, 1972); and David Crystal, "American English in Europe," in Bigsby, *Superculture*, 57–68.

17. For the association of concepts of modernity with the urban milieu, see Marshall Berman, *All That Is Solid Melts into Air: The Experience of Modernity* (London: Verso, 1983).

18. Christopher Booker, *The Neophyliacs: The Revolution in English Life in the Fifties*

and Sixties (London: Pimlico, 1992 [1st pub. 1969]); Bernard Levin, *The Pendulum Years: Britain and the Sixties* (London: Jonathan Cape, 1970); William O'Neill, intro. to the 2005 ed. of *Coming Apart: An Informal History of America in the 1960s* (Chicago: Ivan R. Dee, 2005), xviii; Doug Rossinow, *The Politics of Authenticity: Liberalism, Christianity, and the New Left in America* (New York: Columbia University Press, 1998). For a positive reading, see Sohnya Sayres, Anders Stephanson, Stanley Aronowitz, and Fredric James (eds.), *The 60s without Apology* (Minneapolis: University of Minnesota Press, 1984); the negative case has been put by, for instance, Allen J. Matusow, *The Unraveling of America: A History of Liberalism in the 1960s* (New York: Harper and Row, 1984); and Stephen Macedo (ed.), *Reassessing the Sixties: Debating the Political and Cultural Legacy* (New York: W. W. Norton, 1997). Or, from a liberal perspective, John Morton Blum, *Years of Discord: American Politics and Society, 1961–1974* (New York: W. W. Norton, 1991); and David Burner, *Making Peace with the 60s* (New Haven: Princeton University Press, 1996).

19. Stuart Hall and Tony Jefferson (eds.), *Resistance through Rituals: Youth Sub-Cultures in Post-War Britain* (London: Hutchinson, 1976) and other publications of the once-in-fluential Birmingham Centre for Contemporary Cultural Studies group; John Davis, *Youth and the Condition of Britain: Images of Adolescent Conflict* (London: Athlone Press, 1990). The most recent academic study, David Fowler's *Youth Culture in Modern Britain, c.1920–c.1970: From Ivory Tower to Global Movement—A New History* (London: Palgrave Macmillan, 2008), largely echoes the skepticism of Davis and others while admitting that middle-class youth were central to a diminished, largely London-inscribed culture revolution of the period (197–8).

20. Arthur Marwick, *The Sixties: Cultural Revolution in Great Britain, France, Italy, and the United States, c.1958–c.1974* (Oxford: Oxford University Press, 1998), 801–2.

21. Anthony Sampson, *New Anatomy of Britain* (1971), as quoted by Dominic Sandbrook, *White Heat: A History of Britain in the Swinging Sixties* (London: Abacus, 2007 [1st pub. 2006]), 202.

22. Sandbrook, *White Heat*, 492–3, 500.

23. These and other examples in ibid., 411–3, 437, 443, 524; and in Sandbrook, *Never Had It So Good: A History of Britain from Suez to the Beatles* (London: Little, Brown, 2005), 341, 682.

24. James Jupp, "The Discontents of Youth," *Political Quarterly* 40, 4 (October–December, 1969), 411.

25. In 1973 a General Powers Act (sec. 25) gave the GLC the authority to prevent conversion of residential accommodation to short-stay use. On tourism generally, see the reports by various committees and "steering groups" assembled by the GLC, *Tourism and Hotels in London: A Paper for Discussion* (London: GLC, 1971), *Tourism in London: Towards a Short Term Plan* (London: GLC, January, 1973), and *Tourism in London: A Plan for Management* (London: GLC, April, 1974).

26. Mariel Grant, "'Working for the Yankee Dollar': Tourism and the Festival of Britain as Stimuli for Recovery," *Journal of British Studies* 45 (July, 2006), 585–6, 592, 596, 600–1.

27. *International Tourism Quarterly* 1 (1971). It had been about 170,000 in 1951.

28. Simon Jenkins, *Landlords to London: The Story of a Capital and Its Growth* (London: Constable, 1975), 229; H. Robinson, *A Geography of Tourism* (London: McDonald and Evans, 1976), 112; Alisdair Fairley, "Why Nobody Loves Us," *The Listener*, 9 January 1969, 62–3.

29. Alisdair Fairley, "Tourism," *The Listener*, 2 March 1973, 599. See also Fairley, "Tourist

Trouble," *The Listener*, 22 July 1971, 127; and Fairley, "This Other Eden: A Survey of Tourism in Britain," *Economist* 25 (September, 1971), i–xxxi [supplement].

30. Bigsby, *Superculture*, 2.

31. Piri Halasz, *A Swinger's Guide to London* (New York: Coward-McCann, 1967), 19, 39–43.

32. Fairley, "This Other Eden," vii, xx.

33. V. S. Pritchett, "Tourists," *The Listener*, 22 July 1971, 113–4.

34. Clancy Sigal, "America's Great Trauma." *The Listener*, 24 September 1970, 424.

35. GLC, *Tourism in London: A Plan for Management*, 39; Morrison Halcrow, "Tourism: The Hidden Assets," *Daily Telegraph*, 15 September 1972, 18; Alfred Sherman, "Are Tourists Really Worth It?" *Daily Telegraph*, 2 June 1973, 16.

36. The 1952 enquiry was conducted by a BBC researcher using a sample of 203 upper-class Londoners (William A. Benson, *The Impact of Television: Methods and Findings in Program Research* [London: Crosby Lockwood, 1967], ch. 9, 84–92); the 1963 survey was of 205 male students at Oxford and Manchester universities (Ferdinand Zweig, *The Student in the Age of Anxiety: A Survey of Oxford and Manchester Students* [London: Heinemann, 1963], 74–5, 143).

37. A recent example of the need to make London familiar to tourists is the reimaging of a modern public house off of Kingsway. "The George" was originally named for George VI and bore for many years his portrait on its sign-board. It now advertises itself with a painting of George III.

38. Colin MacInnes, *Absolute Beginners* (London: New English Library, 1960 [1st pub. 1959]), 14.

39. Fairley, "This Other Eden," vi, xxxi.

40. GLC, *Tourism in London: A Plan for Management*, 40.

41. GLC, *Tourism and Hotels in London*, 5.

42. A survey taken by the British Tourist Board in July and August of 1973 revealed that nearly one in three visitors to central London were North American (GLC, *Tourism in London: A Plan for Management*, 43).

43. Muriel Beadle, *These Ruins Are Inhabited* (London: Robert Hale and Co., 1970 [pub. in Britain in 1963, and reprinted seven times, 1963–67]), 27–8, 71, 74, 101, 102, 116, 125, 128–9, 154, 188.

44. Brenda Maddox, *Beyond Babel: New Directions in Communications* (London: Deutsch, 1972), foreword; Susan Marling, *American Affair: The Americanisation of Great Britain* (London: Boxtree, Ltd., 1993), 2.

45. Ulf Hannerz, "Cosmopolitans and Locals in World Culture," in Mike Featherstone (ed.), *Global Culture: Nationalism, Globalization and Modernity* (London: Sage, 1990), 242, 246–8; Alistair Cooke, *The American in England: Emerson to S. J. Perelman* (Cambridge: Cambridge University Press, 1975), 21–2.

46. Giles Scott-Smith, "Her Rather Ambitious Washington Program: Margaret Thatcher's International Visitor Program Visit to the United States in 1967," *Contemporary British History* 17, 4 (Winter, 2003), 66. See also Pells, *Not Like Us*, 22; Lawrence Black, "'The Bitterest Enemies of Communism': Labour Revisionists, Atlanticism and the Cold War," *Contemporary British History* 15, 3 (Autumn, 2001), 40.

47. GLC, *Tourism in London: A Plan for Management*, 43; GLC, *Tourism in London: Towards a Short Term Plan*, 11, 23.

48. Amis (21–2) and Pritchett (281), in Peter Firchow (ed.), *The Writer's Place: Interviews*

on the Literary Situation in Contemporary Britain (Minneapolis: University of Minnesota Press, 1974). The interviews were done in 1969.

49. Derwent May, *Critical Times: The History of the Times Literary Supplement* (London: Harper Collins, 2001), 143, 394, 405.

50. I am indebted to a paper read by David Hendy, "A 'Home Service' in a Global World? BBC Radio 4 and American Broadcasting in the 1960s and 1970s," at a conference on "Crosstown Traffic" at Warwick University in 2004.

51. Tom Jaine, obituary for Robert Carrier, the *Guardian*, 28 June 2006.

52. As quoted by Anthony Sampson, *Anatomy of Britain* (London: Hodder and Stoughton, 1962), 17.

53. In a Radio 4 address in 1971 (Pritchett, "Tourists," 114). Snowman, *Britain and America*, 236.

54. Lodge quoted by Daniel Ammann, *David Lodge and the Art-and-Reality Novel* (Heidelberg: Carl Winter, 1991), 87–8. See also Bernard Bergonzi, *David Lodge* (Plymouth: Northcote House Publishers, 1995); and David Lodge, *Changing Places* (London: Penguin, 1992 [1st pub. 1975]).

55. ITV had a self-policed quota of 14 percent imports; by 1971 the BBC had about 12 percent, though mostly on BBC1, the more popular channel, rather than on BBC2, which tended to air exclusively domestic productions (Tunstall, *The Media Are American*, 278–9).

56. Alan Clayson, *Beat Merchants: The Origins, History, Impact and Rock Legacy of the 1960's British Pop Groups* (London: Blandford, 1995), 18–9. See also Asa Briggs, *The History of Broadcasting in the United Kingdom*, Vol. V: *Competition* (Oxford: Oxford University Press, 1995), 143; Sandbrook, *Never Had It So Good*, 363–4; Geoffrey Lealand, *American Television Programmes on British Screens* (London: BFI, 1984), 13–14; schedules in the weekly *Radio Times* and *The Listener*.

57. Stuart Laing, "The Television Revolution in Britain," in David Allan Mellor and Laurent Gervereau (eds.), *The Sixties: Britain and France, 1962–1973: The Utopian Years* (London: Philip Wilson, 1997), 169–70. See also Tim O'Sullivan, "Television Memories and Cultures of Viewing, 1950–65," in John Corner (ed.), *Popular Television in Britain* (London: BFI, 1991). By far the most successful media entrepreneur of the era was Lew Grade, who developed a network of contacts in New York and on the West Coast and in Las Vegas before organizing a commercial television company in the mid-fifties and securing a broadcasting license for ATV (where the important Sunday evening schedule began with *I Love Lucy*). He had a huge success with an American-scripted and American-acted series, *The Adventures of Robin Hood*, in Britain and, after it was bought by CBS, also in America (Lew Grade, *Still Dancing: My Story* [Glasgow: William Collins, 1987]).

58. Quoted in Lealand, *American Television Programmes on British Screens*, 24. See also *The Listener*, 18 December 1969, 868–9; 2 January 1969, 27–8; 13 November 1969, 679–80; 27 April 1972, 567.

PART I

1. *Time Magazine*, 87, 15 (15 April 1966), "London: The Swinging City." Cover (by the British artist Geoffrey Dickson) and cover story (by Piri Halasz): "You Can Walk across It on the Grass," 32–41.

2. Ibid., 41. See also Simon Rycroft, "The Geographies of Swinging London," *Journal of Historical Geography* 28, 4 (2002), 577, 579.

3. David Alan Mellor, *The Sixties Art Scene in London* (London: Phaidon Press, 1993), 120.

4. Ibid., 14, 45–50, 77, 97. See also David Bailey and Peter Evans, *Goodbye Baby & Amen* (London: Conde Nast Publications, 1969), 41.

5. *Time Magazine* (15 April 1966), 11, 32.

6. Tom Wolfe, *The Mid-Atlantic Man, and Other New Breeds in England and America* (London: Weidenfeld and Nicolson, 1969 [written 1964–68], 49–50. See also Mellor, *The Sixties Art Scene in London*, 54 and biographical appendix; Rycroft, "Geographies of Swinging London," 573–6.

7. Mim Scala, *Diary of a Teddy Boy: A Memoir of the Long Sixties* (Dublin: Sitric Books, 2000), 23, 28 and passim.

8. Ibid., 109.

9. Rycroft, "Geographies of Swinging London," 257.

10. Quoted by Grant, "Working for the Yankee Dollar," 590.

11. See Becky Conekin, "'Here Is the Modern World Itself': The Festival of Britain's Representation of the Future," in Conekin et al., *Moments of Modernity: Reconstructing Britain 1945–1964* (London: Rivers Oram Press, 1999), 246.

12. Booker, *The Neophiliacs*, 273–4, 32–3.

13. Lodge, *Changing Places*, 210.

14. Conekin et al., *Moments of Modernity*, 2–3.

CHAPTER 1

1. Identification of modernism with high-rise architecture may be to caricature it, as Nigel Whiteley has reminded us ("Modern Architecture, Heritage and Englishness," *Architectural History* 38 [1995], 222–3), but it was an identification that was commonly made beyond the architectural profession.

2. Iain Chambers, *Popular Culture: The Metropolitan Experience* (London: Methuen, 1986), 17, 35, 185; Serge Guilbaut, *How New York Stole the Idea of Modern Art: Abstract Expressionism, Freedom, and the Cold War* (Chicago and London: University of Chicago Press, 1983), 1. On architectural modernism, see Whiteley, "Modern Architecture, Heritage and Englishness," 223; William Whyte, "The Englishness of English Architecture: Modernism and the Making of a National International Style, 1927–1957," *Journal of British Studies* 48 (April, 2009), 450–1.

3. Quoted in Oliver Marriott, *The Property Boom* (London: Hamish Hamilton, 1967), 5.

4. Duncan Macbeth, "Piccadilly Goldmine," *New Left Review* 2 (March–April, 1960), 14. From 1945 to 1961, 50 million square feet was added to London's office accommodation, five times the amount destroyed by bombing (Jenkins, *Landlords to London*, 215, 228).

5. An exception is Charles Holden's Senate House tower in Bloomsbury. Edward Jones and Christopher Woodward, *A Guide to the Architecture of London* (London: Phoenix Illustrated, 1997), 127, 249, 250; J. M. Richards, *Memoir of an Unjust Fella* (London: Weidenfeld and Nicolson, 1980), 122, 130.

6. In 1954 the Liverpool Council sent a deputation to explore multistory projects in New York (John R. Gold, *The Practice of Modernism: Modern Architects and Urban Transformation, 1954–1972* [London and New York: Routledge, 2007], 184).

7. Jenkins, *Landlords to London*, 209; Nikolaus Pevsner and Bridget Cherry, *The Cities of London and Westminster* (Harmondsworth: Penguin, 1973, 112.

8. Lodge, *Changing Places*, 110.

9. J. M. Richards, "High London," *Architectural Review* 124 (July, 1958), 5–8.

10. Nikolaus Pevsner, *The Cities of London and Westminster* (Harmondsworth: Penguin, rev. ed., 1962); Pevsner and Cherry, *The Cities of London and Westminster* (1973), 113, 285, 618.

11. Bigsby, "Europe, America and the Cultural Debate," in Bigsby, *Superculture*, 3 and 3n.

12. Conrad Hilton, *Be My Guest* (Englewood, NJ: Prentice-Hall, 1957), 285, 287, 330.

13. Ibid., 288–9.

14. Quoted in Marriott, *The Property Boom*, 140.

15. Ibid., 196–7, 203, 204.

16. David Clutterbuck and Marion Devine, *Clore: The Man and His Millions* (London: Weidenfeld and Nicolson, 1987), 57–58.

17. Charles Gordon, *The Two Tycoons: A Personal Memoir of Jack Cotton and Charles Clore* (London: Hamish Hamilton, 1984), 47; Sampson, *Anatomy of Britain*, 421.

18. Raphael Samuel, "'Bastard' Capitalism," in E. P. Thompson (ed.), *Out of Apathy* (London: Stevens and Sons, 1960), 27, 31–2, 33. See also Samuel, "Born-again Socialism," in Robin Archer, et al. (eds.), *Out of Apathy: Voices of the New Left Thirty Years On* (London: Verso, 1989), 42.

19. Quoted in Samuel, "'Bastard' Capitalism," 33.

20. L. Gelman, Clore's secretary, 1966 (quoted in Marriott, *The Property Boom*, 271).

21. *The Times*, 3 July 1957.

22. Hilton, *Be My Guest*, 285, 330.

23. Richards, "High London," 8; *The Times*, 7 November 1957.

24. *The Times*, 9 and 12 November 1957.

25. Ibid., 13 November 1957.

26. Gold, *The Practice of Modernism*, 47; *The Times*, 15 May and 17 June 1958; 13 July 1962.

27. *The Times*, 13 July 1962; Pevsner and Cherry, *The Cities of London and Westminster*, 618; Jones and Woodward, *A Guide to the Architecture of London*, 192.

28. Conrad Hilton was briefly married to Zsa-Zsa Gabor; his elder son Nick, to Elizabeth Taylor.

29. Mildred H. Comfort, *Conrad Hilton, Hotelier* (Minneapolis, MN: Denison, 1964), 214, 220–1.

30. Gordon, *The Two Tycoons*, 133.

31. Hunter Davies, *The New London Spy: A Discreet Guide to the City's Pleasures* (London: Anthony Blond, 1966), 26; Halasz, *A Swinger's Guide to London*, 57–9.

32. Halasz, *A Swinger's Guide to London*, 61–2.

33. The Post Office Tower in exclusively horizontal Fitzrovia provided a *revolving* restaurant and cocktail bar near its 580-foot top when it opened in 1966.

34. *The Times*, 22 April 1963; *Daily Telegraph*, 22 April, 1963.

35. David Crawford, *The City of London* (Cambridge: Woodhead-Faulner, 1976), 11.

36. In a 1959 "Letter from America" (while visiting Britain), as cited by Nick Clarke, *Alistair Cooke: The Biography* (London: Orion, 2000), 387.

37. Richards, "High London," 6–7; Macbeth, "Piccadilly Goldmine," 13, 17.

38. Robin Winks, *An American's Guide to Britain* (New York: Charles Scribner's Sons,

1977), 145. Visiting the States after the war, Benn married an American from Cincinnati and in 1949 took a job with the BBC's North America service.

39. For American influence on Paul Boissevain, Sydney Greenwood, Max Gordon, and Patrick Garnett, see Marriott, *The Property Boom*, 232; Pevsner and Cherry, *The Cities of London and Westminster*, 514; and Jonathan Glancey's obit. for Garnett (the *Guardian*, 8 June 2006). For Peter Carter and Michael Blee, see Gold, *The Practice of Modernism*, 25, 36, 39–40.

40. *The Listener*, 7 January and 18 February 1965.

41. See Reyner Banham, *The New Brutalism: Ethic or Aesthetic?* (London: Architectural Press, 1966), and Sutherland Lyall, *The State of British Architecture* (London: Architectural Press, 1980).

42. Reyner Banham, "Mediated Environments Or: You Can't Build That Here," in Bigsby, *Superculture*, 74–9; see also Nigel Whiteley, "The Puzzled *Lieber Meister*: Pevsner and Reyner Banham," in Peter Draper (ed.), *Reassessing Nikolaus Pevsner* (Aldershot: Ashgate Publishing, 2004), 213–3.

43. Jenkins, *Landlords to London*, 228–38. The New York property boom had already collapsed.

44. Marriott, *The Property Boom*, 166.

45. Jenkins, *Landlords to London*, 253–4.

CHAPTER 2

1. *The Times*, 20 February 1956; at the beginning of the century the embassy had occupied an undistinguished site in Victoria Street. In 1938 it moved into an "unpretentious" building in Grosvenor Square that proved inadequate for the expanded U.S. wartime presence.

2. Jane C. Loeffler, *The Architecture of Diplomacy: Building America's Embassies* (New York: Princeton Architectural Press, 1998), 5, 8, 197–200; Allan Temko, *Eero Saarinen* (London: Prentice-Hall International, 1962), 26.

3. *The Times*, 20 February, 6 June 1956; 26 January 1957; Diary, 15 June 1960 (in A. B. Saarinen [ed.], *Eero Saarinen on His Work* [New Haven: Yale University Press, 1968 (rev. ed.)]; Rupert Spade, *Eero Saarinen* (London: Thames and Hudson, 1971), 17.

4. Temko, *Eero Saarinen*, 31; Marcus Lipton, Labour MP, in the House of Commons, 29 March 1960, and in *The Times*, 8 June; Saarinen Diary, 15 June 1960.

5. *The Times*, 28 October 1960; "Controversial Building in London," *Architectural Forum* 114, 3 (March, 1961), 80–5; Pevsner and Cherry, *The Cities of London and Westminster*, 584–5.

6. Fello Atkinson, "U.S. Embassy Building, Grosvenor Square, London," *Architectural Review* 129 (April, 1961), 253–65; Jones and Woodward, *A Guide to the Architecture of London*, 191; Saarinen Diary, 4 August 1961.

7. John Updike, "An American in London," *The Listener*, 23 January 1969, 97–9.

8. Ibid.; *The Times*, 6 June 1961. During the war Bruce had been head of the OSS in London.

9. *The Times*, 4 January, 15 February and 3 May 1961, 19 March and 31 August 1962; 12 January and 12 March 1963; 28 December 1965; 13 and 22 April, 23 June 1966.

10. Jeff Nuttall, *Bomb Culture* (London: MacGibbin and Kee, 1968), 55; *The Times*, 4 April, 6 November 1961; 19 March, 23, 24, 27, and 28 April, 24 October 1962.

11. Richard Taylor, *Against the Bomb: The British Peace Movement 1958–1965* (Oxford: Clarendon Press, 1988), 89; *The Times*, 24 and 25 October 1962; 12 March, 6 April, and 18 October 1965; 19 February 1968.

12. Collins quoted in Christopher Driver, *The Disarmers: A Study in Protest* (London: Hodder and Stoughton, 1964), 111; Taylor in 1983, quoted in Meredith Veldman, *Fantasy, the Bomb, and the Greening of Britain: Romantic Protest, 1945–1980* (Cambridge: Cambridge University Press, 1994), 140. See also Mark Pythian, "CND's Cold War," *Contemporary British History* 15, 3 (Autumn, 2001), 133–56; John Callaghan, "The Cold War and the March of Capitalism, Socialism and Democracy," *Contemporary British History* 15, 3 (Autumn, 2001), 1–25.

13. Samuel, "Born-again Socialism," in Archer, *Out of Apathy*, 46. Kubrick came to Britain in 1962 to film *Lolita*, and stayed.

14. Richard Taylor and Ian Pritchard, *The Protest Makers: The British Nuclear Disarmament Movement of 1958–1965, Twenty Years On* (Oxford: Pergamon Press, 1980), 39, 77; Driver, *The Disarmers*, 50, 55; Sheila Rowbotham, *Promise of a Dream: Remembering the Sixties* (London: Penguin Press, 2000), 69.

15. Sandbrook, *Never Had It So Good*, 250, 257, 259. See also Frank Parkin, *Middle Class Radicalism: The Social Bases of the British Campaign for Nuclear Disarmament* (Manchester: Manchester University Press, 1968).

16. Driver, *The Disarmers*, 50; Taylor and Pritchard, *The Protest Makers*, 158; Nuttall, *Bomb Culture*, 191; Rowbotham, *Promise of a Dream*, 69.

17. Tariq Ali, *Street Fighting Years: An Autobiography of the Sixties* (London: Collins, 1987), 48–9; Ralph Schoenman, "Bertrand Russell and the Peace Movement," in George Nakhnikian (ed.), *Bertrand Russell's Philosophy* (London: Duckworth (1974).

18. Driver, *The Disarmers*, 112; Peter Brook et al., *The Book of US* (London: Calder and Boyors, 1968), 143; *The Times*, 13 April 1966.

19. Ali, *Street Fighting Years*, 46, 61; *The Times*, 13 April 1966.

20. Nuttall, *Bomb Culture*, 7, 69; *The Times*, 21 August, 4 September 1967; 5 March 1968. The shooting and the bombing may have been the work of a Spanish anarchist group—or so *The Times* claimed.

21. *The Times*, 17 October 1967 (which reported that about sixty Americans in London had performed the ritual of handing in their draft cards); 23 and 24 October 1967; Rowbotham, *Promise of a Dream*, 114; Robert Hewison, *Too Much: Art and Society in the Sixties 1960–75* (London: Methuen, 1988), 160; Ali, *Street Fighting Years*, 160, 177.

22. Ali, *Street Fighting Years*, 177–8; Vanessa Redgrave, *Autobiography* (London: Hutchinson, 1991), 139.

23. Redgrave, *Autobiography*, 48, 146, 153–5; Jane Fonda, *My Life So Far* (New York: Random House, 2005), 165, 203.

24. Ali, *Street Fighting Years*, 177–81; Redgrave, *Autobiography*, 139–41; Mick Farren, *Give the Anarchist a Cigarette* (London: Pimlico, 2002), 176, 180–1; *The Times*, 18 March 1968; the *Daily Mail*, 18 March 1968; the *Sun*, 18 March 1968; the *Guardian*, 18 March 1968.

25. *The Times*, 18, 19, 21, 22 March; the *Sun*, 19 March, 1968.

26. Rowbotham, *Promise of a Dream*, 170; Farren, *Give the Anarchist a Cigarette*, 185; Ali, *Street Fighting Years*, 180–1; Raymond Williams, "The Decadence Game," *The Listener*, 22 October 1970, 557–8.

27. *The Times*, 7 June, 22 July, 3 August 1968; James D. Halloran, Philip Elliott, and Graham Murdock, *Demonstrations and Communication: A Case Study* (Harmondsworth:

Penguin, 1970), 41. By August one could buy a Bobby Kennedy poster at Big O Posters, 49 Kensington High Street—as well as psychedelic posters of Bob Dylan, Frank Zappa, Jimi Hendrix, and Spiderman.

28. *The Times*, 25 October 1968; "BBC on This Day, 27 October 1968," at http://news. bbc.co.uk/; Halloran, Elliott, and Murdock, *Demonstrations and Communication*, introduction.

29. *The Times*, 5 July, 19 December 1966; 22 May, 4 September 1967; Paul Barker, Humphrey Taylor, Emanuel de Kadt, and Earl Hopper, "Portrait of a Protest," *New Society* 31 (October, 1968), 631–4.

30. Or so *The Times* claimed (16 October 1969). About 300 turned up with a few Labour MPs.

31. Ibid., 7 July, 24 December 1970; Nigel Fountain, *Underground: The London Alternative Press 1966–1974* (London: Routledge, 1988), 96, 111.

32. Sandbrook, *White Heat*, 382, 532–7.

CHAPTER 3

1. Perry Anderson, editor's comment introducing Andrew Kopkind's article "The Special Relationship," *New Left Review* 51 (September–October, 1968), 3.

2. Samuel, "Born-Again Socialism," in Archer, *Out of Apathy*, 42–3; Norman Birnbaum, "Foreword," in Thompson, *Out of Apathy*, xii; David Riesman, *The Lonely Crowd* (1950); William Whyte, *The Organization Man* (1956); Vance Packard, *The Hidden Persuaders* (1957); John Kenneth Galbraith, *The Affluent Society* (1958); C. Wright Mills, *The Power Elite* (1956); Michael Harrington, *The Other America* (1962).

3. Francis Hope, "The Intellectual Left," in Gerald Kaufman (ed.), *The Left* (London: Anthony Blond, 1966), 100. See also Michael Kenny, *The First New Left: British Intellectuals after Stalin* (London: Lawrence and Wishart, 1995), 124, 141.

4. Roy Hattersley, *Who Goes Home? Scenes from a Political Life* (London: Little, Brown and Company, 1995), 102; Perry Anderson, "The Left in the Fifties," *New Left Review* 29 (January–February, 1965), 7; Bevan quoted by Lawrence Black in *The Political Culture of the Left in Affluent Britain, 1951–64: Old Labour, New Britain?* (London: Palgrave Macmillan, 2003), 87. Healey first visited the United States in 1949 and returned annually; Gaitskell a year later on a Ford Foundation lecture tour; Jenkins in 1953 and Crosland in 1954, both as Smith-Mundt fellows. Crosland, who (like Shirley Williams, David Owen, and Tony Benn) married an American, "drew liberally on American research" for his influential *The Future of Socialism* (1958). For the revisionists' debt to American social thought, see Black, "The Bitterest Enemies of Communism"; Stephen Brooke, "'Atlantic Crossing?': American Views of Capitalism and British Socialist Thought 1932–1962," *Twentieth Century British History* 2, 2 (1991); and Steven Fielding, "'But Westward Look, the Land Is Bright': Labour's Revisionists and the Imagining of America, c. 1945–64," in Jonathan Hollowell (ed.), *Twentieth-Century Anglo-American Relations* (London: Palgrave, 2001). See also Hattersley's mid-sixties essay "New Blood," in Kaufman, *The Left*, 141–66.

5. Terry Eagleton and Brian Wicker (eds.), *From Culture to Revolution* (London: Sheed and Ward, 1968), 16.

6. Marshall Berman, *The Politics of Authenticity: Radical Individualism and the Emergence of Modern Society* (New York: Atheneum, 1972), xvii; Rossinow, *The Politics of Authenticity*, 5.

7. For some examples of how American sociological thinking affected the work of

some of the New Left in Britain, see G. R. Arnold, "Britain: The New Reasoners," in Leopold Labedz (ed.), *Revisionism: Essays on the History of Marxist Ideas* (London: Allen and Unwin, 1962), 306; Stuart Hall, "The New Revolutionaries," in Eagleton and Wicker, *From Culture to Revolution*, 206.

8. *New Left May Day Manifesto* (London: Goodwin Press, [1967]), 1, 23, 31; the expanded version is Raymond Williams (ed.), *May Day Manifesto* (Harmondsworth: Penguin, 1968).

9. *May Day Manifesto*, 53–63, 106, 189, and passim, chs. 14–17; Madeleine Davis, "'Labourism' and the New Left," in John Callaghan, Steven Fielding, and Steve Ludlam (eds.), *Interpreting the Labour Party: Approaches to Labour Politics and History* (Manchester: Manchester University Press, 2003), 51.

10. *New Left May Day Manifesto*, 31; and Williams, *May Day Manifesto*, 11. For Marcuse, see "The Question of Revolution," *New Left Review* 45 (September–October, 1967), 3–7. The *New Left Review* ignored the American campus rebellions until rather late in the day (Martin Nicolaus, "S.F. State: History Takes a Leap," *New Left Review* 54 [March–April, 1969], 27–34).

11. *May Day Manifesto Bulletin* 2 (February, 1968) and 4 (April, 1968).

12. Peter Sedgwick, "The Two New Paths," *International Socialism* 17 (August, 1964), reprinted in David Widgery (ed.), *The Left in Britain 1956–68* (Harmondsworth: Penguin Books, 1976), 134, 141, 144, 149; Perry Anderson, "Origins of the Present Crisis," *New Left Review* 23 [January–February, 1964], 26, 44–5, and "The Left in the Fifties," 17.

13. *May Day Manifesto Bulletin* 5 (May, 1968); Raymond Williams, "Why Do I Demonstrate?" *The Listener*, 25 April 1968, 521–3, and "The British Left," *New Left Review* 30 (March–April, 1965), 25–6.

14. Bryan Palmer, *E. P. Thompson: Objections and Oppositions* (London: Vero, 1994), 14, 108–9; Rowbotham, *Promise of a Dream*, 169; E. P. Thompson, "C. Wright Mills, the Responsible Craftsman," *Peace News* 22 and 29 (November, 1963); Robin Blackburn, "Edward Thompson and the New Left," *New Left Review* 201 (1993), 4; E. P. Thompson, "William Morris and the Moral Issues To-Day," in *The American Threat to British Culture* (London: Arena Publication, n.d. [1951]), 25. Nevertheless, Thompson spoke on Blake at Columbia during the troubles there in 1968.

15. Eric Hobsbawm, *Interesting Times: A Twentieth-Century Life* (London: Allen Lane, 2002), 70, 248–51, 386; *Industry and Empire: An Economic History of Britain since 1750* (London: Weidenfeld and Nicolson, 1968), 275.

16. David Caute, *The Great Fear: The Anti-Communist Purge under Truman and Eisenhower* (London: Secker and Warburg, 1978); Perry Anderson, "Components of the National Culture," *New Left Review* 50 (July–August, 1968), 3, 57; no. 52 (November–December, 1968) was devoted entirely to the crisis in France.

17. Rowbotham, *Promise of a Dream*, 24, 57–8, 68, 85, 98–9.

18. Ibid., 122, 124–5, 161–2; Ali, *Street Fighting Years*, 216. Wortis, a Marxist who had been thrown out of the University of Wisconsin, joined the Stop It! group of antiwar Americans.

19. Raymond Williams, *Television, Technology and Cultural Form* (London: Fonatana, 1974), 39, 133; Raymond Williams, *Britain in the Sixties: Communications* (Harmondsworth: Penguin, 1962), 74–5; Raymond Williams, "Television in Britain," *Journal of Social Issues* 18, 2 (1962), 8–11.

20. For his own retrospective account of the New Left years, see Stuart Hall, "The 'First'

New Left: Life and Times," in Archer, *Out of Apathy*, 11–38; Hall, "The New Revolutionaries," 182; Stuart Hall, "The Hippies: An American 'Moment,'" in Julian Nagel (ed.), *Student Power* (London: Merlin Press, 1969), 170–202.

21. Eagleton and Wicker (eds.), *From Culture to Revolution*, 16–17; Terry Eagleton, *The Gatekeeper: A Memoir* (London: Penguin, 2001), 20, 147–50.

22. See Davis, "'Labourism' and the New Left," 51.

23. *New Left May Day Manifesto* 18, 31.

24. Marwick, *The Sixties*, 341–2.

25. Peter Brook, *The Shifting Point: Forty Years of Theatrical Exploration 1946–1987* (London: Methuen, 1988), 56.

26. See Michael Kustow, *Peter Brook: A Biography* (London: Bloomsbury, 2005), 307–8.

27. See John Gielgud, *An Actor and His Time* (Harmondsworth: Penguin Books, 1981), 171; also Richard Mangan (ed.), *Sir John Gielgud: A Life in Letters* (New York: Arcade Publishing, 2004).

28. Gielgud, *An Actor and His Time*, 171; Mangan, *Sir John Gielgud*, passim; Scala, *Diary of a Teddy Boy*, 67.

29. Charles Marowitz, *Burnt Bridges: A Souvenir of the Swinging Sixties and Beyond* (London: Hodder and Stoughton, 1990), 1, 19, 36, 140–4. Also, Kustow, *Peter Brook*, 124, 138.

30. Marowitz, *Burnt Bridges*, 54; Hewison, *Too Much*, 195.

31. Nicholas De Jongh, *Politics, Prudery and Perversions: The Censoring of the English Stage 1901–1986* (London: Methuen, 2001), 238–9. The London cast was British, not American; Richard Neville claims that the scene in which the cast made love under the stars and stripes was cut when American tourists walked out (*Hippie Hippie Shake: The Dreams, the Trials, the Love-Ins, the Screw-Ups . . . the Sixties* [London: Bloomsbury, 1995], 224).

32. Mark Boyle and Jeff Nuttall, in Jonathan Green (ed.), *Days in the Life: Voices from the English Underground 1961–1971* (London: Pimlico, 1998 [1st pub. 1988]), 43. See also Alan Sinfield, "The Theater and Its Audiences," in Sinfield (ed.), *Society and Literature 1945–1970* (London: Methuen and Co., 1983), 186. The term "happening" was coined by the New York artist Allan Kaprow in 1959 for multimedia performance events that broke down boundaries between art and ordinary life.

33. Brook, *The Shifting Point*, 50–66, 208, 210.

34. Tariq Ali claimed that Morley Safer's reports for CBS—when broadcast in Britain—had a much greater impact than the BBC's own coverage (*Street Fighting Years*, 46–7).

35. Brook et al., *The Book of US*, 7, 10, 14–21.

36. Ibid., 174–5, 180; Brook, *Shifting Point*, 62, 210; see also Albert Hunt and Geoffrey Reeves, *Peter Brook* (Cambridge: Cambridge University Press, 1995), 96–120. The butterfly idea was taken from the American composer John Cage, whose "Composition 1960 number five" involved musical representation of wings fluttering as a butterfly was turned loose in the concert hall (Kustow, *Peter Brook*, 161).

37. Brook et al., *The Book of US*, 143; De Jongh, *Politics, Prudery and Perversions*, 146–54.

38. De Jongh, *Politics, Prudery and Perversions*, 151; Jim Haynes, *Thanks for Coming! An Autobiography* (London and Boston: Faber and Faber, 1984), 146.

39. De Jongh, *Politics, Prudery and Perversions*, 154; Marowitz, *Burnt Bridges*, 93; John Lahr (ed.), *The Diaries of Kenneth Tynan* (London: Bloomsbury, 2001), 325.

40. Brook, *Shifting Point*, 210; Brook et al., *The Book of US*, 207–12.

41. Stuart Laing, "The Production of Literature," in Alan Sinfield, *Society and Literature 1945-1970*, 165–71; and Sinfield, "The Theater and Its Audiences," 193; see also Michael Coveney, obituary for Dan Crawford in the *Guardian*, 15 July 2005.

42. Nuttall, *Bomb Culture*, 173–4; Farren, *Give the Anarchist a Cigarette*, 102–3; Kustow, *Peter Brook*, 114–5, 138; Eileen Blumenthal, *Joseph Chaikin: Exploring the Boundaries of Theater* (Cambridge: Cambridge University Press, 1984), 5, 14–15, 23, 216.

43. Eric Rhodes, "Newsreel," *The Listener*, 10 April 1969.

44. David Caute, *The Demonstration: A Play* (London: Andre Deutsch, 1970), 7.

45. *The Hornsey Affair* (Harmondsworth: Penguin Books, 1969), 9.

46. Lisa Tickner, *Hornsey 1968: The Art School Revolution* (London: Francis Lincoln, 2008), 56–7; Tom Nairn, "Hornsey," *New Left Review* 50 (July–August, 1968, 65–9); the same issue had two other favorable reports on student rebellion, Tom Fawthrop on "Hull," and David Triesman on "Essex."

47. Carl Davidson, "Campaigning on the Campus," in Alexander Cockburn and Robin Blackburn (eds.), *Student Power* (Harmondsworth: Penguin, 1969), 327.

48. In 1963 the Robbins Report pointed out that 20 percent of school leavers went on to university in the United States, while only 4.6 percent did so in Britain (cited in Tickner, *Hornsey 1968*, 20).

49. The modernism of the buildings, however, was not matched by much modernization of the rituals and hierarchies of academic life—indeed, these were sometimes architecturally entrenched.

50. Basil Spence, "Building a New University," in David Daiches (ed.), *The Idea of a New University* (London: Andre Deutsch, 1970), 201–5; Samuel, "'Bastard' Capitalism," 46–7; E. P. Thompson (ed.), *Warwick University Ltd.: Industry, Management and the Universities* (Harmondsworth: Penguin, 1970), 17, 44, 59–60.

51. David Daiches, *A Third World* (Brighton: Sussex University Press, 1971); John Calder, obituary for Daiches, the *Guardian*, 18 July 2005; Dennis Cox, "The Library for a New University," 165, and Daiches, "The Place of English Studies in the Sussex Scheme," 94, in *The Idea of a New University*.

52. Philip Abrams and Alan Little, "The Young Voter in British Politics," *British Journal of Sociology* 16, 2 (June, 1965), 95, 108; F[rank] Musgrove, *Youth and the Social Services* (London: Routledge and Kegan Paul, 1964), 19, 20n.; Zweig, *The Student in the Age of Anxiety*, xiii–xvi.

53. See CAB 151/66, Student Protests, 1967–69, as cited by Fowler, *Youth Culture in Modern Britain*, 163–4.

54. For deflating revisionism, see Nick Thomas, "Challenging Myths of the 1960s: The Case of Student Protest in Britain," *Twentieth Century British History* 13, 3 (2002), 282, 287, 296–7; Sandbrook, *White Heat*, 541–3; or Fowler, *Youth Culture in Modern Britain*, 160–64. For contemporary analysis, see, for example, Jupp, "The Discontents of Youth," 411–8.

55. David Martin, "Trouble in the University," *The Listener*, 7 March 1968, 291–3 (Third Programme).

56. Shils served in the OSS and was attached to the British Army during the war; for years he held joint appointments at the L.S.E. and later Cambridge (King's and Peterhouse). An influential Weberian scholar, he was not sympathetic to student radicalism.

57. Blackburn, in Green, *Days in the Life*, 251.

58. For the early stages at the L.S.E., see Ben Brewster and Alexander Cockburn, "Revolt at the LSE," *New Left Review* 43 (May–June, 1967), 11–25; and Gareth Stedman Jones, Anthony Barnett, and Tom Wengraf, "Student Power: What Is to Be Done?" *New Left Review* 43 (May–June, 1967), 3–9; David Adelstein, *Teach Yourself Student Power* (Radical Student Alliance, [1968?]). The L.S.E.'s case was put by Harry Kidd, *The Trouble at L.S.E. 1966–1967* (London:Oxford University Press, 1969). Bloom would later commit suicide when threatened with conscription.

59. From May 1968, civil servants kept the Cabinet Office informed about American activist "missionaries," and in January 1969 Education Secretary Edward Short confirmed in the Commons that Americans were behind much of the protest in Britain—though, according to David Fowler, who has closely studied the archives, government was determined not to over-react to what they regarded as a short-term, overblown, and limited phenomenon (*Youth Culture in Modern Britain*, 160–2).

60. Kidd, *The Trouble at L.S.E.*, 26, 30, 37, 120–2.

61. Patrick Wall and John Smith, *Student Power* (London: Monday Club, 1968), 13; Ali, *Street Fighting Years*, 117; Paul Hoch and Vic Schoenbach, *LSE: The Natives are Restless* (London: Sheed and Ward, 1969), vii–ix.

62. David Triesman, "Essex," *New Left Review* 50 (July–August, 1968), 70–2; Tom Fawthrop, "Hull," *New Left Review* 50 (July–August, 1968), 59–64; Halloran, Elliott, and Murdock, The *Demonstrations and Communication*, 35; *The Times*, 8 and 9 March 1968; Rowbotham, *Promise of a Dream*, 181, 185.

63. Eagleton, *The Gatekeeper*, 95; *The Times*, 25 October 1968.

64. The next year Caute published a piece on the divisions within the American left ("No Common Language," *The Listener*, 7 May 1970).

65. Caute, *The Demonstration*, 21, 58, 70–1, 75, 84, 92, 100.

66. Peter Linebaugh, "From the Upper East Side to Wick Episcopi," *New Left Review* 201 (September–October, 1993), 23; Thompson, *Warwick University Ltd.*, passim; E. P. Thompson, "The Business University," in *Writing by Candlelight* (London: Merlin, 1980), 13–27; Palmer, *E. P. Thompson*, 100–10; and Robert W. Malcolmson, John Rule, and Peter Searby, "Edward Thompson as a Teacher: Yorkshire and Warwick," in Malcolmson and Rule (eds.), *Protest and Survival* (London: Merlin Press, 1993), 1–23.

67. Ali, *Street Fighting Years*, 50–1. See also Fountain, *Underground*, 17, 19.

68. Rowbotham, *Promise of a Dream*, 181; Ralph Keyes, "The Free Universities," *The Nation* (2 October 1967), 294–9; interviews with Peter Jenner, Joe Boyd, Graham Keen, Courtney Tulloch, in Green, *Days in the Life*, 61–2, 95–7, 103; Andrew Wilson, "Moving Times—New Words—Dead Clocks: Sigma, London Counter-Culture," in Mellor and Gervereau, *The Sixties*, 259–60; and Joe Boyd, *White Bicycles: Making Music in the 1960s* (London: Serpent's Tail, 2005), 134–5.

69. Frank Kermode, "Antiuniversity," *The Listener*, 29 February 1968, 257–9; *May Day Manifesto Bulletin*, no. 2 (February, 1968), 18. See also Fountain, *Underground*, 260.

70. Rowbotham, *Promise of a Dream*, 171; *The Hornsey Affair*, 42; Thompson, *Warwick University Ltd.*, 44.

71. See, for instance, Jeremi Suri, "The Rise and Fall of an International Counterculture, 1960–1975," *American Historical Review* 114, 1 (February, 2009).

72. An exception was BBC-1's "Students in Revolt," a current affairs program broadcast in June of 1968 featuring "Danny the Red" Cohn-Bendit and other activists from Europe, a

somewhat feeble affair that Fowler (*Youth Culture in Modern Britain*, 148–58) rather oddly regards as influential. For a dismissive contemporary view, see Francis King, "Student Prince," *The Listener*, 20 June 1968, 814–5.

73. Alasdair Clayre, "Dissenting Intellectuals in America," *The Listener*, 13 March 1969, 334–7; and Christopher Ricks' unsympathetic comment, ibid. 329–30.

74. Tom Nairne, "On the Subversiveness of Arts Students," *The Listener*, 17 October 1968 (491–2); Robin Blackburn, "Student Reformers," 5 June 1969 (739–4), also "Revolutions in Our Time: Robin Blackwell Talks to Joan Bakewell," 22 January 1970 (116–8); Richard Gilbert produced a sympathetic account of the Hornsey rebellion for BBC's External Services ("Wisdom Working," *The Listener*, 4 July 1968, 12–3); John Sparrow, "Revolting Students," *The Listener*, 4 July 1968, 1–4, and "Civilisation," 8 May 1969, 629–31; also the professor of English at Bristol University, Christopher Ricks, "Student Thought," 13 March 1969, 329–30.

75. Alistair Cooke, *Letter from America*, "SS and SDS," 8 May 1969, 632; Sparrow, "Revolting Students," "Civilisation," and "Egalitarianism and an Academic Elite," published in a 1969 pamphlet and republished in C. B. Cox and A. E. Dyson (eds.), *The Black Papers on Education* (London: Davis-Poynter, 1971), 41–5. His indignation at being challenged "in a minatory tone" by undergraduates led him to reflect on the need for standards that would privilege those from the superior public schools.

76. Richard Hoggart, "1968–1978: The Student Movement and Its Effects in the Universities," *Political Quarterly* 50 (1979), 178, and *An Imagined Life* (London: Chatto and Windus, 1992), 97, 138, 179.

77. "Special Issue on Protest and Discontent," *Political Quarterly* 40, 4 (October–December, 1969), 354–6; Colin Crouch and Stephen Mennell, *The Universities: Pressures and Prospects* (London: Fabian Society, 1972), 11, 21, 37, 41, 94.

78. Fowler, *Youth Culture in Modern Britain*, 160–1.

79. G. F. Hudson, "The Berkeley Fashion," in Cox and Dyson, *The Black Papers*, 180. See also Kingsley Amis, "Pernicious Participation," 170–2; A. E. Dyson, "The Sleep of Reason," 84–6; and Bryan Wilson, "Youth Culture, the Universities and Student Unrest," 189–204.

80. Theodore Roszak, *The Making of a Counter-Culture* (Berkeley: University of California Press, 1969), and "On Academic Delinquency," in T. Roszak (ed.), *The Dissenting Academy* (Harmondsworth: Penguin Books, 1969), 11–44.

81. Wall and Smith, *Student Power*, 1–3, 16; Cockburn and Blackburn, *Student Power*, 20–1.

82. *The Hornsey Affair*, 9.

83. Simon Maddison, "Mindless Militants? Psychiatry and the University," in Ian Taylor and Laurie Taylor (eds.), *Politics and Deviance* (Harmondsworth: Penguin, 1973), 111; for the maverick critique, see Thomas Szasz, "The Psychiatrist as Double Agent," first published in *Transactions* in 1967 and reprinted in Howard S. Becker, *Campus Power Struggle* (New Brunswick, N.J.: Transaction Books, 1973).

84. Anthony Ryle, *Student Casualties* (London: Allen Lane, the Penguin Press, 1969), 13, 16, 44, 127, and passim.

85. Myre Sim, *Tutors and Their Students: Advice from a Psychiatrist* (Edinburgh: E. and S. Livingstone, 1970), 46–7; *Guide to Psychiatry* (1963, with several editions); *Basic Psychiatry* (with E. B. Gordon, 1968, with further editions in 1972 and 1976).

PART II

1. Farren, *Give the Anarchist a Cigarette*, 119–20, 136, 168, 170, 226; Barry Miles, *In the Sixties* (London: Jonathan Cape, 2002),181–4.

2. Simon Frith, *Sound Effects: Youth, Leisure, and the Politics of Rock and Roll* (London: Constable, 1983), 46; McKay, *Yankee Go Home*, 41.

3. Nuttall, *Bomb Culture*, 170; Mellor, *The Sixties Art Scene in London*, 134; Boyd, *White Bicycles*, 2; David Alan Mellor, "'Tomorrow Starts Now': Utopian Visual Culture in Britain," in Mellor and Gervereau, *The Sixties*, 21–3; Rycroft, "Geographies of Swinging London," 567.

4. Rycroft, "Geographies of Swinging London," 581; for an informed interpretation emphasizing difference, see Chad Andrew Martin, "Paradise Now: Youth Politics and the British Counterculture, 1958–1974" (Ph.D. dissertation, Stanford University, 2003).

5. Hewison, *Too Much*, 86; Marshall Berman, "The Signs in the Street: A Response to Perry Anderson," *New Left Review* 144 (March–April, 1984), 123.

CHAPTER 4

1. Quoted in Green, *Days in the Life*, 62–3.

2. Barry Miles, *Hippie* (London: Cassell Illustrated, 2003), 9.

3. Miles, *In the Sixties*, 172.

4. Boyd, *White Bicycles*, 67–8.

5. *Rolling Stone,* 4 February 1971; Clinton Heylin, *Bob Dylan: Behind the Shades. Take Two* (London: Penguin, 2001), 186.

6. Barry Miles, *Ginsberg: A Biography* (London: Viking, 1989), 370–1, 535–6, and *In the Sixties*, 53–4, also 31–7, 44.

7. Miles, *In the Sixties*, 53–4, 65.

8. Ibid., 57–8; Barry Miles, "Foreword," *Ginsberg in London: Photographs by John Hopkins* (London: Andrew Sclanders, 2000); Michael Horovitz (ed.), *Children of Albion: Poetry of the Underground in Britain* (Harmondsworth and Baltimore: Penguin Books, 1969), 337. Trocchi, an Italo-Scot novelist and "cultural provocateur," grew up in 1940s Glasgow, drifted to Paris where he was involved with the Situationists, and then on to New York and the fifties Beat scene (Andrew Murray Scott, *Alexander Trocchi: The Making of the Monster* [Edinburgh: Polygon, 1991]).

9. Farren, *Give the Anarchist a Cigarette*, 58; Nuttall, *Bomb Culture*, 192; Miles, *Hippie*, 76, *In the Sixties*, 59, and "Foreword," *Ginsberg in London*; Alexis Lykiard, "Introduction," *Wholly Communion: The Film by Peter Whitehead* (London: David Osler and Frank, 1965), 5–6; Scott, *Alexander Trocchi*, 141–2. Michael Horovitz, in Green, *Days in the Life*, 19.

10. Andrew Loog Oldham, the son of a U.S. Air Force officer killed in the Second World War.

11. Stephen Crofts, "Peter Whitehead Talks about His New Film—*The Fall*," *Cinema* 1 (December, 1968), 18–23; Peter Whitehead Archive (http//www.contemporaryfilms.com/archives/peter.htm).

12. Marowitz, *Burnt Bridges*, 65, 154; Miles, *In the Sixties*, 60; Lykiard, *Wholly Communion*, 25–33; Scott, *Alexander Trocchi*, 140–2, 147.

13. Miles, "Foreword," *Ginsberg in London*; *Long Hair* 1, 1 (1965).

14. Elizabeth Nelson, *The British Counter-Culture 1966–73: A Study of the Underground Press* (London: Macmillan, 1989), 39.

15. George McKay, *Senseless Acts of Beauty: Cultures of Resistance since the Sixties* (London and New York: Verso, 1996), 2–3. See also Nuttall, *Bomb Culture*, 171, 175, 181, 191; Hewison, *Too Much*, 82; George Melly, *Revolt into Style: The Pop Arts in Britain* (Harmondsworth: Penguin, 1970), 228–9.

16. Ali, *Street Fighting Years*, 127; Bernice Martin, *A Sociology of Contemporary Cultural Change* (Oxford: Basil Blackwell, 1981), 2.

17. They developed their skills playing for U.S. servicemen at East Anglian airbases and were the first British group to undertake a full-scale North American tour. See Dave Laing's obituary for Denis Payton, the *Guardian*, 5 January 2007; and Clayson, *Beat Merchants*, 183–4, 188.

18. See Sandbrook, *Never Had It So Good*, 476–7, 680.

19. Jonathan Gould, *Can't Buy Me Love: The Beatles, Britain and America* (New York: Harmony Books, 2007), 253, 258–9, 267, 283, 287, 299, 323, 332, 489, 502–3, 516, 524–5.

20. Barry Miles, *Paul McCartney: Many Years from Now* (London: Vintage, 1998), x, xiii, 211; Ian Macdonald, *Revolution in the Head: The Beatles' Records and the Sixties* (London: Pimlico, 1998), xii–xiii, xv, xvii; Gould, *Can't Buy Me Love*, 317, 319, 388; Kenneth Gloag, "Situating the 1960s: Popular Music—Postmodernism—History," *Rethinking History* 5, 3 (2001), 405–6, quoting Frederick Jameson, *Postmodernism: or, The Cultural Logic of Late Capitalism* (London: Verso, 1991).

21. Miles, *Paul McCartney*, 347, and *In the Sixties*, 171–2; Gould, *Can't Buy Me Love*, 347; Bruce A. Beatie, "The Tolkien Phenomenon: 1954–1968," *Journal of Popular Culture* 3, 4 (Spring, 1970), 694; Dave Laing, "Chet Helms: Promoter of Janis Joplin," obituary in the *Guardian*, 27 June 2005.

22. Ian Birchall, "The Decline and Fall of British Rhythm and Blues," in John Eisen (ed.), *The Age of Rock: Sounds of the American Cultural Revolution* (New York: Random House, 1969), 94–102; Joe Boyd, in Green, *Days in the Life*, 61–2; Boyd, *White Bicycles*, 42–3.

23. George McKay, *Circular Breathing: The Cultural Politics of Jazz in Britain* (Durham: Duke University Press, 2005), ix.

24. Michael Brocken, *The British Folk Revival 1944–2002* (Aldershot: Ashgate Publishing, 2003), ix, 13, 26–7, 33, 36, 39–40; McKay, *Circular Breathing*, 33; "Ewan MacColl: 1915–1989, A Political Journey," The Working Class Movement Library, *www.wcml.org.uk*; Ewan MacColl, *Journeyman: An Autobiography* (London: Sidgwick and Jackson, 1990). For an example of the popularity of American protest folk among the younger of the Labour Party, see Roy Hattersley, *Who Goes Home?*, 21.

25. Brocken, *The British Folk Revival*, 84–5. In the spring of 1964 an "American Folk, Blues and Gospel Caravan" toured London, Bristol, Portsmouth, Liverpool, Birmingham, Leicester, Sheffield, Manchester, and Brighton with Muddy Waters, Cousin Joe, Otis Spann, Sister Rosetta Tharp, Sonny Terry, Brownie McGhee, and Rev. Gary Davis (Simon A. Napier, in *Jazz Monthly*, July, 1964, 6–7).

26. David Stuckey, *The Spinners: Fried Bread and Brandy-O!* (London: Robson Books, 1983), 41; see also Derek Schofield's obituary of Hall in the *Guardian*, 30 June 2008. Dylan had two half-hour Saturday-night programs on BBC-TV in June of 1965, and had made an appearance the previous year on an ITV Sunday program called "Halleluiah" (Heylin, *Bob Dylan*, 153).

27. Frith, *Sound Effects*, 27; Derek Schofield, obituary for Cyril Tawney, the *Guardian*, 27 April 2005.

28. Boyd, *White Bicycles*, 56–7; "Ewan MacColl: 1915–1989, A Political Journey," 2.

29. Brocken, *The British Folk Revival*, 95.

30. Simon Frith and Howard Horne, *Art into Pop* (London and New York: Methuen, 1987), 95–6; Gould, *Can't Buy Me Love*, 97, 375, 485, 506; Miles, *In the Sixties*, 98–100; Jenner, in Green, *Days in the Life*, 111.

31. Mellor, *The Sixties Art Scene in London*, 120; Miles, *Paul McCartney*, 513–6.

32. Nik Cohn, *Pop from the Beginning* (London: Weidenfeld and Nicholson, 1969), 191. On the Anglo-American rock music industry, see Frith, *Sound Effects*, chs. 5 and 6.

33. Mary Whitehouse, *Cleaning-Up TV: From Protest to Participation* (London: Blandford Press, 1967); Richard Merton, "Comment," *New Left Review* 59 (January–February, 1970), 90.

34. Frith, *Sound Effects*, 99; Fountain, *Underground*, 122.

35. For Pryce-Jones, see May, *Critical Times*; and John Willett's obituary in the *Guardian*, 9 February 2000; John Birt, *The Harder Path: The Autobiography* (London: Time Warner, 2002), 103–4; Neville, *Hippie Hippie Shake*, 232; *The Listener*, 27 April 1972, 567.

36. Clive James, *The Book of My Enemy: Collected Verse 1958–2000* (London: Picador, 2003), 338–9, and "Under the Counter," *New Society*, 12 March 1970, 449–50, "Views," *The Listener*, 30 April 1970, 574; Charles Davis, "Religious Pluralism and the New Counter-Culture," *The Listener*, 9 April 1970, 478–80.

37. Wilfred De'Ath, "Notes from the English Underground," (*The Listener*, 20 August, 244–6; 27 August, 277–9; 3 September, 309–11; and 10 September, 1970, 346–7). He first achieved notice in 1964 for his documentary about a juvenile delinquent drawn into the jazz and cannabis scene in Soho. He subsequently became a media resource on authority-rejecting teens and other deviants (Wilfred De'Ath, *Just Me and Nobody Else* [London: Hutchinson, 1966] and *Down and Out: The Collected Writings of the Oldie Columnist* [London: Andre Deutsch, 2003], 146, 177); "A Confidence Trickster in Conversation with Wilfred De'Ath," *The Listener*, 14 September 1967, 325–6.

38. Wilfred De'Ath, "Coming to the End of America," *The Listener*, 24 February 1972 (242–4); "The Disneyland of the Dead," *The Listener*, 2 March 1972 (276–8); "Black Rage and White Guilt," *The Listener*, 9 March 1972 (308–10); "Getting It Together," *The Listener*, 13 September 1973 (337–41); Robin Page, "Pop Philosophy and Fact," *Daily Telegraph*, 18 September 1971.

39. Carstairs, a distinguished academic, was also a familiar voice on BBC radio. In 1962 he delivered the annual Reith Lectures, broadcast on the Home Service, with the catch-all topic "This Island Now," focusing on the delinquency, psychopathy, and social and personal disorganization of the various subcultures of "our society" (*The Listener*, 15 November, 791–4; 22 November, 853–6; 29 November, 891–4; 6 December, 947–50; 13 December, 1001–3; and 20 December, 1035–8, 1962).

40. G. M. Carstairs, "Living and Partly Living," *The Listener*, 13 December 1962, 1001–3.

41. G. M. Carstairs, "Youth: The New Constituency," *The Listener*, 14 September 1972 (329–30), "Liberating Acts," 21 September 1972 (362–3), and "Characteristics of the Counter-Culture," 28 September 1972 (398–400).

CHAPTER 5

1. Interviewed by Charlotte Philby in "1967: The Summer of Love," *The Independent*, 5 May 2007.

2. Laing, interviewed by Chris Stephens, "Art and the 60s: This Was Tomorrow," Tate

Online (www.tate.org.uk/); Robert Hewison, *Culture and Consensus: England, Art and Politics since 1940* (London: Methuen, 1995), 134.

3. Rowbotham, *Promise of a Dream*, 124.

4. Quoted by Hewison, *Too Much*, 124; see also 43, 133–4.

5. Ibid., 108; Miles, *In the Sixties*, 87–90; Ali, *Street Fighting Years*, 211 (Hockney, as well as Ron Kitaj and Jim Dine, donated paintings to support Ali's radical magazine *Black Dwarf*); Mellor, *The Sixties Art Scene in London*, 129; John A. Walker, *Left Shift: Radical Art in 1970s Britain* (London: I. B. Tauris, 2002), 53; Tim Hilton on the Hayward Gallery show, *The Listener*, 28 October 1971, 599–600.

6. Edward Lucie-Smith, *Art in the Seventies* (Oxford: Phaidon, 1980). See also Walker, *Left Shift*, 30, 139.

7. Tony Ray-Jones, *A Day Off: An English Journey* (London: Thames and Hudson, 1974), 7. See also Russell Roberts, *Tony Ray-Jones* (London: Chris Boot, for the National Museum of Photography, Film and Television, 2004).

8. Liz Jobey, "The English Seen," the *Guardian*, 2 October 2004; Ray-Jones, *A Day Off*, 10, 12; Veronica Horwell, obituary for Claude Virgin, the *Guardian*, 13 December 2006.

9. Quoted in Jobey, "The English Seen."

10. Iain Sinclair, *The Kodak Mantra Diaries: October 1966 to June 1971* (London: Albion Village Press, 1971); Marwick, *The Sixties*, 455, 481–2, 496.

11. Roger Hutchinson, *High Sixties: The Summers of Riot and Love* (Edinburgh: Mainstream Publishing, 1992), 76.

12. Frith and Horne, *Art into Pop*, 52–3, 55; Frith, *Sound Effects*, 99.

13. Richard Neville, *Play Power* (London: Jonathan Cape, 1970); Mike [*sic*] Farren and Edward Barker, *Watch Out Kids* (London: Open Gate Books, 1972); *The Daily Telegraph*, 21 February 1967; *The Daily Mail*, 26 September 1969.

14. Harford Thomas (ed.), *The Permissive Society: The Guardian Enquiry* (London: Panther Books, 1969), 9–13.

15. Ibid., 35–9, 44–5, 61.

16. Cited by Aubrey Walter in *Come Together: The Years of Gay Liberation (1970–73)* (London: Gay Men's Press, 1980), 10–11.

17. Roger Perry, *The Writing on the Wall: The Graffiti of London* (London: ElmTree Books, 1976); Richard Mills, *Young Outsiders: A Study of Alternative Communities* (London: Routledge, 1973), 1.

18. Timothy Miler, *The 60s Communes: Hippies and Beyond* (Syracuse, NY: Syracuse University Press, 1999), 26–9.

19. Clem Gorman, *Making Communes* (London: Whole Earth Tools, 1971), 45.

20. Craig Sams, "About Macrobiotics, the Craig Sams Story," *The Microbiotic Guide* (June, 2004).

21. Farren, *Give the Anarchist a Cigarette*, 80, 127–8; Boyd, *White Bicycles*, 143–4; Miles, *In the Sixties*, 98–100.

22. Thomas, *The Permissive Society*, 12; Richard Hoggart, "Proper Ferdinands?" in ibid., 74–9; Hutchinson, *The High Sixties*, 87–8, 192; Farren, *Give the Anarchist a Cigarette*, prologue; Marowitz, *Burnt Bridges*, 2–3, 5; Frith and Horne, *Art into Pop*, 97.

23. Marowitz, *Burnt Bridges*, 2–3, 5; Alistair Cooke, "Where the Difference Begins," in Thomas (ed.), *The Permissive Society*, 60; Thomas (ed.), *The Permissive Society*, frontispiece.

24. De'Ath, "Notes from the English Underground—The Last of Four Reconnaissances,"

10 September 1970, 346–7; Farren, *Give the Anarchist a Cigarette*, 242; Nelson, *The British Counter-Culture*, 45.

25. Nelson, *The British Counter-Culture*, 45, 51; Frith and Horne, *Art into Pop*, 52–3; Hewison, *Culture and Consensus*, 143; Frith, *Sound Effects*, 171–2; D. A. N. Jones, *The Listener*, 24 February 1972, 229–31.

26. Jones, *The Listener*, 24 February 1972, 229.

27. Nuttall, *Bomb Culture*, 181; Adam, in Green, *Days in the Life*, 117; Neville, *Play Power*, 18.

28. Nuttall, *Bomb Culture*, 191; Farren, *Give the Anarchist a Cigarette*, 87, 119–20, 125; Neville, *Hippie Hippie Shake*, 88; Catherine Itzin, *Stages in the Revolution: Political Theatre in Britain since 1968* (London: Eyre Methuen, 1980), 9–10; Haynes, *Thanks for Coming!*, 139–41, 154–61; Fountain, *Underground*, 25.

29. Fountain, *Underground*, 33; Nelson, *The British Counter-Culture*, 153 n.; Neville, *Hippie Hippie Shake*, 88, 224; Neville, in Green, *Days in the Life*, 147, 149; Miles, *In the Sixties*, 163.

30. De'Ath, "Notes from the English Underground—The Last of Four Reconnaissances," 346–7.

31. Robins, in Green, *Days in the Life*, 210–11. See also Nelson, *The British Counter Culture*, 72; Miles, *In the Sixties*, 141, 166, 195; Miles, in Green, *Days in the Life*, 125; Fountain, *Underground*, 25, 30, 33.

32. Nelson, *The British Counter Culture*, 55, 60, 62, 66, 82, 120; David Huxley, *The Growth and Development of British Underground and Alternative Comics 1966–1986* (Ph.D. dissertation, Loughborough University, 1990), 17; Fountain, *Underground*, 193.

33. Frith, *Sound Effects*, 168–9; Nuttall, *Bomb Culture*, 207–8; Nelson, *The British Counter Culture*, 46; Fountain, *Underground*, 43; Tony Palmer, *The Trials of OZ* (Manchester: Blond and Briggs, 1971), 257.

34. Huxley, *Growth and Development*, 17–18.

35. Mellor, "Tomorrow Starts Now," 24; Farren, *Give the Anarchist a Cigarette*, 124. The Bronx-born cartoonist Bud Handelsman, who moved to London in 1963, published his polished work in *Punch*, the *New Yorker*, and *Playboy* as well (see Susan Jeffreys, obituary for Handelsman, the *Guardian*, 21 July 2007).

36. Farren, *Give the Anarchist a Cigarette*, 296–7, 303–6; Roger Sabin, *Comics, Comix & Graphic Novels: A History of Comic Art* (London: Phaidon Press, 1996), 110, 117; Huxley, *Growth and Development*, 38 n.; Fountain, *Underground*, 143.

37. Rowbotham, *Promise of a Dream*, 210; Ali, *Street Fighting Years*, 233–4; Sabin, *Comics, Comix & Graphic Novels*, 104–5, 111.

38. Roger Lewis, "Captain America Meets the Bash Street Kids: The Comic Form in Britain and the United States," in C. W. E. Bigsby (ed.), *Super-Culture: American Popular culture and Europe* (London: Paul Elek, 1975), 187; Huxley, *Growth and Development*, 131–2.

39. Sabin, *Comics, Comix & Graphic Novels*, 118; Gilliam's interview with Ken Plume for IGN Entertainment (http://filmforce.ign.com/articles/); Graham Chapman et al., *The Pythons: Autobiography* (London: Orion, 2003), 193–5; Palin, *Diaries*, 5, 13; Ian Christie (ed.), *Gilliam on Gilliam* (London and New York: Faber and Faber, 1999), 22, 27, 37–8, 50, 52.

40. Widgery quoted in Fountain, *Underground*, 214.

41. Fountain, *Underground*, 33, 43–4, 214.

42. Ibid., 73, 78.

43. James L. Spates, "Countercultural and Dominant Cultural Values," *American Sociological Review* 41, 5 (October, 1976), 881.

CHAPTER 6

1.　Boyd, *White Bicycles*, 143, 159; Farren, *Give the Anarchist a Cigarette*, 80, 126; Haynes, *Thanks for Coming!*, 144; Andrew Wilson, obituary for Mark Boyle (the *Guardian*, 10 June 2005).

2.　Miles, *In the Sixties*, 151; Nuttall, *Bomb Culture*, 210; Farren, *Give the Anarchist a Cigarette*, 119–20, 123, 126–8, 150–1.

3.　Miles, *In the Sixties*, 130.

4.　Frith, *Sound Effects*, 167; see also *Melody Maker*, 1960–70.

5.　Williams, "Television in Britain," 10–11; Updike, "An American in London," 97–9; Robert Chapman, *Selling the Sixties: The Pirates and Pop Music Radio* (London: Routledge, 1992), 129–30.

6.　*Ready, Steady, Go!* was the invention of Elkan Allan, who toured the United States after the war, then returned to a career at BBC Radio and ITV; he retired to L. A. (Neil Lyndon, obituary for Allan, the *Guardian*, 30 June 2006); Scala, *Diary of a Teddy Boy*, 67, 91; John Cronnolley, "Interview with Ronan O'Rahilly," at www.offshoreechos.com/; Peter Moore, "Radio Caroline," at www.caroline.uk-plc.net/; I am also indebted to Richard Rudin's paper read at the University of Warwick in 2004, "Tracks across the Pond: How UK Radio Has Been Influenced by . . . US Radio Stations."

7.　Nuttall, *Bomb Culture*, 129; Tania Branigan, "Radio's Pirate Queen Still Rules at 40," the *Guardian*, 27 March 2004; Briggs, *The History of Broadcasting in the United Kingdom*, Vol. V, 514–5 and 621–2 n.

8.　Lodge, *Changing Places*, 71–2.

9.　Among the other DJs who had some experience in North America were Rick Dane (Phoenix), Simon Dee (Ottawa), Peter Drummond (Kansas), Duncan Johnson (Canada), Tom Lodge (Canada), John Peel (Dallas, Oklahoma City, and California), "Emperor" Rosko (son of a Hollywood producer), and Tommy Vance (L. A.). See Keith Skues, *Radio Onderland: The Story of Radio One* (Lavenham: The Landmark Press, 1968), passim; Bill Williamson, *The DeeJay Book* (London: Purnell, 1969), 51, 100.

10.　Frith, *Sound Effects*, 124; Cohn, *Pop from the Beginning*, 70.

11.　A concept deployed by Frith (*Sound Effects*, 7–8), with regard to record playing.

12.　John Peel and Sheila Ravenscroft, *Margrave of the Marshes* (London: Bantam Press, 2005), 47, 140; Michael Heatley, *John Peel: A Life in Music* (London: Michael O'Mara Books, 2004), 21–2, 30; see also Martin ("Paradise Now," 120–47) for unpublished Peel interviews with Jonathan Green. For Cooke's accent, see below, p. 272.

13.　Peel and Ravenscroft, *Margrave of the Marshes*, 233–4, 401; Farren, *Give the Anarchist a Cigarette*, 90; Chapman, *Selling the Sixties*, 125.

14.　Loris Valvona remembering the 1968 Isle of Wight Festival [http://tinpan.fortunecity.com/ebony/546/ iow1968]; Gould, *Can't Buy Me Love*, 249, 281.

15.　Gould, *Can't Buy Me Love*, 561; Michael Clarke, *The Politics of Pop Festivals* (London: Junction Books, 1982), 11, 15, 30–1; Birt, *The Harder Path*, 109; *The Times*, 11 December 1973; Farren, *Give the Anarchist a Cigarette*, 283–9.

16.　Martin, *A Sociology of Contemporary Cultural Change*, 158. The first Isle of Wight concert, featuring San Francisco's Jefferson Airplane, attracted 8,000 to 10,000; Woburn drew 40,000 to hear Jimi Hendrix; the second Isle of Wight event with Bob Dylan, the Band, and the Who, perhaps 100,000; the third, with the Doors, Jimi Hendrix, Joni Mitchell, Sly and the Family Stone, Miles Davis, and Tiny Tim as well as the Who, drew perhaps 600,000.

17. The Beatles may not have played Woodstock, but Havens led with his own versions of "With a Little Help from My Friends," "Strawberry Fields Forever," and "Hey Jude."

18. Clarke, *The Politics of Pop Festivals*, 23; Nelson, *The British Counter-Culture*, 98.

19. Jefferson Airplane, at the first Isle of Wight Festival and Parliament Hill in London in 1968, the Roundhouse in 1969, and Bath in 1970; the Doors at the Roundhouse in 1969; the Grateful Dead, at the Hollywood Festival near Newcastle-under-Lyme in 1970, and in 1972 and 1974; Frank Zappa's The Mothers of Invention, at the Royal Festival Hall in 1968 and the Bath Festival in 1970; Creedence Clearwater Revival, Santana, and Crosby Stills and Nash at the Albert Hall in 1970, among others.

20. Steve Marriott, of the band Humble Pie (*New Music Express*, 24 July 1971).

21. Michael Schumacher, *Crossroads: The Life and Music of Eric Clapton* (London: Warner Books, 1998), 33; Eric Clapton, with Christopher Simon Sykes, *Eric Clapton: The Autobiography* (London: Century, 2007), 19, 23.

22. Schumacher, *Crossroads*, 82–3; Clapton, *Eric Clapton*, 83–5; Ian MacDonald, *The People's Music* (London: Pimlico, 2003), 64–5.

23. Noel Redding and Carol Appleby, *Are You Experienced? The Inside Story of the Jimi Hendrix Experience* (New York: Da Capo Press, 1996), passim; obituaries for Redding in the *Guardian*, 15 May 2003, and *The Independent*, 14 May 2003.

24. Scala, *Diary of a Teddy Boy*, 106; Paul Gilroy, *The Black Atlantic: Modernity and Double Consciousness* (London: Verso, 1993), 94–5; Boyd, *White Bicycles*, 118; Mellor, "Tomorrow Starts Now," 24.

25. Cohn, *Pop from the Beginning*, 133–4; Mick Farren, "The Titanic Sails at Dawn," *New Music Express*, 19 June 1976, 5–6.

26. Farren and Barker, *Watch Out Kids*.

27. Haynes, *Thanks for Coming*, 142–3.

28. Miles, *In the Sixties*, 135–7; Marowitz, *Burnt Bridges*, 151–2; Haynes, *Thanks for Coming*, 142–3; Fountain, *Underground*, 27.

29. Marowitz, *Burnt Bridges*, 151–2; Boyd, *White Bicycles*, 159.

30. *Cinim* 1 (n.d., 1967?), 8; Stephen Dwoskin, *Film Is . . . The International Free Cinema* (London: Peter Owen, 1975), 63.

31. Gordon Page, Abbott Meader, Bill Wees, and Sandy Daly, among others (see *Cinim* 3 [1969?], 31; Dwoskin, *Film Is . . .*, 64–5). Mekas's statement was published in an open letter in *Cinim* 1.

32. Dwoskin, *Film Is . . .*, 63, 65–76; Margaret Dickinson, *Rogue Reels: Oppositional Film in Britain, 1945–90* (London: BFI, 1999), 42; *Cinim* 3, 31; P. Adams Sitney, *Visionary Film: The American Avant-Garde* (New York: Oxford University Press, 1974), vii.

33. For one version of what is still a sensitive issue, see Stephen Dwoskin, "A Little Bit of Then," *Filmwaves* 3 (February, 1998).

34. David Curtis, "English Avant-Garde Film: An Early Chronology," in David Curtis and Deke Dusinbere (eds.), *A Perspective on English Avant-Garde Film* (London: Arts Council of Great Britain, 1978), 9–10; Michael Mazière, "Interview with Malcolm Le Grice" (www.studycollection. co.uk/maziere/interviews/LeGrice).

35. John Russell Taylor, *The Times*, 29 January 1971; Mazière, "Interview with Malcolm Le Grice."

36. *The Times*, 26 June–1 July 1967.

37. Hewison, *Too Much*, 161; Dickinson, *Rogue Reels*, 39, 227–30.

38. John Clay, *R. D. Laing: A Divided Self* (London: Hodder and Stoughton, 1996), 84;

Sinclair, *The Kodak Mantra Diaries*, Book I, 15 July, 17ff.; David Cooper (ed.), *The Dialectics of Liberation* (Harmondsworth: Penguin, 1968), 7–11; *The Times*, 19 July 1967; Hewison, *Too Much*, 135–8; Farren, *Give the Anarchist a Cigarette*, 102–3; Ali, *Street Fighting Years*, 128.

39. Among Laing's American clinical sources were Nathan Ackerman in New York, the Gregory Bateson group in Palo Alto (Bateson himself was formerly British), Ross Speck in Philadelphia, and Russell Lee of the Palo Alto Medical Clinic. Adrian Laing, *R. D. Laing: A Life* (Phoenix Mill, Gloucestershire: Sutton Publishing, 2006), xxix–xxx, 65, 100–3, 108, 119; Clay, *R. D. Laing*, 102, 131; Sinclair, *The Kodak Mantra Diaries*, Book II (25 July).

40. R. D. Laing, *The Divided Self* (London: Tavistock, 1969 [1st pub. 1960)]); Cooper, *Dialectics of Liberation*, 9–10; Rowbotham, *Promise of a Dream*, 145.

41. Cooper, *Dialectics of Liberation*, 9; Sheila Rowbotham, *Woman's Consciousness, Man's World* (Harmondsworth: Penguin, 1973), 22–34.

PART III

1. Regina Nadelson, *Who Is Angela Davis? The Biography of a Revolutionary* (New York: Peter H. Wyden, 1972), 120; Angela Davis, *An Autobiography* (New York: Random House, 1974), 149–50.

2. Kobena Mercer, *Welcome to the Jungle: New Positions in Black Cultural Studies* (New York and London: Routledge, 1994), 289; Rossinow, *The Politics of Authenticity*, 19; Trevor Pateman (ed.), *Counter Course: A Handbook for Course Criticism* (Harmondsworth: Penguin Books, 1972), 9; Beverley Bryan, Stella Dadzie, and Suzanne Scaafe, *The Heart of the Race: Black Women's Lives in Britain* (London: Virago Press, 1985), 143; Elizabeth Wilson, *Mirror Writing: An Autobiography* (London: Virago, 1982), 1, 153–4.

3. William L. Van Deburg, *New Day in Babylon: The Black Power Movement and American Culture, 1965–1975* (Chicago: University of Chicago Press, 1992), 9, 58. There has been a wealth of recent scholarship reassessing the American Black Power movement in its historical and local contexts. See, for instance, Peniel Joseph, *Waiting 'til the Midnight Hour: A Narrative History of Black Power in America* (New York: Holt and Co., 2006); and Peniel Joseph (ed.), *The Black Power Movement: Rethinking the Civil Rights-Black Power Era* (New York and London: Routledge, 2006).

CHAPTER 7

1. David Reynolds, *Rich Relations: The American Occupation of Britain, 1942–1945* (New York: Random House, 1995), 228 and passim.

2. Edward Pilkington, *Beyond the Mother Country: West Indians and the Notting Hill White Riots* (London: Taurus, 1988), 70–1, 127, 133; Madge Dresser, *Black and White on the Buses: The 1963 Colour Bar Dispute in Bristol* (Bristol: Bristol Broadsides, 1986), 27 and 64 n.

3. Mark Bonham Carter, "Measures against Discrimination: The North American Scene," *Race* 9, 1 (July, 1967), 1, 1 n.; Chris Mullard, *Race, Power and Resistance* (London: Routledge, 1985), 94–5, 98.

4. "British and U.S. Responses to Minority Demands—A Comparison," *Race Today* 3, 4 (April, 1971), 115, 117, 125; Mullard, *Race, Power and Resistance*, 105.

5. Alan Brien, "New York Nightmare," *Sunday Times*, 6 April 1969. See also Henry Brandon, "The Disunited States," *Sunday Times*, 10 March 1968. Both are cited in Stuart Hall et al., *Policing the Crisis: Mugging, the State, and Law and Order* (London: Macmillan, 1978), 18–19.

6. Ionie Benjamin, *The Black Press in Britain* (Stoke-on-Trent: Trentham Books, 1995), 101; Ken Pryce, *Endless Pressure: A Study of West Indian Lifestyles in Bristol* (Harmondsworth: Penguin, 1979), 68–9).

7. Douglas M. Haynes, "The Whiteness of *Civilization*: The Transatlantic Crisis of White Supremacy and British Television Programming in the United States in the 1970s," in Antoinette Burton (ed.), *After the Imperial Turn: Thinking With and Through the Nation* (Durham, N.C.: Duke University Press, 2003), 324–5; Bryan, Dadzie, and Scaafe, *The Heart of the Race*, 223–4; Pryce, *Endless Pressure*, 163 n., 167 (based on research completed in 1974).

8. Roger Hewitt, *White Talk Black Talk: Inter-Racial Friendships and Communication among Adolescents* (London: Cambridge University Press, 1986), 73, 115–6.

9. Ferdinand Dennis, *Behind the Front Lines: Journey into Afro-Britain* (London: Gollancz, 1988), 112.

10. Hall et al., *Policing the Crisis*, introduction (see also Centre for Contemporary Cultural Studies, *The Empire Strikes Back: Race and Racism in Seventies Britain* [London: Hutchinson, 1982]); Dick Hebdige, "Reggae, Rastas & Rudies," and Iain Chambers, "A Strategy for Living," in Stuart Hall and Tony Jefferson (eds.), *Resistance through Rituals: Youth Sub-Cultures in Post-War Britain* (London: Hutchinson, 1976), 135–66.

11. Mercer, *Welcome to the Jungle*, 29, 289 [these essays were written 1985–92].

12. Gilroy, *The Black Atlantic*, 15, 35, 87, 109.

13. Claire E. Alexander, *The Art of Being Black: The Creation of Black British Youth Identities* (Oxford: Clarendon Press, 1996), iv, 15, 31; see also Claire E. Alexander, *The Asian Gang: Ethnicity, Identity, Masculinity* (Berg, 2000).

14. King's statue, designed by Tim Crawley, is one of ten "modern martyrs" unveiled there by the Archbishop of Canterbury in 1998.

15. For example in April 1972, when BBC2 aired a major documentary "King—Montgomery to Memphis," or on "Man Alive" in May of 1974.

16. Dilop Hiro, *Black British, White British* (London: Eyre and Spottiswoode, 1971), 53; Dresser, *Black and White on the Buses*, 15–17, 32; Mike Phillips, *London Crossings: A Biography of Black Britain* (London: Continuum, 2001), 32, 45, 50–1.

17. Phillips, *London Crossings*, 24, 56, 143, 193.

18. Pilkington, *Beyond the Mother Country*, 105. See also Marika Sherwood, *Claudia Jones: A Life in Exile* (London: Lawrence and Wishart, 1999), 150–62; Bill Schwarz, "Crossing the Seas," in Schwarz (ed.), *West Indian Intellectuals in Britain* (Manchester: Manchester University Press, 2003), 1–30; Benjamin, *The Black Press in Britain*, 42; Jessica Watson-Crosby, "Claudia Jones—Dynamic Champion of Equality," *People's Weekly World Newspaper*, 28 February 2004 [www.pww.org].

19. Sherwood, *Claudia Jones*, 100–1, 104; Pearl Connor-Mogotsi, "Our Olympian Struggle," March, 1995 [www.chronicleworld.org]; John D'Emilio, *Lost Prophet: The Life and Times of Bayard Rustin* (New York: Free Press, 2003), 364, 395–6; David J. Garrow, *Bearing the Cross: Martin Luther King Jr. and the Southern Christian Leadership Conference* (London: Jonathan Cape, 1988), 351–2, 364.

20. Schwarz, "Crossing the Seas," 17; Connor-Mogotsi, "Our Olympian Struggle."

21. Sherwood, *Claudia Jones*, 144–5; Martin Luther King, Jr. (ed. by Clayborne Carson), *Autobiography of Martin Luther King, Jr.* (London: Abacus, 2000), 258.

22. Benjamin W. Heineman, *The Politics of the Powerless: A Study of the Campaign Against Racial Discrimination* (Oxford: Oxford University Press, 1972), 16–19.

23. On Malcolm X, see *The Autobiography of Malcolm X* (Harmondsworth: Penguin, 1966); Peter Goldman, *The Death and Life of Malcolm X* (London: Victor Gollancz, 1974); Perry Bruce, *Malcolm: The Life of a Man Who Changed Black America* (Barrytown, NY: Station Hill, 1991); Jan Carew, *Ghosts in Our Blood: With Malcolm X in Africa, England and the Caribbean* (Chicago: Lawrence Hill, 1994); and Taylor Branch, *Pillar of Fire: America in the King Years 1963–65* (New York: Simon and Schuster, 1998). Baldwin's much-acclaimed *The Fire Next Time* (1963) made him a somewhat lionized figure; he had a house in Chelsea; Dennis, *Behind the Front Lines*, 126.

24. Branch, *Pillar of Fire*, 539; Ali, *Street Fighting Years*, 40–2; Carew, *Ghosts in Our Blood*, viii; Hiro, *Black British, White British*, 55–6.

25. Schwarz, "Crossing the Seas," 17; Branch, *Pillar of Fire*, 585–6; *The Times*, 12 February 1965.

26. *The Times*, 13 February 1965; Goldman, *The Death and Life of Malcolm X*, 255; Arun Kundnani, "Remembering Malcolm's Visit to Swethwick," *Independent Race and Refugee News Network*, 10 February 2005 [www.irr.org.uk].

27. Schwartz, "Crossing the Seas," 17; Hiro, *Black British, White British*, 64.

28. Garrow, *Bearing the Cross*, 482–5, 568; Branch, *Pillar of Fire*, 394, 436, 612. Martin Luther King, Jr., *Where Do We Go from Here, Chaos or Community?* (New York: Harper and Row, 1967); Stokely Carmichael and Charles V. Hamilton, *Black Power: The Politics of Liberation in America* (New York: Random House, 1967) [the 1968 London editions were published by Hodder and Stoughten and Cape, respectively].

29. Adrian Laing, *R. D. Laing*, 131; Clay, *R. D. Laing*, 144; Roszak, *The Making of a Counter Culture*, 64–5; Sinclair, *The Kodak Mantra Diaries*, 22 July; Stokely Carmichael, with Ekueme Michael Thelwell, *Ready for Revolution* (New York: Scribner, 2003), 572–3, also *Stokely Speaks: Black Power Back to Pan-Africanism* (New York: Random House, 1971), 100.

30. Stephen Jessel, *The Times*, 19 July 1967; Carmichael and Thelwell, *Ready for Revolution*, 572–3; Anne Walmsley, *The Caribbean Artists Movement 1966–1972: A Literary & Cultural History* (London and Port of Spain: New Beacon Books, 1992), 93.

31. Davis, *An Autobiography*, 150; Carmichael and Thelwell, *Ready for Revolution*, 578; David Cooper, "Beyond Words," in Cooper, *The Dialectics of Liberation*, 195; Sinclair, *The Kodak Mantra Diaries*, 22 July (italics in original).

32. Schwarz, "Crossing the Seas," 17; Hiro, *Black British, White British*, 65; *The Times*, 25 July 1967, blamed Carmichael's incendiary rhetoric for the riots in Detroit and other American cities.

33. Broadcast in March and again in June of 1968 (*The Listener*, 21 March 1968, supplement).

34. *The Times*, 5 August 1967, 3 March and 6 May 1970; Neville, *Play Power*, 20; Mercer, *Welcome to the Jungle*, 303; For Brown, see Walmsley, *The Caribbean Artists Movement*, 136; for Seale, Hillyeard, and Cleaver, see, for instance, *The Listener*, 3 July 1969, 11–2. The two versions of *Soul on Ice* were published in London by Jonathan Cape in 1969; a cheap Panther paperback version appeared in 1971.

35. Not until issue 56 (July–August, 1970) did the Black Panthers appear in the *New Left Review* and then only obliquely in a reprinted resolution passed by the SDS national council in Austin, Texas.

36. *The Times*, 14 and 16 March 1968.

37. Miles, *In the Sixties*, 143; and Neville, *Play Power*, 140; Mike Phillips, obituary for

Tulloch, the *Guardian*, 13 December 2006; Ray Gosling, *Personal Copy: A Memoir of the Sixties* (London: Faber and Faber, 1980), 84–5.

38. Charles Shaar Murray, *Crosstown Traffic: Jimi Hendrix and Post-war Pop* (London: Faber and Faber, 1989), 100–1; Hall, "The New Revolutionaries," 198–200; Tulloch in Green, *Days in the Life*, 10–11.

39. Editorial, *Race Today*, 6, 1 (January, 1974). See also Mullard, *Race, Power and Resistance*, 24; Paul Gilroy, *"There Ain't No Black in the Union Jack": The Cultural Politics of Race and Nation* (Chicago: University of Chicago Press, 1991), 119; Ali, *Street Fighting Years*, 128, 235.

40. Carmichael and Hamilton, *Black Power*, 12, 51.

41. See Van Deburg, *New Day in Babylon*, 181–2; Walmsley, *The Caribbean Artists Movement 1966–1972*, 28, 119, 164, 236, 244, 249; Louis James, "The Caribbean Artists Movement," in Schwarz, *West Indian Intellectuals in Britain*, 209–27.

42. Michael Abdul Malik, *From Michael De Freitas to Michael X* (London: Andre Deutsch, 1968), 143 (while De Freitas no doubt exaggerated his closeness to Malcolm X, there is no reason to doubt the veracity of this passage); Carew, *Ghosts in Our Blood*, viii.

43. In 1972 there was an hour-long documentary on the BBC, and the *Sunday Times* ran a special feature written by Naipaul; Phillips, *London Crossings*, 56; Sam Selvon, *Moses Ascending* (Salisbury: Cox and Wyman, 1984 [1st pub. by Heinemann, 1975]), 10–2, 81–3, 98; Derek Humphry and David Tindall, *False Messiah: The Story of Michael X* (London: Hart-David, MacGibbon, 1977); and James Sharp, *The Life and Death of Michael X* (Waterford: Uni Books, 1981) rely excessively on hearsay; Gordon K. Lewis, "Protest Among the Immigrants," *Political Quarterly* 40, 4 (October–December, 1969), 432. We now have a fuller and more balanced life in John L. Williams, *Michael X: A Life in Black and White* (London: Century, 2008), which, informed by rambling and diffuse recollections, nevertheless confirms the need for a substantial revision.

44. Humphry and Tindall, *False Messiah*, 53; Boyd, *White Bicycles*, 134–5, 160; Malik, *From Michael De Freitas to Michael X*, 116–7, 126–7, 166, 171; Haynes, *Thanks for Coming!*, 154–9; Fountain, *Underground*, 53; Nuttall, *Bomb Culture*, 208–9. Williams claims that De Freitas attended but did not read at the Albert Hall event, but see Horovitz (*Children of Albion*, 315).

45. *The Times*, 25 July 1967; Humphry and Tindall, *False Messiah*, 65; A. Sivanandan, *From Resistance to Rebellion: Asian and Afro-Caribbean Struggles in Britain* (London: Race and Class, 1986), 122, 125; Carmichael and Thelwell, *Ready for Revolution*, 574.

46. Harry Goulbourne, *Caribbean Transnational Experience* (London: Pluto Press, 2002), 90, 115–6.

47. Mullard, *Race, Power and Resistance*, 110. See also Raj Pal, "An Interview with Sivanandan," *Birmingham Black History*, 18 August 2006 [www.birnighamblackhistory.com].

48. Goulbourne, *Caribbean Transnational Experience*, 90.

49. Obi Egbuna, *Destroy This Temple: The Voice of Black Power in Britain* (London: MacGibbon and Kee, 1971), 18. Also *The Times*, 14 March 1968.

50. Egbuna, *Destroy This Temple*, 69, 90, 139.

51. Sivanandan, *From Resistance to Rebellion*, 126. See also Anne-Marie Angelo, "The Black Panthers in London, 1967–1972: A Diasporic Struggle Navigates the Black Atlantic," *Radical History Review* 103 (Winter, 2009), 17–35, for a recent treatment of the British Panthers.

52. Michael Banton, *Racial Minorities* (London: Fontana, 1972), 37; Heineman, *The Politics of the Powerless*, xi, 181, 193.

53. Chris Mullard, *Black Britain* (London: George Allen and Unwin, 1973), 141, 149; Sivanandan, *From Resistance to Rebellion*, 136–7; *The Times*, 3 March and 27 April 1970; Angelo, "Black Panthers in London," 17.

54. A name suggested, perhaps, by the Grassroots Conference in Detroit in 1963 at which Malcolm X laid out his ideas about Black nationalism.

55. Sivanandan, *From Resistance to Rebellion*, 126–35; Goulbourne, *Caribbean Transnational Experience*, 79–88; Julia Sudbury, *"Other Kinds of Dreams": Black Women's Organisations and the Politics of Transformation* (London and New York: Routledge, 1998), 6–7; *Black Liberator* 1, 1 (September/October, 1971) and 2, 4 (January 1975/August 1976).

56. Malik, *From Michael De Freitas to Michael X*, 171, 204; Carmichael and Thelwell, *Ready for Revolution*, 576.

57. Michael Grade, *It Seemed Like a Good Idea at the Time* (London: Macmillan, 1999), 99; Benjamin, *Black Press in Britain*, 5; Haley addressed the Radio 3 audience with his "Search for an Ancestor" in January, 1974 (*The Listener*, 10 January 1974); Gilroy, *"There Ain't No Black in the Union Jack*, 165; Les Back, *New Ethnicities and Urban Culture: Racisms and Multiculture in Young Lives* (London: UCL Press, 1996), 213–4.

58. The *Daily Mirror*, 17 August, and the *Sunday Express*, 2 May 1972, cited in Hall et al., *Policing the Crisis*, 3, 25. See also, for instance, Wilfred De'Ath's article in *The Listener*, 9 March 1972, 308–10, on "Black Rage and White Guilt," which focuses on crime in Washington, DC.

59. Andrew Salkey, *Come Home, Malcolm Heartland* (London: Hutchinson, 1976), 15.

60. Tariq Modood, "'Difference,' Cultural Racism and Anti-Racism," in Pnina Werbner and Tariq Modood (eds.), *Debating Cultural Hybridity: Multi-Cultural Identities and the Politics of Anti-Racism* (London: Zed Books, 1997), 154–72; Desai quoted from *Race Today* by Prathiba Parmar, "Gender, Race and Class: Asian Women in Resistance," in Centre for Contemporary Cultural Studies, *The Empire Strikes Back*, 268.

61. Mullard, *Black Britain*, 148–9.

62. Banton, *Racial Minorities*, 181.

63. Dennis, *Behind the Front Lines*, 176.

64. Peter Stevens, *British and American English* (London: Collier-Macmillan, 1972), 39, 61–2.

65. Van Deburg, *New Day in Babylon*, 15.

66. Owen Bowcott, "MoD Kept Race Details on Troops," the *Guardian*, 4 January 2005.

CHAPTER 8

1. Halasz, *A Swinger's Guide to London*, 34; Michele Roberts, *Paper Houses: A Memoir of the '70s and Beyond* (London: Virago, 2007), 15.

2. Elaine Aston, "Finding a Voice: Feminism and Theatre in the 1970s," in Bart Moore-Gilbert (ed.), *The Arts in the 1970s: Cultural Closure?* (London: Routledge, 1994), 99, 104.

3. Juliet Mitchell, *Woman's Estate* (New York: Pantheon Books, 1971), 50; Hadley in Michelene Wandor, *Once a Feminist: Stories of a Generation* (London: Virago Press, 1990), 72, 74–5.

4. Rosie Boycott, *A Nice Girl Like Me: A Story of the Seventies* (London: Pan Books, 1985), 38; Lynne Segal, *Making Trouble: Life and Politics* (London: Serpent's Tail, 2007), 57;

for the influence of Laing among British feminists, see Thomas Mathew, *Psychological Subjects: Identity, Culture, and Health in Twentieth-Century Britain* (Oxford: Oxford University Press, 2006), 278–83.

5. Mitchell, *Woman's Estate*, 49–50; *The Listener*, 1 April 1971, 419; Williams, *Siege of Trencher's Farm*, 40–1, 199.

6. Sheila Rowbotham, "The Beginnings of Women's Liberation in Britain," in Wandor, *Once a Feminist*, 23, 27; on feminist expectations, see D. L. Le Mahieu, "Imagined Contemporaries: Cinematic and Televised Dramas about Edwardians in Great Britain and the United States, 1967–1985," *Historical Journal of Film, Radio and Television* 10 (1990), 249; Joyce Gelb, "Feminism in Britain: Politics without Power?" in Drude Dahlerup (ed.), *The New Women's Movement: Feminism and Political Power in Europe and the USA* (London: Sage, 1986), 103–21.

7. See, for example, David Bouchier, *Idealism and Revolution: New Ideologies of Liberation in Britain and the United States* (London: Edward Arnold, 1978), 106, 133, and *The Feminist Challenge: The Movement for Women's Liberation in Britain and the USA* (London: Macmillan Press, 1983), 3, 117.

8. Rowbotham, *Promise of a Dream*, xii–xiii.

9. Rowbotham, *Woman's Consciousness, Man's World*, 39; *Promise of a Dream*, 241.

10. bell hooks, *Ain't I a Woman* (1981), cited in Nira Yuval-Davis, "Intersectionality and Feminist Politics," *European Journal of Women's Studies* 13, 3 (2006), 193; Ranu Samantrai, *AlterNatives: Black Feminism in the Postimperial Nation* (Palo Alto, CA: Stanford University Press, 2002), 5; for examples of women in the American Black Power movement, see Cynthia Griggs Fleming, "Black Women and Black Power: The Case of Ruby Doris Smith Robinson and the Student Nonviolent Coordinating Committee," in B. Collier-Thomas and V. P. Franklin (eds.), *Sisters in the Struggle* (New York: NYU Press, 2001), 197–213; Stephen Ward, "The Third World Women's Alliance" and Ronda Y. Williams, "Black Women, Urban Politics, and Engendering Black Power," in Joseph, *The Black Power Movement*.

11. Anne Coote and Beatrix Campbell, *Sweet Freedom: The Struggle for Women's Liberation* (Oxford: Blackwell, 1987), 5; Angela Neustatter, *Hyenas in Petticoats: A Look at Twenty Years of Feminism* (London: Harrap, 1989), 13; Cleaver, *Soul on Ice*, 15, 17; Tracye A. Matthews, "'No One Ever Asks What a Man's Role in the Revolution Is': Gender Politics and Leadership in the Black Panther Party, 1966–71," in Collier-Thomas and Franklin, *Sisters in the Struggle*, 233, 237, 247; Williams, "Black Women," 89.

12. Bryan, Dadzie, and Scaafe, *The Heart of the Race*, 1, 145. See also Sudbury, *"Other Kinds of Dreams,"* 100; Ward, "The Third World Woman's Alliance," 120, 144; Kimberly Springer, "Black Feminists Respond to Black Power Masculinism," in Joseph, *The Black Power Movement*, 106, 115; McLeod, *Postcolonial London*, 93–4, 125.

13. Yasmin Alibhai-Brown, *Who Do We Think We Are: Imagining the New Britain* (London: Allen Lane, Penguin Press, 2000), 12, 201.

14. Terri Quaye, "Taking It on the Road," in Sarah Maitland (ed.), *Very Heaven: Looking Back at the 1960s* (London: Virago Press, 1988), 29, 33; interviewed by Marion Fudger, *Spare Rib* 26 (August, 1974), in Marsha Rowe (ed.), *Spare Rib Reader* (Harmondsworth: Penguin, 1982), 291–95.

15. Irma Kurtz, "The Third World War: Women against Men: Make War Not Love," *Sunday Times*, 14 September 1969 (magazine, 18–33); Bouchier, *The Feminist Challenge*, 98–9.

16. Eva Figes, *Patriarchal Attitudes: Women in Society* (London: Virago, 1978), 7;

Rowbotham, *Woman's Consciousness, Man's World*, 5; Mitchell, *Woman's Estate*, 52, 81; Battersby interview in *Spare Rib* 69 (April, 1978), reprinted in Rowe, *Spare Rib Reader*, 568.

17. Juliet Mitchell, "Women: The Longest Revolution," *New Left Review* 40 (November/ December, 1966), 11–37.

18. See Jeffery S. Miller, *Something Completely Different: British Television and American Culture* (Minneapolis: University of Minnesota Press, 2000), 51.

19. Jackie Stacey, *Star Gazing: Hollywood Cinema and Female Spectatorship* (London: Routledge, 1994), 118, 235, 238; Beverly Skegg, *Formations of Class and Gender: Becoming Respectable* (London: Sage, 1997), 110–1; Elizabeth Wilson, *Only Halfway to Paradise: Women in Postwar Britain 1945–1968* (London: Tavistock, 1980), 11, 184; Margaret Walters, "Images of Janis Joplin," *Spare Rib* 37 (July, 1975); Ali, *Street Fighting Years*, 231.

20. Bouchier, *The Feminist Challenge*, 56, 68–9; Neustatter, *Hyenas in Petticoats*, 8, 13; Rowbotham, *Promise of a Dream*, 251.

21. Janet Hadley, Val Charlton, and Sue O'Sullivan, in Wandor, *Once a Feminist*, 75, 160–70, 214–26; Segal, *Making Trouble*, 62–3, 144; Rowbotham, *Promise of a Dream*, 222.

22. Lois Graessle, in Wandor, *Once a Feminist*, 126–37.

23. Ibid., 55–70, 113–20, 138–44. Anna Koedt's essay, Susan Lydon's "The Politics of Orgasm," and Mary McCarthy's *The Tyranny of the Orgasm* were widely discussed in British feminist groups.

24. Kate Millett, *Sexual Politics* (London: Virago Press, 1977), frontispiece (italics added).

25. Shulamith Firestone, *The Dialectic of Sex: The Case for Feminist Revolution* (London: Paladin, 1972), 11–2, 105 (italics in original), 192–5.

26. Ibid., 20, 23, 38n; Mitchell in Wandor, *Once a Feminist*, 109; *Woman's Estate*, 50.

27. *Woman's Estate* opened with a quotation from Blake and acknowledged communes that "accorded women the newly glorious role of emotionality and creativity" (title pg, 13 n.–14 n., 38, 43); Elizabeth Gould Davis, *The First Sex* (New York: G. P. Putnam's Sons, 1971), 339; Firestone, *The Dialectic of Sex*, 224.

28. Juliet Mitchell, *Psychoanalysis and Feminism* (London: Allen Lane, 1974), xix, 398; Germaine Greer, "Lib and Lit," in *The Listener*, 25 March 1971, 355–6; Gillian Hannah, cited by Aston, "Finding a Voice," 112; Robin Morgan (ed.), *Sisterhood Is Powerful: An Anthology of Writings from the Women's Liberation Movement* (New York: Random House, 1970).

29. Eric Morley, *The "Miss World" Story* (Maidstone: Angley Book Company, 1967), 25, 138, 140–1; [Anon.], *Why Miss World?* ([London], n.p., n.d. [1971]), 1.

30. Morley, *The "Miss World" Story*, 111–2, 201–2; Charles Thompson, *Bob Hope: The Road from Eltham* (London: Thames Methuen, 1981), 155–7; *Why Miss World?*, 9.

31. Morley went to the States to learn from the bigger, more lavish American event (Morley, *The "Miss World" Story*, 58–63, 65–6); for a recent collection of essays on the Miss America pageant, see Elwood Watson and Darcy Martin (ed.), *"There She Is, Miss America!" The Politics of Sex, Beauty and Race in America's Most Famous Pageant* (New York: Palgrave Macmillan, 2004); Morley, *The "Miss World" Story*, 48.

32. Thompson, *Bob Hope*, 158–9; "The Beauty . . . and the Bovver Girl," the *Daily Mail*, 21 November 1970; the *Daily Express*, 21 November 1970. The success of Miss Grenada, a black woman, suggests the judges were struggling to legitimize the event in the face of radical criticism. Hope should have been prepared for trouble. In October, in the States, feminists "took over" a show of his at the NBC studios.

33. "Miss World Uproar," *Daily Express*, 21 November 1970; *Why Miss World?*, 11–4.

34. Michelene Wandor, *Carry on Understudies: Theatre and Sexual Politics* (London: Routledge, 1986), 37; Segal, *Making Trouble*, 67; *Why Miss World?*, 13; Aston, "Finding a Voice," 103.

35. Roberts, *Paper Houses*, 34, 37, 38, 54. Pell also became her "sexual mentor." See also Marwick, *The Sixties*, 356; Hewison, *Too Much*, 151, 219–20; Fountain, *Underground*, 152–3.

36. Eve Setch, "The Face of Metropolitan Feminism: The London Women's Liberation Workshop, 1969–79," *Twentieth Century British History* 13, 2 (2002), 173–4.

37. Ibid., 179–80, 186.

38. Ibid., 173, 184; Fountain, *Underground*, 104, 158.

39. Bouchier, *The Feminist Challenge*, 59; Brian Braithwaite, *Women's Magazines: The First 300 Years* (London: Peter Owen, 1995), 81, 96–103. The most popular radical feminist title, *Spare Rib*, never printed more than 20,000 copies of any run.

40. Kurtz, "The Third World War [Part Two]," *Sunday Times*, 21 September 1969 (magazine, 20–30). See also Lucie-Smith, *Art in the Seventies*, 9, and chs. 6, pt. 2, and 7, pt. 1; Lisa Tickner, "The Body Politic: Female Sexuality and Women Artists since 1970," *Art History* 1, 2 (1978), 236–51; Hewison, *Culture and Consensus*, 181; Dickinson, *Rogue Reels*, 38, 41, 230–1.

41. Kurtz, "The Third World War [Part Two]," 20–30.

42. Wilson, *Only Halfway to Paradise*, 196; Mitchell, "Women: The Longest Revolution," 15–17, 34–5, and passim. Italics in the original.

43. Rowbotham, *Promise of a Dream*, 230. Fountain has observed that at the time few noticed Mitchell's article and "its impact had been slight" (Fountain, *Underground*, 70).

44. Mitchell, "Women: The Longest Revolution," 19, 24, 33.

45. Mitchell, *Psychoanalysis and Feminism*, xviii–xix, 300, 319–27, 340–55, 398. Her attempt to retrieve Freud annoyed many on the left (see, for example, Jeffrey Weeks, "Discourse, Desire and Sexual Deviance: Some Problems in a History of Homosexuality," in Kenneth Plummer [ed.], *The Making of the Modern Homosexual* [London: Hutchinson, 1981], 95).

46. Mitchell, *Psychoanalysis and Feminism*, 300.

47. Ibid.

48. Figes, *Patriarchal Attitudes* (introduction to 1978 edition), 7–8.

49. Ibid., 8.

CHAPTER 9

1. Millet, *Sexual Politics*, 336–7; *Come Together* 3 (January, 1971).

2. Marwick offers only seven pages on gay liberation in a text of over 800 (*The Sixties*, 725–32).

3. Samuel, "Born-again Socialism," in Archer, *Out of Apathy*, 52; Dennis Altman, *Homosexual Oppression and Liberation* (London: Angus and Robertson, 1972), 207; David Fernbach, in Lisa Power, *No Bath but Plenty of Bubbles: An Oral History of the Gay Liberation Front, 1970–73* (London: Cassell, 1995), 80–1; Pateman, *Counter-Course*, passim; for Evans, see Toby Marotta, *The Politics of Homosexuality* (Boston: Houghton Mifflin Company, 1981), 147; and David Carter, *Stonewall: The Riots That Sparked the Gay Revolution* (New York: St. Martin's Press, 2004); for Young, see Bob Cant and Nigel Young, "New Politics, Old Struggles," in Gay Left Collective (ed.), *Homosexuality: Power and Politics* (London: Allison and Bushby, 1980), 116–7.

4. Carl Whittman, *A Gay Manifesto* (London: Agitprop, n.d. [1972]), 5 [orig. pub. San Francisco, 1971]; Wilson, *Mirror Writing*, 117, 118; Altman, *Homosexual Oppression and Liberation*, 154–5; Neville, *Play Power*, 224.

5. Power, *No Bath*, 17; Walter, *Come Together*, 10–11.

6. Ray Gosling, "Homosexuals Now," *New Society* 29 (August, 1968), 293–4; Fountain, *Underground*, 79, 91.

7. Abner Cohen, *Masquerade Politics: Explorations in the Structure of Urban Cultural Movements* (Oxford: Berg, 1993), 19; Power, *No Bath*, 102; for the North Beach beat and gay scene, see John D'Emilio, *Sexual Politics, Sexual Communities* (Chicago: University of Chicago Press, 1983), 179–82.

8. Marotta, *The Politics of Homosexuality*, 328. See Andy Medhurst, "Perverse Pop: From Joe Meek to David Bowie," in Mellor and Gervereau, *The Sixties*, 96–103, for the relationship of the Beatles and Stones to what he calls the "queer sensibilities" of the period.

9. Simon Watney, "The Ideology of the GLF," in Gay Left Collective (ed.), *Homosexuality*, 65.

10. Donn Teal, *The Gay Militants* (New York: Stein and Day, 1971), 297–301; Power, *No Bath*, 90–1, 97; see also Rebecca Jennings, "'The Most Uninhibited Party They'd Ever Been To': The Postwar Encounter between Psychiatry and the British Lesbian, 1945–1971," *Journal of British Studies* 47, 4 (October, 2008).

11. Power, *No Bath*, 3; Cleaver, *Soul on Ice*, 98–9, 102–3, 110, 184; Marotta, *The Politics of Homosexuality*, 128–9.

12. Samantrai, *AlterNatives*, 126; Duchess Harris, "From the Kennedy Commission to the Combahee Collective: Black Feminist Organizing, 1960–1980," in Collier-Thomas and Franklin, *Sisters in the Struggle*, 280–305; Springer, "Black Feminists Respond to Black Power Masculinism," in Joseph, *The Black Power Movement*, 112; Gail Carmen and Pratibha Shaila, "Becoming Visible: Black Lesbian Discussions," *Feminist Review* 17 (Autumn, 1984), 70.

13. Mitchell, "Women: The Longest Revolution," 36, and *Woman's Estate*, 36, 70–1.

14. Simon Watney, "The Ideology of GLF," in Gay Left Collective, *Homosexuality*, 69; Power, *No Bath*, 117 (the GLF Women's Group was, she says, rebuffed by "the Maoists of women's liberation").

15. Frank Mort, "Essentialism Revisited?: Identity Politics and Late Twentieth-Century Discourses of Homosexuality," in Jeffrey Weeks (ed.), *The Lesser Evil and the Greater Good: The Theory and Politics of Social Diversity* (London: Rivers Oram Press, 1994), 202–3.

16. Chris Waters, "Disorders of the Mind, Disorders of the Body Social: Peter Wildeblood and the Making of the Modern Homosexual," in Conekin et al., *Moments of Modernity*, 137; Ken Plummer, "Awareness of Homosexuality," in Roy Bailey and Jock Young, *Contemporary Social Problems in Britain* (Farnborough: Saxon House, 1973), 103, 120–1 n.

17. Altman, *Homosexual Oppression and Liberation*, xiv.

18. In Green, *Days in the Life*, 321.

19. Marotta, *The Politics of Homosexuality*, 136, 144, 307; Arthur Bell, *Dancing the Gay Lib Blues: A Year in the Homosexual Liberation Movement* (New York: Simon and Schuster, 1971), 15.

20. Marotta, *The Politics of Homosexuality*, 89–90, 135; Don Milligan, *The Politics of Homosexuality* (London: Pluto Press, 1973), 3–4.

21. Frank Mort, "Sexuality: Regulation and Contestation," in Gay Left Collective (ed.), *Homosexuality*, 38; see also other essays in Gay Left Collective, *Homosexuality*.

22. Altman, *Homosexual Oppression and Liberation*, xiv and 22–3.

23. Whittman, *A Gay Manifesto*, 2; *Gay News* 1 (June, 1972).

24. The BBC broadcast a documentary on male homosexuality in 1964 and one on lesbianism in 1965 (Bryan Magee, *One in Twenty: A Study of Homosexuality in Men and Women* [London: Secker and Warburg, 1966], 7).

25. Waters, "Disorders of the Mind, Disorders of the Body Social," 147; Frank Mort, "Mapping Sexual London: The Wolfenden Committee on Homosexual Offences and Prostitution 1954–57," *New Formations* 37 (Spring, 1999), 103, 108–10.

26. Marotta, *The Politics of Homosexuality*, 9. Characterization of the homophile organizations as liberal, respectable, and irrelevant has been challenged, not entirely convincingly, by Martin Meeker ("Behind the Mask of Respectability," *Journal of the History of Sexuality* 10, 1 [January, 2001], 78–116).

27. Sandbrook, *Never Had It So Good*, 563; Jennings, "The Most Uninhibited Party," 899–900. See also Magee, *One in Twenty*, 182–5.

28. David Eisenbach, *Gay Power: An American Revolution* (New York: Caroll and Graf, 2006), 24, 27; D'Emilio, *Sexual Politics, Sexual Communities*, 112, 145 n., 149.

29. Eisenbach, *Gay Power*, 75.

30. Diana Trilling, "British Television," *The Listener*, 22 February 1968, 225–8, instancing a BBC TV program on homosexuality, "Consenting Adults," without the forced moral lessons and white-coated doctors and psychologists that could be expected from an American network.

31. Mary McIntosh, "The Homosexual Role," in Plummer (ed.), *The Making of the Modern Homosexual*, 30–49 [including interview]. See also Jeffrey Weeks, "The 'Homosexual Role' after 30 Years: An Appreciation of the Work of Mary McIntosh," *Sexualities* 1, 2 (May, 1998), 135; the Mary McIntosh Papers (L.S.E. Archives), MCINTOSH/6/6; also Mary McIntosh, in Power, *No Bath*, 179–80.

32. Jeffrey Weeks, "Discourse, Desire and Sexual Deviance," in Plummer, *The Making of the Modern Homosexual*, 94; K. Plummer, *Sexual Stigma: An Interactionist Account* (London: Routlegde, 1975), vii, 11–2, 19–20; Carole Warren, *Identity and Community in the Gay World* (New York: John Wiley, 1974).

33. Jeffrey Weeks, *Coming Out: Homosexual Politics in Britain from the Nineteenth Century to the Present* (London: Quartet Books, 1990 [rev. ed.]), 189; Patrick Higgins, *Heterosexual Dictatorship: Male Homosexuality in Postwar Britain* (London: Fourth Estate, 1996), 47; Mort, "Mapping Sexual London," 103; Davies, *The New London Spy*, 221; Halasz, *A Swinger's Guide to London*, 188–9.

34. Jules Cassidy and Angela Stewart-Park, *We're Here: Conversations with Lesbian Women* (London: Quartet Books, 1977), 59–63; Philip Derbyshire, "Personal Politics—Ten Years On," *Gay Left* 8 (Summer, 1979), 6–7, and "Right to Rebel," in Gay Left Collective, *Homosexuality*, 20.

35. For the Stonewall story, see Carter, *Stonewall*; also Marotta, *The Politics of Homosexuality*, ch. 4; Teal, *The Gay Militants*; Bell, *Dancing the Gay Lib Blues*; Eisenbach, *Gay Power*, 80–98; and John D'Emilio, "Stonewall: Myth and Meaning," in John D'Emilio, *The World Turned: Essays on Gay History, Politics, and Culture* (Durham, N.C.: Duke University Press, 2002), 146–53.

36. Walter, *Come Together*, 10.

37. Ibid., 10–1; listings of university gay societies can be found in *Gay News*; also MCINTOSH/7/3: Trevor Locke's "Report on Gay Student Societies."

38. *Come Together* 3 (GLF meetings were sometimes held at the Arts Lab in Camden, where a film "Come Together" was made about the movement); D'Emilio, *Sexual Politics, Sexual Communities*, 181; Wilson, *Mirror Writing*, 39, 123; Walter, *Come Together*, 23; John Phillips, "Coming to Terms," in Bob Cant and Susan Hemmings (eds.), *Radical Records: Thirty Years of Lesbian and Gay History 1957–1987* (London: Routledge, 1988), 60, 63–4; Weeks, *Coming Out*, 191.

39. Don Milligan, "Homosexuality: Sexual Needs and Social Problems," in Roy Bailey and Mike Brake (eds.), *Radical Social Work* (London: Edward Arnold, 1975), 96–111.

40. Power, *No Bath*, 23–4, 28, 33; Marotta, *The Politics of Homosexuality*, 116–7; Eisenbach, *Gay Power*, 135; Walter, *Come Together*, 12–4.

41. Bartlett, *Who Was That Man? A Present for Mr Oscar Wilde* (1988), in Mark W. Turner, *Backward Glances: Cruising the Queer Streets of New York and London* (London: Reaktion Books, 2003), 48.

42. Eisenbach, *Gay Power*, 103; Power, *No Bath*, 210–3; *Come Together*, Spring, 1973 (reprinted in Walter, *Come Together*); Weeks, *Coming Out*, 202–4.

43. Ken Plummer, "Gay Cultures/Straight Bodies," in Morley and Robins, *British Cultural Studies*, 393; Jeffrey Weeks, Michael James, and Cloud Downey in Power, *No Bath*, 261–3; *Gay News* 1 (June, 1972).

44. *The Times*, 28 August 1971; in January Robert Chesshyre told *Observer* readers: "The idea for the [Gay Liberation] Front [has] crossed the Atlantic"; the *Evening Standard* noticed GLF protests in February, and in April the *Guardian* ran an article and photos (newspaper clippings in MCINTOSH/7/1); Keith Birch, "A Community of Interests," in Cant and Hemmings, *Radical Records*, 51–4.

45. According to Power, *No Bath*, 25; Walter (*Come Together*, 10–1) however claimed that the *Sennet* action occurred in September, taken by a small group just prior to the formal organization of GLF.

46. David Fernbach, in Power, *No Bath*, 28; Marotta, *The Politics of Homosexuality*, 102–3, 105; Eisenbach, *Gay Power*, 132; *Come Together*, 1–15 (1971–73).

47. Notes from the GLF coordinating committee, 19 July [1971?] in MCINTOSH/7/1; Lumsden, in Power, *No Bath*, 208–9; *Gay News* 25 (June, 1973), and passim 1972–73.

48. *Gay News*, issues 25 and 27 (1973); Gilian Hanscombe and Andrew Lumsden, *Title Fight: The Battle for Gay News* (London: Brilliance Books, 1983), 8, 9, 25, 30, 53, 56–8, 62; Peter Burton, *Parallel Lives* (London: GMP Publishers, 1985), 116.

49. Power, *No Bath*, 3; Birch, "Politics of Autonomy," 86; Walter, *Come Together*, 7–8. For a contemporary account of the origins of lesbian feminism, see Sidney Abbott and Barbara Love, *Sappho Was a Right-on Woman: A Liberated View of Lesbianism* (New York: Stein and Day, 1977).

50. "Women-Identified Women [*sic*]," in *Gay News* 18 (1973); also Radicalesbians, "The Woman-Identified Woman," from Documents from the Women's Liberation Movement, On-line Archival Collection, Special Collections Library, Duke University [http://scriptorium.lib.duke.edu/wlm/womid/].

51. Karla Jay, quoted in Eisenbach, *Gay Power*, 138. See also Marotta, *The Politics of Homosexuality*, 231, 242, 244–5.

52. Coote and Campbell, *Sweet Freedom*, 242; Julie Bindel, obit. for Susan Lydon, the *Guardian*, 26 July 2005.

53. Fountain, *Underground*, 172–3; Boycott, *A Nice Girl Like Me*, 75.

54. For the Gateways zap, see a leaflet, "We Are Lesbians—And We Are Beautiful," in the McIntosh Papers (MCINTOSH/7/1); also *Come Together*, issue no. 2; Power, *No Bath*, 233, 242.

55. "Gay Liberation—What Happens Next?" in MCINTOSH7/1; Wilson, *Mirror Writing*, 127–8.

56. Aston, "Finding a Voice," 109; Weeks in Power, *No Bath*, 241; for Dusty Springfield's lesbianism, see Penny Valentine and Vicki Wickham, *Dancing With Demons: The Authorized Biography of Dusty Springfield* (London: Hodder and Stoughton, 2000).

57. Veronica Pickles and Judy Barrington on coming out, in Cassidy and Stewart-Park, *We're Here*, 22, 33, 36; Janet Dixon, "Separatism: A Look Back in Anger," in Cant and Hemmings, *Radical Records*, 77–80; see also Coote and Campbell, *Sweet Freedom*, 242–3.

58. Marotta, *The Politics of Homosexuality*, 309; Weeks, *Coming Out*, 199–200; Walter, *Come Together*, 35.

59. *Gay News* 2 (July?, 1972), 6.

60. Phillips, "Coming to Terms," 66; Rebecca Jennings, *Tomboys and Bachelor Girls: A Lesbian History of Post-War Britain 1945–71* (Manchester: Manchester University Press, 2007), 100–2; Wilson, *Mirror Writing*, 74–5; Elizabeth Wilson, "Memoirs of an Anti-heroine," in Cant and Hemmings, *Radical Records*, 44.

61. Marotta, *The Politics of Homosexuality*, 112.

62. Milligan, *The Politics of Homosexuality*, 9–11; Walter, *Come Together*, 13–4, 22–3.

63. Eisenbach, *Gay Power*, 46–7; Walter, *Come Together*, 146–7; "The Pubs—Some Suggestions from a Small Group [4 October 1971]," MCINTOSH/7/1.

64. Kenneth Leech, *Keep the Faith Baby: A Close-Up of London's Drop-Outs* (London: SPCK, 1973),58–9; Thorneycroft, Weeks, and Sreeves, "The Liberation of Affection," 162; Frank Mort, "Archaeologies of City Life: Commercial Culture, Masculinity, and Spatial Relations in 1980s London," *Environment and Planning D: Society and Space* 13 (1995), 582, and "Essentialism Revisited," 206; Marotta, *The Politics of Homosexuality*, 193–4; Burton, *Parallel Lives*, 46–8.

65. Gregg Blachford, "Male Dominance and the Gay World," in Plummer, *The Making of the Modern Homosexual*, 192–3; Dennis Altman, "What Changed in the Seventies?" in Gay Left Collective, *Homosexuality*, 52; on saunas, see *Gay News* 112 and 114 (February and March, 1977).

66. Frank Mort, *Cultures of Consumption: Masculinities and Social Space in Late Twentieth-Century Britain* (London: Routledge, 1996), 175–6, 179; Jon Savage, *England's Dreaming: Anarchy, Sex Pistols, Punk Rock and Beyond* (New York: St. Martin's Press, 1992), 139, 147, 183, 186; Ian Taylor and Dave Wall, "Beyond the Skinheads: Comments on the Emergence and Significance of the Glamrock Cult," in Geoff Mungham and Geoff Pearson (eds.), *Working Class Youth Culture* (London: Routledge, 1976), 105–23.

67. *Gay Left* 10 (1980), 24–6; *Gay News* 166 (3–16 May 1979); Charles Silverstein and Edmund White, *The Joy of Gay Sex* (New York: Simon and Schuster, 1978); Turner, *Backward Glances*, 56.

68. Dereka Rushbrook, "Cities, Queer Space, and the Cosmopolitan Tourist," *Gay and Lesbian Quarterly* 8, 1–2 (2002), 183–206; Warren, *Identity and Community*, 19. Current

scholarly interest in "transnational" history continues to influence work on cross-cultural sex and sexualities. See, for instance, Margot Canaday, "Thinking Sex in the Transnational Turn: An Introduction"; and Joanne Meyerowitz, "Transnational Sex and U.S. History," *American Historical Review* 114, 5 (December, 2009), 1250–7 and 1273–86.

69. George Melly, *Philip Core* (London: Gay Men's Press, 1985), 5–13; Lucie-Smith, *Art in the Seventies*, 84–6.

70. Altman, "What Changed in the Seventies?" in Gay Left Collective, *Homosexuality*, 57–9, 61; Bill Osgerby, *Youth in Britain since 1945* (Oxford: Blackwell, 1998), 78–9.

71. Rushbrook, "Cities, Queer Space, and the Cosmopolitan Tourist," 193; also Burton, *Parallel Lives*, 49–50; Weeks, *Coming Out*, 232. For a recent consideration of the problem of dialectical approaches to "modernism," see Michael Saler's perceptive historiographic review "Modernity and Enchantment," *American Historical Review* 111, 3 (June, 2006).

PART IV

1. See Raphael Samuel, *Theatres of Memory*, Vol. 1: *Past and Present in Contemporary Culture* (London: Verso, 1994).

CHAPTER 10

1. Reyner Banham, *The Listener*, 22 August (235–6), 29 August (267–8), 5 September (296–7), and 12 September (330–1), 1968; Reyner Banham, *Los Angeles: The Architecture of Four Ecologies* (London: Allen Lane [Penguin Press], 1971), 16, 36, 244; Cameron is quoted in *Los Angeles*, 16.

2. Harold Jackson, obituary for Charles Wheeler, the *Guardian*, 4 July 2008.

3. Beside *The Neophiliacs* (1969), there are Booker's journalistic pieces republished in Christopher Booker, *The Seventies: Portrait of a Decade* (Harmondsworth: Penguin, 1980); for Johnson, see *Enemies of Society* (London: Weidenfeld and Nicholson, 1977).

4. John Selwyn Gummer, *The Permissive Society: Fact or Fantasy?* (London: Cassell, 1971), 21–2, 25, 89, 95, 118, 120–1, 128–9, 131, and passim.

5. Newman, *The Listener*, 7 March 1974, 295–8. His book on reducing crime through urban planning (*Defensible Space*) was published in the United States in 1972, and in Britain in 1973.

6. On the literature of dystopia, see Stephen Brooke and Louise Cameron, "Anarchy in the U.K.? Ideas of the City and the *Fin de Siecle* in Contemporary English Film and Literature," *Albion* 28, 4 (Winter, 1996), 635–56; and Bart Moore-Gilbert, "Apocalypse Now? The Novel in the 1970s," in Moore-Gilbert, *The Arts in the 1970s*, 152–75.

7. James Allen [Richard Allen], *Skinhead* (London: New English Library, 1970), 5–6, 13, 58–9, 113; Richard Allen, *Suedehead* (London: New English Library, 1971),10–1, 43, 45–6, 52, 83–5.

8. Allen, *Suedehead*, 5; Howard Brenton, *Revenge* (London: Methuen and Co, 1970), 5, 35–6, 49–51.

9. Martin Amis, *Dead Babies* (London: Vintage, 1991 [1st pub. 1975]), frontispiece, 20, 43–4, 67–8, 153, 179–80.

10. Hewison, *Too Much*, 256.

11. Anthony Powell, *Hearing Secret Harmonies* (London: Arrow, 2005 [1st pub. 1975, the twelfth and last novel in the series *A Dance to the Music of Time*]), 42–3, 46, 87, 109–11.

12. Margaret Drabble, *The Ice Age* (Harmondsworth: Penguin, 1978 [1st pub. 1977], 26, 49–50, 51, 66, 166, 175, 215, 252–3; Muriel Spark, *The Takeover: A Parable of the Pagan*

Seventies (Harmondsworth: Penguin, 1978 [1st pub. 1976]); John Osborne, *Watch It Come Down* (Playbook, July, 1974), Act I, Scene 1, page 10.

13. Paul Theroux, *The Family Arsenal* (Boston: Houghton Mifflin, 1976), 15, 37, 47, and passim; Ian McEwan, *The Cement Garden* (London: Vintage Books, 1994 [1st pub. 1978]), 28 and passim.

14. Caryl Churchill, *"Not Not Not Not Not Enough Oxygen" and Other Plays* (London: Longman, 1993), 24–42; Eve Figes, "Cuckolds," in *The Listener*, 15 July 1971, 91–2; Ballard in a 1975 interview in Goddard and Pringle, *J. G. Ballard*, 9, 11; also J. G. Ballard, *Miracles of Life: Shanghai to Shepperton, an Autobiography* (London: Fourth Estate, 2008), 4, 129, 165, 187.

15. Ballard, *Miracles of Life*, 235, 239–40; Bruce Weber, obituary for Ballard, the *New York Times*, 21 April 2009; Diane Johnson, "J. G. Ballard: The Glow of the Prophet," *New York Review of Books* 55, 15 (9 October 2008); J. G. Ballard, *High-Rise* (London: Granada, 1977 [1st pub. 1975]), 35–6, 52–3, 69, 133; David Pringle's review and a 1975 interview, in Goddard and Pringle, *J. G. Ballard*, 9, 11–2, 76.

16. Booker in an essay on an early-fifties housing estate in East London designed by Denys Lasdun, republished in *The Seventies* in a section titled "The Death of Progress," 300.

17. See, esp., the influential work of the German social psychologist then at the L.S.E., Hilde Himmelweit (H. T. Himmelweit, A. N. Oppenheim, and P. Vince, *Television and the Child: An Empirical Study of the Effect of Television on the Young* [London : Oxford University Press, 1958]).

18. Whitehouse, *Cleaning-Up TV*, 15.

19. William A. Belson, *Television Violence and the Adolescent Boy* (Farnborough: Saxon House, 1978), vii–viii, x, 4–5, 15, 20 (Belson often published in U.S. journals).

20. James D. Halloran, "Studying the Effects of Television," and "The Social Effects of Television," in J. D. Halloran (ed.), *The Effects of Television* (London: Panther Books, 1970), 9–23, 25–68; Alasdair Milne, *DG: The Memoirs of a British Broadcaster* (London: Coronet, 1989), 86–7; Alasdair Clayre, "Violence on Television," *The Listener*, 28 December 1972, 885–7.

21. Clive James, in *The Listener*, 17 February 1972, 203–4.

22. Alistair McGown, "Lindstrom, Freda (1893–1981)," BFI Screenonline (*www.screenonline.org.uk*); Briggs, *The History of Broadcasting in the United Kingdom*, Vol. V, 175–82; Jeremy Potter, *Independent Television in Britain*, Vol. 4: *Companies and Programmes 1968–80* (London: Macmillan, 1990), 256–7.

23. Richard M. Polsky, *Getting to Sesame Street: Origins of the Children's Television Workshop* (New York: Prager, 1974); Potter, *Independent Television*, Vol. 3, 76, and Vol. 4, 256–7. Within a year or two, Thames was producing *Rainbow* (from 1972); by the next year there was ATV's *Inigo Pipkin*, Yorkshire's *Mr Trimble*, and Granada's *Hickory House*.

24. Raymond Williams, in *The Listener*, 18 November 1971, 700; Brenda Maddox, in *The Listener*, 9 March 1972, 295–7; see also Maddox, *Beyond Babel*, 135–6. A negative review also appeared in *Race Today* echoing some American blacks who saw the program as an attack on black culture (Bradley Martin, "Sesame Street: Pattern for Pre-School TV?" *Race Today* 3, 12 [December, 1971], 399–400).

25. Des Wilson (ed.), *The Environmental Crisis: A Handbook for All Friends of the Earth* (London and Exeter, NH: Heinemann, 1984), foreword, x–xi.

26. Wilson, in ibid., 1; John Sheail, *An Environmental History of Twentieth-Century Britain* (London: Palgrave, 2002), 138–40.

27. Royston Landau, *New Directions in British Architecture* (London: Studio Vista, 1968); Lyall, *The State of British Architecture*; Ian Jeffrey, "The Cult of Creativity: Young British Architects," in Mellor and Gervereau, *The Sixties*, 124–31; Tickner, *Hornsey 1968*, 37, 89.

28. "Sons of the Earth," *New Statesman*, 3 August 1973, 146–8.

29. Veldman, *Fantasy, the Bomb, and the Greening of Britain*, 205–24; see also S. K. Brookes, A. G. Jordan, R. H. Kimber, and J. J. Richardson, "The Growth of the Environment as a Political Issue in Britain," *British Journal of Political Science* 6 (April, 1976), 245–55; and Walt Patterson, "A Decade of Friendship: The First Ten Years," in Wilson, *The Environmental Crisis*, 140–54.

30. For Shurcliff, see Adam Bernstein's obituary in the *Washington Post*, 28 June 2006; for Wiggs, see Jerry Ravitz's obituary in *The Independent*, 8 August 2001.

31. S. K. Brookes et al., "The Growth of the Environment as a Political Issue in Britain," 253–4; Richard Wiggs, *Concorde: The Case Against Supersonic Transport* (London: Ballantine, 1971), 27–42, 176.

32. Larkin, from "Going, Going," in *High Windows* (London: Faber and Faber, 1974 [orig. pub. in *How Do You Want to Live?* (H.M.S.O., 1972)]), 21–2; Tony Aldous, *Goodbye Britain?* (London: Sidgwick and Jackson, 1975), 6–7, ch. 7; *The Illustrated London Times Book of London's Villages* (London: Seeker and Warburg, 1980), xii, xviii–xix.

CHAPTER 11

1. John, Duke of Bedford [John Robert Russell, 13th Duke], in collaboration with George Mikes, *How to Run a Stately Home* (London: Deutsch, 1971), 65.

2. Christopher Dunn, "The Book Drain," *The Listener*, 275–6; Alisdair Fairley, "National Heritage," *The Listener*, 26 November 1970, 763.

3. Eric Paice, "Costumed," *New Statesman*, 27 July 1979, 139–40; Antoinette Burton, "When Was Britain? Nostalgia for the Nation at the End of the 'American Century,'" *Journal of Modern History* 75, 2 (June, 2003), 360; Dominic Strinati, "The Taste of America: Americanization and Popular Culture in Britain," in Strinati and Wagg, *Come on Down?*, 57–8 (the same point was made by Christopher Hitchens in *Blood, Class and Nostalgia: Anglo-American Ironies* [London: Vintage, 1991], 5).

4. Booker, *The Seventies*, 272.

5. Parts of this section were previously published as "Nostalgia, Heritage and the London Antiques Trade: Selling the Past in Thatcher's Britain," in George K. Behlmer and Fred M. Leventhal (eds.), *Singular Continuities: Tradition, Nostalgia, and Indentity in Modern British Culture* (Palo Alto, Cal.: Stanford University Press, 2000).

6. Cited in Sandbrook, *White Heat*, 400–1.

7. Samuel, *Theatres of Memory*, Vol. 1, 92. See also, esp., Patrick Wright, *On Living in an Old Country: The National Past in Contemporary Britain* (London: Verso, 1985). On American buyers of antiques, see Hart M. Nelson, "The Democratization of the Antique," *Sociological Review* 18, n.s. [1970], 407–19.

8. Bedford, *How to Run a Stately Home*, 42, 54; E. R. Chamberlin, *Preserving the Past* (London: J. M. Dent and Sons, 1979), 57; David Lowenthal and Marcus Binney (eds.), *Our Past Before Us: Why Do We Save It?* (London: Temple Smith, 1981), 9; *The Times*, 24 September 1983, 8.

9. *Art and Antiques*, 8 September 1979.

10. John A. Walker, *Arts TV: A History of Arts Television in Britain* (London: John Libby, 1993), 63.

11. Haseler, *The English Tribe*, 57; Samuel, "Mrs. Thatcher's Return to Victorian Values," 18, 24; Fred Davis, *Yearning for Yesterday: A Sociology of Nostalgia* (New York: The Free Press, 1979), 11–5.

12. *Antiques Collector*, February, 1976, i.

13. Deborah Stratton, *Collecting in the '70s* (London: Sunday Telegraph, 1975), 5, 7, 117; Chamberlin, *Preserving the Past*, 70; *The Antique Collector*, March, 1979, 1.

14. Ronald Pearsall and Graham Webb, *Inside the Antique Trade* (Shaldon, Devon: Keith Reid, Ltd., 1974), 53.

15. Jeremy Cooper, *The Complete Guide to London's Antique Street Markets* (London: Thames and Hudson, 1974), 23, 81; Ronald Pearsall, *The Joy of Antiques* (Newton Abbot: David and Charles, 1988), 9; Anna Shaw, "Off to Market," *The Antique Collector*, July, 1982, 8, 12.

16. *The Antique Collector*, February, 1982, 96; men predominated among the younger, high-flyers, though older women were common stall-holders in some sections, like bijouterie.

17. Ibid., April, 1982 and July, 1983.

18. Pearsall and Webb, *Inside the Antique Trade*, 113; Chamberlin, *Preserving the Past*, 72; *Sunday Times*, 29 November 1981, 18.

19. *Art and Antiques*, 14 July 1979, 3; Pearsall and Webb, *Inside the Antique Trade*, 115; Cooper, *The Complete Guide*, 80.

20. Clarke, *Alistair Cooke*, 349.

21. Ibid., 1.

22. Ibid., 123–7, 145.

23. Ibid., 278, 299, 389–90; Leonard Miall, obituary for Alistair Cooke in *The Independent* (31 March 2004); also Nick Clarke in the *Guardian* (31 March 2004).

24. Cooke to A. P. Wadsworth, 24 November 1952; Hetherington to Cooke, 5 February 1970 (in Helen Pidd, "Letters to [and from] America," the *Guardian*, 31 March 2004).

25. William Hardcastle, "Mid-Atlantic," *The Listener*, 13 November 1969, 679–80; also "Television's Co-Productions," *The Listener*, 3 December 1970, 756–7.

26. Michael Pilsworth, "Buddy, Can You Spare a Dime," *Sight and Sound* 49, 1 (Winter, 1979–80), 51; Le Mahieu, "Imagined Contemporaries," 244; *The Listener*, 20 January 1972, 92–3; 27 January 1972, 114; 3 February 1972, 150; 1 February 1973, 151. Though (adjusted for inflation) production costs for television rose by nearly 70 percent from 1965 to 1985, the license fee for color TV did not increase (Le Mahieu, "Imagined Contemporaries," 243).

27. Dennis Scuse, in *The Listener*, 1 January 1970, 18; Briggs, *The History of Broadcasting in the United Kingdom*, Vol. V, 712–3.

28. Clarke, *Alistair Cooke*, 514; Leahy's letter in *The Listener*, 11 May 1972, 624.

29. Alistair Cooke, *Masterpieces: A Decade of Masterpiece Theatre* (New York: Alfred A. Knopf, 1981), 21; Miller, *Something Completely Different*, 96; Clarke, *Alistair Cooke*, 493–9, 513–4, 537; see also Clarke's obituary for Cooke in the *Guardian*, 31 March 2004.

30. Haynes, "The Whiteness of *Civilisation*," 331.

31. For the Pilkington Committee's remit and report, see Briggs, *History of Broadcasting*, Vol. V, 257–308; Grade, *Still Dancing*, 221–3, 279–80.

32. Grade, *Still Dancing*, 255; Potter, *Independent Television in Britain*, Vol. 4: *Companies and Programmes 1968–80*, 4–5.

33. Herb Schmerz, *Goodbye to the Low Profile* (London: Mercury Books, 1986), 191.

Also Gillard, *The Listener*, 6 July 1972, 1–3; Miall, *The Independent*, 31 March 2004; Clarke, *Alistair Cooke*, 520–1.

34. Briggs, *History of Broadcasting*, Vol. V, 144, 713; Rawleigh Warner, Jr., "Ideals in Collision: The Relationship between Business and the News Media," in R. Warner and L. S. Silk, *Ideals in Collision: The Relationship between Business and the News Media* (Pittsburgh: Carnegie-Mellon University Press, 1979), 36; Laurence Jarvik, "PBS and the Politics of Quality: Mobil Oil's 'Masterpiece Theatre,'" *Historical Journal for Film, Radio and Television* 12, 3 (1992), 253–74.

35. Cooke, *Masterpieces*, 9, 42; Schmerz, *Goodbye to the Low Profile*, 191, 193–5; Miall, *The Independent*, 31 March 2004; Clarke, *Alistair Cooke*, 523; Miller, *Something Completely Different*, 92.

36. Schmerz, *Goodbye to the Low Profile*, 195.

37. Ibid. See also Cooke, *Masterpieces*, 181–2; Le Mahieu, "Imagined Contemporaries," 246; Miller, *Something Completely Different*, 106–7.

38. Andrew Higson, "Heritage Cinema and Television," in Morley and Robins, *British Cultural Studies*, 253, 258; Miller, *Something Completely Different*, 89; Timothy Brennan, "Masterpiece Theatre and the Uses of Tradition," *Social Text* 12 (Fall, 1985), 103, 108, 111. See also Carl Freedman, "England as Ideology: From 'Upstairs, Downstairs' to *A Room with a View*," *Cultural Critique* 17 (Winter, 1990–91), 79–106, for an analysis of English self-representation, on the one hand, and America's "narcissistic identification" with England on the other.

39. *New Yorker*, 20 May 1974; May, *Critical Times*, 400–401, 405.

40. Freedman, "England as Ideology," 88–9.

41. In 1969 Ford's popular sport car, the Mustang, was available in "Wimbledon White."

42. H. A. Harris, *Sport in Britain: Its Origins and Development* (London: Stanley Paul, 1975), 155–7; the same Kipling stanza ("If you can meet with Triumph and Disaster/And treat those two imposters just the same") appears above the entrance to the stadium court at Forest Hills in New York.

43. He became tennis coach to Hollywood stars. See Jon Henderson, *The Last Champion: The Life of Fred Perry* (London: Yellow Jersey, 2009).

44. Briggs, *The History of Broadcasting*, Vol. V, 857; Steven Barnett, *Games and Sets: The Changing Face of Sport on Television* (London: BFI Publishing, 1990), 5, 7; Max Robertson, *Wimbledon 1877–1977* (London: Arthur Barker, 1977), 6; Central Office of Information, *Sport in Britain* (London: H.M.S.O., 1972), 20; Laver and Collins, *The Education of a Tennis Player*, 248, 299–300, and passim.

45. Bud Collins, "Foreword," in Evonne Goolagong and Bud Collins (with Victor Edwards), *Evonne* (London: Hart-Davis, MacGibbon, 1975), 15–6.

46. Barnett, *Games and Sets*, 118; Joan M. Chandler, *Television and National Spirit: The United States and Britain* (Chicago: University of Illinois Press, 1988), 165, also 82 and ch. 8.

47. Ronald Atkin, *The Book of Wimbledon* (London: Heinemann, 1981), 50–3; Alistair Cooke and Stuart Hood in *The Listener*, 27 September 1973, 398, 430–1.

48. Chandler, *Television and National Spirit*, 157–9.

49. Ibid., 73–93, 160–4; Harris, *Sport in Britain*, 157–8; Hans Keller, "Tennis Violence," in *The Listener*, 13 July 1972, 63.

50. Goolagong and Collins, *Evonne*, 136.

51. The U.S. viewing peak was in 1980, with nearly 8.5 million viewers, a 6.6 Nielsen rating, and 26 percent of audience share (Nielsen TV Ratings Data, as cited by Bill Gorman at tvbythenumbers.com/2008/07/04/wimbledon-tennis-viewership-1973–2008/4209); Atkin, *The Book of Wimbledon*, 9.

52. The *Guardian*, 22 June 2005.

53. Ibid., 23 June 2008.

CHAPTER 12

1. *London House Magazine* 3, 7 (1972), 20–1; Peter Pepper, *A Place to Remember: The History of London House, William Goodenough House and the Burn* (London: Ernest Benn, Ltd., 1972), 18. Some of this chapter is based on my own experiences.

2. See Pevsner, *The Cities of London and Westminster* (Harmondsworth: Penguin, 1957), 103–4.

3. Bridget Cherry (ed.), *The Buildings of England. London 4: North* (London: Penguin, 1998), 267.

4. *London House Magazine* 2, 1 (January, 1957), 7.

5. Pepper, *A Place to Remember*, 16–17, 30, 32.

6. *The Times*, 31 October 1951; Pepper, *A Place to Remember*, 20, 99, 70, 114–5.

7. Hitchens, *Blood, Class and Nostalgia*, 298.

8. Updike, "An American in London," 97–9; See *London House Magazine* 1957–76, passim, for lists of long-stayers and alumni; most of the "short-stayers" in the summer were probably American.

9. One American played tennis, 1972, one cricket, 1973, one rugby, 1974. Annually 50 or 60 male residents in the sixties and seventies were on the cricket, squash, rugby, hockey, and tennis teams.

10. Interview with author, April, 2008.

11. Richard Hackman, "London House & Willy G, 40 Years On," *Goodenough College News* 8 (January, 2008), 15; *London House Magazine* 3, 4 (October, 1969), 12; 3, 5 (October, 1970), 5–7.

12. Dominion Students' Hall Trust v. Attorney General (1946–47); *The Times*, 13 November 1946, 14 February 1947.

13. Pepper, *A Place to Remember*, 95–6.

14. Dominion Students' Hall Trust v. Attorney-General. In Re Dominion Students' Hall Trust. Charity Division. Ch D. Evershed J. 25 November 1946; *London House Magazine* 2, 2 (October, 1957).

15. Ironically, the proto-liberationist Caribbean Artists Movement was founded just across the square in Edward Braithwaite's basement flat in 1966 (James, "The Caribbean Artists Movement," 209–27).

16. *London House Magazine* 3, 5 (October, 1970), 5–6.

17. Ibid. 3, 4 (October, 1969), 12; and 3, 6 (October, 1971).

18. Interview with the author, April, 2008.

19. *London House Magazine* 3, 4 (October, 1969).

20. Turner, *Backward Glances*, 71; Robert L. Calder, "The Barrier of English as a Common Language," *London House Magazine* 3, 6 (October, 1971).

21. Charles C. Murrah, "Visits," *London House Magazine* 3, 5 (October, 1970), 11: noting the "unmistakable 'Englishness' of [Battcock's] personality and mode of lecturing"; *London House Magazine* 3, 4 (October, 1969), 13, 46; Crawford, *The City of London*, 9.

22. *London House Magazine* 3, 6 (October, 1971); Calder, "The Barrier of English."

23. Haseler, *The English Tribe*, 58; Phyllis Hatfield, *Pencil Me In: A Memoir of Stanley Olson* (London: Andre Deutsch, 1994), 1, 4, and passim; obituary by Eric Pace in the *New York Times*, 14 December 1989.

24. *The Times*, 20 April 1963.

25. Dennis Severs, *18 Folgate Street: A Tale of a House in Spitalfields* (London: Chatto and Windus, 2001), 4–7, 32–6, 138, and passim.

26. Maev Kennedy's profile, the *Guardian*, 4 May 2007; see also Tim Dowling's interview with Bryson, "How Clean Is My Valley," 5 May 2007; Raymond Seitz, *Over Here* (London: Weidenfeld and Nicolson, 1998), 7–8, 13, 20–1, 23.

27. Winks, *An American's Guide to Britain*, x; GLC, *Tourism in London: A Plan for Management*, 17–18.

POSTSCRIPT

1. For Kehoe, see Gloria Negri's obituary in the *Boston Globe*, 28 August 2008.

2. *Boston Globe* (4 June 1975). The American English-Speaking Union—there were seventy-five branches by the seventies—was separate from that in Britain.

3. *The Times*, 4 June, 28 June, 9 July 1976; Thompson, *Bob Hope*, 163.

4. *Boston Globe*, 12 July 1976.

5. Lahr, *The Diaries of Kenneth Tynan*, 269–70; Clarke, *Alistair Cooke*, 558–9; Cynthia Hearn and Dennis Hartshorne (eds.), *1976 Declaration of Interdependence* (Wollaston and Washington, DC, 1976), 4–5.

6. Foreword to John Brooke, *King George III* (London: Constable, 1972), ix.

7. *The Times*, 23 February, 8 May, 4, 29, 30 June, 3 July 1976. On the 4th of July, BBC1 aired a program on the festivities in the United States and ended with two American films—*True Grit* and *Davy Crockett*; BBC2 had its own series of Bicentennial Summer programs, and on the 4th ITV broadcast "America 1776."

8. *The Times*, 16 February 1976.

9. *The Boston Globe*, 12 July 1976, 2.

10. 11 July 1976. Margaret Manning reviewing Jo Durden-Smith, *Who Killed George Jackson?* (New York: Knopf, 1976).

CONCLUSION

1. Robin Denselow, *When the Music's Over: The Story of Political Pop* (London and Boston: Faber and Faber, 1989), 26, 28.

2. Birchall, "The Decline and Fall of British Rhythm and Blues," 94–102.

3. Marowitz, *Burnt Bridges*, 8.

4. And remained so beyond our period. See Marie Gillespie, *Television, Ethnicity and Cultural Change* (London: Routledge, 1995), on Punjabi youth in Southall and their aspirational response to television's "tropes of advertising, notably . . . the American/global teenage dream of freedom, fun, beauty and love" (14).

5. Martin, *A Sociology of Contemporary Cultural Change*, 15–6.

6. Leon Hunt, *British Low Culture: From Safari Suits to Sexploitation* (London: Routledge, 1998), 2.

Index